Politics and the Environment

From theory to practice

James Connelly and Graham Smith

London and New York

First published 1999
by Routledge
11 New Fetter Lane, London EC4P 4EE

Simultaneously published in the USA and Canada
by Routledge
29 West 35th Street, New York, NY 10001

Typeset in Baskerville by
Ponting–Green Publishing Services, Chesham, Bucks
Printed and bound in Great Britain by
Creative Print and Design (Wales), Ebbw Vale

British Library Cataloguing in Publication Data
A catalogue record for this book is available from the British Library

Library of Congress Cataloging in Publication Data
Connelly, James.
    Politics and the environment: from theory to practice / James Connelly
and Graham Smith.
    Includes bibliographical references and index.
    1. Environmental policy.   2. Environmental ethics.
    I. Connelly, James.   II. Smith, Graham.   III. Title.
    GE170.C6426   1999
    363.7'056 – dc21   98–28002

ISBN 0–415–15067–1 (hbk)
ISBN 0–415–15068–X (pbk)

Contents

Conclusion   305

Tables

Acknowledgements

A number of people have helped to shape the structure, content and tone of this book and we are grateful to them all. We would like to thank our editors at Routledge: both Caroline Wintersgill, who initially commissioned the book, and Patrick Proctor, who most ably prompted and cajoled when we needed it. The readers, who included Stephen Young, Tim Gray and Mike Kenny, also deserve thanks for their perceptive comments on the structure of the initial proposal and the content of the final draft. Other useful criticisms of draft chapters were offered by undergraduate students at Southampton Institute who took the course on which much of this material is based. We would also like to thank friends and colleagues from a variety of backgrounds – academics, policy officers, environmental activists – who have inspired us with their ideas and friendship; and thanks to Kate Joliffe for help with compiling the index.

James would like to thank his parents for their love, rivalry and encouragement, Tom and Ruth for their firm and eloquent reminders that writing books is not the only thing in life, and Rajni and Pauline for being there. Graham would like to thank his family for their constant love and support and, most of all, Susan for laughter and inspiration.

Finally, our thanks to Blackwell Publishers for permission to use examples drawn from I. McLean's *Public Choice* in Chapter 4.

Introduction

WHY ENVIRONMENTAL POLITICS?

While we have been thinking about this question, committed activists have been tunnelling underground, engaged in protests against road and airport extension schemes; governments have been negotiating the stabilising and reduction of greenhouse gases; and Greenpeace has been at sea protesting against nuclear testing and oil exploration in Antarctica. Such issues are habitually treated as though they were unconnected; but this is a serious misconception. Despite appearances, there are clear links between different environmental, social and political problems, be they local or global issues. This book will explore the nature of these links and will do so through exploring the question of whether there is anything distinctive about environmental issues as such and, hence, whether there is anything distinctive about the concept of environmental politics. There are those who argue that environmental issues, although serious and perhaps of pressing current concern, are no different in kind from any other important issues. Thus a book on environmental politics would differ from other books simply in respect of its subject matter. In our view this is a serious mistake and we argue, on the contrary, that the distinctive nature of environmental issues and hence of environmental politics must be recognised. Environmental concern spans a range of interlocking issues from the local to the global. It challenges our thinking on fundamental questions concerning human beings and the natural world. It challenges us to engage in acts of collective sacrifice and to cooperate in ways which have never previously been achieved. It challenges us to adopt new technologies, new methods of working together and new ideas of international relations. Environmental politics is not, therefore, merely the substitution of one policy focus for another: it is necessarily radical because it challenges some of our most basic and entrenched ways of seeing, understanding and acting within the world.

To give some examples. Until recently issues such as car ownership, industrialisation and continued economic growth were unreservedly believed to be 'good things'. But these fundamental beliefs have been challenged, and it is greens[1] leading the challenge. But why? Why is it that greens believe that conventional political approaches to these issues are inadequate? What is it that greens bring to the realm of politics that is so different and so challenging? It is our contention that there are two fundamental insights that are offered by green politics and which provide the impetus for a searching re-examination of existing political practices. These are, first, an attention to the ethical dimension of humanity's relations with the non-human world; and second, a recognition of the finite nature of the planet's resources. A recognition of the standing of non-human nature and the Earth's finitude is common to all greens, although the interpretations and implications of both of these insights are contested. For example, which aspects of the non-human world have ethical standing and on what grounds? Should we be concerned with sentient beings, all life forms, inanimate entities; with individuals, species or whole ecosystems? Is the value of such entities merely instrumental or is it intrinsic? Is the natural world of value only in so far as it serves human purposes or does it possess value independently of those purposes? Such debates are common currency within environmental thinking and act as a spur to different types of environmental action. Even where beliefs on these matters are not explicitly stated, they none the less have implications for political thinking and action.

Equally, the recognition of the 'limits to growth' – the notion that we have only finite resources in terms of both raw materials and waste assimilation capacity – is central to the green view. There is, however, debate as to what follows from this. This claim amounts to more than the obvious fact that the world is finite; the point is that we are exhausting its resources, using them at a faster rate than they can be replenished. What follows from this? Does a recognition of these limits imply simply a refocusing of capitalism, leading to an increased sensitivity to environmental problems through modifying production and consumption processes? Or does it imply a fundamental restructuring or rejection of industrial society, together with a call for decentralisation and a move to small-scale economic, political and social practices?

SUSTAINABLE DEVELOPMENT

Green ideas are becoming increasingly prevalent and influential and as such have been taken up to varying degrees by those both inside and outside the green movement. This is perhaps most obvious in the frequent use (and abuse) of the term 'sustainable development'. In its original usage, the term 'sustainable development' constituted a serious challenge to orthodox political and economic arrangements. However, its use has become increasingly broadened and in the process lost much of its radical cutting edge. People have even used it to defend existing practices such as continued patterns of economic growth and industrialisation. Perhaps the most well-known and oft-quoted definition of sustainable development comes from the Brundtland Report, *Our Common Future*: 'development that meets the needs of the present without compromising the ability of future generations to meet their own needs' (WCED, 1987, p. 43). This is a broad definition, and everything hinges on its interpretation. Interpreted loosely it can be used to justify almost any activity in the present so long as we leave broadly equivalent means and resources to those in the future. Interpreted more rigorously it implies that virtually all of our activities in the present should be subject to the closest possible scrutiny to ascertain their full environmental effects, and that many of them might fail the simple test of long-term sustainability. Even though it has been misused, we believe that it remains an important concept – perhaps the most fundamental concept –against which the success of green transformations can be judged. The fact that it is part of common political currency and hence subject to the marketplace of political bargaining and counter-definition may paradoxically be an advantage. If there is political commitment to the idea of sustainable development because all sides want to appropriate it in justification of their own activities, greens can insist that the various parties concerned explain their interpretation and demonstrate how their policies embody the principle. Greens can point to the core ideals that it embodies and challenge alternative interpretations, thereby reclaiming its radical thrust. Different actors will at least be contesting the issue using the same vocabulary, and will be faced with the challenge of justifying their favoured interpretation if they wish to continue to appropriate the term in political discourse. The core ideals embodied within sustainable development are thus central to the arguments developed within this book.

Core ideals and themes within sustainable development

1 *Economy–environment integration*: economic decisions to have regard to their environmental consequences.

2 *Intergenerational obligation*: current decisions and practices to take account of their effect on future generations.

3 *Social justice*: all people have an equal right to an environment in which they can flourish.

4 *Environmental protection*: conservation of resources and protection of the non-human world.

5 *Quality of life*: a wider definition of human well-being beyond narrowly defined economic prosperity.

6 *Participation*: institutions to be restructured to allow all voices to be heard in decision making.

(Adapted from Jacobs, 1995a, p. 1471)

The concept of sustainable development is fundamental because it embodies a range of ideals and principles whose realisation is necessary to a green future. The idea of sustainable development will be a running theme linking the parts and chapters of the book.

THE STRUCTURE OF THE BOOK

The book is divided into three parts. At the end of each chapter is a case study which draws out a particular theme raised in the previous discussions. Part I addresses issues central to environmental thought and political action. It begins, in Chapter 1, with a philosophical examination of the way in which we reason about environmental issues and it considers our moral obligations to the natural and human world. In Chapter 2, the focus shifts to the conflicting ideological positions held by greens. The tensions between the political beliefs and assumptions found within environmental politics are explored. Chapter 3 concludes this section by looking at the environmental movement as a whole, its key actors and the parties, people and groups active in contemporary environmental politics. This chapter also endeavours to show the way in which ideas which perhaps seemed merely theoretical and abstract when considered independently of practice, have a real impact on the thought and action of activists, governmental policy makers and the general public.

Part II is concerned with analysing some of the background issues which must be faced in the development of environmental policy. Environmental problems have certain unique characteristics which mean that governments are forced to face hard decisions and to revise their standard and deeply ingrained policy responses. Thus we look in Chapter 4 at the problem of collective action: why is it that even where everyone knows that there is a problem they are reluctant to act? Policy makers, at whatever level, have to take account of this fact otherwise their policy making will founder on the rock of human intransigence. Chapter 5 returns to the theme of the way in which we value the environment, examining the present drive towards the inclusion of environmental values within the methods and techniques developed by economists. In Chapter 6, we consider the variety of means which might be adopted in seeking to cure or ameliorate environmental problems.

In Part III, the focus shifts to an examination of environmental policy as developed and implemented at all levels, from global to local. Throughout this section we shall illustrate the necessity for action to occur at all levels. Chapter 7 addresses the international dimension, focusing on the principles of international politics and examining the challenges facing policy makers attempting to secure global environmental agreements. The role of the Rio Earth Summit in 1992 is analysed and returned to in the chapters that follow. Chapter 8 looks at the emergence of Europe as a key intermediate player. The European Union often acts in its own right on the international scene and stands in a supranational relation to its member states on many environmental issues. In Chapter 9, we look at national responses and the different ideas and principles which lie behind the policy styles adopted in different countries. In the final chapter, we look at the way in which local government has responded to the emerging environmental agenda, in particular the development of Local Agenda 21, a product of the Rio Earth Summit.

Finally, in our Conclusion, we draw together the strands of the arguments that have been developed, stressing that it is imperative that we respond to both the practical and theoretical challenges thrown up by the emergence of environmental politics.

Part I

Environmental thought and political action

1   Environmental philosophy

Underlying environmental arguments are beliefs, not always explicitly formulated, about the relative priorities of human, animal and plant life, and the whole ecology of the planet.

(Peacocke and Hodgson, 1989, p. 87)

Responsible environmental action requires serious reasoning about environmental issues. We need a clear grasp of the terms we use, the values we espouse, and our beliefs about what we consider it morally proper to do. Do we have responsibilities towards the environment? What might these responsibilities be? From what sources are they derived? The chapter begins with a brief examination of some of the basic terms and concepts, such as 'environment' and 'nature', followed by a discussion of the relationship between human beings and the natural world. Next, the relationship between environmental ethics and conventional approaches in ethics is analysed in order to situate the demand for a new, environmentally sensitive ethic. What possibilities and resources are offered by different philosophical approaches and traditions? The discussion then turns to a consideration of the values we associate with the non-human world; values which inform the way we act towards the environment, be it direct action protests or environmental policy making. However, our considerations need to go beyond purely environmental values and the chapter concludes with an analysis of global distributive justice and justice to future generations. Reasoning about environmental issues requires us to attend to our duties towards present generations, future generations and the non-human world.

REASONING ABOUT NATURE AND THE ENVIRONMENT

Terms and concepts

The terms 'nature' and 'environment' are, of course, central to any discussion. What is 'natural' is usually defined as that which takes place independently of human agency; it is contrasted with the artificial, with the results of human skill or artifice. The natural, in total, constitutes a single world or system of nature

(Collingwood, 1946, p. 30). In this sense the term is broader than the term 'natural' in 'natural history'; it refers not merely to natural objects as they appear to us, but to the underlying principles governing their being and organisation. However, as J.S. Mill recognised, there is also a sense in which everything is natural:

> It thus appears that we must recognize at least two principal meanings in the word nature. In one sense, it means all the powers existing in either the outer or the inner world and everything which takes place by means of those powers. In another sense, it means, not everything which happens, but only what takes place without the agency, or without the voluntary and intentional agency, of man.
>
> (Mill, 1874, p. 8)

John Passmore discusses a related issue in distinguishing the terms 'nature' and 'environment':

> I shall, of necessity, be using [nature] in that sense in which it includes everything except man and what obviously bears the mark of man's handiwork. For what is in question is man's moral relationships to a nature thus defined. In another fundamental sense of the word – 'whatever is subject to natural law' – both man and man's artifacts belong to nature; nature can then be contrasted, if at all, only with the supernatural. And sometimes it will be necessary to use the word in that broader sense. The word 'environment' is often substituted for the collective 'nature'. But other people, their actions, their customs, their beliefs are the most important ingredient in our environment.
>
> (Passmore, 1980, p. 5)

Passmore here introduces the further point that 'nature' is not synonymous with the 'environment'; we can, for example, contrast the 'natural environment' with the 'built environment'. The term 'environment' in this narrow sense implies an environment for some creature or collection of creatures, whether plant or animal. Here, an 'environment' is an 'environment' for something. But we also frequently use the term 'environment' more broadly to refer to the whole of the natural world – from ecosystem to biosphere – within which human beings and all other parts of the plant and animal world have their being. 'Environment', then, is not coterminous with 'nature', and 'nature' itself has several meanings, not all of direct relevance to environmentalism.

Again, although they are often used interchangeably, we frequently need to distinguish terms such as 'preservation' and 'conservation'. Preserving something implies keeping it exactly as it is without human interference; conserving something, on the other hand, might imply managing its existence through human intervention. Thus, saving of natural resources for later consumption can be conveniently referred to as 'conservation', while saving from the adverse effects of human action might be better referred to as 'preservation'. Passmore points out, however, that preservationists and conservationists will not necessarily see eye to eye:

On a particular issue, conservationists and preservationists can no doubt join hands, as they did to prevent the destruction of forests on the West Coast of the United States. But their motives are quite different: the conserver of forests has his eye on the fact that posterity, too, will need timber, the preserver hopes to keep large areas of forest forever untouched by human hands. They soon part company, therefore, and often with that special degree of hostility reserved for former allies. So it is as well that they should be clearly distinguished from the outset.

(Passmore, 1980, p. 73)

Typically, conservation requires human intervention whereas preservation requires its complete absence: hence, when environmentalists talk of 'wilderness' they are referring to the idea of a region from which human activity and its effects are absent. For preservationists, the natural world is assigned a value in itself, an intrinsic value; for conservationists the concern is with its value for human purposes.

Human beings and the natural world

Human duties to the natural world arise both from our ability to consider our place in relation to nature and from the fact that we can exercise enormous power, for good or ill, over it. We consume resources; we pollute the environment with waste products; and we create landscapes or reclaim land from the sea. And not least it might be said that man 'has certainly won the contest between animal species in that it is only on his sufferance that any other species exist at all, amongst species large enough to be seen at any rate' (Quinton, 1982, p. 217). Second, human beings not only cause environmental destruction, they are also able to develop and implement solutions to that destruction. Although we are 'natural' in origin we cannot hide behind the 'natural' and deny responsibility for our actions and their consequences. Our capacity for reasoning does not lift us clean out of the natural world, but it enables us to do what those without this capacity cannot: to reason about the natural world and our place within it. The ability to manipulate the natural world in accordance with our own ends goes together with the ability to reason about our exercise of that power; but as it would appear that our ability to reason about our responsibilities still lags behind our ability to manipulate nature, we are currently faced with the challenge of generating an ethics suitable for our predicament. Of course, the recognition of human responsibility does not necessarily result in our doing the right thing: before we act we need to be clear about what we are trying to do.

Does this mean that we need a new environmental ethic comprehensive enough to provide a justification for all our environmental duties? The call for a comprehensive new ethic should be examined carefully. There are two reasons to be sceptical of such a demand. The first is that it may be the case that our existing moral values and traditions already provide (or could be reasonably adjusted to provide) what those who call for a new ethic are asking for. The second is to query whether a new ethic is possible even in principle. From where could a 'new ethic' emerge and how could people possibly be persuaded to adopt it? In what sense, that is, could a 'new ethic' be new? Surely if we mean something entirely other than, and independent of, our current ethic then either this is inconceivable; or if conceivable, it is impossible to imagine anyone being given good reasons for adopting it. On the other hand, we could perhaps translate the call for a new ethic into a demand for a fundamental shift in the focus and priorities of our existing moral concerns. As such, a new ethic would emerge from what we already have, drawing on resources implicit within our moral tradition. This move, if successful, has the merit that the moral radical would be appealing to beliefs and values we already implicitly possess. Understood as a plea for a significant shift in the focus of our moral concerns, the demand for a new environmental ethic expresses a justifiable doubt in the ability of our traditional systems of thought and belief (as they currently stand) to provide us with a satisfactory framework within which we can situate our environmental concerns. By gathering our newly emerging intuitions concerning the environment into a coherent and systematic whole, moral theory may provide us with a comprehensive environmental ethic which is both rooted in our moral traditions and sensitive to concerns they are incapable of addressing in their unrevised form. We need, then, to examine our moral traditions to see how well they are suited to (or can be adapted to) our new moral concerns.

THREE MORAL TRADITIONS AND THE ENVIRONMENT

Which, if any, of the theories and traditions characteristic of the Western world can support an environmentally sensitive ethic? Which is best able to provide intellectual support to our sense of having a duty to preserve nature, to conserve resources for future generations and to act justly towards those in the South affected by our economic and environmental policies? Clearly a lot is being asked for here, because the feature common to most hitherto existing types of moral theory is their exclusive focus on human concerns. It is reasonable to expect, therefore, that they will be better equipped to deal with questions of (say) distributive justice than the intrinsic value of nature. A complete environmental ethic, by contrast, has to reach beyond those concerns and extend its range to cover the sentient, the living and the non-living. It will modify our entire scale of values: human beings and their interests will still be important, but their interests will no longer be the only interests worthy of consideration. Environmental ethics, then, presents a challenge to traditional ethics: it raises questions about duties not only to animals but also towards plants and inanimate objects and natural phenomena. In the Western world we are the inheritors of a wide variety of forms of moral thinking. It would not be possible to discuss all of these strands of thought and so we shall briefly examine three moral traditions which have currency in contemporary debates: stewardship, utilitarianism and respect for life. Later in the chapter we will discuss the contractarian tradition, a more explicitly anthropocentric form of thinking, in relation to questions of distributive and intergenerational justice.

Stewardship

In the West our moral values are still largely shaped by a broadly Christian tradition. This is true irrespective of our individual religious affiliations, or lack of them: the Christian ethic permeates the fabric of our moral life and history. The Christian attitude towards nature in general splits into two strands: one in which the natural world is regarded as being there essentially for man's sole instrumental use; and another in which we have duties of stewardship to the natural world. The former view, in which nature is regarded as something to be exploited for its materials, as a source of knowledge leading to power and control over it, is typical of the modern scientific attitude. In paganism the natural world is understood as populated by spirits or gods and hence to be approached in a spirit of reverence and awe. By contrast the Christian view regards nature as created (but not 'inhabited') by God. This provides the ideal conditions for natural science and its associated technology to emerge and to dominate nature (White, 1994; Foster, 1992). This is the legacy of the 'scientific revolution' typified by the work of sixteenth- and seventeenth-century figures such as Francis Bacon, which largely took the view that human beings stood over and above nature. Nature was there solely for man's use. Human needs and wants were paramount and nature, in one way or another, existed to satisfy them. This is a classic formulation of what is frequently termed 'strong anthropocentrism'.

The alternative view, based on the principle of stewardship, has coexisted with the first and is rooted in a different reading of the book of Genesis. However, the issue here is not which is the correct biblical reading, but which attitude has been dominant. White argues forcefully that Christianity in practice has been committed to an exploitative attitude, sowing the seeds of the contemporary environmental crisis. But the alternative interpretation has never been entirely absent and its insights have much to offer contemporary thinking. Attfield argues that the Christian tradition should be viewed as one in which the injunction to be master of the natural world implies not a rapacious attitude towards it, but the contrary. It implies that we should have dominion in the sense of being a steward appointed by God to look after and cherish both the garden he has given us to cultivate and the creatures who live in it (Attfield, 1991, pp. 20–33). We do not unconditionally own parts of the planet, but hold them on trust. Such a view leads naturally to an ethic of environmental concern. It is certainly likely to be environmentally superior to a view in which property rights are held to be absolute, in which all parts of the natural world are held to be merely means to human ends, and where we have a right to do exactly what we want with our property even at the expense of those who come after us. The principle of stewardship is an example of 'weak' or 'enlightened anthropocentrism'.

The key biblical passage here is the book of Genesis in which man was commanded to 'Be fruitful and multiply and replenish the earth and subdue it and have dominion over the fish of the sea, and over the fowl of the air, and over every living thing that moveth upon the earth' and that man was put 'into the garden of Eden to dress it and to keep it' (Genesis, 1:28; 2:15). It is clear from these passages that human beings are permitted to use nature. However, it is far from clear that they have been granted an unlimited right of exploitation, such that they have no duties towards the natural world. A word like dominion needs to be considered carefully: 'man's dominion' should perhaps be interpreted as the granting of trust to humans, giving them stewardship to look after nature on behalf of God. It should not be thought of as justifying despotism or tyranny, but as the responsible exercise of a trust. The tradition of stewardship derives from this interpretation. Human beings, although they have a privileged place in nature, are exhorted to act responsibly and with consideration towards the natural world.

> In the first place, creation is God's and humans are simply a part of it. Nature is seen as a whole, interdependent in its basic diversity and variety. Human beings, like other creatures, are created 'out of the earth'.
>
> (Watson and Sharpe, 1993, pp. 222–3)

Human beings were created in God's image, but what does this imply? The World Council of Churches commented recently that this meant that humans should be seen as 'reflecting God's creating and sustaining love' and that 'any claim to the possession and mastery of the world is idolatrous' (ibid., p. 223). In the light of this, 'dominion refers specifically to the task of upholding God's purposes in creation rather than imposing humanity's self-serving ends' (ibid.). Thus the symbolism of the garden is important: humanity's role is to tend and keep the garden which God has granted it dominion over; the injunction to replenish implies that it should be kept fertile and not overworked.[1] The concept of stewardship has thus moved to the centre of modern Christian thinking. As Watson and Sharpe argue:

> stewardship is today the generally accepted understanding within Christianity ... of the role given to humanity in creation, in its relations with the rest of nature. This can be interpreted as co-worker with God in creation, but in no sense as co-equal. For it signifies that humanity's position is that it is tenant and not owner, that it holds the earth in trust, for God and for the rest of creation, present and to come.
>
> (ibid., 1993, pp. 223–4)

Principles of stewardship include responsibility for the whole Earth; solidarity of all people; the need to take a long-term view. As such they offer a critique of existing capitalist relations and are congruent with broad principles of sustainable development.

Of course, this tradition is anthropocentric, and it has rarely been used to justify radical environmental thought and action (although much protest concerning cruelty to animals could be traced to its influence). But it should not be overlooked as a source of environmental concern. At the very least it resonates with the sense that certain things should not be done, despite their undeniable human benefits, and that wanton acts of despoliation or cruelty or over-exploitation of natural resources should be avoided as exceeding the legitimate role that mankind has been granted in relation to the natural order.

Utilitarianism

For utilitarianism, actions should be judged by their consequences, not their intrinsic rightness. Desirable consequences typically include pleasure (or the avoidance of pain), happiness, well-being, or simply the satisfaction of preferences. The moral goal is held to be the maximisation of welfare in a society through calculation of which actions[2] will bring about the greatest aggregate benefit, or, as Jeremy Bentham phrased it, 'the greatest happiness of the greatest number'.

Clearly much of our practical reasoning is intuitively utilitarian, and it is important both to recognise this and to appreciate the scope and limits of utilitarianism, especially as it applies to debates in matters of public policy.[3] For the moment, however, we shall look at one interesting application of utilitarianism – the justification of vegetarianism. Although utilitarianism has traditionally been applied to solely human concerns, there is nothing in principle preventing its extension to the non-human world. Given its focus on maximising welfare in a society, the question now becomes who counts as belonging to that society. Peter Singer, in his influential book *Animal Liberation* (1983, originally published in 1975), argues that the relevant moral community comprises all those able to feel pain or pleasure. He picks up on one aspect of utilitarianism – the promotion of pleasure and the avoidance of suffering –and combines it with Bentham's dictum 'each to count for one and none for more than one'. From this starting point he constructs an account of our obligations to animals by recognising our kinship with other sentient beings. Animals, like humans, can feel pain and suffer and this simple fact means that we can include them in our calculations of aggregate welfare. The reason for this inclusion is not their intellectual abilities or powers of reason. Just as having a higher degree of intelligence does not entitle one human to use another for their own ends so it does not entitle humans to exploit non-humans. The right question to ask, insisted Bentham, was not 'Can they reason? Can they talk? but, Can they suffer?' (Bentham, 1960, p. 412). It is the capacity for suffering and/or the enjoyment of happiness which generates the right to moral consideration. This capacity is a prerequisite for having interests, and for Singer animals have interests which we should consider:

> If a being is not capable of suffering, or of experiencing enjoyment or happiness, there is nothing to be taken into account. This is why the limit of sentience (… a convenient … shorthand for the capacity to suffer or experience enjoyment or happiness) is the only defensible boundary of concern for the interests of others.
>
> (Singer, 1983, p. 9)

This line of reasoning might appear to lead to the conclusion that we should regard all animals as deserving equal consideration to each other and to ourselves.

But this does not follow: Singer is arguing for treatment as an equal, not for equal treatment. Pains and pleasures have equal significance; but this leaves open the question of identifying relative levels of pain or pleasure. The key point here is that his argument implies that we should not treat other sentient beings merely as means to our ends: they are sentient beings with interests which we should take into account. In so far, for example, as our dietary practices cause avoidable suffering to animals, and in so far as this suffering is not a necessary precondition for our own survival, any utilitarian calculus leads to the conclusion that we should cease those practices. He is not arguing that animals should be treated equally to human beings, but that their interests should be taken into account in a way in which they currently are not.

Singer's utilitarianism thus enables him to generate a powerful argument against the exploitation of animals for human purposes. At the minimum this provides grounds for the cessation of intensive factory farming; at its strongest, an argument for vegetarianism. However, Singer has to allow that this cannot be an absolute prohibition, because utilitarianism aims at maximising aggregate net welfare, and his utilitarianism thus does not provide a principle which would absolutely prohibit any particular act. Even the dictum 'each to count for one and none for more than one' needs to be carefully understood. On the one hand it has the effect of addressing attention to the interests of creatures which otherwise we might ignore in moral calculation; on the other it is not so much a call to equality of treatment as an insistence that the suffering of each creature counts as one unit in the overall calculation of aggregate welfare. Hence it serves as no protection of the interests of any individual creature, including humans.[4] It is merely an insistence that their capacity for pain and pleasure be taken into account in the calculation of welfare as a whole. Singer's inclusion of animals and their capacity for pleasure and pain within our moral framework is important because it quite rightly directs attention to that suffering and away from the view that human beings are quite separate from, and do not need to concern themselves with their impact on, the animal kingdom. But, by the same token, Singer's argument cannot give us any absolute respect for animal life as such. Neither can it provide us with the other elements which we would regard as necessary for a comprehensive environmental ethic. In its emphasis on individual sentience, it can provide no clear guidance for our concern with protecting species, non-sentient life forms or natural objects. Singer's argument thus works well, but only within its self-imposed constraints. It can offer nothing outside the framework of sentience and suffering. But this is not to diminish its importance. It has had an enormous practical effect in generating debate about animal–human relationships, converting many people to vegetarianism and leading them to further consideration of other environmental issues.

Utilitarian arguments are in general open to a further range of criticisms, perhaps the most important being that they can lead to the justification of conclusions which we would find morally repugnant. As Scheffler puts it in a discussion of classical utilitarian doctrine: 'because it is concerned to maximise total aggregate satisfaction or utility, classical utilitarianism demands that we channel resources to the relatively well-off whenever that will lead to the required maximisation' (Scheffler, 1994, p. 10). The point is that a concern with the aggregate level of satisfaction can end up justifying ill treatment of individuals precisely because individuals as such are not important within the theory. Only the aggregate level of satisfaction is important. Considerations of this sort lead philosophers such as Bernard Williams (1973; 1985) to a wholesale rejection of utilitarianism in both this and other more modern and subtle forms. It is easy to think of examples in which we could increase overall well-being by treating a particular person as a means to our ends, by redistributing their goods or even their bodily parts so as to improve the welfare of others. In so far as such a redistribution increases the net level of welfare, utilitarianism, it is argued, should embrace it. By contrast, in everyday life we would object because we are inclined to insist that there are limits which are based on the intrinsic worth or value of people.

Again, we can see that it would be difficult to extend utilitarianism in such a way as to generate a full environmental ethic. While it has a place in our moral reasoning, utilitarianism is not usually assumed to be a fully satisfactory answer to our environmental concerns. In so far as it attaches absolute value to one end – welfare – utilitarianism is incapable of dealing with other considerations satisfactorily. For example, it is hard pressed to account for the value we might wish to place on the existence or well-being of things independently of our own individual welfare. Again, it cannot easily adapt itself to our moral intuitions concerning the value of life, the value of ecological systems and the existence of species, as well as the more anthropocentric concerns of justice.

The significance of life

Another possibility might be to ground an ethic on the notion of respect for life, irrespective of sentience. The notion of 'reverence for life' is indelibly associated with the life and work of Albert Schweitzer. However, there are problems with such an approach. On what grounds do we have this respect? Where does it come from? Is it a feeling natural to all thinking beings able to reflect on the complex subtleties of living organisms? It certainly cannot come from any sympathy, any sharing of suffering or feeling if the organism is not itself sentient. A related problem is what the idea implies for us, it can hardly be an injunction not to consume or use living organisms, because we need to eat to live. Perhaps it is an injunction to recognise the value of what sustains us, a reminder that we should not be wasteful, wanton or destructive without good cause. In other words, it is an insistence on the moral considerability of living things; not an absolute prohibition on use or consumption. Such an interpretation has value: like Singer's argument, it draws our attention to what we otherwise might overlook and extends the bounds of moral consideration. Hence it would appear to have a role to play in any environmental ethic. But there are still two problems. First, it fails to establish priorities: what, for example, is the relative worth of animals and plants? What are the occasions on which we can consume either or both of these things? Second, it fails to extend our obligations to the non-living world.

Thus 'reverence for life' cannot provide the ethic we need. It leaves too many unanswered questions. For example, life may have intrinsic value, but this claim cannot account for the value we assign to other natural features such as mountains, rivers and lakes, and it ignores the problem of what 'life' is. But it is important to value life even though we cannot perfectly preserve it: to live a life is necessarily to take other life. It is important to recognise that we should take account of living things in considering the effects of our actions. Granted its limitations, can this approach be developed and used as part of a wider environmental ethic?

One way is to argue that all objects, whatever their outward appearance, are really in some sense alive or conscious. Such a view would get around the problem of the attribution of value to non-living objects by insisting that there are no non-living objects. Whatever the metaphysical merits of this point of view, even its proponents doubt that it can help in our moral reckonings as we must necessarily be largely ignorant of the character of this consciousness (Sprigge, 1997, p. 130). It seems far better simply to accept that we have duties and not to try to base them on life or sentience alone. There is, however, one ingenious way of resurrecting the 'life' argument so that it applies to everything: by granting honorary life to inanimate objects as part of a whole organism. If, for example, we were to accept the Gaia hypothesis propounded by James Lovelock (1979) to the effect that the world as a whole is a living self-regulating biosystem, comparable with other biological organisms, then we can of course apply a life-ethic to all of the Earth and to every part of it, including those parts of it usually regarded as not living. Such an approach challenges the tendency to regard things in isolation, neglecting their interrelatedness. Rocks and rivers, considered in isolation, are non-living things, but considered as part of a wider organism they should be granted the respect we grant to life as such. However, this position stands or falls with the tenability of the Gaia hypothesis itself.

Independently of the truth of the Gaia hypothesis, however, it might be possible to establish an intermediate position. By considering the matter at the level of ecosystems and interdependence we can achieve essentially the same results as if we adopted the Gaia hypothesis, without a commitment to the view that the whole Earth is a living organism. Thus we could argue that rivers, rocks, forests and species should be assigned value because, through their interactions, they form and support ecosystems which are as fundamental to our considerations as any individual animal or plant. Any entity within an ecosystem can be seen to be morally considerable in virtue of its position as part of a wider 'living' whole. Each item has honorific life status where it is not already a living being. Living beings themselves derive some of their importance from the role they play within the ecosystem. The interrelatedness of living and non-living entities becomes central to our considerations. Aldo Leopold's 'Land Ethic' can be seen to have a place here. He declares that: 'A thing is right when it tends to preserve the integrity, stability and beauty of the biotic community. It is wrong when it does otherwise' (Leopold, in Dobson, 1991, pp. 240–1). This is a broader conception than mere reverence for life, as it includes reference to the whole biotic community and thereby escapes some of the strictures already noted. However, it perhaps tends too far in the opposite direction (as does the idea of Gaia in its own way) by assigning too little value to the individual and too much to the whole.

This more holistic understanding of value in nature has important consequences for the relation between the self and the environment (Mathews, 1991). Arne Naess, the inspiration behind deep ecology, exhorts us to adopt an intuitive sense of 'life' which would encompass the biological/geological whole in which we are embedded. The deep ecological conception of self rejects 'the man in the environment image in favour of the relational, total-field image'; it tends towards the principle of 'biospherical egalitarianism'; it emphasises ecological concepts of 'diversity and symbiosis' (Naess, 1973, pp. 95–100).[5] Bringing Naess and Leopold together, we arrive at the view termed 'autopoietic intrinsic value theory', in which intrinsic value is attributed to all entities that are 'primarily and continuously concerned with the regeneration of their own organization activity and structure' (Eckersley, 1992, pp. 60–1). Such entities are ends in themselves and hence have intrinsic value. Combining the recognition of intrinsic value with an expanded notion of the self brings together the biocentric (life regarding), ecocentric (ecosystem regarding) and anthropocentric views through a reconsideration of the way we understand and experience the world.

The interrelatedness of all living and non-living entities could be seen as the basis of an inbuilt human sense of oneness with the environment in which we are embedded. Transpersonal ecology, as expounded by Warwick Fox (1990), seeks to comprehend this sense by looking at the question of the self. We tend to think of the self as isolated, opposed to other selves and separate from the rest of the world. But this atomistic understanding is in many ways false, as anyone who feels strongly for another knows when faced with their pain, fear or struggles. The fact that we can empathise with other humans is important, and lies at the heart of moral motivation. But we can also empathise with other animals in their suffering and joy. Transpersonal ecology seeks to show that we have and should develop a wider sense of self. If we can cultivate this wider sense of self by identifying with other human beings, Fox argues that we can extend the boundaries of our selves outwards to embrace the larger ecological whole. This is not the imposition of our 'selfish', strong anthropocentric self on the rest of the world. On the contrary, a wider self transcends our particular desires and wishes by emphasising empathy with the selfhood of other beings with which we share the world (Eckersley, 1992, pp. 61–2).

Although deep and transpersonal ecology emphasise the interrelatedness of all entities, it is not clear how this expanded consciousness helps us to approach ethical conflicts and the practical problems that flow from them. Human beings necessarily make interventions in the natural world in order to survive. Non-intervention is not an option. When we intervene we need to weigh the effect of alternative courses of action. It is not clear that such ecological consciousness can help with the details of such considerations. We must make choices about which entities are significant, which are to be given priority, which direction our development should take. How are we to weigh the claims of different living and non-living entities? In these terms deep ecological thinking may be limited. However, if we are to develop a more ecologically enlightened ethics, it must be rooted in a transformed, embedded sense of self. Transpersonal and deep ecological approaches may offer certain insights of value to this project of transformation.

We have examined three different approaches to the moral questions of the environment. Each approach can be associated with different ways of valuing the world. Utilitarianism lays the emphasis on sentience, on the ability to suffer or feel pleasure, and hence on how we treat animals displaying these features. Animals are seen as being equal with humans in respect of their sentience, but the consequence is that a gulf arises between sentient and non-sentient beings. The stewardship tradition generates a broader view in which human beings are seen as benevolent. It is precisely because humans are conceived of as standing over and above nature, and are thought of as rational beings made in God's image, that they are given the responsibility of caring for the natural world and the creatures within it. Respect for life, in its wider sense, emphasises the continuity of humans with the whole of the natural world. There is no great gulf between human and non-human nature, sentient or non-sentient being. All are part of a wider whole. Each moral tradition makes a distinctive contribution to the way in which we value the natural world, and in looking at the issue of value in more detail we may draw on each to a greater or lesser extent. We have inherited a plurality of value orientations towards the natural world and all have something to offer.[6] The theoretical task is how to combine these different aspects of our ethical heritage into a coherent theory able to underpin practice.

THE NATURE OF VALUE AND THE VALUE OF NATURE

The centrality of value to environmental ethics becomes apparent as soon as we start asking ourselves serious questions about why we want to protect the natural environment. Broadly there is a division between three categories of value: instrumental, inherent and intrinsic.

We attribute instrumental value whenever we regard the non-human world as valuable in so far as it is of use to human beings. Strictly speaking this should be referred to as anthropocentric instrumental value, since all living entities use their environment for food and habitat. However, as we are principally concerned with the actions of human beings, we shall adopt the shorthand form. What follows from an insistence that all values are or should be instrumental to the purposes of humankind? In so far as the well-being or survival of people is dependent on the survival or well-being of the natural environment, people have a strong incentive for protection and preservation. But there is an important consequence: human action in maintaining any aspect of the natural world is made contingent upon the interests people happen to have (or think they have). If they do not have (or do not think that they have) those interests there would be no purely instrumental reason for preserving or protecting certain parts of the natural world. While environmental concern based on people's interests alone might be practically effective in gaining support for certain policy outcomes, it is a perilously weak foundation for an environmental ethic. The role of enlightened self-interest in environmental politics as a spur to environmental action is of the greatest importance and its practical political value should not be underestimated; but it does not amount to an environmental ethic. Whilst including such instrumental concerns, an environmental ethic needs to go beyond contingent human interests and the direct relation between the environment and human welfare.

By contrast, it is possible for people to appreciate aspects of the natural world without interfering with or consuming them. A person might say that the sight of a flock of geese flying overhead is of inherent value in that they appreciate it spiritually and aesthetically and value it accordingly. Interference with the spectacle would spoil it. We wish only to appreciate as a spectator. To think of the geese aesthetically in this way is to ascribe them inherent value; to think of the geese merely as a food resource would be to think of them purely instrumentally.

A different approach again would be to argue that even if certain things had no aesthetic or inherent value they should still be protected and preserved for their own sake. This would be to assign intrinsic, non-anthropocentric value to the aspect of the environment concerned, be it an individual animal or an ecosystem. The term 'intrinsic value' has a number of senses.[7] In everyday life we are likely to use the term in either of two different ways. First, to mean that values are objective, that is to say, found in the object and not simply imputed by an observer. To say that beauty lies in the object is to say that beauty is a property of the object and that the observer, in ascribing beauty, is recognising it as located in the object, not simply in the eye of the beholder. Second, the term might be used to indicate that the value something possesses is not only objective but is independent of its instrumental value to something else. It has freestanding, self-sufficient value in its own right simply for being what it is in itself. Thus we often say that human life is intrinsically valuable and therefore should be protected, preserved and enhanced; human beings should be treated with respect in virtue of their humanity alone and not treated simply as means to the ends of other people.

In environmental debate the term intrinsic value is typically used in ways which combine the above characteristics and it is also used rhetorically to extend the range of moral attention beyond human concerns. It is not denied that human beings have intrinsic value, but they are not held to be the only things which possess such value. Typically, in discussions concerning the moral status of animals, for example, sentient creatures are granted intrinsic value. However, as we have shown in our earlier discussion, it can also be argued that living, non-sentient beings and non-living natural objects, such as rivers, forests, and wilderness, possess intrinsic value. If so, they deserve to be granted moral considerability and their interests or well-being should be taken into account and might very well divert, prevent or modify our actions, whether they be building a road through a particular landscape or building a dam and destroying the habitat of a small fish.

The inescapability of anthropocentrism: who values?

To think clearly about the values we associate with the environment we need to distinguish clearly *who* values from *what* is valued. The value of something depends on human consciousness in the sense that, beyond the purely instrumental response that we associate with animals satisfying their basic needs, only human beings can ascribe and determine value. Without human beings there would be (in the relevant sense) no value. However, this does not mean that objects cease to have value when they cease to be thought about. Some things have not yet been valued, but this does not mean that they suddenly change from being valueless to being valuable at the very instant that they are valued by a conscious entity (Attfield, 1994, p. 204). Human beings ascribe value, and to this extent value is rooted in human consciousness, but when they make valuations they are recognising value rather than arbitrarily creating it. To show that values are not arbitrary one can simply ask how one would respond if asked to attribute a greater value to a pebble than to a bird or to a piece of grass than to a tree. There is a scale of value, the precise details of which can be debated and revised, but in which the broad outlines are firm. We neither value everything equally nor assign things no value at all.

Anthropocentrism is often taken to be the view that only human beings have moral standing or that it is only the interests of human beings that in the end matter. However, there is also a weaker sense in which it is recognised that the interests of other beings should be taken into account. To make this clear we need to make a further distinction between the claim that it is human beings who assign value, and the separate claim that it is only humans and their interests that are *of* value. The first is necessarily true; the second is the real ecological point at issue. Environmental ethicists, responding to what they take to be strong anthropocentricism, often make the claim that there is value in nature itself separate from the process of valuation. Such a belief in the existence of objective intrinsic value is termed non-anthropocentrism. Such a position appears incoherent as it seems to fail to recognise the necessity of human consciousness in recognising value (Hayward, 1995, pp. 62–72; Thompson, 1990, pp. 147–60). The important distinction, then, is between different forms of anthropocentrism: strong and weak.

The fact that value is assigned or recognised by human beings does not in itself imply that values are anthropocentric in the sense of privileging human beings over the rest of nature. There is nothing inconsistent, that is, in human beings valuing the interests of other natural objects or beings above the interests of human beings. In other words it is important to distinguish who is *asking* the questions from who benefits from the answer given (Williams, 1995, p. 234). Only human beings ask these sorts of questions and values are to that extent human-based or anthropocentric in a weak sense. In this context a better term than anthropocentric is anthropogenic. Anthropogenic value originates from, but is not necessarily beneficial to, human beings. In this sense even the intrinsic value attributed by deep ecologists to the natural world is anthropogenic or weakly anthropocentric. As Andrew Dobson recognises:

> If there were no human beings there would be no such conceptualized thing as intrinsic value, and it is an open question whether there would be any such thing as intrinsic value at all. In this sense, any human understanding will be (weakly) anthropocentric, including the green movement itself.
>
> (Dobson, 1995, p. 66)

What is valued?

Holmes Rolston suggests that there are at least ten different areas of value associated with nature. They are worth consideration as they extend our tripartite classification into a spectrum of value allowing for a subtle appreciation of a wide range of human and non-human activities.

Aspects of environmental value

Economic: provider of resources for humans.

Life support: sustains and enhances life.

Recreational: recreation, contemplation and activity.

Scientific: the development of scientific inquiry.

Aesthetic: enjoyment of beauty; awe, wonder and humility in the face of the sublime.

Life: variety of living entities.

Diversity and unity: complexity and simplicity; relation of the parts to the whole.

Stability and spontaneity: continuity and change.

Dialectical: the interrelatedness of the social and the natural.

Sacramental: religious awe.

(Rolston, 1981, pp. 113–28)

Rolston is drawing attention here to the enormous variety of ways in which nature can be valued: our categories of instrumental, inherent and intrinsic value provide the primary colours on the spectrum; these further categories, the intervening shades. This variety serves to encourage us to seek out the different values that we associate with nature. It is a mistake to suppose that there is only one form of environmental value; we need to be open to a plurality of possible sources.

In what we have said with respect to our inherited traditions of thought and the variety of values that can be associated with the natural world, we have shown that all aspects of the natural world should be seen as morally considerable. This is not to say that everything is of equal value, or that the significance of different aspects is obvious. What we have tried to show is that the onus of justification has shifted. Good reason now needs to be given by those who wish to exploit the environment. They will have to show that the significance of the developments they propose outweighs the significance of the natural entities that their activities would affect.

DUTIES TO THE HUMAN WORLD

Thus far we have focused on moral responsibilities to the natural world; we now turn to responsibilities to humanity. The above discussion of the relation between humanity and nature simplified the issue by speaking of humanity's relationship with the natural world. But 'humanity' is not a single entity: it is divided into nations and classes. Hence issues of justice between nations and between classes have a bearing on the question of the way we treat nature. Some radical environmentalists appear to take the view that only our obligations to the natural world have significance, or that, given the size and urgency of the environmental crisis, they should take priority over human affairs: but this is not our view. The challenge faced by environmental ethics is to balance the competing claims of the natural and the human worlds, not to ignore one set of claims entirely. To do so would be to make a comparable mistake to that made by those who insist only on the importance of human well-being in the world. Both extremes are morally flawed.[8] We now turn to a consideration of our duties to present and future humanity.

Global distributive justice

There are great disparities in wealth and income between the world's nations, and this informs our deliberations about aid, trade and development and our concern with famine, poverty and suffering. But what, if anything, does this have to do with environmental issues? What links the morality and politics of global inequality to specifically environmental concerns? A general answer is that human settlements exploit their environment in various ways, and some patterns of resource use are environmentally damaging whereas others (relatively) are not. Some patterns of living are sustainable in that there is no reason in principle why they cannot be continued indefinitely; others are not sustainable given scarce resources and modes of consumption which over-exploit the resources available and destroy the environment with their detritus. Some environmental destruction is the consequence of affluence, for example carbon dioxide emissions as a result of car use; other forms of destruction are the consequence of poverty, for example destruction of forests for fuel or shelter where clearance leads to erosion. Distributive and environmental concerns are therefore intrinsically interconnected at this level.

Certain forms of environmental degradation can neither be contained nor solved purely at a local level. Global warming and ozone depletion, for example, affect the planet as a whole and their solution requires global cooperation. Isolated local action is simply insufficient. Environmental policy is thus faced with the dilemma that while the environmental problems caused by prosperity, such as global warming, ozone depletion and acid rain, are well recognised, the North is unwilling to jettison or modify the lifestyle which creates the problems. At the same time the South actively wishes to adopt some of the environmentally damaging aspects of that lifestyle as it develops. It is this, with its implied steep increase in consumption of fossil fuels and use of non-renewable resources, which will magnify the very problems we are trying to solve. If solutions have to be global, and if this requires a change in the way people live and develop, we need to generate international environmental regimes which will solve the problem of collective action by securing worldwide agreement on key issues. Agreement will not be secured unless the settlement is seen and felt to be fair by those affected, and this brings in the issue of global distributive justice. Thus the relationship between environmental policy, environmental ethics and questions of global distributive justice becomes clear. An unjust world will not succeed in solving global environmental problems.[9]

From the South's perspective it frequently appears that the North is demanding a degree of restraint and sacrifice which it is not prepared to submit to itself. The demand to forswear the benefits of industrialisation so long enjoyed can easily be construed as hypocrisy, and there is a view that the problem is very much of the North's own creation and that therefore the onus should be on the more industrialised nations to take responsibility. This leads to the South making conditions for their having to accept stringent universal environmental standards and to a demand for material compensation for forgone benefits and technological assistance in finding and providing environmentally sensitive alternatives. If, for example, burning coal pollutes the atmosphere, creates acid rain and leads to global warming, then the onus is on the North to provide alternative, environmentally sensitive technologies. Again, if it is not thought desirable to use refrigerators which contain CFCs, contributions will have to be made towards developing new forms of technology which will overcome the problem. The South cannot be denied its right to develop in whatever direction it sees fit. The view that the North should not simply make demands but should provide compensation and alternative forms of technology was expressed very sharply by the Indian Environment Minister in 1990, over demands for the less industrialised nations to refrain from using ozone-depleting technology. Her view was that India should not sign the Montreal Protocol unless she was promised both financial assistance and the technology to make alternative chemicals (*The Economist*, 7 July 1990).

Thus humanitarian moral concern with global distributive justice is frequently allied to a pragmatic political imperative: no justice, no cooperation; no cooperation, no solution. The South may be economically weak, but it can have, on occasion, the power of veto in global environmental policy affecting patterns of production and consumption. This forces a proper consideration of global distributive justice. However, in practical terms, the South may not have the bargaining or veto power to force the issue. Here we can only appeal to moral considerations. What is required, perhaps, is an impartial set of principles which can be subscribed to by all, including the weakest of the world's nations. In so far as environmental concern is rooted in the adverse effects of environmental degradation on human health and well-being, such principles must apply equally to all human beings irrespective of their location. We cannot be morally justified in solving environmental problems by exporting them. There is no moral reason to deny others the welfare we would wish to enjoy ourselves; it cannot be morally right to inflict the adverse consequences on other people merely because they are in no position to object. To test our good faith we should perhaps be prepared to consider the extent to which we would be willing to accept the principles governing international policy if we were situated elsewhere.

Take the issue of natural resources. The distribution of natural resources around the globe is uneven. Some countries are sitting on large oilfields and others are sitting on an empty desert; some countries have good supplies of fertile land and water and others do not. What follows from this uneven and unequal distribution of resources? Does it follow that each country has an absolute right to the resources situated within its territory? Or does it follow, on the other hand, that they should be shared? There is a broad agreement that certain uninhabited parts of the world – the poles and the oceans – belong to the world as a whole and their exploitation is regulated or prevented through international agreement. Clearly this approach does not currently prevail in respect of inhabited countries: but none the less the issue of ownership, responsibility and control is a live debate. This will be picked up in Chapter 7. Does Brazil have the right to do just what it likes with its rain forests, or can international intervention be justified to protect them? Does the lucky accident of proximity to fuel or food stocks allow a country to enjoy a monopoly of that resource? How far are we justified in applying certain basic principles of justice to these cases?

The dominant ethical approach to these issues is drawn from the contractarian tradition in moral and political theory. This analyses rights and duties as the outcome of a hypothetical contract in which we try to understand what our rights and duties would be if we were able to stand back and look carefully at the matter without the intrusion of personal interests and selfish desires. Such a theory attempts to justify moral principles by showing that they would be agreed upon by rational agents in certain ideal circumstances. Its purpose is to exhibit the rationality of moral rules (Carruthers, 1992, p. 36).

In his *Theory of Justice* (1972), John Rawls challenges us to think through the principles of justice we would choose if we did not know what our situation in life was, what we were going to be, and what benefits or burdens we have in life. He assumes that people's moral judgements are more likely to be unprejudiced if the peculiarities of their own situation and interests are unknown at the point of discussing general principles of justice; if we do not know who or what we are, we cannot bias the conclusion in our own favour. He refers to this condition of choice, and the associated lack of knowledge about ourselves and our circumstances as, respectively, the 'original position' and the 'veil of ignorance'. They are designed simply to clarify our thinking on these issues by forcing us to be impartial, by positing a situation in which, although we want the best for ourselves, we cannot directly choose a way of ensuring that we will emerge better off than anyone else. Rawls assumes that we are prepared to commit ourselves to whatever principles emerge out of our deliberations and he maintains that rational actors would choose principles of justice which would act as yardsticks for assessing the basic structure of a society.

The general conception of justice that Rawls claims we would accept is that 'all social primary goods – liberty and opportunity, income and wealth, and the bases of self-respect – are to be distributed equally unless an unequal distribution of any or all of these goods is to the advantage of the least favoured' (Rawls, 1972, p. 303). More specifically, he argues that this could be further subdivided into two basic principles. The first is that each person is to have an equal right to the most extensive total system of equal basic liberties compatible with a similar system of liberty for all; the second that social and economic inequalities should be arranged so that they are both (1) to the greatest benefit of the least advantaged, and (2) attached to offices and positions open to all under conditions of fair equality of opportunity. For present purposes the most important of these principles is the idea that social and economic inequalities should be to the greatest benefit of the least advantaged. This he terms the 'difference principle' and the basic point is that it assumes equality and holds that inequalities can only be justified if to the benefit of the least well-off in society.

These principles of justice can be used in our evaluations of the distribution of wealth and income. Rawls remarks that 'the natural distribution is neither just nor unjust; nor is it unjust that men are born into society at some particular position. These are simply natural facts. What is just and unjust is the way that institutions deal with these facts' (ibid., p. 102). The issue, then, is how we respond to the natural distribution, and we can do this in a Rawlsian fashion by asking what principles would be agreed to by countries which were denied knowledge of certain particular facts about themselves. Or, to put it more concretely, what principles would be chosen by representatives of the world's nations if they did not know whether they were the USA, Somalia, Sweden or Bangladesh? It is not hard to imagine that globally acceptable principles of distributive justice might look something like Rawls' principles and that they would justify and endorse some forms of global redistribution through aid and trade, perhaps the writing off of various forms of international debt, and perhaps a more widespread sharing of the world's resources. In return, various forms of intervention in the hitherto sovereign affairs of nations would be justified and accepted: the over-exploitation of a country's natural resources (forests or flora or fauna, for example) would no longer be tolerated and the countries affected would accept this consequence as the outcome of a fair international regime from which they in turn benefit. Elements of such an interpretation of justice can at times be found in the discussion and output of some international agreements, although it is still far from being a central consideration of all parties. There would of course be enormous implications for international relations and specifically for thorny issues such as sovereignty. Aid, for example, is typically given directly to governments, but this is to ignore the internal distribution of power, wealth, income and opportunities within each state. However, if we try to give aid directly to individuals or groups within a state and ignore governments, we create all sorts of ethical and political problems. Whichever way these arguments go, it is at least obvious that any globally successful environmental policy must issue in a rethinking of our attitudes towards sovereignty and ownership and point in the direction of the recognition of the world as a resource common to all its inhabitants.

Justice and future generations

The actions of those living in the present will affect those living in the future. In the past we were probably confident that the effects of our actions would be (on the whole) benign and that those coming after us would be the privileged and grateful beneficiaries of our research, technology and investment. This assumption is no longer prevalent. People worry about the world in which their children or grand-children will grow up. They worry that their future is bleak. Nor can we simply reverse our patterns of behaviour, thereby removing this fear and restoring our lost optimism: what future generations will inherit is in large part already determined by what has already been done. We cannot take away the carbon dioxide or the chlorofluorocarbons from the atmosphere, although, given political will and wis-dom, we can reduce future levels of emissions. In some instances we have already imposed a requirement on future generations to find alternatives for the energy sources that we are close to exhausting and we have also bequeathed to posterity the task of clearing up the consequences of our inadequate knowledge of toxic waste disposal. We are currently storing nuclear waste which will remain highly toxic for a million years; we are doing this despite the fact that we do not yet know for certain how best to store it safely. Our obligations to future generations depend-ing on the safe storage of nuclear waste extend to at least 30,000 generations.

Intergenerational justice is only one aspect of environmental ethics, but it stands at the junction of numerous environmental policy issues, particularly when we reflect on the requirements of sustainable development which requires, in the words of *Our Common Future*[10] that we meet 'the needs of the present without compromis-ing the ability of future generations to meet their own needs' (WCED, 1987, p. 43).

Intergenerational justice concerns what we ought to leave to the generations who will succeed us in respect of resources, pollution and environmental damage, flora and fauna, biodiversity, wildernesses, and so on. But what sort of obligations are these? It is generally accepted that there is a strong obligation to avoid harm to others, but it is sometimes held that we also on occasion have obligations to go beyond this and to improve the welfare of others. This raises the question of whether we are obliged to make our successors better-off than we are or ensure that they are no worse off. Should we, for example, ensure that pollution and environmental degradation get no worse, or try to restore environments (so far as possible) to their 'original' state? Related questions include what constitutes harm; what constitutes benefit; and what substitutions future generations will find acceptable where we cannot pass on to them exactly the same mixture of environmental resources as we ourselves inherited. Whatever the precise nature of the answers, surely it is possi-ble to agree that we have some obligations to future generations? An affirmative answer immediately raises the question of how far into the future we should think of our obligations stretching. How far into the future should we set our sights? Should we focus only on generations immediately following ours, or should we set our sights on 30,000 generations? The answer depends on, first, the source of our obligations, and second, on whether our priority is to avoid harm or promote positive good. If the priority is to avoid harm, it is plausible to argue that this must be a relatively open-ended commitment, especially in the case of irreversible, non-remediable damage, such as the extinction of species or the poisoning of the planet through nuclear radiation. Here, because the actions or their effects are non-reversible, what affects one generation will affect all those succeeding it. The present generation can help or harm future generations, but future generations cannot help or harm us, at least not in the same sense.[11] We have power over them in that we can promote our own interests at the expense of theirs, if we so choose. Future generations are, it might be said, both powerless and vulnerable.

Why do we have obligations to future generations?

The boundaries of our moral concern extend outwards as we include our contemporaries, other species, and perhaps other aspects of the natural world, within the bounds of a relevant moral community. We are now being asked whether or not to include currently non-existent members of future generations within the relevant moral community. Some argue that we can have no obligations to non-existent entities; others argue that our priority ought to be the needs and interests of the generation to which we belong and that justice begins in our own time. This is not necessarily a selfish response, as it could include the acceptance of important and costly obligations to other members of our current generation. Lying behind these issues are further questions: are obligations to people remote from us in time or space weaker than those to people closer to us? Is there a significant moral difference between remoteness in time and in space? Most people would agree that we do, in fact, have obligations to those remote from us in space; and we do also behave as if we have obligations to those remote from us in time as well. However, it might be argued that the obligations are of different degrees of strength or intensity: even so, to allow that we have any obligation at all to future generations makes a difference to what we ought to do in the present.

Whatever we do we cannot duck the question, because increased knowledge of the likely consequences of our actions inevitably brings in its train the sort of imaginative sympathy which generates a sense of moral responsibility. For example, we possess a great deal of knowledge about the plight of peoples in the South and we accept obligations to help in various ways. We know about famine and suffering and this generates moral sentiments. It does not necessarily follow that we do what we think we ought to do, but the recognition that there is a problem leads us to search for the causes and to consider possible remedies. In this respect we are in a vastly different position to people 200 years ago, who can hardly be blamed for not helping people in other parts of the world when they were ignorant of the fact that they were suffering. We are familiar with media representations of people suffering in other countries: to turn away from the pictures unmoved is an act of a different nature from simply not knowing that the suffering existed at all. However, there are no media representations of future generations and we are in that sense in the position of those 200 years ago ignorant of suffering elsewhere in the world; but we do know that people will suffer, even if we shall not live to see that

suffering for ourselves. Are we not morally responsible for the foreseeable consequences of our actions, irrespective of whether we live to witness them for ourselves? Surely simple recognition of this responsibility generates obligations to
future generations?

There are some things about which one cannot know today that one will have an
obligation to tomorrow. For example, tomorrow an old lady might need to be helped
across the road, or a child to be saved from drowning. We do not know that this will
be the case but we can agree that if it were the case then there would be an obligation
to do something about it. By parity of reasoning, if we did not know that future
generations were going to exist then we could not know that we had an obligation to
them. However, we do know that future generations are going to exist; we do know,
that is, that the generational equivalent of the old lady or the drowning child will
exist; and we know this now. We know it before they exist, and this means that we
have to act on this now. If I knew the child was going to place itself in danger of
drowning tomorrow then I would have an obligation to do what I could today to
prevent that happening. Future generations are, in this respect, like the child who is
in danger of drowning tomorrow. And it does not matter that we do not know who
the future generations are; after all, it makes no difference who the drowning child is
either. A sceptic might argue that future generations might not exist: true; but so
what? It is irresponsible and stupid to act as if they will not. Furthermore it is only at
the moment that they cease to exist that our obligations to them will in turn cease.

This is a general argument which establishes, if successful, a broad conclusion.
Another argument might be to again draw on the work of Rawls by using the
contractarian model. One obvious way of doing this is to imagine that the positions
were reversed and that our generation swopped places with a future generation:

> If we were living 500 years hence, do we think we would wish that in respect
> of a particular problem we had been living now instead of then? If we do
> then our present way of acting is a selfish one.
>
> (Cameron, 1989, p. 72)

In this way, Rawls' theory could be applied to the consideration of obligations
to future generations: all we would have to imagine is that the participants in the
original position do not know to which generation they belong and that they might
belong to any generation. This approach, however, goes beyond what Rawls himself argued for in *A Theory of Justice*. There he postulated that the participants in the
original position were contemporaries, although they did not know to which generation they actually belonged. This prevented him from generating obligations to
future generations out of the central premise of his theory. Brian Barry suggests
that Rawls should simply have followed through the internal logic of his own
argument and scrapped that part specifying that all people in the original position
are contemporary and know that they are.[12] The veil of ignorance could then be
employed to conceal from participants which generation each of them belonged
to, and out of this procedure principles of intergenerational justice would be
chosen. These principles would inevitably apply to and between generations many

generations removed from each other: it would be much more far-reaching than Rawls' theory of justice would allow.

Despite the attractions of the extended Rawlsian approach it has often been argued by some that we should be concerned only with immediate posterity. Rawls himself actually holds that responsibilities to posterity are based on ties of affection to the next generation (Rawls, 1972, pp. 128–9).[13] Broadly, it is argued that moral obligations arise from within life in a community within which one becomes entangled in a network of mutual dependencies and comes to accept the corresponding rights and duties. Obligations arise out of actual relations with people, and thus there can be no obligations to those who will live long after we are dead. An extension of this view is to argue that obligations rest on a sense of moral community. Obligations can be extended outwards to include members of communities recognisably similar to our own. Whether or not we have obligations to future generations depends, on this view, on whether we expect them to live in ways that would lead us to regard them as part of our moral community. If we think they will develop in ways we disapprove of then we have no obligations to them. Thus Golding (1972) argues that we have obligations to those in a community with its reciprocal relationships; and that there may be possible obligations to future people, but only where they have a conception of the good life with enough in common with ours. He then goes on to argue that as we do not know what the interests and desires of people in the far future will be, it is therefore pointless worrying about them. We want to protect the natural world to provide our descendants with resources for them to enjoy, or because we think they will share our values concerning the value of the natural world. But what grounds do we have for assuming that people in the far future will adhere to the same values and desires and have the same needs? It is a fair assumption to make for those living in the immediate future – but is it not dangerous to be too sure about what those coming after that will want? And is it not possible that they might choose to live in ways which we could never regard as being acceptable in terms of our own moral community? Given these possibilities, why then should we impose obligations on ourselves to conserve, preserve, protect, maintain or enhance things which people in the future might simply not want or deserve?

But, to take issue with Golding's argument, the point about intergenerational justice is not reducible to whether we share other people's conception of the good life; we can agree that conceptions of what constitutes the good life can and will differ from our own. Nor is it about their interests in the sense in which this is related to their conception of the good life. It is something more fundamental: it is about the possession of life itself, not so much concerned with the conception of the good people choose, as with the very possibility of them being able to choose a conception of the good at all. This point is forcefully made by Brian Barry when he argues that future generations will be alike in certain key respects.

> It is true that we do not know what the precise tastes of our remote descendants will be, but they are unlikely to include a desire for skin cancer, soil erosion, or the inundation of all low-lying areas as a result of the melting of the

ice caps. And, other things being equal, the interests of future generations cannot be harmed by our leaving them more choices rather than fewer.

(Barry, 1991, p. 248)

This point can be generalised: if, for ourselves, we would prefer that earlier generations had left us a greater amount of choice and variety in the natural world, environment and resources, is it not the case that generations following us would appreciate being left the same variety? True, we do not know exactly what they will want and value; but precisely for that reason it is better to widen their choice rather than to narrow it, to give them more opportunities rather than fewer.

Practical doubts

In general it is rare to find anyone arguing against the existence of obligations to future generations, although some argue that our obligations extend only to the generations immediately succeeding ours. In the latter case the expectation is that, as and where it is appropriate and possible, the torch of intergenerational justice will be passed down the generations, thereby ensuring continuity over many generations. In this sense the difference between those advocating a limited and those advocating an extended conception of intergenerational justice is easy to overstate. However, what constitutes passing the torch depends on the issue. If our obligations are relatively open-ended this may generate a sharp clash between justice for those living in the present against justice for those living in the future. Given that resources are finite, any consumption will have an effect on choices available for those in the future. This raises a tangled web of problems going far beyond what can be dealt with here, although some, in particular the question of the substitution of natural and man-made resources, will be dealt with in later discussions of sustainable development. It is worth commenting that the answer to the question partly depends on the distinctions made earlier between avoiding harm and promoting welfare (as did Barry's riposte to Golding), between reversible and irreversible damage, between certain and probable harm. As has already been argued, an obligation to avoid certain types of actual harm is open-ended; an obligation to promote the welfare of others presupposes that we in fact know what constitutes their welfare. Here Golding's argument is a telling one. But the point about natural resources, for example oil or coal, is not so much whether later generations inherit stocks so much as that they inherit sufficient energy means, irrespective of what form this energy takes. If we take seriously the view that each generation has obligations only to its immediate successors, each generation would have the duty of ensuring that it passed on to its successor the equivalent in energy terms to that it itself inherited. This could be a heavy duty and one better shared over several generations – a possibility which presupposes a much greater continuity of environmental concern over time and hence a concern not only with immediate posterity but also with distant posterity. As Cameron argues: 'Our obligation to the generations after this immediately succeeding one can be thought of as mediated through our obligation to enable that next generation to discharge its obligation to all its successors' (Cameron, 1989, p. 72). Of course any action we take now may be in vain. Future generations may simply not care, may believe that different issues are more significant, or develop technologies which make our actions redundant. But we cannot know any of this and hence we should act on the limited knowledge that we have.

CONCLUSION

We can affect other generations, but is there not a prior obligation to the needs and interests of this generation? Is there a legitimate concern that there may be a clash between intragenerational and intergenerational justice? Trying to be fair to people in the future might preclude being fair to people living now. What sorts of sacrifices are we justified in asking people to make in the present for the good of future generations? Is it possible to share the burden of these sacrifices fairly? A short answer might be that, as argued above, global environmental policy will not succeed unless questions of global distributive justice are settled first: in this sense *inter*generational justice presupposes *intra*generational justice. We will never secure justice for future generations unless we can also act justly towards all members of our own generation. Further, this is made still more difficult when we consider the claims associated with the non-human world, which at times may clash with both present and future human well-being.

Some argue that we should discriminate on the basis of time, and discriminate in favour of the present generation. The present generation is the last one which can help those alive in the present; all previous generations to our own have already done their work for good or bad. On the other hand, people in the distant future can be helped by a number of succeeding generations as well as by the present one – responsibility can be shared. Therefore the obligation of the present generation should primarily be to itself. One obvious answer to this is that there are many actions which we can take now which will engender risks or harms to future generations whatever anyone does in the future; and in these cases it makes no difference what our successors do or do not do. If we pollute the world with nuclear waste then it cannot be undone by any action taken in the future. There are always some who will argue that science will find the answer to this (and to every other problem) at some point. This is a terrible burden to leave: it amounts to not only leaving the original problem, but also the problem of finding a solution which we have admitted we cannot find ourselves.

We have to be careful, especially when considering questions of resource depletion, to distinguish needs from wants.[14] Our priority has to be to meet the needs of the present; this must take precedence over considerations for the future and non-human obligations. However, despite this, there are different ways in which we can fulfil our basic needs, some being more sensitive to future-regarding and environment-regarding duties. It should be stressed that this edict applies to present needs, not wants or superfluous desires. It must be recognised that in many cases meeting the needs of future generations or giving due consideration to environmental

7126

obligations will result in a reduced ability to fulfil wants. With the Brundtland definition of sustainable development in mind, we must try to satisfy our needs in the present in ways which neither compromise the ability of future generations to satisfy their needs, nor adversely impact on the integrity of the natural environment.

Here it can be seen how the concept of sustainable development, which we argue to be central to the environmental agenda, emerges as a complex web of theoretical, practical and ethical issues. A simple definition such as Brundtland's presupposes the answer to a range of questions, questions which arise at the intersection of the natural world, human well-being, and intragenerational and intergenerational considerations. Questions of value, obligations and principles all come into play in any deliberation, and this shows that despite the seemingly abstract nature of the preceding discussion, it is central to any serious attempt to generate solutions and agree on policies on issues as diverse as global warming, the ozone layer, the development of Antarctica, global development patterns, population, resource use or toxic waste disposal.

CASE STUDY: ANIMAL RIGHTS

Chapter 1 has explored a number of issues in environmental philosophy and ethics. It was argued that the development of an environmental ethic required the extension of our already existing moral resources and reasoning to beings and things currently outside their scope. An examination of some of the reasoning typical of debate about animal rights will show how this can be done and also raise some questions about whether the language of rights is appropriate in this sphere.

Concern with animal welfare has a long tradition, most recently being the focus of protest against animal experimentation and the export of live animals. Part of the debate about the status of animals centres on the possibility (or otherwise) of attributing rights. Notoriously there are a number of problems with this suggestion. For example, the attribution of rights to non-human beings may be meaningless; it may be practically ill-judged to focus on animal rights as the rallying cry of the animal welfare movement; animal rights may be insufficient to capture the full range of the moral relationships we have with animals; animal rights, by focusing on individual members of a species, might divert attention from the fate of the species as a whole; and so on. It is impossible to enter into all of these questions here, but it is worthwhile taking a look at some of the arguments put forward and to ask one or two questions about the political value of ascribing rights to animals. This discussion is also significant in showing how the various moral theories examined earlier in this chapter can be brought to bear on a specific moral issue.

Rights

First some preliminary comments about the concept of rights. Rights can be of different types. A moral or natural right is one which we think ought to be the case even if, in fact, a society or a legal system does not explicitly recognise it. A positive right is one which would be generally upheld by a community; and a legal right is one which is granted by law and where those holding the right are protected by law.

If someone has a right this is generally taken to imply that someone (or something) else has a corresponding duty to uphold that right. Rights and duties are correlative. Again, but more contentiously as we shall see, it is often argued that if, say, a person has a right to something this is because they are part of a society in which they also have duties to others and that if they are not prepared to shoulder the burden of having duties they should not be allowed to have rights either. Rights correspond to responsibilities. It is obvious, though, that not everyone can carry out duties or even be said to have them. We would normally argue that babies, people in comas and people with learning difficulties have rights, despite the fact that they might be unable to understand what they are or to carry out duties as part of a society. And we might go further and say that it is precisely these groups, the weak and powerless who are unable to look after themselves, who stand most in need of the protection offered by rights. To this list we might add animals.

Pain and suffering

Although there are those who have denied and those who continue to deny that animals feel pain or suffer (at least in the same sense as humans),[15] most of us would accept that animals do feel pain and can suffer. At the same time we might argue that the degree of pain felt is probably less in some animals than in others, and also that there are forms of suffering peculiar to human beings because of their capacity to form conceptions of themselves, their lives and their futures. Given the capacity for suffering, there are many who would argue, following Peter Singer (1983), that on utilitarian grounds we have direct duties to animals: their suffering entitles them to our moral concern and should be taken into account in our moral calculations. Singer grants that some creatures may suffer more and others less for a variety of reasons, but given that they suffer, the utilitarian view is that suffering should be minimised. Proponents of this view would not typically advocate rights for animals, although Singer allows that the use of the term 'animal rights' may be politically advantageous.

Rights and agency

There is an often expressed view that if a rights-bearer cannot understand the notion of a 'right' then it follows that it cannot possess rights: 'it is the capacity for moral autonomy ... that is basic to the possibility of possessing a right' (Carruthers, 1992, p. 144). This view arises from a contractarian approach to morality in which only those able to contract can be moral agents and possess rights and duties. Further, as noted above, to have rights a being must also be able to assume duties. If this is so, while humans still might have some responsibilities towards animals, these will fall outside a contract theory. Hence animals cannot be said to have rights. Rawls, for example, argues that animals are not entitled to strict justice, but that it is none the less wrong to be cruel to animals and to destroy species: we have duties of compassion and humanity towards animals, but they fall outside the scope of rights as understood within contract theory (Rawls, 1972, p. 512).

Rawls' view is similar to that of Kant, who denied that there can be direct duties to animals, although he argued that we should treat animals carefully and responsibly. If morality is a transaction between rational beings, animals lie outside that sphere of consideration. Towards animals we have indirect, but not direct duties, because animals are not self-conscious. Our duties are to humans and one reason for being considerate towards animals is that 'he who is cruel to animals becomes hard also in his dealings with men' (Kant, 1963, p. 239). The question to consider here, however, is whether it is reasonable to say that merely because an animal cannot itself be a moral agent, we have no direct duties towards them. Feinberg suggests that:

> Almost all modern writers agree that we ought to be kind to animals, but that is quite another thing from holding that animals can claim kind treatment from us as their due. Statutes making cruelty to animals a crime are now very common, and these, of course, impose legal duties on people not to mistreat animals; but that still leaves open the question whether the animals, as beneficiaries of those duties, possess rights correlative to them. We may very well have duties *regarding* animals that are not duties *to* animals, just as we may have duties *regarding* rocks, or buildings, or lawns, that are not duties *to* the rocks, buildings or lawns.
>
> (Feinberg, 1991, p. 372)

Direct and indirect duties

Singer claims that our duties towards animals are direct, simply because of their capacity to suffer. The contrasting view, as we have seen, is that duties towards animals are indirect. Further, some argue that they can actually be brought into a contract theory. For example, Carruthers contends that:

> Since many people have concerns for animals, and are deeply distressed at seeing an animal suffer, this may place on us an obligation not to cause suffering to animals, except for powerful reasons. This would not be because needlessly causing such suffering would violate the rights of the animal, any more than someone who defaces a beautiful building violates the rights of the building. On this approach animals, like buildings, would have no direct rights or moral standing. Rather, causing suffering to an animal would violate the right of animal lovers to have their concerns respected and taken seriously.
>
> (Carruthers, 1992, pp. 106–7)

This is one argument; another, already mentioned, is that often attributed to Kant, which is that cruelty to animals has an adverse effect on our moral character and in our dealings with other people; and a third is based on the fact that animals might belong to human owners, whose rights would be violated if we mistreated them. These views do not seem very satisfactory. The first seems arbitrary in that we would not treat all claims on the ground of sensibility as of equal worth, and what we would therefore need is some way of deciding which should be acted on and which not. In the second it is easy to deny the connection between cruelty to animals and cruelty to human beings; besides, if suffering or cruelty is to be our primary consideration, and if humans and animals can both suffer, it is hard to avoid the conclusion that Singer is right and there is a direct duty to both human and non-human animals. In the third the problem is the contingent nature of the protection offered: no one doubts that property rights can provide protection, but morally this is a weak argument as animals are treated as objects protected if their owners happen to want them to be, but not otherwise.

So, in what sense, if any, is it possible to say that animals ought to have moral rights? And, if they do, should some or all of them become positive or legal rights? Clearly this is only possible if we allow that we can have direct duties towards those who are not rational beings, who do not understand the concept of a 'right' and who we cannot expect to have duties towards us. Tom Regan argues in *The Case for Animal Rights* that talk of animal rights is both possible and desirable.

Regan draws on a distinction between acquired and unacquired duties and rights, the former being those which arise from our voluntary acts or our place in institutional arrangements; the latter being natural duties which:

apply to us without regard to our voluntary acts. … they have no necessary connection with institutions or social practices. … Thus we have a
natural duty not to be cruel, and a duty to help another, whether or not
we have committed ourselves to these actions. It is no defence or excuse
to say that we have made no promise not to be cruel or vindictive, or to
come to another's aid.

(Rawls, 1972, pp. 114–15)

Regan argues, therefore, that we should distinguish between having a valid
claim and being able to make that claim or recognise that claim on one's own
behalf. Further, if we were always to insist that the being protected by a right
was a rational moral agent as well as a moral 'patient', we would be ignoring
precisely the sort of occasion on which rights might be most necessary:

When, as in the case of moral patients, they have rights but are themselves incapable of claiming or defending them, then the duty 'society'
has to do this for these individuals is, one might say, all the greater.

(Regan, 1984, p. 284)

At this point it is sometimes argued that if we were to ascribe rights to
animals we would then have to 'police' nature to ensure that other animals
do not violate those rights. This clearly would be absurd. But the point is,
surely, that if we accept that animals could be given rights despite not being
fully rational agents able to engage in a social contract, they would by definition not have duties. Only moral agents can understand and take on duties
and be held morally accountable for their actions. In other words, human
beings, as moral agents, can grant animals rights; but animals, not being
moral agents, cannot be morally praised or blamed for their actions. If this
is acknowledged, there would seem to be nothing intrinsically absurd about
the granting of rights to animals. This conclusion is of considerable importance as it would seem to have serious implications for both political and
legal practice. But there still remain some questions about the workability
and practical value of ascribing moral or legal rights to animals.

Some practical considerations

One practical difficulty with granting legal rights to animals is simply how it
would be done. This, it can be argued, is simply a matter of legal practice
and by no means insoluble. The historical fact that the law does not recognise the rights of animals and has no procedures for their represention is
neither here nor there. We do not have to abide by the way law currently

conceives of animals and their rights; and, if we wish to put these rights into law, the problem is simply the issue of how the bearers of these rights will be represented. In principle this might not be so very different from the way in which minors or those incapable of acting on their own behalf have their rights and interests represented in the existing legal system (Midgley, 1983, pp. 54–5).

But what of more general political considerations? The language of rights has great rhetorical power; that much is obvious. But surely this power is dependent, both conceptually and practically, upon the relative scarcity of its use? And if this is so, is there not a corresponding danger that this power would be lost if talk of rights becomes indiscriminate? While it might be wise to permit some extension to the catalogue of rights we currently possess, it might be unwise to permit any and every suggested extension. Given that the conception, ascription and observance of basic *human* rights is still a matter of considerable debate and disagreement, any extension of rights to even more contested areas may undermine the plausibility of rights as such.

Having said this, it is not incoherent or unreasonable to talk of the rights of animals. But this still leaves open other questions centring, on the one hand, on the moral force and persuasiveness which the language of animal rights can have, and, on the other, whether or not the ascription of rights will actually make any real difference to the way in which animals are treated.

To take the latter first, if we think of rights as 'trumps' (Dworkin, 1977), then the possession of a right overrides other considerations such as general welfare. As it turns out, the rights which Regan (for example) grants animals differ from rights ascribed to humans in two respects: first they are thinner in content, and second they are weaker in that less is required to override them. It seems that they are not so much trumps as just quite good cards to have in one's hand. Regan argues that:

> the principal negative duty we have in their case is not to treat them disrespectfully, and the correlative negative right they have against us is not to be treated in ways that ignore their equal inherent value. But just as our negative duty not to interfere in the lives of others does not consist merely in our minding our own business, so our duty regarding the respectful treatment of animals involves more than our taking care to treat them with respect. Since they have a valid claim to respectful treatment, we have a *prima facie* duty to assist them when others treat them in ways that violate their rights.
>
> (Regan, 1984, p. 282)

In other words, 'the right of animals not to be harmed is a *prima facie*, not an absolute right. In saying this we concede that there are circumstance in which this right may justifiably be overridden' (Regan, 1984, p. 330). Similarly, Warren argues that animal rights are different from human rights in both strength and content, and that animal rights can be easily overridden by environmental and utilitarian reasons, reasons that would not suffice to override stronger human rights (Warren, 1991, p. 395).

If animals can be rights-bearers then perhaps it follows (as Regan would argue) that we should ascribe rights to them irrespective of whether this will in fact better their condition overall. But there seems no compelling reason to ascribe rights merely because one can: restraint might be better. Of course, the recognition of rights or the ascription of legal rights probably would make a difference: at the very least, the hand of those who seek to uphold and improve animal welfare would be considerably strengthened. But the extent of the protection which would ensue is still uncertain and contestable. This brings us back to rhetoric. It can easily be argued that animal rights provide a strong rhetorical force for animal protection, and even Singer, who is opposed philosophically to the use of rights talk, allows that it might have political value. However, rhetoric lives or dies by its ability to persuade, and if both those who think that extending rights to animals weakens the force of rights language, and those who argue that animal rights can be more easily overridden than human rights are correct, should we not accept that the use of the concept and language of animal rights is, in practice, misconceived and misplaced? Misconceived and misplaced because, by weakening the force of the language of rights and thereby perhaps bringing it into disrepute, it weakens the very claim for greater animal protection which it invokes the language of rights to support. Hence it might be wise for even the sincerest believers in animal rights to accept that they might best serve their purposes by not invoking or pressing for them.[16]

SUGGESTIONS FOR FURTHER READING

Two useful collections are Robert Elliot (ed.), *Environmental Ethics* (1995) and Robin Attfield and Andrew Belsey (eds), *Philosophy and the Natural Environment* (1994). Elliot's collection includes a number of 'classic' articles which have shaped the development of environmental ethics. Attfield and Belsey's book is more contemporary and broader in scope. One of the most thorough and engaging contributions in this field is Robin Attfield's *The Ethics of Environmental Concern* (1991). The journal *Environment Ethics* includes both mainstream and more radical contributions; it has been joined recently by *Environmental Values*, which is becoming a well-regarded journal in the field of environmental philosophy.

2 Green ideology

Ecocentrism preaches the virtues of reverence, humility, responsibility, and care; it argues for low impact technology (but it is not anti-technological); it decries big-ness and impersonality in all forms (but especially in the city); and demands a code of behaviour that seeks permanence and stability based upon ecological principles of diversity and homeostasis. ... The technocentric ideology, by way of contrast, is almost arrogant in its assumption that man is supremely able to understand and control events to suit his purposes.

(O'Riordan, 1981, p. 1)

This chapter turns to more political questions within contemporary environmental thinking. For example, what might a future sustainable society look like? Can we derive a specifically green set of institutional arrangements? Who are the agents of green political change? Is there a coherent green political ideology?[1] Within green political thought, it is common to find such questions answered with reference to two considerations: first, our ethical relationship with the natural world; and second, the limits placed on development by the finite nature of physical resources and the ability of ecosystems to withstand damage from pollution. However, neither reflection on our relations with the natural world nor scientific arguments concerning the carrying capacity of ecosystems will in themselves lead to a comprehensive green political position. To understand the emerging form of contemporary green political thought, it is also necessary to reflect on more traditional values, such as justice, democracy and equality; to engage in a critical dialogue with other political traditions. By analysing the evolving relationship between green politics and the more established traditions of Western political thought, it can be seen that some form of environmental considerations has played a part in the development of most political traditions and that such considerations have at times been utilised to justify green political arrangements ranging from fascist to anarchist.

There remain tensions within green political thinking concerning such issues as the structure of political institutions and strategies for change. These tensions will be highlighted with reference to the themes implicit within the concept of sustainable development. Although there appears to be an emerging consensus centred on this concept, there are none the less widely divergent interpretations of what sustainable development actually requires. Perhaps the fact that actors as far apart as environmental direct action groups and business associations appeal to the same concept in support of their activities should serve as a warning that usage does not always imply precise agreement on meaning.

POLITICS, ETHICS AND *THE LIMITS TO GROWTH*

From ethics to politics

In the previous chapter, arguments were developed to show how our relationship with the natural world might be understood philosophically and ethically. What becomes clear is that it is extremely difficult to accurately describe the ethical relationships involved and the duties and obligations that these generate. That such ethical considerations are central to the commitment of many green activists is not in doubt; the point now at issue is whether political strategies and institutional arrangements can be derived directly from such reflections and commitments. Could the belief in, for instance, the intrinsic value of all natural entities tell us anything about the ideal form of institutions? Is it possible to 'read off' political arrangements from reflections on natural processes? For example, is it plausible for political ecologists to claim that diversity in nature equates to toleration; stability to democracy; interdependence to equality; and longevity to tradition (Dobson, 1995, p. 24)? Are these claims that features of the natural world equate to social and political forms and principles coherent?

There are a number of sceptical points that need to be made here which are crucial to the development of green politics. The first is as true for green politics as it is for environmental ethics: it is simply not possible to 'read off' ethical and political principles direct from scientific concepts such as diversity, symbiosis or complexity. Normative concepts cannot be drawn directly from descriptive ecological concepts. To argue that we can 'because they are natural' is to argue in a circle. As John Barry comments, 'non-human nature gives us no determinate prescriptions about how we ought to live' (Barry 1994, p. 383).[2]

Further, it is far from obvious that ethical commitments to the non-human world, such as a belief in the moral worth of sentience or the intrinsic value of aspects of the non-human world, can tell us anything about whether we should commend democratic or authoritarian solutions to political questions. The link between ethical and political commitments is rarely clear-cut. In fact it is a fair criticism of environmental philosophy that it provides little in the way of practical guidance in the area of political change. This is not to say that ethical reasoning and ecological insights are a waste of time and play no part in political considerations. All that is being stressed is that there is no necessary one-to-one connection between ethical and political commitments. What such ethical reasoning can provide us with, however, is a critical standpoint from which to assess political arrangements and decision-making processes. Such reflections can help us to make judgements about the environmental sensitivity of institutional designs, for instance in contributing towards criticism of purely economic decision-making processes such as cost–benefit analysis (CBA), which cannot adequately represent such ethical commitments. For more on this see Chapter 5.

In the previous chapter our everyday moral considerations were widened to take into account duties to present and future human generations. Considering these issues may help to articulate the point that is being made here. Such considerations do not simply stem from a particular view of values in nature, from, for example, the assertion of intrinsic value, but from a commitment to justice – a typically anthropocentric concern. Studying ecological relations will not lead us to a precise definition of what our duties and obligations to present and future generations entail; that requires adherence to beliefs beyond such reflections. However, environmental considerations and values help us to deepen our understanding of humanity's relations with the non-human world and of our political and social institutions, but without offering us the basis for a complete blueprint for a future sustainable society.

The limits to growth debate

If an ethical commitment to non-human nature provides a basic building-block of green political thought, the debate over the ecological limits of social and economic arrangements has provided another. In 1972, the Club of Rome, a group of prominent scientists, educators, economists, humanists, industrialists and national and international civil servants, published its report *The Limits to Growth*.[3] The report was based on an investigation of the interconnected nature of five trends that the Club of Rome believed to be of global concern: 'accelerating industrialisation, rapid population growth, widespread malnutrition, depletion of nonrenewable resources, and a deteriorating environment' (Meadows *et al.*, 1972, p. 21). Using a computer-generated world model, a series of scenarios was developed by inputting different rates of change for each factor. Central to the report, and to much green analysis that followed, is the emphasis on the exponential, as opposed to linear, pattern of growth associated with the trends highlighted. A particular characteristic of such exponential growth is the suddenness with which it approaches fixed limits. It is this characteristic that led to the pessimistic conclusion of the Club of Rome that the post-war rate of economic expansion and population growth could not be sustained without widespread poverty and famine, exhaustion of global natural resources and irreparable environmental damage. There is a decidedly neo-Malthusian feel to *The Limits to Growth* in line with the concerns for population growth expressed in books such as *The Population Bomb* by Paul Ehrlich, published in the same year.[4]

Conclusions of *The Limits to Growth*

1 If the present growth trends in world population, industrialisation, food production, and resource depletion continue unchanged, the limits to growth on this planet will be reached sometime within the next hundred years.

The most probable result will be a rather sudden and uncontrollable decline in both population and industrial capacity.

2 It is possible to alter these growth trends and to establish a condition of
ecological and economic stability that is sustainable far into the future.
The state of global equilibrium could be designed so that the basic needs
of each person on earth are satisfied and each person has an equal opportunity to realise his individual potential.

3 If the world's people decide to strive for the second outcome rather than
the first, the sooner they begin working to attain it, the greater will be their
chances of success.

(Meadows *et al.*, 1972, pp. 23–4)

Since its publication, the report has been widely criticised and a number of its
predictions have failed to materialise. In retrospect, some of its conclusions and
modelling proved overly simplistic and pessimistic. Wilfred Beckerman, for example, in his recent book *Small is Stupid* (1995a), is scathing about such resource depletion scare stories, pointing out that *The Limits to Growth* failed to allow for the
various feedback mechanisms operative within an economy – if a good or resource
becomes scarce its price rises, which signals a search for new sources of that good
or for suitable substitutes.[5] Beckerman's critique in many ways exposes the pessi-
mism of the Club of Rome's report, although it clearly requires there to be suitable
substitutes, a claim that may not always be true with certain environmental goods.
(We shall return to this point in our case study of weak and strong sustainability at
the end of Chapter 5.) However, despite its rather overstated conclusions and
simplistic computer modelling, the report managed to focus attention on growing
global tensions surrounding resource depletion, and its central theme – that infi-
nite growth in a finite system is impossible – has become a 'foundation stone of
Green political thinking' (Dobson, 1991, p. 13).

In the same year, the editorial board of *The Ecologist* magazine co-wrote *A Blueprint for Survival* (Goldsmith *et al.*, 1972) and this was followed two years later by E.F.
Schumacher's *Small is Beautiful* (1973). Following in the steps of the Club of Rome,
these two seminal texts emphasise the need to restructure society and economy to
a 'human scale'. Decentralisation is seen as fundamental if society is to become
more congenial and develop within ecological limits. However, as with ethical
considerations, commitment to the tenet that societies must adapt to living within
ecological limits does not entail any particular political arrangement. There is no
direct and necessary link between the finite nature of the Earth's resources and the
prescription of decentralisation. In fact, as we shall see later, the recognition of
physical limits has led a number of theorists and activists to call for centralised
authoritarian solutions to environmental problems. Taking these qualifications on
board, the limits-to-growth thesis still remains a critical green standpoint in relation to other traditions of thought. This is especially true when we consider that
the thesis can be taken to go beyond a simple physical interpretation – many greens

would want to talk about moral limits to growth, a socio-economic critique of the inequalities and environmental insensitivity of liberal capitalist political economy (Barry, 1994, pp. 372ff).

It is important to note that there is also no necessary connection between the ethical basis of our obligations to the non-human world and acceptance of the limits to growth arguments. As we shall see later in this chapter, this very issue leads to tensions between some ecosocialists, who have accepted that there must be ecological restrictions to the forces of production, and greens, who believe that they must also widen their ethical commitments beyond purely human well-being. It is to such tensions that we now turn.

GREEN THOUGHT AND WESTERN POLITICAL TRADITIONS

Any survey of green political texts from the last two or three decades will reveal that there is a wide variety of political institutions and strategies for change endorsed as the way forward to a sustainable future. From democratic to authoritarian regimes, centralised states to decentralised communities, planned to free-market economies, party politics to grassroots activism – all have found support at some time or another.[6] Such endorsements have often been a response to particular contexts and situations: Robyn Eckersley, for instance, highlights three interconnected 'preoccupations' within green political thought, which can be seen as a response to particular circumstances (Eckersley, 1992, pp. 8–20). The first preoccupation, the crisis of participation, evolved primarily during the 1960s in the civil rights movement. Its central concern is with participation in decision-making processes and issues of resource distribution, leading to a recognition of democracy and social justice as important themes within the green movement. The second preoccupation, the crisis of survival, was originally inspired by the publication of *The Limits to Growth* and *A Blueprint for Survival* and 'marked the emergence of the *global* dimensions of environmental degradation and the *common fate* of humanity' (Eckersley, 1992, p. 12). The apparent urgency of the survivalist message led many writers to call for authoritarian solutions to the environmental crisis, thereby contradicting the democratic thrust of earlier commentators. The third and final preoccupation is the belief that environmental concerns are as much a crisis of culture and human character as a crisis of nature or the use of natural resources. If this is so, a broader ecological understanding of human needs, technology and self-image becomes essential with a recognition that it is in our interests, understood in a comprehensive manner, to become less dependent on technological responses to environmental and social problems.

These preoccupations need to be recognised and each given due weight: but it is important to realise that they may be in tension with each other. For example, green concerns often stress the need for a holistic or organicistic approach to the solution of environmental problems, but these may in turn be markedly at odds with the concern for egalitarianism and the associated demands for social change which also form part of the agenda. If these tensions can be successfully addressed, green politics might then be linked with other emancipatory political projects that call for cultural renewal and the revitalisation of civil society. As Eckersley has argued:

> This new theoretical project is concerned to find ways of overcoming the destructive logic of capital accumulation, the acquisitive values of consumer society, and, more generally, all systems of domination (including class domination, patriarchy, imperialism, totalitarianism, and the domination of nature).
>
> (ibid., 1992, pp. 20–1)

This is an extremely ambitious and radical remit for any political project and it would be an oversimplification to think that the values and attitudes it embodies have been developed purely from an analysis of our ethical relationship with the natural world or from the need to live within ecological limits. Equally, to view these developments as having occurred only within the last three decades would ignore a long history of attitudes to nature which have played a part in various streams of political thinking. As Andrew Vincent points out, the attitudes associated with ecology:

> did not spring upon us in the 1970s with pure radical credentials. Rather, they relate to a subtle and immensely potent conjunction of attitudes to nature which have been present in European thought since the late nineteenth century. Despite their widespread promotion by different and politically diverse groups throughout the twentieth century, it is the accidental conjunction of circumstances, individuals and events in the 1970s which has provided a dynamic refocus for the ecological vocabulary.
>
> (Vincent, 1992, pp. 214–15)

We need to survey briefly some of the traditions within Western political thought in order to understand how they have helped shape green political thinking. All the traditions have something to say about human–non-human relations and, in some cases, critical reassessment has occurred in the light of green critiques. One of the central issues we need to consider is whether green political thought has developed an entirely autonomous response to our circumstances or whether it still depends on the insights of other political streams. We shall sketch historical associations between traditions and ecological thinking and highlight tensions to be found with current environmental concerns, specifically the ethical considerations of the non-human world and questions arising from the limits-to-growth debate. We shall also consider whether the central values of these traditions are compatible with green thinking. Ecological politics has developed from a critical relationship with many other streams of thought, and because of this it incorporates a number of diverse and contradictory tendencies.

Authoritarianism and fascism

> If scarcity is not dead, if it is in fact with us in a seemingly much more intense form than ever before in human history, how can we avoid reaching the conclusion that Leviathan is inevitable? Given current levels of population and technology, I do not believe that we can. Hobbes shows why a spaceship earth must have a captain. Otherwise, the collective selfishness and irresponsibility produced by the tragedy of the commons will destroy the spaceship, and any sacrifice of freedom by the crew members is clearly the lesser of two evils.
>
> (Ophuls, 1973, p. 224)

As this quotation shows, it is very easy to move from a perception of the seriousness of the environmental problems towards a view in which, as Ophuls argues, the choice is between 'Leviathan and oblivion'. In responding to the problems identified by *The Limits to Growth* and similar reports, writers such as William Ophuls and Robert Heilbroner, whilst at a personal level committed to liberal and democratic values, envisaged an environmentally benevolent Leviathan as the only political arrangement that could stop human societies from developing beyond environmental carrying capacities. Restrictions on levels of production, consumption and population growth could not be achieved quickly enough through democratic processes, and individuals' rights and freedoms would have to be overridden in the short term in order to achieve long-term survival and lessen ecological damage. Perhaps the most consistent and influential advocate of this position has been Garrett Hardin, whose 'Tragedy of the Commons' thesis (Hardin, 1968) espouses strong, centralised leadership if self-interested individuals are not to despoil environmental resources. Along with his later, more controversial 'Lifeboat Ethic' (Hardin, 1977) – which seems to many to suggest that if the developed, Western nations are to survive then they should cut off aid links with the Third World and leave them in poverty – such authoritarian ideas have often found their way into green proposals concerning population control, resource distribution and immigration. It is essential for greens to realise that many of their concepts and much of their rhetoric can have authoritarian and imperialistic overtones.

Green theorists frequently appeal to concepts of the natural, using organic metaphors, elevating the spiritual over the rational, and justifying a holistic politics which elevates the community and the state over the individual. Such ecological doctrines have often been appealed to by authoritarian and fascistic movements: for instance, pantheistic ecological considerations were fundamental to the ideology of the Nazis. Although few greens would now espouse such political arrangements, they would do well to recognise that authoritarian solutions are often lurking in the background.

Conservatism

Many of the concerns of environmentalists appear to have their roots in central conceptions within traditional conservatism. Congruence can be found with respect to ideas of tradition, continuity, stability, organic change, prudence, rejection of totalitarianism and appeals to community. Traditional conservative and ecological theorists often share an anti-capitalist stance and romantic visions of non-human nature. In a recent defence of the deep affinity between ecological theory and conservative philosophy, John Gray adopts a common criticism of neo-liberal market philosophy, stressing the similarities of the two streams of thought (Gray, 1993, pp. 124–77). Both share a multi-generation perspective, give primacy to the common life, see danger in novelty and give a central place to the virtue of prudence. There is considerable scepticism about the possibility, inevitability or desirability of 'progress' and an emphasis on continuity and change as occurring within a developing tradition rather than in the light of a rational blueprint for society. The ideals of harmony and stability are central conceptions to both traditional conservatism and green political thought. As Freeden remarks, 'conservative arguments cannot be completely disentangled or excluded from all green positions' (Freeden, 1995, p. 15).

Although there are indeed many areas of congruence, Gray's analysis can easily be construed as focusing selectively on particular areas of green thought and conservatism. Clearly the conservation and preservation streams of the environmental movement owe much to conservative and romantic visions of nature. As we shall see in the next chapter, it is often the case that in specific local environmental campaigns traditional conservatives are found in alliance with more radical, emancipatory greens. However, contemporary green analysis of social relations appears to part company with much conservative thought on various issues, although even here the case is not clear-cut. Where conservative thinking tends to emphasise order, tradition and community over what it sees as abstract criteria such as social justice and egalitarianism, contemporary green political analysis typically takes these later ideas as central and is critical of apparent conservative apologies for hierarchical social arrangement. Here we find a paradox in green thinking, with calls for universal standards of justice and democracy coexisting with a desire to defend indigenous communities and their practices. But what if those practices, which may be environmentally sustainable, are themselves based on the dominance of a particular social group? It is with such questions that green political thought must come to terms and perhaps it would be more accurate to see conservatism and romanticism as modes of thought out of which a more comprehensive green critique is developing.

Liberalism

Environmental thought again shares a mixed relationship with the liberal tradition. Although influenced in many ways by early liberal thought, particularly ideas of rights, freedom and democracy, the most recent turn in liberal thought, namely neo-liberalism and *laissez-faire* free-market economics, appears incompatible with the central tenets of green thinking. In the previous chapter on ethics the influence of two early liberals, Jeremy Bentham and John Stuart Mill, has already been noted. Bentham's utilitarian views on public policy have found favour amongst animal rights theorists, where sentience and the ability to suffer pain are central to considerations of the proper treatment of animals. Many of Mill's ideas are similarly resurfacing in green texts. Herman Daly (1991), for instance, has championed the steady-state economy (see the case study at the end of Chapter 5), which was first adumbrated in Mill's *Principles of Political Economy*. Liberal approaches to environmental problems have been used to argue for the extension of rights to both future generations and other living things (Eckersley, 1995b; 1996). Appeals to nineteenth-century liberal ideals such as public space and deliberation, civic virtue and civil society show that certain streams of liberal thought are central to green visions of future sustainable societies (Sagoff, 1988, pp. 146–70).

However, it would be fair to say that where many connections can be made to these classic liberal values, the rise of neo-liberal or New Right thought in recent times has been viewed with horror by the majority of environmentalists.

> Individualism, the pursuit of private gain, limited government and market freedom are contradicted by radical ecology commitments to the resolution of environmental problems as a collective good and to the intervention and restrictions on economic and personal freedoms to deal with them. Liberal economy is seen to underpin the commitment to economic expansion and accumulation and to the identification of wealth and material advancement with progress and improvement.
>
> (Martell, 1994, p. 141)

Such material accumulation is seen by many green writers as spelling ruin and destruction for human and ecological communities, putting increasing pressure on social and environmental relations (Dryzek, 1992, pp. 18–26). Further, the neo-liberal conception of well-being as a correlative of material acquisition is viewed as a complete misrepresentation of what is important to a human life. There would appear to be serious contradictions between neo-liberal market logic and environmental imperatives. Recently, though, there has been a response to such criticisms by advocates of 'free-market environmentalism'. For such neo-liberals, ecological problems such as Hardin's 'Tragedy of the Commons' are the result of a lack of well-defined property rights and price mechanisms; rather than reducing the impact of the market we need to extend its role (Anderson and Leal, 1991). This is very much a counter move by the New Right in order to deflect greens' anti-free-market claims and to rework environmental problems in neo-liberal rhetoric. It is important, however, to note that the rejection of a free-market approach to environmental problems does not necessarily mean that greens must be totally anti-market: the market and price incentives and disincentives can be used as part of environmental policy without being seen as the whole of policy (see Chapter 6 for a fuller discussion of this issue).

In more general terms, the individualism which lies at the heart of liberalism, whether in its political expression (the insistence on rights and liberties) or in its economic expression (the insistence on markets) creates a problem for environmentalists who are attempting to develop new forms of community and political participation relevant to a sustainable society. Much green thinking has a greater affinity with various forms of communitarianism, both in its insistence on the essential relationship of an individual to a society (as opposed to the liberal conception of society as being nothing more than the creation of pre-existing bearers of rights) and in its insistence on responsibilities rather than merely on the assertion of rights.

Marxism and socialism

It is very common to find the criticisms levelled at capitalism and liberal free-market ideology mirrored in discussions on socialism and communism. As Jonathon Porritt argues: 'Both [capitalism and socialism] are dedicated to industrial growth, to the expansion of the means of production, to the materialistic ethic as the best means of meeting people's needs, and to unimpeded technological development' (Porritt, 1984, p. 44). For writers such as Porritt, both are forms of the 'super-ideology' of industrialism, with the former communist states displaying a record of environmental protection as bad as (if not worse than) Western nations. Although socialists share green concerns for poverty relief and egalitarian redistribution of resources, increased wealth generation is often seen as essential in order to finance such policies. Greens argue that socialist thought does not take into account the physical limits to wealth production, seemingly believing in the ability of science and technology to overcome scarcity. Further, it is argued that the environment is considered only in terms of its direct impact on the well-being of humans. Socialists have responded by accusing greens of having an idealised vision of the non-human world and providing 'in essence a defence of middle class privilege and exploitative class and neo-colonialist relationships' (Hay, 1988, p. 26). However, between these rather polarised positions the continuing debate between greens and socialists has in the last few years resulted in the re-examination of their shared attitudes in light of the apparent hegemony of neo-liberal thinking. It is both simplistic and narrow either to take the former communist bloc as the basis of criticism of all Marxist and socialist ideas, or to view greens as only interested in the ecological effect of production.

There are at least four areas where fruitful connections have been made and where the green analysis has been deepened by socialist reflections – and vice versa. First, in the area of political economy, socialist thought exposes in some depth the destructive power of capitalist societies. Such an analysis has helped to deepen and refocus the ecological critique of industrialism. Socialists have often adopted the sceptical view that greens have seemed willing to ameliorate the ecological impact of capitalism rather than call for a full-scale transformation of economic structures. As André Gorz argues:

> It is ... time to end the pretence that ecology is, by itself, sufficient: *the ecological movement is not an end in itself, but a stage in the larger struggle.* It can throw up obstacles to capitalist development and force a number of changes. But when, after exhausting every means of coercion and deceit, capitalism begins to work its way out of the ecological impasse, it will assimilate ecological necessities as technical constraints, and adapt the conditions of exploitation to them.
> (Gorz, 1980, p. 3)

The centrality of growth, the injustice of the existing distribution of wealth and the short-term interest in profit maximisation of free-market ideology might be seen as common elements within socialist and green thought. However, for more mainstream socialists the generation of material wealth is not in itself a problem, rather the method of its production and distribution. Here we do find a tension between those socialists who are willing to accept the ideas of natural limits to economic expansion and an ecological dimension in political economy (Hayward, 1995, pp. 115–27) and those who seem overly optimistic and share the Promethean belief that the problems of poverty, injustice and inequality can be solved through the abolition of scarcity by technical means.

Marx largely viewed nature as something to be dominated and used for human purposes. Where he identified and denounced exploitation it was the exploitation of class by class through their different places within the relations of production (the pattern of ownership, property, law and control over the forces of production); the forces of production and their domination over nature he much admired. The task, as he saw it, was to harness the technological possibilities of exploiting nature in the service of a fundamental change in the social relations of production in which the surplus labour value of the worker no longer accrued solely to the benefit of the capitalist class. For Marx, the question of the desirability of exploiting nature, or the limits to such exploitation, was not a matter of concern, and nature as such was not ascribed value independently of its instrumental value to human beings in allowing them to develop and progress. The ecological dimension cannot, therefore, be straightforwardly grafted on to orthodox Marxism, requiring as it does a reorientation of human relations with the natural world.

The second area of interest is the question of agents of change. Although often providing clear prescriptions for a future sustainable society, green political thought has often been rightly criticised for inadequately theorising strategies for change. On the other hand, orthodox Marxism has a ready-made explanation of both the causes of change and the agents of change. With its emphasis on the forces of production and its analysis of the social relations of production, it could confidently state that the main agent of change would inevitably be the working class. But the Left is now in a position of turmoil on this issue, with the traditional Marxist emphasis on the working class as the vanguard of political revolution becoming increasingly unconvincing. Both green and socialist writers have turned their attention to political strategies that incorporate, for instance, new social movements, the unemployed, communes, and more traditional parliamentary routes. We shall return to this issue in Chapter 3.

The third area of critical debate centres on the role of institutions, particularly the state, both in processes of change and in any future society. Many ecosocialists tend to view the green commitment to a decentralised society as a romantic, Utopian ideal that is doomed to failure, would result in further inequalities, and be unable to tackle large-scale environmental problems because of a lack of coordination. An enlightened state is often seen to be essential if a sustainable future is to be achieved.

If one is honest, however, about the objectives which an ecologically enlightened state would set itself, it is difficult to avoid concluding that the state, as
the agent of the collective will, would have to take an active law-making and
enforcing role in imposing a range of environmental and resource constraints.

(Ryle, 1988, p. 60)

It is worth noting, however, that there are streams of socialist thought based on
decentralist values which do not put so much stress on statism. Writers such as
William Morris, Erich Fromm and Ivan Illich, whose work has often been ignored
within left-wing thought dominated by reformist and revolutionary statist political
thinking, are now being reinterpreted and given their due in the light of the ecological imperative to restructure societies.

Finally, much has been written about the Marxist attitude to the non-human
world. The early writings of Marx can be interpreted as showing an awareness of
the interconnectedness and dialectical relationship of humanity with the rest of
nature and the alienation of both under systems of capitalism. However, even with
such a positive interpretation and the concept of nature as 'man's inorganic body',
it is clear that Marx's dialectics are orientated specifically at the self-realisation of
humanity through the domination and transformation of nature (Benton, 1993,
pp. 23–57). Socialists are often charged with being interested in environmental
concerns only in so far as there is a direct effect on human well-being. In response,
greens are often vilified for a tendency towards mysticism and romanticism. But do
differences in orientation of this sort necessarily issue in differing policy implications? For the most part it might not seem so. However, it is easy to see how on
specific issues, for example species extinction, there might be no relation between
human well-being and the threatened species. Socialists could then apparently
offer no reason for protection. But this may not be the final position: socialist
beliefs do not necessarily rule out consideration of non-human entities, even if in
practice they have focused their attention primarily on human welfare. There are
certainly a number of post-Marxists, such as Herbert Marcuse, who recognise the
link between the domination of man by man and nature by man and look forward
to the re-enchantment of the non-human world. More recently, writers such as
André Gorz, David Pepper, Ted Benton, Tim Hayward and Michael Jacobs have
done much to reconcile the apparent differences between socialist and green political thought. The ecological dimension to political economy has been generally
accepted as a paramount concern and 'red–green' dialogue on political, social and
economic arrangements is an area of extremely fruitful work.

Anarchism and decentralised communitarianism

The political arrangement supported by many radical greens is along anarchist
lines, where the ideals of egalitarianism, non-hierarchy, local empowerment and
democracy, self-reliance and diversity are often central concerns. This arises out of
a deep mistrust of traditional forms and bearers of political authority, a desire to
challenge them and to reassert that power and authority lie with people and their

communities. The writings of late nineteenth- and early twentieth-century anarchists, such as Peter Kropotkin, can be seen as precursors to the more recent *A
Blueprint for Survival* (Goldsmith *et al.*, 1972). Anarchist arguments for decentralisation of social and political institutions are taken to be absolutely necessary if a
sustainable society is to emerge. This vision can be contrasted with the authoritarian responses to *The Limits to Growth* report discussed earlier.

As with other traditions of thought, the ecoanarchist stream is not unified and
can be subdivided into social ecology and ecocommunalism (Eckersley, 1992, pp.
145–69). The most influential social ecologist is undoubtably Murray Bookchin,
whose analysis of environmental problems is based on a perceived connection
between the exploitation of nature and the exploitation of human beings.[7] Contemporary society is seen as socially, economically and politically irrational and
anti-ecological in that the competitive capitalist system is based on hierarchical
relations of command and obedience within which nature is commodified. It is
only when the domination of human over human is overcome that the domination
of nature can be transcended. This will only occur in decentralised, autonomous
and radically democratic communities.

Such an analysis is very different from that of the ecocommunalists, who draw
extensively on deep ecology (Naess, 1973; 1989). Here it is the humanity–nature
relation that is central. Under the influence of deep ecological insights, bioregionalists,
such as Kirkpatrick Sale, hold that communities must learn to live within the carrying capacity of their specific bioregion. In many ways there is a resonance within
bioregionalism of certain 1970s survivalist views that self-sufficient, small-scale
communities are the only feasible response to an imminent environmental catastrophe.

The deep ecological position is frequently criticised for simply 'reading off'
ethical and political principles from ecological concepts such as diversity, symbiosis and complexity: on what grounds can we derive ethical or political principles
direct from such scientific concepts? Naess's conception of deep ecology, and particularly his commitment to 'biospherical egalitarianism', has been vociferously
challenged by Bookchin, who argues, at times polemically, that the decentring of
humans in such a political position has a tendency towards anti-humanism and
misanthropy. For Bookchin, too much emphasis is placed on the mystical qualities
of the human–non-human relationship, on the development of an ecological self
or consciousness, while the social, political and economic roots and realities of the
environmental crisis are ignored.[8] It is true that both social and deep ecology wish
to confer the 'maximum political and economic autonomy on decentralised local
communities', that their 'anarchism is grounded in, or otherwise draws its inspiration from, ecology' and that both positions provide a strong defence of 'the grass
roots and extra-parliamentary activities of the Green movement' (Eckersley, 1992,
p. 145), but the important differences between deep and social ecology must also
be recognised.

The anarchist belief that the state must be either bypassed or abolished leads to
much heated debate within green political thought. The state is viewed as the
prime example of an oppressive agent and a defender of hierarchical social and

political power relations. Also it is seen to be too far removed and centralised to deal with local environmental and social problems. However, for many critics, and particularly ecosocialists, the removal of the state and subsequent emergence of autonomous communities is viewed as overly idealistic and Utopian and fails to take account of fundamentally important state functions.

First, there is some concern over how the internal political structure of decentralised communities would be controlled. For social ecologists, radical participatory democracy is fundamental. But, for bioregionalists it is living within the ecological carrying capacity of a bioregion that is of prime importance rather than the political arrangements of a society. This is clearly implied by Sale:

> Bioregional diversity means exactly that. It does not mean that every region of the north-east, or North America, or the globe, will construct itself upon the values of democracy, equality, liberty, freedom, justice, and other such like *desiderata*. It means rather that truly autonomous bioregions will likely go their own separate ways and end up with some quite disparate political systems – some democracies, no doubt, some direct, some representative, some federative, but undoubtedly all kinds of aristocracies, theocracies, principalities, margravates, duchies and palatinates as well. And some with values, beliefs, standards and customs quite antithetical to those that the people in this room, for example, hold dearest.
>
> (Sale, in Dobson, 1991, pp. 80–1)[9]

Thus the stress placed on the value of diversity can be interpreted to mean a radical diversity of institutional forms. Hence, some of the more politically sensitive questions concerning authoritarian solutions to population, immigration, punishment and the like return to the fore. There is a further issue surrounding the value of diversity which is so central to the rhetoric of anarchists – could a small-scale society support physical and cultural diversity and difference internally? Do not small, self-contained communities often lead to conformity and ostracise difference? In this respect the state may be viewed as the guarantor of democracy and the defender of political freedoms and difference.

Second, there is a question of distribution of resources: is it just that some communities or bioregions would be environmentally more abundant than others? This reflects issues of intragenerational justice between the North and the South raised in Chapter 1. Is there not some obligation for those who live in resource-rich locations to redistribute to those less fortunate? A similar issue is raised in terms of transboundary and large-scale environmental impacts. A small-scale community is likely to respond to local environmental problems more sensitively than a more centralised authority, but without some form of over-arching authority, how are cumulative, supra-community problems such as acid rain or global warming to be faced? How are claims between communities over the impact of transboundary pollution to be settled?

Finally, the question of strategy is perhaps underdeveloped. How are we to get to this Utopia of decentralised communities from the present state structure and the increasing globalisation of capital and culture? Many radical greens are funda-mentally at odds with the idea of achieving this outcome through parliamentary means. Such processes necessitate concessions and leave too much power with too few individuals. If the means must be consistent with the ends then it is no surprise that potentially corrupting processes are vilified and in general lifestyle changes and the development of alternative communities and practices are endorsed. Although the wider political significance of such extra-parliamentary activities may at times be limited, the influence of anarchist thought, with its belief in local political action and its challenging of existing institutions and the interests they represent, is evident in much green political thinking.

Feminism

'Ecological feminism' is an umbrella term which captures a variety of multicultural perspectives on the nature of the connections *within* social sys-tems of domination between those humans in subordinate positions, particu-larly women, and the domination of non-human nature. … Ecofeminist analy-ses of the twin dominations of women and nature include considerations of the domination of people of color, children, and the underclass.

(Warren, 1994, p. 1)

Ecofeminist analysis shares the broad concern of the feminist movement as re-gards the elimination of gender bias – or more widely, all forms of bias towards subordinated groups –and the development of non-gendered or non-interest domi-nated political, social and economic practices and institutions. Values and characteristics usually conceived of as feminine, such as humility, care and nur-ture, are seen to be seriously undervalued in patriarchal societies, with a detrimental effect on how we conceive of our relationships with non-human nature. In addi-tion, ecofeminists argue that there are connections between the domination and oppression of women and of nature. This leads not only to a variety of ecofeminist positions that have strong political connections to existing political traditions, for example liberal, Marxist and socialist feminisms (Warren, 1987), but also varia-tions based on the interpretation of the link between the domination of women and nature (Plumwood, 1986, p. 121).

The various accounts of the source of the links between the subordination of women and domination of the natural world seem to fit into two main categories. First, there is an argument that dominant philosophies have traditionally operated on the basis of various dualisms in which women and nature are both allocated an inferior position with respect to men and their projects. It is argued that this differ-entiation has had real historical consequences across all forms of human knowl-edge and practice, be it in art, science, education, ethics or politics. These consequences have led to attitudes justifying the exploitation of women and the natural world and can be seen as an expression of what is often termed strong anthropocentrism. Second, there is an account of domination which stresses the physiological and psychological difference between men and women. Here women are taken to be biologically closer to the natural order by virtue, for example, of their capacity for childbirth and nurture.

It is these conceptual connections that in many cases cause tensions and disagreements both within ecofeminist analysis and within the wider feminist movement. The second stream of ecofeminism highlighted often promotes the idea of a biologically and psychologically determined connection between women and nature. Women must be in the vanguard of environmental change simply because they are closer to and understand the natural world in a way that men can never achieve. Such biological and psychological determinism, however, emphasises a fundamental difference between the sexes which for many critics could be used as the basis for further domination and servitude. Clearly there are controversies within ecofeminist thought, with other commentators simply wishing to argue that a more environmentally sensitive society needs to articulate those principles, values and characteristics traditionally associated with the feminine, but potentially accessible to all humanity. This later position is invaluable in highlighting the power relations that lead to the marginalisation and exclusion of women, indigenous peoples and others, and the possibilities for radical institutional change called for by many within the green movement.

A new ideology?

Should green political thought be understood as an ideology in its own right? It is common to find writers claiming that green thinking represents an overcoming of Right–Left distinctions and, on occasions, that it represents a complete break from traditional political thought; for others it is a new ideology that can take its place alongside the more established ideologies such as conservatism, socialism, liberalism or anarchism. It would seem, however, that the answer to our question is problematised by the fact that there is wide disagreement as to the meaning of the term 'ideology': it is an essentially contested concept within political theory.[10]

Michael Freeden (1995) analyses ideologies in terms of the core, adjacent and peripheral concepts of which they are composed. Given such an understanding, one should expect an overlap between different ideologies in that they may share many concepts in common. However, the place assigned to these concepts within the whole, and hence their relative significance and meaning, will vary from ideology to ideology. In analysing green ideology then, one should not expect that all its values and principles will be completely different from other ideologies; rather, one should expect to find some features in common, but contained within a whole whose overall thrust is substantially different. In this chapter, we have argued that at the core of green political thinking is the belief that our ethical relations with non-human nature and the finite character of resources need to be central in political reflections; beyond these two core ideas, green political thought must rely on insights from other traditions. So, are these core themes enough to demarcate green political thinking sufficiently from other ideologies and doctrines?

Of the green political theorists who have argued that it is possible to demarcate a green ideological position, one of the most significant and influential is Andrew Dobson. He argues that 'ecologism' does represent a new ideology since it provides a description of the present political and social climate, a prescription of how the world ought to be arranged and the motivation for change (Dobson, 1995, p. 2). The ideological form Dobson identifies is somewhere 'within a broadly left-emancipatory framework' (ibid., p. 85) and can be clearly differentiated from 'environmentalism'; from the attempt to assimilate environmental concerns into more traditional political positions:

> environmentalism argues for a managerial approach to environmental problems, secure in the belief that they can be solved without fundamental changes in present values or patterns of production and consumption, while ecologism holds that a sustainable and fulfilling existence presupposes radical changes in our relationship with the natural world, and in our mode of social and political life.
>
> (ibid., p. 1)[11]

In a similar manner, Andrew Vincent holds that 'the ecology perspective ... tends to combine, uniquely, both respect for local autonomy in communities and a global message' (Vincent, 1992, p. 225). However, both writers seem to over-emphasise a particular stream within a wide range of possible coherent green political positions that can be understood as a reaction against the domination of a strong anthropocentric or technocentric attitude, where nature is simply seen as something to be mastered and controlled. Might it not be better to understand green political thought as a critical perspective which has forced existing political traditions to undergo an internal analysis and re-think of their fundamental premises and concerns, as well as providing a critical space for convergence and debate between traditions? Rather than attempting to define the definitive ideological form for green politics, we would be wise to be cautious and to reflect on Martin Ryle's warning that 'the mere invocation of "ecology", crucial as it is, does not in itself determine in a positive sense the future development of social and political reality' (Ryle, 1988, p. 7).

Tensions and mutual distrust, both theoretical and practical, abound within green political thought, for instance over the role of the state and the limits of decentralisation, or the identification of agents and processes of change. Political commitments such as justice, democracy and liberty cannot be developed from purely ecological considerations, although ecological ideas can have implications for their preferred form. It is perhaps easier in many ways to draw out what contemporary green political thinking rejects, such as authoritarian solutions and free-market capitalism, than provide an unambiguous account of a unitary green ideological position. Contemporary green ideas can perhaps best be understood as developing from a fluid, critical reflection on traditional areas of political thought, particularly areas of socialist, anarchist and feminist thinking, with ecological concerns as a necessary, but not complete, part of that reflection.

SUSTAINABLE DEVELOPMENT, DEMOCRACY AND THE ENVIRONMENT

Having looked at some of the traditions of political thought that have influenced green politics, this final section will investigate the connections between two concepts that are central to much contemporary green political thinking – sustainable development and democracy. How do greens interpret the concept of sustainable development and what is the relationship between democratic and environmental challenges? The idea of sustainable development grew out of green political thought but has been popularised and corrupted by other actors. At the same time, as we have seen above, certain elements of the heritage of green politics have a fairly ambiguous, if not hostile, relationship with the idea of democracy. Can the competing demands of sustainable development and democracy be reconciled?

Much rests on how the concept of sustainable development is to be interpreted and employed by those interested in environmental problems. Agreement on the importance of the concept of sustainable development can be found across the ideological spectrum. Groups as diverse as neo-liberal free-marketeers and radical bioregionalists agree that it is significant, but disagree about its implications. Consensus on the importance of a concept such as sustainable development can disguise the extent of the divergence in the ways in which it is understood by different people and interests. Different groups share the concept, but have different conceptions of sustainable development – sometimes it would seem that all there is in common between them is the very phrase 'sustainable development' itself. It is an essentially contested concept – institutional arrangements and policies and strategies for change do not simply follow from its invocation. It is the fact that the term has been corrupted by political opponents, leading to the loss of its radical edge, that has led many greens to disown the principle. The concept of sustainable development was initially attractive because it offered grounds for a fundamental critique of existing practices. Rather than rejecting the concept outright, however, perhaps greens would be better advised to reclaim its radical nature. Let us then return to the ideals and themes implicit within the concept which we laid out in the Introduction (se page 5).

Within the concept of sustainable development we find a number of further concepts which are central to green political thought, but which themselves are equally contested. The manner in which these different themes and concepts are themselves understood and then balanced against one another leads to the different conceptions of sustainable development. First, the recognition that social and economic practices are inseparable from the natural environment requires integration of economic development and environmental protection. But what is the relative importance given to environmental protection? Can we 'trade off' environmental loss against economic gain? Are man-made and natural capital substitutable or is there a critical level of natural capital that sustains life? Second, what is the nature of obligations to future generations and what do they entail practically? What sacrifices do we need to make? Third, what is the meaning of 'environmental protection'? Is it merely a conservation ethic based on what humans find appealing in some way? A commitment to live within limits or the carrying capacity of bioregions? A recognition of the independent value and status of non-human nature? Fourth, is a commitment to social justice based on desert, merit or needs and does it clash with intergenerational obligations? Fifth, what does quality of life entail? Is economic welfare an accurate indicator of well-being? If not, how is it to be measured? Finally, what sort of political institutions can support participation? Is participation simply consultation or a more radical empowerment? Does it necessitate decentralisation? Is the market the most effective form of individual sovereignty and direct democracy or is it a mechanism of political disenfranchisement? As can be seen from the variety of questions that have been raised, it is not surprising that sustainable development is a contested concept, since almost all the themes of environmental ethics and political thought are played out in terms of its core ideas. However, by focusing on the dominant interpretations of the concept a coherent and radical understanding can be seen to emerge.

Ecological modernisation

> The modern sustainable development debate has tended to shift the focus away from growth *versus* the environment to one of the potential *complementarity* of growth and environment.
>
> (Pearce *et al.*, 1989, p. 21)

At present, the dominant interpretation of sustainable development is that associated with the idea of ecological modernisation, which has challenged 'the fundamental assumption of conventional wisdom, namely that there was a zero-sum trade-off between economic prosperity and environmental concern' (Weale, 1992, p. 31). Undoubtedly, the seminal text promoting such a view has been the Brundtland Report, *Our Common Future*, published in 1987, a document which we shall discuss in more detail in Chapter 7. The report gave rise to the most quoted and widely accepted notion of sustainable development as 'development that meets the needs of the present without compromising the ability of future generations to meet their own needs' (WCED, 1987, p. 43).

The Brundtland Report emphasises the mutual reinforcing of economic growth, social development and environmental protection. As with *The Limits to Growth* report, environmental degradation is linked with patterns of economic development. However, Brundtland concludes that continued economic growth is essential for environmental protection. This interpretation of sustainable development has been widely endorsed at all levels. It is easy to understand why such a definition of sustainable development could be supported by many different and often antagonistic parties in that it apparently offers the panacea of combining economic growth and environmental protection. It is undoubtably this conception of sustainable development as 'ecological modernisation' and the widespread political support that it has received that is forcing many radical greens to disown the concept they originally generated in order not to be drawn into an apparent consensus which might legitimise the status quo and existing institutional order.

Critiques of ecological modernisation

The most vociferous rejection of the ecological modernisation model of sustainable development tends to come from campaigners whose work reflects the plight of Southern nations. Writers such as Martin Khor, Vandana Shiva and Edward Goldsmith are critical of the primacy given to economic growth and believe that the development patterns outlined by Brundtland and the like are based solely on Western values and conceptions of what it means to be 'developed'. This Western hegemony leads to mechanistic and patriarchal models of development being universally enforced and hence the domination of indigenous peoples, women and nature through a reduction of all value to an economic or use value. 'The paradox and crisis of development arises from the mistaken identification of culturally perceived poverty with real material poverty, and the mistaken identification of the growth of commodity production as providing better human sustenance' (Shiva, 1992, p. 190).

Dominant accounts of sustainable development are charged with being culturally and ethically insensitive and for failing to comprehend the complexity and interconnectedness of ecological and social relations. Ecological modernisation is seen as legitimising and sustaining the very political and economic institutions that have caused the current levels of environmental degradation and developmental injustices. There is a paradox here: the radical critique can be subverted by its own success. The political pressure and influence of greens may be responsible for making capitalism and economic growth more environmentally sensitive and therefore more resilient to ecological critique. The underlying problem is that ecological modernisation is centred on the avoidance of pollution costs through redesign of processes, rather than on a fundamental reassessment of the need for the products of these processes. In other words, it is green capitalism. For writers such as Khor, we must not lose sight of the role that capitalism plays in the continuation of poverty and environmental degradation:

> This is the ultimate environmental and social tragedy of our age: the scientific knowledge that could be properly used to provide for every human being's physical needs is being applied instead through industrial technology to take away resources from the Third World largely for the production of superfluous goods. Meanwhile, the majority of Third World peoples sink deeper into the margins of survival.
>
> (Khor, 1992, p. 38)

From this position it is vital that an alternative vision of sustainable development is advanced, one that is sensitive to cultural differences, utilises appropriate technology and recognises the importance of traditional knowledge. Such a vision can only be forthcoming, it is argued, if the voices of those marginalised by the dominant paradigm – for instance indigenous peoples and women – can be heard and respected. Such a model would be radically participative, counteracting the domination of particular sectional interests and their interpretations of sustainable development. From this we can begin to see that forms of democratic engagement are in practice inseparable from the call for sustainable development.

Rethinking sustainable development

Critics of the ecological modernisation model are right to question its role in justifying the status quo and further Western-style industrialisation. They look at who
supports such an interpretation of sustainable development and see only the continued domination of those benefiting from contemporary free-market institutional arrangements. It is clear that those endorsing the ecological modernisation
model have not fully comprehended the radical potential of demands for sustainable development.

At a minimum, sustainable development calls for a reinterpretation of needs.
Quality of life goes well beyond simple measures of economic wealth. It also requires strong control of markets in order to safeguard the environment and intra-
and intergenerational obligations. Radical criticisms of ecological modernisation
expose those who use the concept of sustainable development for their own ends,
particularly those groups and institutions whose very practices are at odds with the
ideals inherent within the concept. But even allowing for this, a number of tensions
still remain, which not surprisingly reflect tensions inherent in much green political thinking. These issues tend to be based on who interprets what the abstract and
general principles of sustainable development mean in practice. This in turn raises
the question of the legitimacy of contemporary political institutions and their
ability to manage change. Where environmental concerns are taken into consideration by contemporary political institutions, it is common that it is their economic value that is seen to be significant. In Chapter 5 we shall respond in more
depth to this practice, but for now it is enough to say that such a valuation is limited
and appears to reinforce the technocentric worldview that greens challenge. The
economic valuation of environmental entities fails to attend to the plurality of
values that we associate with the non-human world. The nature of aesthetic and
ethical values is misrepresented if presented in economic terms. However, economists are frequently afforded 'expert' status within decision-making processes and
their calculations and models are often not open to challenge. These questions
concerning the standing of economic knowledge can be seen as problematising
certain types of political arrangements. In particular they challenge the status of
certain policy 'experts'. Being concerned about sustainable development requires
us to ask on whose behalf knowledge is being utilised. Particular groups within
society use forms of 'expertise' to legitimise unreasonable and environmentally
destructive practices. Political decision-making processes lack sensitivity to the plurality
of values we associate with the non-human world.

Extending democracy: a fundamental requirement of sustainable development?

If we are to move towards a more sustainable and equitable future, social, political
and economic institutions will need to adapt to new ways of doing things. On even
a limited conception of needs, contemporary institutions lack legitimacy in that
they have been unable to provide the conditions for the general fulfilment of human well-being. Institutions at all levels are implicated in the growing disparity of

wealth within and between societies, increased environmental degradation and the inability to act within the confines of the global capitalist system (Dryzek, 1987; 1992). Their practices and interpretations of sustainable development are seen to favour the interests of particular politically influential groups within society and are unconcerned with the experiences and needs of the disenfranchised. An example of this is provided by the case study that follows Chapter 3, which focuses on the way that road schemes have been developed in the UK by the Department of Transport (DoT). The DoT's technical decision-making procedures misrepresent and distort the values we associate with the natural world. Further, where opportunities for public participation exist, the procedures and rules explicitly exclude the possibility of challenging these misrepresentations and distortions. Unsurprisingly the motives of the state and other institutions are distrusted, leading to feelings of political alienation and a general apathy towards political institutions. When the values, experiences and interests of citizens are continually misrepresented it should be no surprise that they become cynical of public affairs (Offe and Preuss, 1991, pp. 164–5). How then, in such circumstances, can institutions be trusted to develop sustainable policies and practices? Sustainable development requires radical political restructuring to reflect the experiences and needs of all sectors of society. Opportunities need to be available to challenge the environmental and social implications of current practices.

It would seem, then, that the crisis to which contemporary green politics must respond can best be understood as a crisis of representation or, more accurately, a crisis of misrepresentation. Our knowledge of, and ethical commitments to, non-human nature is frequently misrepresented in technical decision-making processes by so-called experts and by our political representatives. We have argued above that the interests of particular groups frequently dominate in such a way that the experiences and needs of large sections of society are systematically excluded. How then are decision-making processes to be designed to ensure that the voices of the disenfranchised are heard and different interpretations of sustainable development and our relations with the natural world explored? Is it possible to design institutions which can guard against the manipulation of the political agenda by powerful elites?

Certain key themes begin to emerge from our reflections on the relation between sustainable development and democracy. Contemporary capitalism primarily requires governments to protect private capital and to ensure continued economic growth. Under such conditions, environmental considerations will never be given priority where they conflict with capital accumulation. Sustainable development is at odds with the logic of capitalism. Therefore the ecological modernisation model is suspect. Further, sustainable development points towards the priority of democracy over capital accumulation. Greens have good reason to be democrats. However, theorists such as Robert Goodin believe that greens should be concerned primarily with achieving sustainable ends rather than with the justice of the means. 'To advocate democracy is to advocate procedures, to advocate environment is to advocate substantive outcomes: what guarantee can we have that the former procedures will yield the latter sort of outcomes?' (Goodin, 1992, p. 168). But Goodin has overlooked precisely what we have stressed in this chapter: environmental concern can lead to the advocacy of a number of substantive outcomes. There is a range of values and practices subscribed to by greens – there is no single universally agreed green endpoint. What becomes important then is the manner in which we come to agree on which ends to pursue. Political spaces need to be opened up in which alternative conceptions of the future can be offered and challenged. Thus questions of ends are, it turns out, inseparable from questions of means. Sustainable development is as much about democracy as it is about limits to growth and our ethical relationship with the non-human world.

The extension of different forms of democratic participation offers a strong alternative to ecological modernisation, an alternative which connects ecological thinking with other streams of emancipatory thought, such as critical theory and feminism. Making these connections is without doubt politically and theoretically important. As a result of the interchanges between greens and contemporary democratic theorists, alternative conceptions of democracy have emerged. Of particular interest is deliberative or discursive democratic theory, which directly responds to the problems of representation and authority raised earlier.[12] The core idea behind deliberative theories is that decisions are only legitimate if they derive from a process of argument and deliberation in which all citizens have an equal right to be heard and decisions are made through the force of the better argument. Other forms of power and political influence derived from wealth or patronage should have no place. Joshua Cohen provides a useful characterisation of deliberative politics:

> The notion of a deliberative democracy is rooted in the intuitive ideal of a democratic association in which the justification of the terms and conditions of association proceeds through public argument and reasoning among equal citizens. Citizens in such an order share a commitment to the resolution of problems of collective choice through public reasoning, and regard their basic institutions as legitimate in so far as they establish the framework for free public deliberation.
>
> (Cohen, 1989, p. 21)

Hence deliberative institutional designs are participatory in that the values and needs of all groups in society form the basis of political deliberation and the legitimacy of actions and institutions is rooted in reasoned agreement. Only when citizens are able to see that their political and ethical commitments to environmental issues are genuinely taken into account will they begin to regain trust and interest in political debate and action.

Deliberative democracy does not necessarily require complete decentralisation, although clearly more locally based decision-making procedures would allow a higher degree of participation.[13] However, as has already been noted, larger-scale institutions are also necessary to tackle transboundary and global environmental problems. But these too can be deliberative, and as Dryzek argues, deliberative structures are likely to be the most effective in dealing with the 'high degrees of complexity and uncertainty, and substantial collective action problems' arising from our relations

with the natural world (Dryzek, 1995, p. 16). The contemporary world is characterised by the dispersed nature of information and knowledge and the plurality of
values and commitments. Deliberative institutions are designed to respond to this.
Deliberative democracy can also be seen as 'ecological' in so far as it is characterised
by the notion of appropriate scale. The idea of deliberation cuts across existing
political and economic boundaries because, as Dryzek argues, 'the size and scope of
institutions should match the size and scope of problems' (ibid., p. 26).

CONCLUSION

Green politics responds to the lack of attention given on the one hand to the
ethical standing of non-human nature and on the other to the limits to growth
implicit in the finite nature of the planet. As we have seen, recognition of these
concerns is insufficient in itself to generate a comprehensive political doctrine in
its own right. What it does do, however, is provide powerful critical ground from
which to challenge existing and potential practices. We have shown that there is a
variety of possible green positions emerging from critical engagement with pre-
existing political traditions. We have tried to argue, particularly in relation to the
contested nature of sustainable development, that greens need to concern themselves not simply with the more obvious environmental values, but also with related values such as justice and democracy.

CASE STUDY: ASPECTS OF A GREEN POLITICAL PROGRAMME

In the above chapter, we have argued that the two core concepts of a green
political theory are (1) attention to the values associated with the non-human
world and (2) the limits-to-growth thesis. We also drew out contemporary
considerations of decentralisation and democratic deliberation – the need
to make decisions at the appropriate level and to include all voices in the
decision-making process. How then are such values transcribed into a green
political programme? What are some of the features of the political platform of green parties?[14]

Perhaps the central aspect of a green political programme (one which sepa-
rates it from more traditional positions) is the focus on consumption, particularly the need to reduce material consumption. It is not enough simply to
concern ourselves with the distribution of resources (one of the traditional
focuses of difference between political platforms and ideologies); rather we
need to call into question what is being produced, how and why. According to
Paul Ekins, a green economic and political framework needs to be grounded in
the 'satisfaction of needs' rather than wants, a 'reconceptualisation of the

nature and value of work' and a 'commitment to economic self-reliance' (Ekins 1986, p. 97). In all the areas of a green programme below there is a general recognition that our current lifestyles and attitudes are implicated in the environmentally and socially destructive aspects of modern capitalist economies.

Consumption and waste management

Contemporary capitalist economies are geared towards the creation of profit through the satisfaction of ever-increasing wants. Greens recognise that the creation and satisfaction of wants is a continuous process and so believe that economies ought to be refocused on needs.[15] The role of advertising, with its particular ability to transform superfluous wants into apparent needs, becomes a central concern. Such attention on needs is central to the principles that are embedded in the concept of sustainable development: international distributive justice; intergenerational justice; and the recognition that the carrying capacity of the environment – the ecological limiting factor to growth – must be recognised in development patterns.

Capitalist economies tend to be linear in the sense that resources are depleted, products produced and consumed and finally disposed of into the environment as waste, frequently causing pollution. Greens argue that this linear process, which as economies grow becomes more intense, needs to become circular and reduced in size. Products should be more durable and when their initial use is over, they should not be disposed of, but rather repaired or recycled – utilised as resources for other production processes. There is a hierarchy for consumption and waste management which would be central to a green economy.

The waste management hierarchy

First: Reduce overall consumption.

Second: Consume selectively – aim for maximum possible use of secondary materials, durability, reparability and recyclability. Buy second-hand, hire or share.

Third: Minimise the generation of waste.

Fourth: Reuse.

Fifth: Recycle (including composting).

Sixth: Recover energy.

Last: Dispose to properly engineered landfill only as last resort.

(LGMB, 1995a, p. 4)

It is interesting that recycling, which is perhaps one of the most popularised 'shallow green' proposals, is not the primary focus. Recycling can be seen as an attempted technological fix to make capitalist economies less environmentally damaging. A green economy considers recycling only as an option after reduction of consumption, reuse and the like.

The rise in 'green consumerism' is regarded in a similar way to recycling – at best only a partial improvement on present consumption patterns and at worst an attempt to make capitalism appear more ecologically friendly. Where publications such as *The Green Consumer Guide* (Elkington and Hailes, 1988) exhort consumers to wield their consumer power to force manufacturers to develop more ecologically sensitive production processes, the bottom line is that 'genuinely green consumerism ... would focus on reducing rather than simply changing personal levels of consumption' (Irvine 1989, quoted in Dobson, 1991, p. 218).

Technology and energy usage

Greens are often portrayed as 'anti-technologists' or 'neo-Luddites'. Admittedly there are such reactionary tendencies in the environmental movement, but these tend to be peripheral. However, greens are sceptical of technology and its application. There is a recognition that technology seems to shape contemporary society and its wants and desires; its social and ethical impact often leading to a sharp separation of humanity from the natural world. Strong anthropocentric, Promethean attitudes of control and domination abound. For greens this attitude and relation to technology must be reversed. Technology should be used appropriately in a manner which both aids the development of humanity in its widest, enlightened sense and has as little impact on the non-human world as possible.

Perhaps the most obvious example of this concern is nuclear power, which has been a focus of consistent campaigning by almost all sectors of the green movement. A potentially highly destructive energy source has been developed, while low-impact alternatives have consistently been ignored. The potential impact of nuclear technology is not simply a concern of the present generation – we are leaving future generations the legacy of dealing with the highly radioactive waste products of our energy generation. This is perhaps the most obvious example of both the present generation's over-optimistic belief in the promise of science to provide technological solutions to environmental problems and their failure to consider fully their obligations to the future. Inseparable to these considerations is the recognition that the nuclear energy and arms industries are inextricably linked. The idea of a weapon of mass destruction that could obliterate all forms of life on the planet is simply anathema to green thinking. Low-impact, renewable 'soft' energy options, such as wind, sun and wave, which have been consistently ignored and underfunded, would be promoted. Although these energy paths may not themselves generate enough to fulfil current demand, a reduction in consumption and conservation of energy would reduce this demand substantially. Measures such as energy and carbon taxes would be introduced to facilitate this change to a conservation society and the move from non-renewable fossil fuels to renewable sources.

Work and taxation

There needs to be a move away from the connection of meaningful work with paid employment. Outside the formal, paid economy people engage in activities whose worth is undervalued in contemporary society – parenting, housekeeping, volunteering, etc. In recognition that such activities are the basis upon which the wage economy functions, greens argue that there should be a universal basic income scheme through which all citizens would receive a level of income that would be sufficient to cover basic needs. This would do away with the current means-tested benefits system, which often acts as a barrier to those who wish to take part-time employment or work on informal community-based activities. Critics question whether the incentive to work would remain or whether the tax base can deliver such a scheme. This later issue is particularly problematic if economies are to be reduced in scale – there may simply not be enough money to redistribute. However, this is a long-term problem, and in the long term greens would expect our conception of money, work and community relations to have changed significantly. They point to local money and trading schemes, such as LETS (Local Employment and Trading System), which have been particularly applied in deprived areas, as offering the potential for more congenial community-based, not-for-profit forms of trading.

The tax base itself would be altered in other ways. There would be a move away from taxes on work and labour (for instance income tax on the poor and national insurance), to be replaced by taxes on environmentally damaging practices such as intensive energy usage, polluting industrial processes and the use of scarce raw materials. In this sense the tax system would focus on activities that ought to be discouraged from the standpoint of a sustainable future. The polluter-pays principle (PPP) becomes central. For a more detailed discussion of 'green taxes', see Chapter 6.

Agriculture

Industrialisation of agriculture is now prevalent and the effects of this on both the food we eat and the environment in general need to be called into question. Intensive forms of farming are the focus of much criticism, particularly in terms of the Promethean project of the control and domination of nature that it embodies. With respect to crop production, the profit motive has led to the application of higher levels of artificial fertilisers and pesticides, which have affected the quality of food and polluted land and water courses. Organic farming, particularly at a community level, is held up as the way forward for agriculture. Similar arguments hold for the treatment of animals. Although greens do not necessarily believe that eating meat is wrong *per se*, they abhor contemporary factory farming methods. Equally, concern is raised as to the motives and necessity of both animal research and biotechnology. Biotechnology in the agricultural sector is a particular focus of antagonism as diverse ecosystems and plant types are replaced by monocultures which promise higher yields and profits.

Transport and trade

Greens tend to ask why we need to travel to the extent that we do in the modern world. Urban and rural areas, including employment locations, ought to be planned such that the need for long-distance travel is reduced. And when travel is necessary and cycling or walking is not possible, then preference should be given to public forms of transport – trains and buses. Emphasis on the private car is inefficient, polluting and socially divisive – many facilities are currently inaccessible to those without access to a private vehicle.

For similar reasons, global trade should also be reduced such that necessary production occurs at a local level. International trade ought to be the exception rather than the rule. Shipping goods across the world is both polluting and inefficient from an environmental perspective. It also means that transnational corporations tend to have a high degree of influence on world markets, often leaving localities fairly powerless, particularly in the South. This does not mean that more economically developed countries do not have a duty to help such nations to develop, but this development should lead to nations and localities being able to provide for the basic needs of their population. Such an emphasis on self-reliance fits in with calls for decentralisation and local democracy and places greens in obvious opposition to the current trend towards global market liberalisation. Their position is often understood as a form of protectionism. However, it is protectionism of a particular kind – the development of local economies to provide for local needs.

SUGGESTIONS FOR FURTHER READING

The first and most reliable survey of green political theory (now in its second edition) is Andrew Dobson's *Green Political Thought* (1995). Two works which engage more deeply with issues in political theory and ideology are Tim Hayward, *Ecological Thought* (1995) and Robyn Eckersley, *Environmentalism and Political Theory* (1992). The journal *Environmental Politics* often covers related topics.

3 The environmental movement

The ecology movement, when viewed as a whole, draws its force from a range of arguments whose ethical underpinnings are really quite divergent and difficult to reconcile.

(Soper, 1995, p. 254)

Environmental protest in one form or another has scarcely been out of the news over the past few years. The public has become familiar with images of anti-road direct actions; Reclaim the Streets parties; protests against the live export of veal calves; Greenpeace campaigns against the dumping of the Brent Spar, whaling, and the nuclear testing at Mururoa atoll. But this is just the tip of the iceberg. These forms of protest may grab the headlines, but the activities of the environmental movement go well beyond direct action. There is a range of groups with a range of aims and strategies. The 'environmental movement' encompasses a wide variety of people, interests and groups, which differ in the goals they seek and in the means they employ. It comprises green political parties, a vast array of pressure groups, activists in the mainstream political parties, 'green' businesses and consumers, and those seeking alternative lifestyles. What are these people and groups trying to achieve and how are they trying to achieve it? In Chapters 1 and 2 we examined the core ideals of environmental politics with respect to human relationships with the natural world and the limits to economic growth. But these features do not tell us which political approach ought to be employed, although they impose limits on strategy and suggest criteria for accepting or rejecting certain options. This chapter focuses on the nature of the environmental movement, how different sections of the movement aim to achieve their goals and how they see themselves in relation to each other.

An environmental movement?

Is there an identifiable environmental movement? Is there a single unified movement working together harmoniously, with agreement on means and ends? Clearly there is a movement in a loose sense in that there is a range of groups and organisations committed to environmental protection and change. But, as Kate

Soper indicates, within this movement there is a wide range of activities and justifications 'whose ethical underpinnings are really quite divergent and difficult to reconcile' (Soper, 1995, p. 254). Considering the practices of organisations as divergent as the National Trust (NT) and Earth First! (EF!) makes this point: both of these groups can claim to be part of the environmental movement. These divergences can and do result in tensions and clashes. For example, recent attempts to site wind turbines have met with opposition not only on aesthetic grounds but also because they might affect bird sanctuaries and other habitats. There is a clash here between the advocates of alternative energy and the advocates of wildlife. There is not necessarily any way of reconciling their differences, yet both sides claim the mantle of environmentalism. It would seem that it is a mistake to think of the environmental movement as a single actor (Yearley, 1994, p. 156).

From the early 1960s there has been a renewed concern about the environment. Groups established before this time, such as the Royal Society for the Protection of Birds (RSPB) in the UK and the Sierra Club in the USA, have increased their membership substantially and many new organisations, frequently more radical in their approaches and demands, have been formed in the last three decades or so. Although it is hard to ascertain precisely the levels of support that they enjoy, the membership of environmental groups in the UK has roughly doubled each decade since 1960: about 4.5 million people currently belong to an environmental organisation.[1] The table below gives an indication of the increase in membership over the past fifteen years. These figures relate to the more well-known environmental groups. These are only part of the movement as a whole.

Table 3.1 Membership of leading UK environmental groups[2]

	1980	*1985*	*1990*	*1995*
Greenpeace	10,000	50,000	380,000	380,000
FoE	12,000	27,000	110,000	110,000
WWF	51,000	91,000	247,000	220,000
Ramblers	36,000	50,000	81,000	109,000
National Trust	950,000	1,323,000	2,032,000	2,293,000
CPRE	27,000	26,500	44,000	45,000
RSNC	140,000	165,000	250,000	250,000
RSPB	321,000	390,000	844,000	890,000
Total	1,547,000	2,122,500	3,988,000	4,297,000

Source: McCormick, 1991; *Social Trends*, 1992–1997.

As this chapter progresses, the focus will move from attempts to work directly within parliamentary structures in traditional political parties or more recently established green parties, to organisations whose primary aim is to influence policy, to those who eschew the parliamentary road and look towards the transformation of communities and local practices.

PARTY POLITICS

Greening the established parties

In September 1988, Mrs Thatcher surprised the political world by delivering a speech on the environment to the Royal Society. As an astute politician, she recognised that environmental concerns had caught the public imagination. In many ways the speech appeared to be a radical conversion, a recognition that the environment should be at the forefront of any government programme. As it turned out, this new-found environmentalism was more rhetoric than substance; none the less it propelled green considerations into the political mainstream and thereby created space for debate. Traditional parties are now required to respond to the challenges posed by the popularity of green issues, scientific evidence on the depletion of the ozone layer and global warming, and the claims that radical changes in living patterns are necessary.

Although the emergence of the environment as a major issue in the late 1980s appeared to signify a shift in the political terrain, it needs to be recognised that there were and still are activists operating within each of the major parties. Within the UK, for example, perhaps the two most successful internal groupings have been the Socialist Environment and Resources Association (SERA), affiliated to the Labour Party, and the Liberal Ecology Group. Within the Conservative Party there are more informal groupings – typically sympathetic to the conservation and landscape issues at the heart of the ideological roots of conservatism. These groups have been particularly influential in affecting the content of each party's environmental statements and policies; for instance, the Labour Party's critically well-received environmental policy document *In Trust for Tomorrow* (1994).

The old established parties are frequently referred to by greens as the 'grey' parties and often reviled as part of the problem, not part of the solution. Although most parties within liberal democracies have begun to take notice of environmental imperatives, it is frequently charged that they are merely pandering to transient shifts in public opinion, attempting to deflect the challenge of the newly formed green parties and to attract the votes of a more environmentally conscious younger generation. They are accused of 'greenwashing' their policies rather than seriously rethinking and reformulating their political doctrines. Given that the established parties are typified by a commitment to some form of industrialism and economic growth, greening their policies amounts to little more than amelioration, with no serious challenge to the existing patterns of consumption, production and lifestyle. This can be understood as a form of ecological modernisation with its strong conviction that economic growth and environmental protection can be reconciled. A weak form of environmentalism predominates. As an example, responses to global warming and acid rain have been slow where the problems result from existing industrial practices. When solutions have finally been proposed and accepted, they have typically been technocentric: technical solutions tend to be sought. Radical social and economic change is not seen as a plausible political option.[3]

The green parties

The first green party was established in 1972 in New Zealand, followed a year later by 'People' in the UK, which was to become the Green Party in 1985. Perhaps the most successful party, the German Grünen, emerged in 1980. Green parties have been established in almost all liberal democracies, although not all have achieved the same level of electoral success. In this section we will attempt to show some of the reasons why this should be the case. Further, we will investigate the internal factional disputes that have plagued what Petra Kelly termed these new 'anti-party parties'. In a number of ways these new parties see themselves as fundamentally different from the established parties, resulting in tensions between those greens who wish to remain ideologically pure and independent, and those who are prepared to engage in coalitions and pragmatic compromises. A comparison will be made between the UK and Germany. Both countries have a strong tradition of environmental activism, yet the electoral fortunes and influence of the green party in each case has been vastly different.

Success or failure?

Crudely, the measure of success or failure, if taken to be the level of party representation in legislative assemblies, is a function of the electoral system. Although the highest ever vote received by a green party was that achieved in the UK in the 1989 European elections, the party has never had a representative elected in either the national or European legislative assemblies.[4] By comparison, Die Grünen has consistently achieved electoral success. Quite simply this difference is related to the electoral systems operative in each country.

The failure to translate votes into parliamentary seats in the UK arises from the nature of the 'first past the post' system, which militates against small parties with diffuse support. This is a system in which each of the 651 constituencies elects one representative; the candidate with the highest vote wins the seat. Because voting is constituency-based, the Green Party has simply not had enough concentrated support to achieve a breakthrough, except in a small number of local government elections. Even when it achieved its vote of 15 per cent in 1989, a vote that in many ways can be seen as a backlash against the lack of environmental concern in the traditional parties,[5] it did not do well enough in any single constituency to win a European seat. In British politics second place has no electoral impact. Within the European Union the UK's electoral system is unique; if the election had been conducted according to one of the systems of proportional representation in operation in the rest of Europe, the Green Party could have won up to twelve seats. The German system of proportional representation, in which 'first past the post' is supplemented by a party list system resulting in a more proportional outcome, has allowed Die Grünen to achieve its relative electoral success. A vote above 5 per cent automatically secures a level of legislative representation. Apart from the 1990 'reunification' election, Die Grünen has had continuous representation in the Bundestag and the European Parliament since 1983. In recent regional (Länder) elections Die Grünen achieved its best electoral results to date, in certain areas edging out the Free Democrats (FDP) as the third party and reducing the power of the Social Democrats (SPD). In two cases SPD–Grünen ('Red–Green') coalitions have been forged. But are such coalitions the way forward for the green parties?

The formation of the 'red–green' coalition in North Rhine–Westphalia, for example, has led to conflict between the partners over the issue of open-cast mining. This conflict reflects basic ideological differences: the established labour and industrial commitments of the SPD against the economic and social restructuring favoured by Die Grünen. The issue has been fudged by deferring the project, but this is no solution and merely serves to highlight the fact that similar conflicts are likely to occur in almost all policy areas. Greens must ask themselves how far they are prepared to compromise their principled position. Contrary to much popular belief green parties are not single-issue parties attempting to make environmental improvement at the edges; they are committed to wholesale reform. In many ways this is not yet fully understood by the electorate. Even if it was understood, they still have to face the barrier of overcoming the economic short-termism that infects both voting patterns and party programmes. Would people be prepared to vote for a party that does not promise continued economic growth and increased consumption opportunities? How a green party should respond to this challenge is the subject of continuing and often acrimonious debate. Should they compromise to achieve power or adhere to ideological purity? It is paradoxical that the success of green parties may subvert their own principles and goals. As Dryzek remarks: 'it would be ironic indeed if the major impact of the German Greens were to render German capitalism, and German economic growth, more ecologically sustainable – and less in need of a green critique' (Dryzek, 1995, p. 299). The possibility that the ideals of green parties might be neutralised or subverted by conventional political processes has been explicitly recognised by many activists, including Die Grünen's Petra Kelly:

> As Greens, it is not part of our understanding of politics to find a place in the sun alongside the established parties, nor to help maintain power and privilege in concert with them. Nor will we accept any alliances and coalitions. This is wishful thinking on the part of the traditional parties, who seek to exploit the Greens to keep themselves in power. ... We are, and I hope we will remain, half party and half local action group – we shall go on being an anti-party party.
>
> (Kelly, in Dobson, 1991, pp. 193–4)

Internal organisation and factional conflict

The debate over electoral strategy is part of a wider set of disagreements within the internal politics of green parties. It is frequently linked to disagreements over internal party structure. The issue of electoral compromise is mirrored in a debate about leadership and hierarchical forms of organisation. These issues are logically separate, but generally speaking they run together. Crudely, it can be said that activists adopt one of two basic orientations: ideological fundamentalism or pragmatic realism. This is often referred to as the 'fundi–realo' split, a division that has plagued green parties everywhere. For many activists, commitment to grassroots democracy is central, not only to their vision for society, but also to how green parties themselves ought to be organised. This commitment raises important questions concerning party organisation and the nature of leadership. Their radical democratic commitment is at odds with the hierarchical structures of traditional parties and the 'cult of leadership' that this generates. However, pragmatic greens argue that success in electoral politics requires an identifiable leadership: figures that the public trust and recognise. Radicals believe, on the other hand, that structures should be open and non-hierarchical, that leadership and responsibility should be collective.

After its success in the 1989 European elections, the issue of leadership became central to debates about how the UK Green Party should develop. A group of well-known public figures within the party launched Green 2000, a structural reform programme to streamline party organisation. Members such as Jonathon Porritt and Sara Parkin believed that if the party was to capitalise on its success then it needed to adopt a more professional and realistic attitude to leadership, presentation and decision making. There were recognisable and popular figures within the organisation and they should be charged with enhancing its image with the public. But for a sizeable number of party members, specifically many of the party activists, this violated deeply held beliefs and would also have resulted in a loss of grassroots influence, leaving power in the hands of a small executive. A very public rearguard action was fought that not only led to the resignation of some of the most prominent figures, but also to a decline in membership. This acrimonious infighting contributed to the abysmal showing at the 1992 general election, and the party is only just beginning to recover.[6]

For Die Grünen, questions of leadership and organisation have been even more pressing given their representation in the Bundestag. Originally, party policy had been to rotate representatives to ensure and maintain the collective and non-hierarchical nature of their approach to politics. But, like their Green 2000 counterparts, a number of the elected greens, including Petra Kelly, argued that it was necessary for them to continue in a prominent position if they were to work efficiently within the bureaucratic structures of the Bundestag. It took time to acclimatise to the day-to-day demands of, and to work effectively within, the assembly. For others, however, Kelly and her associates had succumbed to the very cult of leadership she had previously preached against and the radical edge of green politics was being blunted. Many radical activists became disillusioned with this accommodation to the political status quo. Rudolf Bahro, a leading 'fundi', was so incensed by what he took to be the inevitable subversion of the ideals of Die Grünen that he resigned. He believed that it was simply impossible for a party of whatever sort, and however self-critical, to escape the common fate of all parties: 'At last I have understood that a party is a counterproductive tool, that the given political space is a trap into which life energy disappears, indeed, where it is rededicated to the spiral of death' (Bahro in Dobson, 1991, p. 198).

The future of green party politics?

Does there continue to be a role for green parties, particularly in those places where they have achieved little electoral success? What is their role in the wider green movement? For a comparatively successful party, such as Die Grünen, it can be argued that it has a leading role. The party is a focus and a voice for environmental politics within the legislature and is considered to be an influential, major part of a wider national movement extending from the grassroots to the Bundestag and on into the European Parliament. But what of its UK counterparts? Its lack of electoral success means that the British environmental movement is unable to capitalise on access to a comparable parliamentary platform. Short of election-time publicity, there seems little that the UK Green Party can offer, since it has no unique access to Whitehall decision making which is not already open to pressure groups.

> In other European countries, where Green parties are represented in parliament, the ecological and environmental cause benefits from enhanced visibility and access and, sometimes, from financial support as well. There, ecologists may use Green parliamentary representatives as a conduit for influence through the formal political process or, as in Germany, they may employ a dual strategy of party and movement, in which the party serves to channel into the formal political process issues which have been raised by the extra-parliamentary movement. In Britain, neither strategy is available; the poor prospects for a Green party under present electoral arrangements compel ecologists and environmentalists to adopt other tactics.
>
> (Rootes, 1995, p. 79)

The role of the UK Green Party has again been subject to debate with the motion at the 1996 party conference to refrain from putting forward candidates in the general election. Given the poor national support for the party in recent elections, is it better advised to focus its limited resources on a few selected constituencies, or even to step back from participating whilst the party rebuilds itself? In the event, the motion was heavily defeated for a number of important reasons. First, what is the point of a party which does not seek election? What then would differentiate it from any other environmental pressure group or organisation? Second, there is justified concern that alternative green parties would spring up to take their place. In particular there are groups without the Green Party's commitment to democratic processes and international justice waiting for just this type of opportunity. Third, for many members the motion was as much a stunt to gain media attention as a serious proposition. After all, the fairly autonomous local branches of the party are free to make these decisions independently. The press coverage of this issue, however, enabled the party to re-establish itself in the public mind.

The claim that an electorally unsuccessful green party is of no value to the wider environmental movement may well be overstating the case. There are important political debates concerning issues of organisational structure as well as the broader green programme as a whole which are rarely aired within individual pressure groups. The party provides a forum for all issues. Where for many the dissension and divisions displayed within green party debate detract attention and are perhaps embarrassing, for others they represent an essential element of democratic practice, itself central to their green vision. But, as Chris Rootes argues: 'As long as the Green Party remains so marginal to the political process, the environmental movement will continue to tread the path of influence rather than that of power' (Rootes, 1995, p. 86).

ENVIRONMENTAL PRESSURE GROUPS

As pointed out in the Introduction, it is environmental pressure groups which tend to be the most visible element of the environmental movement. But what is a pressure group? How are we to characterise the diversity of organisations which are identified by the use of this term? Apart from a loose affinity, what do the RSPB and Reclaim the Streets have in common? Wyn Grant defines a pressure group as:

> an organisation which seeks as one of its functions to influence the formulation and implementation of public policy, public policy representing a set of authoritative decisions taken by the executive, the legislature, and by local government and the European community.
>
> (Grant, 1989, p. 9)

This is a useful working definition, although, as will be shown, not all environmental organisations would claim to be seeking to influence policy. For certain anarchical groups such as Earth First! (EF!), public policy and even the state itself are objects of suspicion, the very cause of the current environmental crisis.

An important distinction is frequently made between different types of group in terms of who or what they represent. First, cause or promotion groups represent a belief or principle; they act to further that cause. Membership is not restricted: anyone who accepts the belief or principle can join. Most of the well-known environmental organisations fit into this category. Friends of the Earth (FoE), the World Wide Fund for Nature (WWF) and the Council for the Protection of Rural England (CPRE) are all committed to particular ideals and as such are best described as cause or promotion groups. Second, by contrast, interest or sectional groups represent a particular section of the community, defending their common private interests. Membership tends to be restricted to that sectional interest. The Country Landowners' Association (CLA), the Society of Motor Manufacturers and Traders (SMMT) and the Confederation of British Industry (CBI) are all well-known interest groups whose political activities are based purely on enhancing the interests of their members.

A further distinction can be made between 'insider' and 'outsider' groups.

Insider groups have gained a degree of legitimacy and may be consulted by government departments and agencies on matters of policy. For example, the RSPB is frequently consulted as a matter of routine by the Ministry of Agriculture, Fisheries and Food (MAFF) and members of the road lobby such as the Automobile Association (AA) and the Road Haulage Association (RHA) by what was until recently the Department of Transport (DoT). However, in itself insider status says nothing about the level of influence that these groups enjoy; rather it simply means that they can be considered part of the department's policy community. Outsider groups do not have this access. For some, this is a problem as they wish to engage in a constructive relationship with officials but have been unable to gain recognition. The New Economics Foundation, for instance, has little or no influence in departments such as the Treasury; Compassion in World Farming (CIWF) has had little consistent impact on MAFF. Other outsiders, as we argued for EF!, are ideologically opposed to any positive relationship with government. However, the distinction is not always clearcut, for two interconnected reasons. First, some groups stand at the threshold of official recognition; their status is unclear and they stand in an ambiguous relationship with Whitehall. Second, it is frequently the case that a group has insider status with one department or agency but not with others. WWF and CPRE are examples in that they clearly had insider status with the former Department of the Environment (DoE), but had a more problematical relationship with the DoT, and no contact with the Treasury.[7] This differential access will no doubt continue, given that the state is becoming more fragmented, as departmental responsibilities become more devolved through the creation of quasi-independent agencies (quangos). For environmental pressure groups with limited resources, this situation creates difficulties in that they campaign across a whole range of issues. This is further exacerbated by the fact that well-resourced sectional interest groups, opposed to the environmental agenda, have insider status, even to the point of having their representatives appointed to quangos.[8]

In response to the power of vested 'anti-environmental' interests, green groups have often mobilised themselves into coalitions. Where pressure groups can overcome their competitiveness and recognise that it is a waste of limited resources to campaign independently on the same issue, much can be gained. When this is particularly successful, an 'umbrella' group emerges. In transport politics, Transport 2000, formed in 1973, is an obvious example comprising (amongst others) FoE, CPRE, rail unions and public transport user groups. More recently, in 1996, the Real World coalition was established to promote the full range of issues implicit within sustainable development: environmental protection, global poverty and security, inequality, and democratic renewal. Thirty-two of the UK's leading pressure groups, including FoE, WWF, Christian Aid, Charter 88, Oxfam and Save the Children Fund, have issued a wide-ranging manifesto, *The Politics of the Real World* (Jacobs, 1996), as a challenge to the existing political establishment. Further, they have issued a direct challenge to the major political parties to implement twelve key reforms.

The Real World coalition's *Action Programme for Government*

- increased public investment in local, community and voluntary enterprises;

- ecological restructuring of the tax system;

- enactment of a Bill of Rights;

- increased international development aid;

- strategy for affordable housing;

- integrated transport programme;

- substantial reduction of the UK's carbon dioxide emissions;

- enforceable code of conduct on international arms transfers;

- strategy to increase consumption of fresh and nutritious food;

- reform of international trade to safeguard social and environmental standards;

- binding legal protection for Sites of Special Scientific Interest;

- alternative social and economic indicators.

(Real World, 1996)

The formation of coalitions, at whatever level, be it policy or grassroots, is a positive step forward in two respects. First, combining resources, knowledge and expertise enables groups to boost their impact and effectiveness. Second, and this is especially true where such coalitions cut across hitherto discrete campaigning areas, it gives the groups involved an opportunity to explore issues of mutual concern; it is a learning process for those participating.

Forms of action

Whilst recognising that the categories used to define pressure group politics are not watertight, knowing where a group stands in relation to the insider/outsider and cause/sectional distinctions is helpful to understanding the tactics and forms of action it chooses or is forced to employ. As the 'Forms of action' box on page 78 demonstrates, pressure group action can range from informal or formal lobbying or petitioning through to large-scale marches and direct action.

While, within their overall strategies, environmental pressure groups may use one or more of these forms of action, their choice of tactics will be dependent upon their status and principles. Approaches may range from moderate or conventional to more radical, hard-edged and conflictual means. The former tactical style is to operate within established procedures, working through dialogue and consultation in a cooperative manner. Typically demands are not absolutist, and

Forms of action

- *Informal contact and influence* through discreet lobbying behind the scenes, often with transfer of personnel. For example, ex-ministers and civil servants from the former DoT often move to positions in the British Roads Federation (BRF).

- *Formal lobbying* through governmental institutions and bodies. For example, FoE makes submissions to standing committees (such as the Standing Advisory Committee on Trunk Road Assessment) as well as having a seat on the UK Round Table for Sustainable Development.

- *Letters and petitions to MPs and ministers* from group members and the general public organised in a concerted manner. For example, in their successful campaign against sow stalls, CIWF inundated MAFF with letters and petitions.

- *Scientific research and reports* to establish the credibility of green concerns. For example, FoE has been responsible for breakthrough reports on the impact of acid rain, the global timber trade and nuclear power.

- *Consumer boycotts* designed to highlight industrial malpractice. For example, a number of development groups have called for a boycott of Nestlé products. The company has been accused of swamping Southern nations with baby milk powder, which people are unable to use safely because water supplies are contaminated.

- *Court action* where it is believed that official procedures have not been adhered to. For example, protestors against the M3 extension through Twyford Down challenged the DoT for its failure to abide by the EC directive on environmental impact assessment.

- *Demonstrations and marches*, which provide obvious visible evidence of public support. For example, the massive numbers that turned out for a series of anti-nuclear demonstrations organised by the Campaign for Nuclear Disarmament (CND) in the 1980s.

- *Media stunts* to gain widespread public exposure. For example, Greenpeace has become famous for its skill in attracting media attention to issues such as whaling and nuclear testing.

- *Non-violent direct action*, where activists engage in acts of civil disobedience and eco-sabotage. For example, EF! has been involved in monkey-wrenching, mass trespass and 'bulldozer diving' on road construction sites.

- *Violent direct action*, where the aim is to injure those directly involved in practices that are environmentally destructive or harmful to animals. For example, the ALF has sent letter bombs to particularly prominent vivisectionists.

groups are prepared to negotiate, frequently willing to compromise to reach agreed solutions. The latter approach is characterised by more confrontational and un-compromising tactics, demands often being absolutist, allowing little or no space for compromise (Young, 1993, p. 23). Clearly, different forms of action can be used in different ways: for instance, the production of a scientific report could be the basis for conventional dialogue and negotiation or, more radically, as the basis of confrontation with, and challenge to, government or industrial experts. Further, these tactics are not necessarily mutually exclusive; environmental pressure groups will frequently adopt an array of approaches in their campaigning. These points can be illustrated by looking at how two of the most well-known organisations, Greenpeace and Friends of the Earth (FoE), have approached campaigning and the problems that their apparent success has brought.

Greenpeace and FoE: the price of success?

Both Greenpeace and FoE have their origins in a repudiation of the moderate, conventional lobbying tactics of more traditional pressure groups. With the rise of environmental concern in the late 1960s and early 1970s, many people saw the need for a new, more direct form of campaigning. The apparent urgency of the environmental crisis was the spur to the creation of these groups, ushering in a new style of environmental protest and a new breed of protester. Activists were com-mitted to confrontational forms of direct action, a style of campaigning that they quickly discovered to be of great interest to the media. This media exposure led to high levels of public support. From radical beginnings both organisations have grown, achieving international standing with an active presence in all parts of the world.

FoE was founded in the USA in 1969 by David Brower, who had become disil-lusioned with the staid traditionalism of the Sierra Club. Although rightly famous for its high publicity campaigns, exemplified by the early, innovative dumping of non-returnable Schweppes bottles outside the company's London headquarters in 1971, FoE has never limited itself to a single form of protest. In the early 1970s it published a number of path-breaking reports, including Ehrlich's *The Population Bomb* (1972). Success came early with RTZ abandoning its plans to mine areas of Snowdonia National Park and the British government banning imports of leop-ard, cheetah and tiger skins. Equally, its campaigns against the nuclear industry and the use of CFCs have been models of imaginative and well-researched action. It has not simply lobbied government but has taken direct action against industry, for instance its leading role in the successful boycott of the DIY stores which im-ported hardwoods from unsustainable rain forest sources.

Over the past twenty-five years the level of commitment and technical exper-tise of FoE has gained the respect, not only of the general public, but, perhaps more importantly, of certain sections of the political establishment. In the UK, for instance, it is impossible now to regard it purely as an outsider group. Whilst FoE activists continue to engage in confrontational activities, and although it provides resources and support for other groups such as the Third Battle of

Newbury,[9] it has assumed a more conventional and, at times, insider role in relation to specific departments and agencies. After the publication of the UK government's response to Rio's Agenda 21, FoE accepted the invitation to sit on the UK Round Table on Sustainable Development. Internationally, FoE has taken advantage of the new-found status of non-governmental organisations (NGOs) in United Nations forums; for example, presenting detailed submissions to the Commission for Sustainable Development (CSD). At the opposite end of the organisational structure, their semi-autonomous local groups have begun to take an active role in local government initiatives such as Local Agenda 21. As an organisation, FoE has recognised that participation in local to global political forums offers a valuable opportunity for change.[10] In many ways this is a far cry from its radical beginnings and it has not always escaped criticism for a per-ceived softening of approach. However, the organisation appears to be doing its best to negotiate a difficult and largely unexplored terrain where governments are recognising some of the implications within a commitment to sustainable development. How should a group such as FoE respond to requests from govern-ment and industry for help in developing programmes of action? FoE appears to be attempting to have the best of both worlds, juggling high-profile actions alongside participation in governmental bodies. At present it appears adept at performing this balancing act, although its more radical edge has been sacrificed in order to grasp the opportunity to participate in policy communities where it perceives a changing climate which promises new possibilities for an environ-mental voice.

Greenpeace was also launched by renegades from the Sierra Club, in 1971, with protests against nuclear testing in the Aleutian Islands to the west of Alaska. Greenpeace took direct action to the limits, frequently shocking the public by the almost heroic audacity of its activities. Images of activists riding the waves in small inflatable dinghies placing themselves between whaling ship and whale, underneath toxic drums suspended from dumping ships and their dumping zone, or riding headlong into nuclear test zones, were soon relayed worldwide. Never before had the reality of environmental issues been so graphically presented. A perhaps naive attempt by young idealistic activists to save the world by their own actions quickly led to the recognition that their activities generated huge media interest, which could be exploited to further their aims. The media were hungry for images such as these and the scare stories they embodied. In recognising the power of the media, Greenpeace began to tailor its actions for maximal effect, with the media being recruited as accomplices in the process. Direct actions undertaken by FoE and others often seemed amateurish by comparison. Discussing the early years of Greenpeace, Fred Pearce comments:

> The stories that Greenpeace weaves are so beguiling that, according to one insider, 'News desks will often suppress stories of campaigning cock-ups be-cause they like the Greenpeace image too much.' ... Greenpeace has over almost two decades maintained an image of swashbuckling success.
>
> (Pearce, 1991, p. 20)

But does this swashbuckling image hide the complexity of the environmental agenda? Critics have often charged Greenpeace with a selective approach to the environment, picking and choosing those issues which are simple and media-friendly.

> To make the image work, Greenpeace needs a clear, simple message. It is good at being against things, but finds being in favour of them harder; and complex issues, such as Third World agriculture or reafforestation, tend to pass it by.
>
> (ibid.)

To a certain extent, where Greenpeace has tended to keep things as simple as possible, FoE appears unafraid of tackling and admitting the complexity of environmental problems. But their direct and uncompromising approach led to huge popular acclaim and rapidly increasing membership levels and financial support. In 1990, Greenpeace UK was receiving around £5 million per annum, which allowed it to branch out into other activities such as research. Although it has steadfastly refused to participate directly in government policy communities, its research has influenced policy discussions both nationally and internationally. In fact, the reports by Greenpeace scientists have in some cases been the most reliable form of evidence available to many countries, particularly those from the South, during international negotiations. Again, with respect to the International Whaling Commission (IWC), Greenpeace's evidence concerning whale numbers and the infringement of international agreements has been influential, particularly when simultaneous large-scale actions are employed to attract media and public attention. For many nations Greenpeace has too much influence and its activities are seen as subversive. Nowhere was this suspicion better illustrated than by the 1985 sinking of the *Rainbow Warrior* in Auckland, New Zealand. Greenpeace activists were preparing to renew their protests against French nuclear testing in Mururoa atoll, a frequent target for the organisation, when French secret service agents planted two limpet mines on the ship, sinking it and more horrifically killing a photographer in the process. The international outcry was enormous; membership and support soared.

Does this success have a price? Greenpeace has become an international multi-million dollar organisation. It is no longer a small group of committed activists with no responsibilities beyond their own commitment to the non-human world. Quite clearly the growth of the organisation has had a substantial impact. Whereas in its formative years, issues could be raised and pursued immediately and with impunity, in the present climate, activists are forced to consider the financial effect of any proposed actions. Perhaps popular success and the financial rewards this brings have become a burden. Hardcore activists, central to the development of Greenpeace's distinctive approach, have increasingly become disillusioned, often resigning from, or being asked to leave, the organisation. To their mind Greenpeace has gone soft, abandoning its earlier radical and courageous cutting edge. Two recent issues illustrate this.

First, although Greenpeace had hitherto steadfastly refused to endorse products and industrial processes, in Germany it has recently backed the development of non-CFC or HCFC-based refrigerators and a low-emission, low-consumption car. Supporters of these initiatives argue that they are developing a new form of direct action: 'solutions-orientated campaigning'. Opponents decry such ventures, believing that they legitimise and capitulate to the very consumer and car-based culture that they are committed to calling into question.

Second, in the early 1990s, as part of its continuing campaign against nuclear reprocessing at Thorp, Greenpeace attempted to stage a concert on the grounds of the Sellafield nuclear site. Sellafield gained an injunction, banning all protesters from entering the site. Greenpeace was concerned that if it broke the injunction its substantial assets would be sequestered. In response the media were treated to the spectacle of the internationally successful pop group U2 standing alongside Greenpeace activists just below the high water mark by the nuclear plant. Greenpeace declared that it could go no further for fear of what the courts might do. But was this really the action of a hardcore direct action organisation? For many it was not. Indeed, for some it symbolises the decline of the original wave of radical campaigning groups. Even though Greenpeace has recognised this predicament and more recently re-engaged in high-profile, daring actions such as its 1995 campaigns against the dumping of the Brent Spar and the latest round of French nuclear testing, in many ways it has been usurped by a new breed of environmental protester and new forms of organisation, which embody the spirit and idealism of the early Greenpeace.

A final point, before we move on to this new wave of direct action, concerns the nature of Greenpeace's relationship with the media. As already noted, much of Greenpeace's success in bringing environmental issues to widespread public attention can be traced to the ways in which it manages or at times even manipulates the media. Quite simply, Greenpeace frequently presents newspapers and television stations with footage and stories which are published and broadcast without proper independent scrutiny. But it appears that Greenpeace might now be the subject of a media backlash. What seemed at first to be an almost perfectly coordinated campaign against Shell's proposal to dump the Brent Spar oil platform at sea turned into a media relations fiasco. Greenpeace combined scientific evidence of toxic residues with the spectacle of activists boarding and occupying the platform, and national campaigns against Shell service stations. Shell backed down, agreeing to dismantle and dispose of the rig on land. The media proved to be willing accomplices in forcing this change of policy. However, Greenpeace's estimate of the level of toxic residues turned out to be seriously flawed, which the organisation was quick to admit. This left various editors rather embarrassed over their previous one-sided uncritical reliance on Greenpeace's interpretation of the situation. The vicious response in the subsequent editorials was unprecedented and it is unclear how the media will respond to future Greenpeace campaigns.[11]

The new wave of direct action and civil disobedience

The early 1990s saw a quite remarkable rise in the level of non-violent direct action (NVDA) in the UK. The beliefs and approaches of those involved can be traced to a range of sources, for instance the emergence of the American group

EF! and its 'monkey-wrenching' tactics, the methods of hunt saboteurs, nuclear and peace protesters, the tradition of civil and political rights activism, and the radical spirit of deep ecology. In defiance of environmentally destructive developments, the slow pace and apparent intransigence of government responses to environmental concerns, and the lack of real democratic opportunities to make a difference, widely disparate groups began to engage in direct action. Nowhere is this more vividly illustrated than by the ferocious protests against roads and the live transport of animals. In many ways this new mood of defiance can be traced to the events surrounding Twyford Down, beginning in 1992, where all sectors of the community were radicalised and became involved in forms of protests in which they would never previously have thought of participating.[12] This radicalisation was further evident in campaigns against the M11 in East London, the M77 through the Pollock Estate in Glasgow, and most recently in Newbury to name but some of the most well publicised. Although the protests have failed to stop the road schemes, they have achieved a certain amount of success in that the policing of direct action has led to the cost of certain proposed projects becoming prohibitive. Perhaps more importantly, involvement in such protests and the media coverage they have enjoyed has politicised a wide range of people, putting the issue of transport and the environment firmly on the political agenda. Indeed, many activists argue that it was the anticipated levels of direct action and the public outcry it would inspire that caused the DoT to withdraw plans for a river crossing through ancient Oxleas Wood in London.

In many ways the rise in direct action can also be traced to a reaction against the activities of more established environmental pressure groups and the apparent 'professionalisation' of environmentalism. As the expertise of groups such as Greenpeace and FoE has grown they have begun to challenge the scientific methods and evidence of national governments and industrial companies. A new breed of 'expert' environmentalist able to articulate environmental concerns and to negotiate competently on a highly technical level has emerged. This has had the effect of creating a gulf between the 'experts' who run the leading environmental groups and both their core supporters and the general public. To a certain extent the debate around climate change, for example, has become a debate between rival sets of experts and has at times alienated concerned citizens. We raised the spectre of political alienation in Chapter 2 and in many ways the rise in direct action can be seen as a practical response by concerned citizens – a reclaiming of the environmental agenda. As Tim Allman of Road Alert! argues:

> There were a lot of people who didn't like what was happening around them, but who didn't see what they could do that would make much difference. Direct action changed all that. It empowers people. It makes them feel that they, as individuals, can make things happen.
>
> (Alarm UK, 1996, p. 21)

The national wave of NVDA has called into question the sceptics' accusation that environmental protest is merely a form of NIMBYism. NIMBY, which translates as 'not in my backyard', is a frequent form of abuse towards those who object locally to development. The sceptics' argument is that protesters do not oppose developments in principle but merely object to their proposed location: their backyard. Certainly, in the roads protests and the actions against live animal exports, a proportion of the campaigners are local people opposed to the immediate local impact. However, for the majority of those involved it has become a matter of principle. Interestingly, this has led the same sceptics to accuse protesters of being outsiders who do not understand the needs of the community. But it seems that NIMBY has become NIABY: 'not in anybody's backyard'. This new-found relationship between local and principled protest is also evident in the way that Welsh villagers have recently welcomed the influx of young EF! protesters against proposed open-cast mining.[13]

How legitimate are these forms of civil disobedience and what has been the UK government's response?

> An act of civil disobedience is an act of illegal, public protest, nonviolent in character. That is to say: the civilly disobedient act must be a knowing violation of the law, else it would not be disobedient; the act must be performed openly, being one of general community concern of which the agent is not ashamed; and the act must be intended as an objection to some law or administrative policy or public act.
>
> (Cohen, 1970, p. 469)

But what counts as justifiable civil disobedience is not always clear-cut. In a liberal democracy most people are clear as to the legitimacy of most actions and forms of protest. Under most circumstances a political rally is recognised as legal; at the other extreme violent actions directed against individuals would be seen as illegal and condemned on moral grounds. But between these extremes lies a disputed area: the realm of civil disobedience. Many people recognise that, although breaking the law is generally wrong in principle, in some cases where a law seems to contravene deeply held beliefs and ideals, or stops people acting on these beliefs, actively disobeying those laws is legitimate.[14] The problem, however, is which laws and which beliefs and ideals? Although not answering this question directly, for an act of civil disobedience to be legitimate, it is generally assumed that it must be non-violent, take place in the open, with a willingness to accept the consequences, and after all the legal means of democratic persuasion have been exhausted. Interestingly, the practice of monkey-wrenching, the disabling of machinery and damage to property, would not in these terms count as justifiable civil disobedience. But some committed activists are willing to accept the consequences of their actions and believe it is legitimate to stop environmentally destructive developments in this manner; as EF! proclaims, there can be 'No Compromise for Mother Earth'. Within the environmental movement as a whole, however, there tends to be general revulsion to the idea of justifying physical harm to persons (militant animal rights activists aside), although there is some sympathy and support for the monkey-wrenchers.

In response to this new wave of NVDA, new forces entered the equation. Under the provisions of the 1994 Criminal Justice and Public Order Act (CJA), the UK government criminalised certain forms of protest: actions that had previously been legal or subject only to the civil law were now classified as criminal. With respect to the environmental movement, the CJA most obviously criminalised forms of trespass, which have direct impact on, for instance, road protests and hunt sabotage.

Criminal Justice Act

The act defines two new offences which will criminalise a variety of peaceful political activities:

* *aggravated trespass*: trespass which occurs with the intention of disrupting or obstructing any lawful activity as defined by the police. It is also a criminal offence to disobey the orders of any police officer who has directed a person to leave land.

* *trespassory assemblies*: this empowers police to obtain an order banning assemblies held on land without the owner's permission which may result either in 'serious disruption to the life of the community' or 'significant damage to a site of historical, architectural or scientific importance'. Police are also empowered to stop people whom they reasonably believe to be travelling to such an assembly.

Ironically, as the then Conservative government's aim was to fragment and disperse protest and its support, the CJA itself became a focal point of resistance and led to the formation of coalitions between different communities and groups. Apart from attacking the rights of environmental protesters, the CJA criminalised the activities of, amongst others, travellers, squatters and ravers. All over the country new alliances and campaigns sprang up both in an attempt to halt the passage of the legislation and to develop even more imaginative forms of protest and community projects as activists exchanged skills and experience. This new grassroots activist movement is often referred to as 'DIY culture'. Rather than putting a stop to protest and frightening off would-be activists, the years since the introduction of the CJA have seen some of the most audacious, inventive and innovative protests. For example, the Reclaim the Streets party held on the M41 in the summer of 1996 in many ways embodied the original spirit of early Greenpeace actions, although involving thousands of politicised people from all walks of life. As a direct action activist contends:

> That's the pull of direct action: in a world where the individual feels increasingly helpless, direct action instils a sense of power and confidence. It brings people together and gives them hope.
>
> (Marman, 1996, p. 5)

TRANSFORMING EVERYDAY LIFE: FROM GREEN CONSUMERISM TO GREEN COMMUNES

Up to this point the activities of the green movement have been investigated with direct reference to its relations with the legislature and policy process. However, this emphasis in no way exhausts the scope of environmental activity. By moving away from more conventional understandings of party and pressure group politics and towards the way individuals and groups have sought to change their everyday practices, other important aspects of the green movement can be brought into focus. There are perhaps three distinct areas of activity that are worth consideration. The first is frequently termed 'green consumerism' and ranges from changing purchase and consumption patterns (for example, buying ecologically sensitive products) through to the establishment of green businesses. The second area of activity is that associated with 'third-force organisations' (TFOs). These tend to be community-based, not-for-profit groups which develop local projects such as wildlife site conservation, neighbourhood recycling initiatives and reclamation of derelict land. Finally, attention will turn to individuals and groups whose practices are a direct challenge to the existing system. This challenge has taken two principal forms: green communes and DIY culture. Green communes, whilst separating themselves from mainstream society, at the same time aspire to be actually existing Utopias: exemplars for future political and social arrangements. DIY culture is a more recent phenomenon. Rather than separation from society, those involved aim to disrupt, and offer alternatives to, conventional practices. An example of this might be the squatting and refurbishing of a derelict building to provide a community space, a place of shelter for the local homeless. Whereas green communes typically seek rural isolation, DIY activists often operate within inner cities. Clearly all the activities mentioned, from green consumerism to DIY culture, can and do affect the formulation and implementation of public policy; however, the point is that for these areas of green action, influencing the policy process is not necessarily the prime concern. It is the alteration of lifestyles, through changing existing everyday practices and patterns of behaviour, that is central.

Green consumerism

Everyone is a consumer of one sort or another. The question that green politics poses is how and what should be consumed? The 1980s saw a rise in what has been termed green consumerism, the easiest, most accessible and culturally acceptable form of green action. The promotion of 'green' products, such as lead-free petrol, and activities such as recycling has become commonplace.

There is no doubt that green consumerism can be very powerful. Through a realisation that their purchasing power can have an impact, people have come to believe that they can make a change for the better; to a certain extent green consumerism has empowered individuals. In principle, the aggregation of individual market transactions forces industry to change its practices, for example by encouraging it to switch from polluting and wasteful products to more environmentally friendly

Principles of green consumerism

The green consumer avoids products which are likely to:

- Endanger the health of the consumer or of others.

- Cause significant damage to the environment during manufacture, use or disposal.

- Consume a disproportionate amount of energy during manufacture, use or disposal.

- Cause unnecessary waste, either because of over-packaging or because of an unduly short useful life.

- Use materials derived from threatened species or from threatened environments.

- Involve the unnecessary use of – or cruelty to – animals, whether this be for toxicity testing or for other purposes.

- Adversely affect other countries, particularly in the Third World.

(Elkington and Hailes, 1988, p. 5)

alternatives. This is an extension of the logic of the consumer boycott, moving from action against a single readily identifiable product (such as the 1988 FoE campaign against aerosols containing CFCs) to the use of consumer pressure in all markets. Alongside existing companies which have responded to green consumer demands by producing additional 'green' products, a space has opened up for green companies and businesses. These can take the form either of established companies recognising the need to change their production processes or of completely new companies formed on the basis of environmental principles. But what does a company have to do to be 'green'? Clearly, it needs to consider the production and retailing process as a whole, from the impact of the extraction of raw materials and the energy efficiency of production through to the environmental and social costs of transport and packaging: for instance, the source of raw materials; the effect and destination of waste products created in production processes; the recyclability and durability of products.

In the late 1980s green consumerism was at its height: the book *The Green Consumer Guide* (Elkington and Hailes, 1988) and the magazine *The Ethical Consumer* both sold well, and companies, most prominently perhaps The Body Shop and the Cooperative Bank, increased their public profile and market share. But within a few years green consumerism began to suffer a backlash from both consumers themselves and green activists. The consumer backlash can be attributed to a number of causes. First, the initial wave of enthusiasm for green issues declined as Western economies moved into recession and traditional concerns – job security and economic opportunity – reasserted themselves. Combined with this, the novelty of 'being green' wore off. Issue attention and the perennial political focus on economic considerations are problems that the green movement has yet to overcome. Second, markets have been flooded by products purporting to be environmentally friendly. This leads to suspicions that existing products are simply being repackaged and that their green claims are spurious. Even when consumers wish to buy green there is no readily understandable standardised information or labelling to enable product comparison.

Perhaps the most fundamental criticisms, however, have emerged from the more radical elements of the environmental movement. The very idea and possibility of green consumerism itself has been challenged. While green consumerism might conceivably make markets less environmentally destructive, it fails to challenge the logic of accumulation and the patterns of consumption inherent in the capitalist system. Simply, green consumerism argues that when choosing between products, the choice should be made according to a scale of green and ethical criteria; which product is 'greenest'? But surely the environmental challenge questions the need for certain types of product in the first place? True, we can judge between the environmental impact of alternative makes and models of cars; we can choose the most environmentally friendly. But is not an 'environmentally friendly car' a misnomer? Is not the prior decision whether to buy a car or not the more fundamental issue? As Sandy Irvine argues:

> A truly green consumer would be asking first and foremost 'do I really need all these things?' It would involve a change to thinking in terms of what is the minimum necessary to satisfy essential human needs, rather than novelty, fashion, status and all the other hooks of materialism.
>
> (Irvine, in Dobson, 1991, p. 224)

Green consumerism does not attend to the demands of sustainable development. It is no more than a first step and if seen as more, as a panacea, there is a real danger of complacency – all that being green would entail is shopping more wisely and recycling waste paper. This is not to disparage the efforts of dedicated green businesses; it is simply to argue that sustainability requires a reconsideration of the role of private companies and the market.

Third-force organisations (TFOs)

> Around the country, in many of Britain's most deprived urban neighbourhoods, in its rural areas, and even in its more affluent suburbs, tens of thousands of voluntary, community-based organisations enable local people to improve the conditions of their localities and take some control over their own lives. … they come in a variety of forms and meet many different kinds of needs, identified by local people. They are already creating jobs, work and incomes. But their activities are barely recognised by mainstream political debate.
>
> (Jacobs, 1996, pp. 96–7)

There are a variety of organisations and activities, particularly at a local level, that do not fit comfortably into the standard categories such as public/private sector and cause/interest pressure group. Much community-based activity cannot be understood purely in terms of public sector policy and funding or private investment and entrepreneurial venture. TFOs have sprung up in fields as diverse as health, housing and homelessness, education, and the arts; for example, drug projects, housing cooperatives, literacy schemes and community carnivals and theatre. Specifically environmental TFOs have also emerged in many communities. These range from local wildlife conservation projects and recycling initiatives, through to local employment and trading systems (LETS) and 'veg boxes', which link residents with local organic farms (Young, 1996; 1997).

Why have TFOs emerged? In fact, such community-based enterprise has always existed, operating in the space between the public and the private. However, in the last decade there clearly has been increased participation and activity in this sector as the potential of TFOs has been recognised. Inaction on the part of government and industry has led to community action filling the vacuum. This inaction can be traced to a number of sources: lack of will and indifference; lack of resources because of tight public expenditure or the absence of profit-making potential; or a principled belief that such initiatives should be relatively autonomous, self-organised community developments. The majority of projects and initiatives are not completely independent: funding and expertise are frequently sought from public and private institutions. The difference is that TFOs are taking responsibility and developing the activities themselves. Many conservation and environmental improvement initiatives fit this pattern, as do wider enterprises such as housing cooperatives and health projects. But, as Michael Jacobs argues: 'Most of them suffer from a severe lack of resources. Given greater support, there is enormous scope for their expansion' (Jacobs, 1996, p. 97).

But some TFOs retain almost complete independence: LETS is an excellent example. LETS operates independently of the existing economy, with members bartering skills, resources, time and goods amongst themselves using their own currency or credit notes. A coordinator logs the interactions, credits and deficits. No conventional money changes hands: when an individual does some work for another, this is credited to the individual's account by the LETS community. The person for whom the work was done then has a general obligation to repay the community; no individuals are ever directly in debt to each other. For this reason, LETS appears particularly attractive to economically deprived sections of the community and has been seen as a potential solution to 'social exclusion, poverty and inability to work' (C. Williams, 1995, p. 4). From its inception in Vancouver in the early 1980s, LETS has gained increasing popularity in many countries. 'In 1992, just five LETS were in operation in the UK. By early 1995, there were over three hundred with at least 20,000 participants trading the equivalent of at least £1.5 million' (ibid.).

For green activists LETS offers a practical example of an alternative to the logic of capitalist markets and the individualism they engender. Work is reconceptualised in terms of community activity. A Utopian ideal drives these developments and in many ways LETS can be seen as a direct challenge to existing market relations.[15]

Green communes and DIY culture

Central to the green critique is a recognition that the creation of a green society requires not only opposition to prevailing patterns of consumption and political values but also the generation of alternatives: alternative technologies, democratic institutions, forms of community, social relations, and conceptions of work. Rather than the established actions of pressure groups or the weak environmentalism of green consumerism, a more fundamental way to counter modern capitalist society is to opt out altogether, to form new communities and counter-cultures with like-minded people. There have always been a number of environmental activists who believe that the only real way forward is to found green communes: actually existing Utopias. In many ways the more recent DIY culture can be seen as a further expression of this impulse. Environmentally sensitive forms of social, political and economic organisation should be small-scale, self-reliant (or even self-sufficient) and autonomous. By comparison with existing societies, these communities would necessarily be frugal, although the face-to-face, direct forms of democratic self-governance that their proponents argue ought to be established would allow space for new forms of cultural creativity and expression.[16]

Many experiments in alternative communities can best be understood in terms of the survivalist views characteristic of the early 1970s, as a response to the perceived imminence of ecological collapse. These communities saw themselves as separate from the doomed conventional system. In contrast, other green communes have been established as exemplars: demonstrations and visions of alternative possibilities. Perhaps the leading visionary of this position is Rudolf Bahro. Disillusioned with conventional party politics, Bahro argued that 'a new Benedictine order' should be founded to act as a spiritual beacon, a green Utopian reality for us to aspire to (Bahro in Dobson, 1991, p. 202). To a certain extent, a number of existing rural, self-reliant communities and cooperatives could be understood in this way; perhaps the most well known and well documented being the Centre for Alternative Technology (CAT) at Machynlleth, Wales. However, green communes have frequently failed to sustain their initial Utopian ideals. Many have had serious internal problems. Living within small communities can have drawbacks, particularly for those premised on the imminence of eco-collapse. For communes established as exemplars other difficulties have emerged, most prominently the tendency to be reabsorbed within the very society in opposition to which they had previously defined themselves. Without doubt, this is the fate that befell CAT. Over the last two decades, as environmental awareness in the general population increased, the attraction of alternative technologies grew. Rather than a green commune, CAT became more of a tourist destination. This is the paradox for such ventures: success in attracting attention tends to diminish the very conditions vital to their own existence. But the idealism of many activists means that the idea of establishing green communes still appeals and their place in the wider environmental movement is assured.

DIY culture is a relatively recent phenomenon. In the UK it emerged from a coming together of like-minded groups in opposition to the Criminal Justice Bill (later the CJA), its roots including the squatting, direct action and the underground dance cultures. Organisations such as the Freedom Network, initially formed in opposition to the CJA, developed broader agendas as those involved recognised common ground. *SchNEWS*, the weekly publication of Justice? in Brighton (one of the most prominent groups in the DIY network), illustrates the wide range of issues extending beyond simple opposition to a single act of parliament (Justice?, 1996). As the compilers of *The Book*, a directory of DIY organisations, argue:

> This Book is symptomatic of a new awareness, a force of empathy, wit, vision and community spirit which has given a fresh sense of empowerment and freedom. The scapegoated have become united like never before. The old channels of protest and party politics are dead. DIY culture is creating homes and entertainment by the people for the people captured in the philosophy of Deeds not Words.
>
> (*The Book*, 1995, pp. 1–2)

For activists such a George Monbiot, the development from single-issue opposition to the active promotion of green alternatives is essential:

> The direct action movement is the most potent popular force of the 1990s, yet it has one fundamental and potentially fatal weakness. So far it has been largely responsive. The Government proposes a road or a bill and the movement opposes it: the Department of Transport and the Home Office have set the direct action agenda. Political change does not take place until the opponents of government fight for what they're for, rather than simply for what they're against.
>
> (George Monbiot, quoted in McKay, 1996, p. 127)

In contrast to green communes, activities tend to be city-based, dealing head-on with the adverse effects of contemporary society. Derelict land and empty properties have been squatted and made available to activists, artists and the community at large. In many cases those involved are committed to supporting people whom society has left behind or forgotten: the homeless, the elderly and the mentally ill. The seeds of new social relations are being sown within some of the most deprived urban areas. Further, through these initiatives, environmentalists have been forced to address issues extending beyond conventional environmental boundaries and to make alliances with other types of activist. This wider recognition is important as it moves green politics beyond single issues; but at present the idealism of many activists is an inadequate preparation for some of the harsh realities that they now face. This was particularly evident in the case of the 'Pure Genius' eco-village in Wandsworth. In May 1996, supporters of The Land is Ours, an organisation committed to challenging established property rights, occupied derelict land owned by Guinness. Over the preceding few years Guinness had been trying to get planning permission to build a supermarket and luxury flats on the site. Taking advantage of the local community's opposition to these plans, the campaigners aimed to build a model sustainable village, a development that would respond to community needs rather than private profit. Five months later Guinness won a court order to remove the protesters, and the dwellings and reclaimed land were flattened. In many ways the establishment of this new community had been successful as it had forced the political issue of local land rights and community needs into the media and public domain. But beneath the veneer of success other tensions were becoming increasingly apparent. 'Pure Genius' was attractive not only to environmentalists, but also to many of those who had nowhere else to go.

> Utopians and protestors had no training in dealing with the mentally disturbed, beyond common sense and sympathy (of which there was a lot). 'How do you deal with people on heroin? People with guns and knives? We have no support network. Some of these people need hospital care, many need professional help,' said Sarah last month. 'We are having to spend more and more time looking after people. That's fine but you can't expect us to build a community in these circumstances.'

> (Vidal, 1996, p. 3)

Traditional pressure groups, notably Greenpeace, often neglect the complex interconnectedness of social, political, economic and environmental issues, focusing on what can be presented as distinct and easily identifiable problems. Environmental concerns become clear-cut, simplified for media and public consumption. DIY activists recognise that the separation of environmental from pressing social concerns is a nonsense and that the development of grassroots actions and coalitions is essential if we are to comprehend and respond to our present situation.

CONCLUSION

This chapter has not sought to provide a compendium of environmental activity; its aim has been to show the range and forms that such activity can take. Although various terms and categories have been introduced to try to makes sense of the diversity of groups, their ideals and approaches, it needs to be recognised that in practice many transcend these boundaries. However, the categories act as useful pointers enabling us to appreciate the tactics and choices open to the green movement.

What is striking is the range of tactics and forms of action deployed. This should not surprise us, given the diversity of ethical and political commitments represented within green thinking. This takes us back to the identity of the green movement as a 'movement'. Its diversity allows the possibility of action in many different forms and at many different levels – from inside the legislature to grassroots community development, all political spaces are exploited. Although coalitions are increasingly being formed, action is not necessarily concerted. Many groups which are in principle campaigning against similar policies and developments would not wish to be seen to be in alliance. For example, the gaze of the National Trust and Earth First! may at times converge on similar issues, but the likelihood of, and desire for, a strong association is non-existent. In many cases the tactics and forms of action favoured by different green organisations are scorned by others in the same 'movement'. Despite this mutual suspicion the different emphases may actually be positively reinforcing. As Dave Foreman, a prominent American Earth Firster!, argues:

> the actions of monkeywrenchers invariably enhance the status and bargaining position of more 'reasonable' opponents. Industry considers mainline environmentalists to be radical until they get a taste of real radical activism. Suddenly the soft-sell of the Sierra Club and other white-shirt-and-tie eco-bureaucrats becomes much more attractive and worthy of serious negotiation. These moderate environmentalists must condemn monkeywrenching so as to preserve their own image, but they should take full advantage of the credence it lends to their approach.
>
> (Foreman in Dobson, 1991, p. 229)

To answer our original question, then, with another: does the environmental movement need to be homogeneous? Diversity, which appeared at first to be a weakness, may turn out to be the green movement's strength.

CASE STUDY: TWYFORD DOWN AND THE FORMATION OF AN ANTI-ROADS MOVEMENT

In the UK, direct action against road construction projects seems commonplace. The images of protesters physically placing their bodies between machinery and environment, being 'cherry-picked' from trees and aerial walkways and more recently taking their protests underground are all familiar. It is perhaps surprising then to consider that such actions are a comparatively recent phenomenon, beginning in late 1992 at Twyford Down in Hampshire. The story of the Twyford Down campaign reaches back over two decades, the initial public inquiry for the extension of the M3 occurring as early as 1971. It is worth dwelling on some of the aspects of the campaign as it was without doubt one of the major influences in the evolution of a national anti-roads campaign and it is an exemplary case of how environmental groups can be 'mobilised out' of the political process, a point that we shall return to in Chapter 4. The events surrounding Twyford Down have become part of campaigning 'folklore'.

M3 public inquiries

The first public inquiry in 1971 endorsed the extension of the M3 near Winchester through the water meadows along the line of the Itchen Valley. Between then and the follow-up inquiry in 1976, local people and organisations came together under the banner of the M3 Joint Action Group. Support was received from powerful landowners such as Winchester College. With the help of John Tyme, a lecturer at Sheffield Polytechnic who had worked with local campaigners to force the abandonment of the M16 inquiry in the Aire Valley, the M3 inquiry was disrupted and the Inspector judged that a full-scale examination of the scheme was necessary. Not only John Tyme, but others including the headmaster of Winchester College, were ejected from the proceedings at various points in what was perhaps the first direct action associated with this scheme (Tyme, 1978, pp. 31–42).[17] In 1980, the Inspector ruled against the M3 extension, only for the Department of Transport (DoT) to offer a new route which would cut through Twyford Down. At the 1985 public inquiry, there was a lack of real opposition since Winchester College itself had offered to sell the Down to the DoT and both Hampshire and Winchester councils were in broad support of the project. However, once local people realised the extent of the damage to the landscape that would be caused by the new route, the Joint Action Group was reformed. After concerted pressure, during which time Winchester District Council was persuaded to come out against the scheme, the inquiry was reopened in 1987. But, this time the inquiry was lost, with the Inspector deciding in favour of the cutting. The proposal of a tunnel, which had widespread local support, was also rejected. In response, members of the newly formed Twyford Down Association (TDA) challenged the DoT in the High Court for failing to implement the EC's environmental impact assessment directive (see Chapter 5) and when that failed they appealed to the European Commission itself. Whilst the European appeal was under way though, construction work began. TDA kept the question of Twyford Down in the political and media spotlight and in the 1992 election the local MP, the then Roads Minister Christopher Chope, lost his seat. However, the Conservative government won the election with the promise of extending the roads programme and was able to affect the outcome of the EC review during the Maastricht negotiations. With construction under way, local activists were faced with the option of resigning themselves to defeat or continuing the campaign in a new form now that all the legal and political institutional processes had been exhausted. For many, the battle was far from over.

The biased nature of the public inquiry process

Before moving on to discuss the wave of direct action that followed, it is worth reflecting briefly on some of the aspects of the public inquiry process which meant that the odds were generally stacked against the anti-road protesters. A public inquiry into a road proposal is the first official opportunity that people in the UK have to deliberate on questions of transport. Generally a decision has already been made as to the preferred route of the proposed road; the DoT has already decided that a road needs to be built.[18] As early as 1936, the Trunk Road Act gave the Ministry the sole authority for initiating and deciding upon trunk road schemes. The Highways Act 1980 continued in the same vein: 'by giving the Ministry a direct executive responsibility for this one aspect of transport only, it inevitably resulted in an organisational commitment to inter-urban road building at the expense of an overall and balanced view of transport needs' (Kay, 1992, p. 18). To further unbalance proceedings and discredit the 'participation' process, inspectors are appointed by the DoT. Thus the DoT is the sole authority for initiating and deciding on trunk road schemes – 'judge and jury of its own case' (ibid., p. 17). It is perhaps informative to note that over a five-year period, only five out of 146 public inquiries have gone against the DoT (Rowell, 1996, p. 332). Because the issues that are open to debate are so narrowly defined, public inquires provide only a 'veneer of participation'. Objectors are not allowed to challenge either government policy or the use of particular decision-making procedures, in this case an elaborate form of cost–benefit analysis (CBA) known as COBA9. Inspectors have always ruled such challenges illegitimate. 'They [objectors] have been told that it is government policy to rely on both COBA and forecasts in making decisions about new roads, and that scrutiny of government policy is the business of Parliament' (Adams, 1995, p. 1). There is much to be said about the use of CBA in decision making and it will be a central theme of Chapter 5. For now a few comments which should expose the dubious assumptions upon which decisions are based will suffice. Such assumptions cannot be challenged at any point in the public inquiry process.[19]

Calculations of time savings are the dominant benefits of any trunk road proposal and represent the foremost quantification of the DoT's policy objective 'to assist economic growth by reducing transport costs' (DoT, 1989, p. 4; 1992, p. 20). 'Typically, time savings account for 85% to 90% of the gross benefits of a trunk road scheme' (DoT, 1991, p. 5). Using economic valuation techniques, the DoT assigns a figure of 153.2 pence per hour per person for non-working time journeys (at 1985 prices) (DoT, 1987, p. 5). There are at least two areas of concern here. First, the time saving valuation within the COBA9 analysis has no regard for those individuals who have strong environmental commitments and may have been prepared to accept a longer journey time in the knowledge that a sensitive landscape such as Twyford Down was being conserved. As Stephen Atkins writes, 'the likelihood is that many people find that their short-term travel behaviour choices

are being used to justify decisions that they would not support "politically" '
(Atkins, 1990, p. 8). Simply because they use a stretch of road, it is assumed
that all drivers will prefer a quicker journey. Second, there is a problem of
aggregating small increments of time such that benefits of £100 million are
apparently achieved. It is assumed in economic analysis that an individual
accords the same value to a large time period as to the equivalent aggregation of small time periods. If, for instance, an individual saves one minute
every day using a proposed road scheme in non-working time, it is assumed
that the aggregation of those small daily savings is valued in the same way as
a single period of six hours. Outside of the limited assumptions of neo-
classical economic theory, it is questionable as to whether such small time
savings are even noticed and even if they are, whether they are of any productive use compared with the longer time span to which they are apparently equivalent. In 1990, the House of Commons Transport Select Committee
argued: 'The assumption that small increments of time have real economic
value when aggregated over a large number of vehicles is unsubstantiated'
(quoted in Bray, 1995, p. 9). When the aggregation of time savings is commonly in the range of £100 million and is the principal quantified benefit of
a scheme, the cogency of such assumptions needs to be challenged.

One of the major costs of road construction is the price of land. However,
it can be shown that the incorporation of market prices for certain types of
land may result in an acute underestimate. Green belt land, Sites of Special
Scientific Interest (SSSIs) and Areas of Outstanding Natural Beauty (AONBs)
are protected areas, ones which have severe development restrictions attached to them. As the DoE states in *This Common Inheritance*, there is an
objective 'to protect the best of urban and rural environments so that we can
pass on to our children what we value most about our own heritage' (DoE,
1990, p. 80). Surely Twyford Down, part of an AONB, an SSSI and home
to two scheduled ancient monuments was such an environment? However,
where a decision is made to propose a road scheme through such environments,[20] the value of the land is then incorporated. But one of the primary
features of such areas is that they have planning restrictions attached to
them, and so the market price is extremely low; a price that clearly misrep-
resents the important scientific, aesthetic or amenity value of the land in
question. Not only is an area of local or national importance to be lost, but
its value is taken to be less than ordinary agricultural land. The DoT's own
standing advisory committee has recognised this paradox: 'the cost of acquired land ... may be a serious underestimate of its social value if the land
is subject to severe restrictions on development' (SACTRA, 1992, p. 96).

Finally, it is frequently argued that when the COBA9 analysis produces apparent benefits to the economy of millions of pounds, the environmental and social impact of schemes tends to be overlooked. As Stephen Atkins points out: 'Recent public policy has been dominated by concerns over "value for money" in public expenditure. In this context a measure that purports to show cash returns from public investment has a greater influence on decision-makers' (Atkins, 1990, p. 7). As discussed in Chapter 2, the expert knowledge of economists is not open to challenge and as such the idea of public participation is degraded. As Ray Kemp contends, 'the professionalisation of planning with the introduction of technical terms and standards, bureaucratic and legal devices, may be seen to have led to merely token public involvement in many important planning matters' (Kemp, 1985, pp. 183–4). The public inquiries that were held on the M3 extension are prime examples of this tokenism.

Direct action on the Down

Following the exhaustion of political and legal procedures and standard forms of protest, the nature of the campaigning began to change. In order to raise public and media awareness, demonstrations took place on the site itself. Actions that stopped short of full confrontation were coordinated by TDA and FoE. The transition from one form of protest to another is described by Barbara Bryant:

> As far as the Twyford Down campaign itself is concerned, the transition from conventional campaigning tactics (consciousness-raising, legal representation at Public Inquiries, political lobbying, high-profile events) to non-violent direct action was not an easy one. The rationale behind such a transition was overwhelmingly clear: in February 1992, TDA activists and Friends of the Earth (who had been working together for more than a year) argued that the Government was itself breaking the law in proceeding with preliminary works *before* the EC has ruled on the complaint before it concerning breaches of the Environmental Impact Assessment Directive. This unlawful behaviour entirely justified the use of responsible, non-violent direct action to slow down or even prevent the work continuing. A railway bridge due for demolition was therefore occupied on 14 February by Friends of the Earth.
>
> (Bryant, 1996, pp. 300–1)

FoE and TDA continued such actions for a couple of weeks, successfully halting construction before an injunction was served against FoE. At this point 'lawyers advised them that to break it would risk contempt of court proceedings, which would result in fines of up to a quarter of a million pounds. This would bankrupt the organisation. FoE left the site, leaving a breach that was soon filled by the direct action protestors' (Lamb, 1996, p. 6). The changing nature of the campaign continued with local people and green activists taking more confrontational but non-violent direct action (NVDA) against the construction. It is interesting that many of the direct action activists felt that FoE had let them down by pulling out. This reflects the tension between the newly emerging direct action (dis)organisations and the more established and well-resourced pressure groups discussed earlier in Chapter 3. As well as the financial and legal problems that they could have faced, the new activists caused a problem for FoE, 'who were anxious about being associated with mass illegal protests over which they had no control' (Doherty, 1997, p. 149).

In late 1992, members of a newly formed local group, Friends of Twyford Down, as well as members of Earth First! and the Dongas Tribe who had camped on the Down, began 'bulldozer-diving' and 'crane-sitting', squatting the proposed route on St Catherine's Hill. What followed was to set the scene for future confrontations around the country. One incident in particular made protesters realise the physical power that could potentially be unleashed upon them. 'Yellow Wednesday', 9 December 1992, saw private security guards (Group 4) hired for the first time to ensure that the site was cleared for the contractors. The violence meted out to the protesters, with the police looking on, shocked those present and those who viewed the footage on national television.

Undeterred, the Twyford campaign continued throughout 1993, slowing down the construction process and in the end adding some £3.5 million in security costs, including the hiring of private detectives by the DoT to gather information on the protesters.[21] 1993 also saw seven activists jailed for breaking court injunctions and returning to the site. Further, the DoT attempted (unsuccessfully) to recoup the £3.5 million by suing a group of sixty-seven protestors indiscriminately picked from a particular action that involved thousands. Although the road was completed in late 1994, Twyford radicalised groups all over Britain where previously they might have given up the fight after the public inquiry had given the go-ahead. As Jonathon Porritt writes:

> The trauma of Twyford Down galvanised thousands of people into a host of actions that might otherwise never have taken place. It was so horrific, so visible, so palpable. Even now, there is no amount of cosmetic landscaping and tree planting that can conceal the sheer scale of

the wound inflicted on the countryside. It screams out at you, and will go on screaming out to all with ears to hear and eyes to see. ... Ruling politicians and their self-serving advisers consistently underestimate the power of symbolism in politics. Long after the Twyford Down campaign was lost, and the Dongas had been brutally routed, Twyford Down continues to work its magic as a symbol of opposition to undemocratic, ecologically wanton road-building, wherever it takes place.

(Quoted in Bryant, 1996, p. 299)

The emergence of a national anti-roads movement

It is important to remember that before the 1990s there was no national anti-roads campaign at a grassroots level. Organisations such as Transport 2000 and FoE had campaigned at policy level against the road-building programme and in support of an integrated transport policy; but at the level of individual schemes there was no real grassroots movement. This began to change in the 1990s. After having successfully coordinated local opposition throughout London against the London Road Assessment Studies in the late 1980s, ALARM, the umbrella body for over 150 London-based groups, went national. *Roads for Prosperity*, published by the DoT in 1989, promised a £23 billion national roads programme. Alarm UK's response strategy was to set up a network supporting local groups fighting proposed road schemes before, during, or after a public inquiry. Alarm UK became 'a central, umbrella organisation which supplies local groups with information on transport, environmental and campaigning matters, which staged occasional nationwide stunts (including a "Stop That Road Week") and which held conferences where the groups could meet' (Alarm UK, 1996, pp. 13–14). By 1995, about 300 local groups opposing particular road schemes were members of Alarm UK.

With their experience of direct action from Twyford Down and the realisation that road schemes were under construction all over the UK, a small group of Friends of Twyford Down members set up Road Alert!, in many ways a sister organisation to Alarm UK. As Rebecca Lush, one of the protesters who went to jail for their actions, explains: 'Many people have been inspired by the protests that have sprung up since Twyford and have wanted to defend their land too. Road Alert! exists to help these people by passing on protest skills and helping others to get involved' (Alarm UK, 1996, p. 21).

Without doubt the actions at Twyford Down acted as a spur to NVDAs at, for example, Pollock, Bath, Leytonstone, Stanworth Woods near Blackburn, and most recently at the Newbury and Exeter–Honiton bypasses and the proposed new runway at Manchester Airport. The courage and commitment of activists is beyond doubt and we are witnessing a new form of flexible, non-hierarchical and spontaneous protest (Porritt, 1984, p. 303). Certainly the techniques and forms of organisation utilised by activists are becoming more and more sophisticated.[22] Direct action offers the possibility of new forms of political action in the face of political institutions that stifle meaningful public participation and that are unresponsive to environmental values. Even with the introduction of draconian legislation such as parts of the Criminal Justice and Public Order Act, the anti-roads movement still embodies the spirit of opposition and a creative and empowering energy. As Tim Allman, another founder of Road Alert!, contends:

> There were a lot of people who didn't like what was happening around them, but who didn't see what they could do that would make much difference. Direct action changed all that. It empowers people. It makes them feel that they are individuals, can make things happen.
>
> (Alarm UK, 1996, p. 21)

Thus the Twyford Down campaign, whilst unsuccessful in its immediate goal of halting the destruction of the Down, was successful as a spur to further direct action across the country. And the direct action that followed has become more sophisticated and generated increasingly widespread public support. Twyford Down showed both that the public inquiry system is seriously flawed and that the standard legal and political channels of influence are weak and unresponsive. Furthermore, concern is no longer limited to particular local schemes but to the roads-building programme as such and the way in which public discussion of road schemes is limited and circumscribed by an inadequate inquiry system. As Chris Gillham, a veteran of the Twyford Down campaign and an individual far removed from the media image of the dreadlocked, unemployed youth, remarks:

> I came from a background of concerned but respectable and restrained involvement. I spent years in formal committees of preservation groups, not achieving very much. Here is the justification, whenever it is needed, for non-violent direct action. The system allowed us to spend decades in argument, and huge sums of money, making an intellectually unshakeable case, only for the system to brush it all aside. When you hear the brazen words 'democratic process' and 'rule of law', reply quietly with 'Twyford Down'.
>
> (Road Alert!, 1997, case history no. 3)

SUGGESTIONS FOR FURTHER READING

On the broad shape of the green movement there is no single comprehensive text that we would recommend. However, a number of books and journals (in particular *Environmental Politics*) often contain relevant material. A lot of work has been done on party politics: on green parties see Dick Richardson and Christopher Rootes (eds), *The Green Challenge* (1995); on the impact of environmental concern on mainstream parties see Mike Robinson, *The Greening of British Party Politics* (1992).

Part II

The background to environmental policy

4 Collective action, power and decision making

> Therein is the tragedy. Each man is locked into a system that compels him to increase his herd without limit – in a world that is limited. Ruin is the destination toward which all men rush, each pursuing his own best interest in a society that believes in the freedom of the commons. Freedom in a commons brings ruin to all.
>
> (Hardin, 1968, p. 1244)

In Chapter 1, we looked at the nature of ethical questions concerning our obligations to the non-human world and to contemporary and future generations; in Chapters 2 and 3, we looked at issues in political theory and the nature of the environmental movement. In this there was a transition from theoretical to practical considerations. In this chapter theoretical and practical considerations will overlap in the discussion of three related issues affecting the making of environmental policy. The first is a body of issues arising from the fact that the solution to environmental problems is necessarily a collective one. As we shall see, there are a number of obstacles standing in the way of achieving collective action and it is important to understand their nature prior to considering the forms that any solution might take. Second is the issue of power. Individuals, parties and pressure groups have different access to the means of making or influencing policies and decisions. Being right about an issue is not sufficient if there is little or no opportunity to ensure that one's viewpoint will be heard. Third, even assuming that the problems of collective action and power can be solved, there still remain issues concerning the timing of any action. Is it better, in conditions of uncertainty, to act now, or to delay action until more knowledge or a better or cheaper solution is available? These issues, dealt with in this chapter in a theoretical manner, emerge out of the discussions in the preceding chapters and point forward to subsequent chapters in which questions concerning the suitability of different policy instruments and the attempts made at different political levels to solve environmental problems will be discussed.

COLLECTIVE ACTION PROBLEMS

Even where we recognise that something ought to be done, there still remain the everyday political problems of agreeing on what is to be done and how best to implement the solution. It may be hard or even impossible to get agreement on what course of action should be taken; and it is also very common to find that all those involved want something to happen but that none the less nothing happens. Why is this? Very often it is because none of us individually is prepared or able to make something happen. Either we do not want to bear the burden ourselves or we take the view that it cannot be done by just one or two people, but only by a concerted effort. We may conclude that it is not worth trying to do anything unless others are involved. Thus, recognising the existence of an environmental problem and its possible solutions constitutes only the first step towards a satisfactory resolution of the problem. A common underlying feature of the political difficulty in achieving a workable solution is the problem of collective action. In many cases, for example over-fishing in the world's oceans, we can see that although there is a general recognition of the problem it is still extremely difficult in practice to prevent it. It remains in the interest of individual countries to continue present practices even though they are aware that this will lead to a diminution of fish stocks. However, they know that if they do not take the fish someone else will. Why, then, should they be the ones to lose out? The same applies to carbon dioxide emissions. Scientific evidence concerning the danger of global warming does not automatically entail that nations or individuals will reduce their own emissions. They might recognise the problem and consider that something should be done, but they are reluctant to contribute to a solution.

Thus, paradoxically, it often seems that cooperation is least likely where those involved stand to lose most. This is particularly the case at the global level. There is open access to the atmosphere and stratosphere – they are common property, priced at zero, and are therefore likely to be overused. We all get the benefits or the disbenefits; that is, no one can be excluded from the benefits of clean air or the disbenefits of increased ultraviolet-B radiation. However, we are reluctant to assume the individual cost of ensuring the benefits or avoiding the disbenefits. Public goods of this type can only exist through cooperative action and yet cooperation in such a case is extraordinarily hard to attain and still harder to enforce. Where there is a public good which can be secured only through the cooperation of a vast number of individual actors, there is always an incentive for individuals to 'free ride' – to benefit from the public good without contributing towards it. It might be argued that so long as the public goods concerned are provided then it does not matter whether or not there is free riding – after all, the future of the planet is at stake. But the problem lies in the fact that where free riding is possible, the provision of the public good itself may be endangered. Our focus here is not the moral one about the ethics of free riding, but the practical one of securing sufficient agreement to act where the threat of free riding undermines the conditions for securing agreement (Pearce *et al.*, 1989, p. 12).

Collective action problems arise where an individual's contribution to the problem or to its solution is at most a tiny part of a much larger whole, and where their actions one way or another seem to make little or no difference. So, every car driver blames every other driver for the traffic jam in which they sit on the way to work; and as they sit immobile in their cars reflecting on the fact that the carbon dioxide they are emitting from their exhausts contributes to global warming, each driver sees little point in reducing their car use unless everyone else does the same. Everyone is waiting for everyone else to act first, the result being that no one acts at all.

We recognise this as an everyday occurrence: the discipline known as rational choice theory[1] extends the analysis by generalising from the assumption that individuals are self-interested, egoistic, rational, utility maximisers, to the conclusion that achieving voluntary collective action is necessarily fraught with difficulty. People are assumed to be, in general, self-interested; they are assumed to be largely concerned with themselves and their immediate family; they are assumed to be rational in the sense that they can act consistently, given the preferences they happen to have; and they are assumed to be interested in maximising welfare rather than in operating according to abstract moral principles. Rationality, then, is defined in terms of the choice of means, not the choice of ends. To be rational is to be able to choose the most effective, most efficient and most economical means of achieving what one wants, whatever that happens to be.[2] We shall investigate two particularly relevant issues within rational choice theory: voting paradoxes and the 'tragedy of the commons'.

Terms and definitions in rational choice

- *Rationality*: the ability to compile a complete, consistent and transitive preference ordering, and to choose actions accordingly.

- *Transitive:* the property that if *a* stands in some relationship to *b* and *b* stands in the same relationship to *c*, then *a* stands in the same relationship to *c*. Thus if I prefer *a* to *b*, *b* to *c*, and *a* to *c*, my preference relationships are transitive.

- *Private good:* a good which is individually produced and consumed, whose consumption by one person prevents it from being consumed by another, and on which it is hence impossible to free ride.

- *Public good:* a good which is jointly produced and consumed, not subject to crowding, and from which it is impossible to exclude free riders.

- *Privileged group:* a group which contains at least one member who gains enough privately from a public good to be willing to supply it on its own if necessary.

- *Collective action problem:* any situation where all actors are better off if they all cooperate than if they do not but where it is not necessarily in each actor's individual interest to cooperate.

(McLean, 1987, pp. 195–7)

Voting paradoxes

Suppose a protest group is trying to decide where and how to campaign but it cannot reach consensus. Whatever decision members make will be binding on all, because they cannot afford to divide their efforts. One or other course of action must be chosen and the tactics agreed. For the sake of argument, let us suppose that everyone in the group is not purely self-interested – they all share the same broad goals and are willing to assume the burden of acting. They will not free ride on the efforts of others. But the problem of collective action does not fall away. The group still has to make a collective decision based on the individual views or preferences of its members: individual preferences have to be aggregated into a collective choice and this raises the question of which formal procedures they use to make the decision. An obvious answer would seem to be that they make a decision by voting. This appears to be a fairly straightforward thing to do – until we reflect a little further. There are of course a number of well-recognised issues associated with choosing an electoral or voting system, some of which are to do with criteria such as fairness to parties or groups of voters. As we saw in Chapter 3, these issues are important in green politics. However, our present concern is the obstacles to securing collective action on environmental issues, and there are other, more technical, aspects of voting theory directly relevant to this issue.

Representative assemblies and committees typically vote to reach decisions, and structures of decision making have evolved which stipulate the way in which votes should be conducted. It might seem intuitively obvious that the only relevant factor determining the outcome of a sequence of votes is the number of votes each proposal attracts, but in fact this is not necessarily so. It is perfectly possible, for example, for circumstances to arise in which there is no overall winner and in which the outcome is entirely dependent on seemingly irrelevant factors such as the order in which the votes are taken. This seems a rather curious possibility which might have significant consequences, so it is worth a look. As an example, let us suppose that a local council is made up of three parties, none of which has overall control, and in which two are needed to form a coalition on any particular issue for it to be adopted as policy. Each party has its own transitive set of preferences. Given this we can consider the way in which different outcomes might arise. The issue under consideration is whether to build council houses, private houses or a park on a plot of vacant land.[3] The parties' preferences are summarised in Table 4.1.

Table 4.1 The parties' preferences

Preference	Party A	Party B	Party C
1	CH	P	PH
2	PH	CH	P
3	P	PH	CH

Key: CH = council houses; PH = private houses; P = park.

Thus, party A prefers council houses to private houses to a park, and because its preferences are transitive, we can infer that it would prefer council houses to a park if given a straight choice between the two. In the table we can see that (in a straight vote between any two alternatives) two parties prefer council houses to private houses; two prefer private houses to a park; and two prefer a park to council houses. Given this, it is clear that there can be no simple question of deciding which policy there is a majority for, because (in a straight contest between two proposals in each round of voting) a majority can be found for each proposal. In most formal voting procedures there are rules governing how votes are to be taken, and this would normally mean that those voting should be given a choice between only two pro- posals at a time. Thus, once all the amendments to the substantive motion have been tabled, the amendments are usually voted on in turn, at each point there being a straight choice between two alternatives. Finally there is a run-off between the remaining two alternatives and whichever gains a majority wins. In the case under consideration the only thing which will determine the outcome is not any particular majority as such, but the order in which the votes are taken. Michael Laver explains how this works:

> If council housing had been presented first, it would have been rejected by a coalition of parties B and C, each of which preferred something else. Once council housing had been rejected, the run-off between private housing and a park would provoke parties A and C to combine and choose private housing. On the other hand, if a park had been presented as the first matter for deci- sion, it would have been rejected by a coalition of parties A and C. This would have resulted in a run-off between council and private housing. Parties A and B would have combined to choose council housing. [Again], if private housing had been presented first, it would have been rejected by parties A and B. The park would have won the run-off with council housing, since it was preferred by parties B and C.
>
> (Laver, 1983, p. 153)

In other words, any of the outcomes might have been chosen, and which was chosen depended solely on the order in which the alternatives were considered. A majority of voters preferred an alternative to each outcome. The final outcome is therefore not independent of the order in which the votes are taken, but on the contrary, entirely dependent on that order. This may seem a surprising result, but it is remarkably difficult to devise systems of voting in which the outcome is inde- pendent of the order of voting. The above example is the simplest version of a voting cycle in which each of the three alternatives can be defeated by another of the three.

The possibility of a voting cycle obviously presents a challenge to anyone who believes that voting is a straightforward matter; but there are also other possible consequences. So far we have assumed that each party will vote in accordance with its preference orderings as shown in the table. However, it might be in someone's interest, if they know the other parties' preferences, to vote tactically. Tactical voting is where a party or person votes against their real preference in order to secure the best outcome possible under the circumstances. To give a different example: a Labour voter is voting tactically when he or she votes Liberal Democrat because they believe that this will keep the Conservatives out. They do this in a seat where they have reason to believe that Labour will not win, and that if they vote Liberal Democrat (their second choice) they will at least prevent their last choice (Conservative) winning. Thus, they vote against Labour (their first choice) and by so doing help to secure their second-best preferred outcome – if they had voted Labour they might have contributed to a Conservative victory, which was their least desired outcome. If we apply the possibility of tactical voting to our council example above we can see that if, for example, the first vote to be taken were private houses against council houses, and Party A votes in line with its true preference ordering by voting for council housing, council housing would win, but it would then lose in a straight run-off against the proposal for a park. But this is Party A's least preferred option. Thus if Party A is canny and has sufficient knowledge of the other parties' preference orderings, it might be wiser for it to vote for private housing (its second preference) in the first round, thus securing a run-off between private housing and a park in which private housing wins. By not voting in accordance with its true preferences in the first round of voting, and in accordance with its true preferences only in the second round of voting, Party A secures the provision of private housing, which, although it was not its first preference, it undoubtedly prefers to a park, which was its last preference. Of course, all of the parties might try to vote tactically by second-guessing the other parties' preferences, at which point the whole matter gets very complicated indeed! What is clear is that greens need to be aware of the way in which voting and other decision-making processes can affect decisions in policy making and how they might be manipulated by other actors.

Collective irrationality: the 'tragedy of the commons'

The example we have just been looking at is concerned with some of the formal problems of decision making – it is an example of that branch of rational choice theory known as social choice theory. As such, it assumes only that people are rational and utility-maximising, not that they are necessarily self-interested or egoistic. However, in looking at the problem of collective action, we can add to this formal problem in aggregating preferences by making additional assumptions about people's motivation. The branch of rational choice theory known as public choice theory applies the methods and assumptions of economics to political decision making. As we saw above, in our earlier example of the traffic jam, the outcome of individuals acting rationally in their own self-interest can lead to a form of collective irrationality which is in no one's interest.

A classic and frequently cited example of this sort of problem is Garrett Hardin's 'The Tragedy of the Commons'. Hardin asks us to imagine a pasture open to all and to accept that each herdsman will try to keep as many cattle as possible on this common pasture. Although under certain conditions the number of people and the number of animals they graze may stay below the carrying capacity of the land, a day will arrive where this is no longer so and where 'the inherent logic of the commons remorselessly generates tragedy' (Hardin, 1968, p. 1244).

> As a rational being, each herdsman seeks to maximise his gain ... he asks, 'What is the utility to me of adding one more animal to my herd?' This utility has one negative and one positive component.
> 1. The positive component is a function of the increment of one animal. Since the herdsman receives all the proceeds from the sale of the additional animal, the positive utility is nearly +1.
> 2. The negative component is a function of the additional overgrazing created by one more animal. Since, however, the effects of overgrazing are shared by all the herdsmen, the negative utility for any particular decision-making herdsman is only a fraction of −1.
>
> Adding together the component partial utilities, the rational herdsman concludes that the only sensible course for him to pursue is to add another animal to his herd. And another; and another ... But this is the conclusion reached by each and every rational herdsman sharing a commons. Therein is the tragedy. Each man is locked into a system that compels him to increase his herd without limit – in a world that is limited. Ruin is the destination toward which all men rush, each pursuing his own best interest in a society that believes in the freedom of the commons. Freedom in a commons brings ruin to all.
>
> (ibid.)

By substituting examples we can see why seas are over-fished, air and water polluted, the ozone layer destroyed and the emission of greenhouse gases hard to reduce. In each case there is a free good, whether a natural resource or an environmental 'sink' into which we pour our pollution. Because the good is free we over-consume it, and although over-consumption and its consequences is not in the interest of everyone collectively, it is in the short-term interest of each individual to continue to consume as much as they can. Thus the tragedy of the commons, the possibility of collective irrationality, lies at the heart of many environmental problems.

To avert the tragedy, Hardin argues that individual property rights in what were previously the commons ought to be created so that people either own their own land or someone owns the land as a whole and charges people for grazing rights. In either case there is an incentive to ensure the long-term provision of grazing, and it is precisely this incentive which is absent in the commons.[4] This is not the only solution, however. Where there is no ownership at all there is certainly a problem of the sort identified by Hardin; but different forms of ownership are possible: private ownership is one and genuine common ownership another. In the latter case the tragedy of the commons can be averted by community or state action, employing economic, regulatory or moral means. The key issue, as Roemer (1989) and others have argued, is whether decisions can be collectively made which are then binding on those using the resource. A collectively owned piece of land can be well managed if people choose to do so. In Chapters 5 and 6 we will examine some of the regulatory, economic and fiscal policy instruments that are commonly suggested as responses to problems of environmental depletion and pollution. Some of these rely on voluntary cooperation, others on state regulation, others on providing economic incentives to environmentally virtuous action and others (following Hardin's lead) on instituting property rights in the environment.

POWER

Political success depends on power and influence: without either, a group, party or individual will achieve nothing, no matter what the intrinsic merits of their case. But what do we understand by the term 'power'? In his book *Power: A Radical View* (1974), Steven Lukes argues that power should be studied in three dimensions.[5] The first is the exercise of power which occurs in observable overt conflicts between actors over key issues; the second is the exercise of power which occurs in observable overt or covert conflicts between actors over issues or potential issues; the third is the power to shape people's preferences so that neither overt nor covert conflicts exist. The first dimension of power corresponds to Robert Dahl's definition of power in which: 'A has power over B to the extent that he can get B to do something that B would not otherwise do' (Dahl, 1957, p. 203). This is the visible exercise of power; it is clear and obvious. We can see when someone is making someone else do something. It is not necessarily physical, but it is tangible. Clearly this covers many of the cases where we would want to say that power was being exercised, but in Lukes' view it is limited as it is blind to the various and less obvious ways in which the political agenda can be controlled in a political system (Lukes, 1974, p. 57).

Thus, the first dimension needs to be supplemented by a second dimension, which Lukes characterises as the exercise of power which occurs in observable overt or *covert* conflicts between actors over issues or potential issues. We should not only look at what is done, at the decisions people and organisations make, but also at the non-decisions which are made when contentious policy issues are avoided or sidelined rather than subjected to obvious and observable challenge and likely defeat. This goes beyond the visible and obvious exercise of power characteristic of the first dimension. It corresponds with what Bachrach and Baratz term the 'second face of power'. In their view power does not simply involve examining key decisions and actual behaviour:

> Of course power is exercised when A participates in the making of decisions
> that affect B. Power is also exercised when A devotes his energies to creating
> or reinforcing social and political values and institutional practices that limit
> the scope of the political process to public consideration of only those issues
> which are comparatively innocuous to A. To the extent that A succeeds in
> doing this, B is prevented, for all practical purposes, from bringing to the fore

any issues that might in their resolution be seriously detrimental to A's set of preferences.

(Bachrach and Baratz, 1962, p. 948)

This is the 'mobilisation of bias', the confining of decision making to safe issues. The phrase is Schattschneider's, who argues that forms of political organisation are inevitably biased in favour of capitalising on some kinds of conflict and suppressing others, because *'organisation is the mobilisation of bias*. Some issues are organised into politics while others are organised out' (Schattschneider, in Bachrach and Baratz, 1962, p. 949).

What this suggests is two faces of power: one operating at the level of overt conflicts over key issues; the other operating through a process which might be termed 'non-decision making' where conflicts are suppressed and prevented from entering the political process. A full analysis of power thus requires the examination of both decision making and non-decision making. A decision is a choice between alternative modes of action, whereas a non-decision is a decision that results in the suppression or frustration of a challenge to the values or interests of the decision maker. Non-decision making is a way of ensuring that demands for political and social change are stifled before they can be articulated, or kept hidden, or eliminated before they can achieve access to the policy process. And if all these ruses fail, a policy can be rendered impotent, ridiculous or irrelevant by inept implementation.

Although Lukes regards the idea of a second dimension to power as a valuable one, he is still not satisfied that it captures all that we mean by the concept of power; some aspects of power have still escaped the net. At this point he introduces a third dimension characterised by the idea of latent conflict and the affecting of interests. Latent conflict exists when there would be a conflict of wants or preferences between those exercising and those subject to power if the latter were to become aware of their interests. The question of interests is very important here: Lukes defines the underlying concept of power, common to all three views, thus: 'A exercises power over B when A affects B in a manner contrary to B's interests' (Lukes, 1974, p. 27). In the first and second dimension it is relatively obvious that interests have been adversely affected because people recognise this directly when their desires are thwarted; but on the third dimension things change because Lukes introduces the idea of a 'real interest'. When we are examining the third dimension it is not necessarily obvious that someone will have gained and someone lost. Power may be exercised even if those affected by it do not feel adversely affected by its exercise. In other words, the existence of a consensus does not indicate that power is not being exercised:

> is it not the supreme and most insidious exercise of power to prevent people, to whatever degree, from having grievances by shaping their perceptions, cognitions and preferences in such a way that they accept their role in the existing order of things, either because they can see or imagine no alternative to it, or because they see it as natural and unchangeable, or because they

value it as divinely ordained and beneficial? To assume that the absence of grievance equals genuine consensus is simply to rule out the possibility of false or manipulated consensus by definitional fiat.

(ibid., p. 24)

It should by now be clear how the above theoretical account might fit actual cases. Some people, groups or organisations obviously and visibly wield power. We might think, for instance, of the state, transnational corporations, the World Bank or even (at times) Greenpeace. This power is sometimes highly visible, for instance where the state uses sanctions to ensure that we keep within the law, or redefines a form of direct action as a criminal offence. The World Bank has considerable power, much of which is obvious, but some is less so. For example, part of its power consists in the way that it shapes the agenda of economic growth and development, insisting that certain approaches to national economies are not acceptable. In other cases power may be much less visible. Even where a pressure group is granted access to a government minister or department, there is not the slightest guarantee that its views will be listened to seriously, much less adopted. The meetings themselves can be used to defuse opposition because they allow government to go on to make the claim that it has consulted all the relevant parties and interests; but its decision can still be just what it always wanted it to be. Again, where an interest lobby such as the National Farmers Union or the British Roads Federation has succeeded in capturing the mind of a department, its practical success consists in simply making alternatives unthinkable. For many years it has been 'obvious' that we need new roads and motorways; to think or say otherwise has been regarded as cranky and absurd. The issue could not be seriously raised in any forum. Even in public inquiries concerning the route of a motorway, discussion is limited to the route itself. It is not possible to raise the question of whether the motorway is needed in the first place. This is an example of the 'mobilisation of bias', where some issues are organised into politics while others are organised out, and it is extraordinarily difficult to fight.[6] Frequently the most successful lobbyists are the quietest, while the ones making the noise are the ones who have been 'organised out' and who can only make an impact by highly visible and public means. Again, as we discussed in Chapter 2, it is clear that there is currently an 'acceptable' interpretation of sustainable development which is dominated by the outlook of ecological modernisation. Sustainable development is interpreted in such a way as to allow for the continuation of economic growth and production and consumption patterns, which are modified to reduce their adverse environmental impact but remain otherwise unchallenged. This interpretation is built into the reasoning of government, business and economists and is virtually impossible to challenge at the points where it matters.

John Gaventa has argued that if actors have consistently been excluded or failed to achieve any degree of success in political decision making, apathy or fatalism may set in and with it acceptance in the face of the demands of powerful actors (Gaventa, 1982, pp. 20ff). Along similar lines, Brian Wynne comments that 'the powerless always tend to rationalise and thus consolidate their own impotence and apathy because to do otherwise would be to expose themselves to the greater pain of *explicit* recognition of their own neglect and marginality' (Wynne, 1996, p. 53).

> This kind of enculturation process *normalises and consolidates* whatever dependency and lack of agency is thought to exist. It obscures the alienation and ambivalence or worse which people may feel in relation to elites and expert institutions.
>
> (ibid., p. 55)

Further, Gaventa suggests that if actors do not participate in decision-making processes they may well have an under-developed or fragmented political consciousness. Such thoughts resonate with issues raised towards the end of Chapter 2, particularly the apathy and fatalism embodied within political alienation. It is important to recognise that the structure of institutions can shape people's opinions and preferences and act as a barrier to participation.

The un-politics of air pollution

As we have seen, the exercise of power consists not only in the ability positively to get things done. It can also consist in the ability to make sure that decisions are not made or are deferred indefinitely. One way of doing this is to ensure that an emergent issue never reaches the agenda, that is, it never becomes an actual issue for a decision-making body. In *The Un-Politics of Air Pollution: A Study of Non-Decisionmaking in the Cities* (1971), Matthew Crenson provides a good example of how a powerful local interest can prevent issues reaching an agenda. The question Crenson asks is why the issue of air pollution was not raised as early or effectively in some American cities as in others. He wanted to discover why in many cities and towns in the United States air pollution failed to become a political issue. His focus was not just on what was done, but more importantly on what was not done: he wanted to study both political activity and political inactivity. A serious investigation required that he had to choose towns which were, so far as possible, very similar in pollution levels and in social composition, otherwise the answer as to why one town or the other had acted on pollution could have been attributed simply to (say) the fact that one was more polluted than the other. He examined two cities in Indiana: East Chicago and Gary. Both were equally polluted and had similar populations. East Chicago took action on air pollution in 1949; Gary did nothing until 1962. So what was the explanation? In brief, it lay in the fact that Gary was largely dominated by US Steel and had a strong party organisation operating in tandem with the steel company and exercising mutually advantageous control over the labour force. The company and the party were the dominant organisations in the city. East Chicago, on the other hand, was host to a number of steel companies and had no strong party organisation. In Gary, therefore, there was a reluctance and an inability to challenge these dominant organisations. Their power was exercised simply by the fear that they could use their influence: people were afraid of their anticipated reactions;

they did not necessarily have to do anything, their reputation was sufficient to prevent the issue being properly raised.

Crenson's conclusion was that US Steel for a long time prevented the issue of pollution control from being raised because it was able to exploit its position as the major employer and wield power as much through reputation or fear of what it might do (for example, relocate production). When an anti-pollution ordinance was finally enacted (as a consequence of the threat of state or federal action), it had a considerable influence on its content. It did this without entering into the political arena or intervening in policy-making forums: its reputation for power was enough to inhibit the emergence of the issue. By not taking a clearly identifiable stand one way or the other, the company frustrated the efforts of environmentalists and others to introduce an effective pollution control ordinance. One activist remarked that:

> The company executives ... would just nod sympathetically 'and agree that air pollution was terrible, and pat you on the head. But they never *did* anything one way or the other. If only there had been a fight, then something might have been accomplished!' What US Steel did not do was probably more important to the career of Gary's air pollution issue than what it did do.
>
> (ibid., pp. 76–7)

Crenson extended his analysis to other cities and reached the conclusion that the issue of air pollution tends not to flourish in cities where industry enjoys a reputation for power. Further, where industry stays silent, the opportunities of raising the pollution issue are diminished. In addition, the role of political parties and politicians makes a difference. Why was the dominant party not interested in clean air? There were some politicians in both towns who tried to raise the issue of dirty air, but they faced stiff opposition from the 'machine' politicians who controlled both towns. Some politicians might be genuinely motivated by ideology; others, by contrast, are 'non-ideological entrepreneurs' in that they deliver private goods such as jobs or contracts in return for votes. But clean air, because it is a public good, does not lend itself to this approach. That was why, in Gary, it was local politicians as much as anybody who kept clean air off the agenda (McLean, 1987, p. 35). Party politicians can manipulate public support by providing goods to particular groups; but they cannot afford to alienate the financial and other support they gain from a dominant company in their locality. Strong and influential party organisations will tend to inhibit the development of issues such as these because acceding to the demand for clean air will harm the party's political and financial support. Clean air is a public good and its costs are concentrated on industry, which is likely, therefore, to be strongly opposed to it. That is why the conjunction of US Steel and a dominant party organisation kept clean air off the agenda. On the other hand, support for pollution control suffers because although all benefit, it is hard to get people together to fight for it. There is a collective action problem.[7]

The task of placing issues on to the political agenda is made still more difficult because they tend to be interconnected. Those policy analysts (typically pluralists) who believe that a plurality of roughly equal voices each has a say in decision making, and who find empirical evidence for this view by looking simply at overt, discrete, separate and unrelated decisions, are unable to see that power could be exercised in many and more insidious ways than through the obvious wielding of force. Thus, it is possible that success in one issue might lead to success in others because it demonstrates the practical possibility of working together with others. Conversely, at a given moment, the pursuit of a particular issue might prevent other issues from reaching the political agenda. Astute politicians realise that they can defuse a situation by acceding to pressure on some issues and ignoring others. They can use the virtue of compromise to disguise the fact that they are stifling the emergence of issues they do not like or do not wish to address. Governments are adept at this. They can pursue 'green' policies or label already existing policies as 'green' and thereby make the claim that they have addressed environmental issues. In reality, the serious issues may have been neatly sidelined by the appearance of environmental concern driving out its substance.[8] There are, Crenson concludes, 'politically imposed limitations upon the scope of decision making' (Crenson, 1971, p. 178) which are achieved by the use of non-decision making. Simply studying the overt actions of decision makers may tell us nothing about the groups and issues which may have been excluded from the political process (ibid., p. 181).

TAKING PRECAUTIONS: ANTICIPATION AND REACTION IN ENVIRONMENTAL POLICY

Having looked at some of the obstacles to securing effective collective action, and at the political impediments to radical environmental action, we can now examine a further set of considerations which come into play even if and when these problems can be overcome. Prior to any discussion of policy instruments, there is the question of knowing when to act. It may be relatively easy to secure agreement to the proposition that action might be necessary if the outlook really is as serious as environmentalists say it is. Typically though, the response is to question whether matters are really that serious. Further, it is argued that perhaps we should act only when there is absolute proof. Again, a common technocentric and optimistic response is to agree that the issue is serious and demands attention, but that we can rest secure in the expectation that some technical solution will be devised if only we wait patiently. Meanwhile we can continue on our current path. It is to these issues that we now turn, because while some of the responses are simply cynical shirking of the issues, others are genuine responses to difficult questions of choosing how to allocate the scarce resources of time and money.

We generally adopt the view that future costs are less burdensome than current costs. We do this in everyday life, and it is something which economists have formalised through the concept of discounting. The general idea is that we tend to worry less about burdens that will fall on us in the future if there is some present advantage. Therefore, while recognising that the costs will have to be paid later, we view them as of little or no immediate concern simply because they lie in the future. An economist expresses this by assigning a lower monetary value to future costs and benefits as compared with costs or benefits that face us now.[9] Whatever the general virtue of this way of looking at things – and it can hardly be denied that in life we often take this view – when we are considering environmental policy we have to look at the issues a little more deeply. This is because one of the central questions to be faced in making environmental policy is not why should we act or how shall we act, but simply when should we act? For example, should we act now to prevent future harm or wait and act later when we are more certain that we know exactly how to prevent that harm? The first approach is to anticipate problems and seek to solve them before they become serious; the second is to react to serious problems when they have already arisen. Both approaches have something to be said for them; much depends on the current state of knowledge and what we think we might come to know in the future. Again, it depends on the nature and seriousness of the problem and the nature and effects of the solution. Clearly a serious problem which requires only a small adjustment in what we do now is easily dealt with. In contrast, the solution to future problems, with potentially serious consequences, may be both technologically expensive and socially disruptive. Here the temptation to opt for reactive policies is almost overwhelming, especially if we believe – whether rightly or wrongly – that some technical fix might emerge which will enable us to solve it painlessly.

The issue, then, is what to do about environmental risk under conditions of uncertainty. When we anticipate problems we seek to estimate their significance, given the best available current understanding about what will happen if we do not alter our behaviour. We might conclude that delay in modifying our behaviour would be disastrous or catastrophically expensive (both in environmental and in economic terms) and if this is so it is rational to incur the costs in advance of the problem occurring. On the other hand, it can genuinely be the case that delay in some instances can generate better information and therefore lead to cheaper and more effective solutions. But how are we to decide which is the right course of action?

In so far as solutions depend on technological progress, we can adopt either an optimistic or a pessimistic view. The problem is that, by definition, before technological progress occurs there is no certainty that it will occur: the problem would be rather different if we knew that if we waited until ten or fifty years' time we could solve all our problems at minimal cost.[10] This is of course something that we do not and cannot know, although occasionally we can make intelligent forecasts. So the problem which arises is the situation in which the optimists turn out to be wrong, but we continue to behave as if they were right. If, on the contrary, the optimists are right and we take a pessimistic view of technological progress, we may miss out on some marginal advantages in welfare in the present. But perhaps this is the safer option and for that reason the one we should adopt? The safest option for the health of the environment is probably to suppose that the optimists are wrong. If we assume that the optimists are right and they are not, we may face a disaster which might have been preventable on an anticipatory approach (Pearce *et al.*, 1989, p. 10). Before looking at an example of these difficulties in the form of the

problem of global warming we shall consider more generally the relationship between scientific and moral expertise in relation to environmental policy making.

Scientific expertise

Within green political thought we find rather ambiguous and at times contradictory attitudes to science. On the one hand greens criticise the 'technocentrism' of
contemporary society, its faith in scientific progress and the domination of a scientific worldview. On the other hand, much green concern and its related rhetoric is
firmly rooted in scientific evidence, observation and predictions. It is senseless to
talk about physical limits to growth, acid rain, global warming or ozone depletion
without reference to scientific methods and evidence. Is there a paradox here with
greens utilising scientific knowledge itself to expose the effects of the application
of the scientific worldview (Yearley, 1991)? The central issue, however, is not the
practice of science *per se*, but rather 'scientism' – the belief that natural science and
only natural science has the answer to everything and nothing falls outside its
remit. Leaving the philosophical issues to one side, one of the problems with scientism
is that it assumes the 'purity' of science and operates on the assumption that scientific practice is neutral and therefore above the political fray. However, such an
understanding of the role of science in contemporary society is misleading. Jacobs,
for example, exposes the dangers inherent in a naive belief in the neutrality of
science, arguing that many of the assumptions made in, for instance, climate change
models emerge out of 'complex socio-political processes in which scientists are
inevitably bound up with the commitments of the political and economic institutions responsible for funding and acting on the research' (Jacobs, 1995a, p. 1473).

The choice of apparently neutral scientific assumptions within global climate
change predictions often reflect political power relations and access to knowledge.
Typically, large-scale scientific models are based on a set of assumptions which,
for international problems, tend to express the interests of the dominant Western
nations. Their 'objective' status needs to be challenged. Thus an important question within green politics must concern who makes the judgement about what is or
is not regarded as significant or worthy of investigation. Politically and economically powerful actors hold the purse strings, promote research and interpret the
results. Decisions have to be made about the effects of global warming and how
much time and resources will be dedicated to finding a solution. But which effects
are taken to be worthy of consideration and what is to count as a solution? Generally the impact of climate change is conceptualised by and for the industrialised
nations, as a technical and cost-effective matter. But would not a small island state
differ in its interpretation of both the problem and the solution? The general point
here is that those who are accorded scientific expertise tend to be operating within
a political and economic framework, a framework which itself needs to be challenged. Scientific criteria and expertise are subject to the pressures of political
negotiation.

These questions concerning the standing of scientific knowledge can be seen
as problematising certain types of political arrangements. In particular they

challenge the status of 'experts' and 'objective' knowledge. Particular groups within society use forms of 'expertise' to legitimise unreasonable and environmentally destructive practices. With these considerations in mind we can now turn to the issue of global warming and ask what our obligations are in conditions of scientific uncertainty.

Uncertainty: the example of global warming

It is important to remember that uncertainty is simply something we have to live with in all spheres of life. Nothing is exempt. As Jacobs remarks:

> The fact that we do not understand the environment perfectly does not mean that we cannot use what understanding we do have as the basis for making decisions about it. No knowledge is ever perfect; society would be paralysed if we waited for certainty before acting.
>
> (Jacobs, 1991, p. 99)

Uncertainty, then, is not equivalent to a complete lack of knowledge, and therefore it should not be used as the basis for postponing all action; if we did that, then we would never act at all. What we need to do is to consider rationally the ways in which we deal with the uncertainty facing us.

If we take global warming as an example, we can identify different types of uncertainty. There is uncertainty about emissions. We do not know exactly which gases we will be pumping out into the atmosphere: it depends on technical change and political progress in securing stabilisations and reductions. There is also uncertainty about climate response. Meteorological models are enormously complex and because of the vast number of interrelated variables it is difficult to make accurate predictions. Further, there is uncertainty concerning the regional impact of global warming: the world as a whole may undergo global warming, but it does not follow that each part of the world will warm up to the same extent – some parts of the world are likely to cool down. Relatedly, there is uncertainty concerning the thresholds at which the effects of global warming become a problem. We might be unconcerned by, or be able to adapt to, even a large rise in sea level; but thereafter, beyond a certain threshold, the problems might be enormous. Sometimes marginal changes have far-reaching consequences. Finally, we cannot easily predict what the political and social responses to global warming will be. Societies and governments can respond in markedly different ways: how easy is it to say how far populations will simply adapt what they do to the new circumstances, and how governments will respond in their policy making to changing circumstances?

Given the variety of types of uncertainty, there are none the less several reasons for acting now rather than delaying. For example, the outcome if the worst happens is likely to be catastrophic and therefore we need to undertake risk-averse policies – the longer we delay the greater is the level of global warming we are already committed to. David Pearce argues that if necessary we can begin with low-cost policies, moving towards more technologically advanced (but more expensive) policies as and when they become available. Further, prevention needs to be international and as there are always time lags in generating international agreement we should start acting now to ensure that we can secure agreement in time to make a difference (Pearce *et al.*, 1989, pp. 13–14).

On the other hand, there are reasons for delaying action. These include both time preference and the time needed to gather information. But clearly the overall balance is in favour of acting sooner rather than later; indeed, any commitment to sustainable development would seem to require this. There are therefore very strong reasons for adopting an anticipatory approach. Further, there are strong reasons for adopting the precautionary principle. This principle requires decision makers to prevent serious or irreversible environmental harm even if the activity or substance concerned cannot be conclusively shown to cause harm. The burden of proof would thus be on industry. In other words we should try to prevent pollution before it happens.

> The precautionary principle places the burden of proof in decision making on establishing that ecosystems will be protected in the face of uncertainty about the impacts of pollution. In other words, scientific uncertainty should not be taken as a reason for postponing preventative actions.
>
> (Kinrade, 1996, p. 94)

The principle was accepted by the UK government in its 1990 White Paper, although there are questions as to how seriously it is taken in practice:

> Where there are significant risks of damage to the environment, the government will be prepared to take precautionary action to limit the use of potentially dangerous materials or the spread of potentially dangerous pollutants, even where scientific evidence is not conclusive, if the balance of likely costs and benefits justifies it. The precautionary principle applies particularly where there are good grounds for judging either that action taken promptly at comparatively low cost may avoid more costly damage later, or that irreversible effects may follow if action is delayed.
>
> (DoE, 1990, p. 11)

Unlike 'normal' cases, where we say that someone is innocent until proved guilty, the precautionary principle insists that potentially harmful substances are guilty until proved innocent. The burden of proof should be on those who wish to engage in polluting activities to prove that they are safe before they do so. If we wait for absolute proof of the impact of a pollutant, the damage will have already been done and it will probably be impossible to reverse. However, it is possible to interpret the principle in a number of ways. O'Riordan and Jordan point out that the weak interpretation tends to be restricted to the 'most toxic and human life threatening substances and activities' (O'Riordan and Jordan, 1995, p. 197). Such an interpretation is embodied in the UK government's definition above, where there is a central role for cost–benefit calculations and a focus purely on technical feasibility and economic efficiency. This appears to expose once again the dominance of the doctrine of ecological modernisation, where the solution to environmental problems is taken to be primarily managerial and technical. As was argued in earlier chapters, this reinforces an exclusively anthropocentric outlook, which avoids more radical commitments to future generations and non-human nature. Bearing in mind the arguments advanced in Chapter 1, we can see that this formulation of the principle fights shy of accepting any deep commitment to the well-being to future generations and the non-human world, except where commitment requires the imposition of relatively low costs on the current generation.

By contrast, the stronger interpretation emphasises the unconditionality of our obligations towards the non-human world and future generations, even where meeting these obligations can only be carried out at considerable cost to ourselves. This interpretation is likely to be more unpopular and more strongly resisted than the former precisely because it requires more of governments, business and the public who are (perhaps understandably) reluctant to accept the radical consequences. But this interpretation may be the only one worth fighting for if we are truly serious about addressing the full range of environmental problems facing contemporary and future generations and the non-human world. Adoption of the precautionary principle is desirable, but there is little or no point in adopting a version which is too weak to make any appreciable difference, especially if its adoption were to displace more radical responses to environmental problems. The problem is that the principle, understood in the strong sense, requires significant sacrifice in the present. It requires strict control of polluting and depleting activities and will therefore be opposed by all who stand to lose in the short term, whether industry, business, workers or consumers.

CONCLUSION

Any strong environmental programme is likely to be contested on many fronts and subjected to responses ranging from downright opposition to subtle exclusion or manipulation. The problems of collective action and insidious forms of power relations will inevitably raise their heads as people and organisations lobby to secure their position and achieve their goals. Successful environmental action requires a knowledge of both environmental goals and of the obstacles standing in the way of achieving them. This chapter has shown what some of these obstacles are. What remains to be done is to discuss alternative ways of overcoming them. In the everyday world of competing pressure groups and interests, power is fought with power, cunning with cunning, knowledge with knowledge, self-interest by rival self-interest. The pluralist view is that in a modern society the public policies adopted are largely the outcome of this competition. Lindblom calls this process 'partisan mutual adjustment' (Lindblom, 1965, p. 33). The test of a good policy is not that it maximises the decision makers' values but that it secures the agreement of the interests involved. This approach is part of Lindblom's wider conception of policy making as 'disjointed incrementalism'. Here policies are only considered and adopted at the margin – there is only incremental movement from the status quo. Radical policies with large-scale unpredictable outcomes are eschewed. Amelioration becomes the norm: 'A policy is directed at a problem; it is tried, altered, tried in its altered form, altered again, and so forth ... incremental policies follow one upon the other in the solution of a given problem' (Braybrooke and Lindblom, 1963, p. 73). Further, decision makers adjust themselves to available means instead of striving for a fixed set of objectives. This emphasis on the workability of policies, and on the need to secure the agreement of all the interests concerned, is important. A policy made in heaven means nothing on Earth if it cannot be successfully implemented; and striving to do too much can result in failure, while trying to achieve less can result in achieving more.

However, there are drawbacks to this pluralist approach in the field of environmental policy. Lindblom himself accepts that a strategy of disjointed incrementalism is unsuited to wars, revolutions, crises and 'grand opportunities' where the need for large-scale change is combined with insufficient knowledge and understanding (ibid., p. 78). Certain contemporary environmental problems may constitute such a crisis. At the general level, if one is considering irreversible damage there is little or no scope for later reconsideration. Furthermore, many environmental problems have reached their current critical state precisely because they are the outcome of a process of 'disjointed incrementalism'. The logic of incrementalism combined with the logic of collective action, where individual rationality leads to collective irrationality, has led to depletion of the world's fish stocks, damage to the ozone layer and changes in climate patterns. The solution to these problems will not be found by 'muddling through'. Again, if all groups and interests actually were roughly equal, the pluralists' conclusions might seem to be otherwise reasonable. However, they are not equal in power, influence or access and even if they were, there is no reason to suppose that the outcome of this mutual bargaining will be the most suitable policy response. If the activity of policy makers lies in securing compromise between competing interests, rather than in the nature of the problem to be faced, there is every likelihood that the policies agreed, while securing the adherence of those most immediately affected, will be irrelevant to the task in hand. The issues most likely to suffer from this bargaining are those concerning future generations or the non-human world, because they cannot directly speak or act on their own behalf and are reliant on the goodwill of others (not necessarily with power) to look after their interests.

Is there any way in which these voices can be brought into the debate on more equal terms? Is it possible to move away from policy making as the outcome of jostling between unequal interests? One answer may be to institute new political forums in which people can deliberate in public about matters of common concern. At this point we can challenge the assumptions of rational choice theory, not by denying their relevance under certain circumstances, but by asking whether they hold in all circumstances. Thus, preferences should not be treated as always given and immutable, but something that can be reflected on in public discussion and modified by reasoned persuasion and exemplary action. To emphasise the democratic theme introduced at the end of Chapter 2, people seek to maximise their own good, but if brought together in a public space to deliberate on the common good and required to give publicly acceptable reasons for their policy choices, they cannot simply state that they approve of something because it is in their own interest. Mere self-interest has no persuasive force where justification is public and has to appeal to publicly acceptable criteria and principles. Deliberative institutions presuppose the capacity of ordinary people to question and reflect on policies and priorities, including policies and priorities directed towards the future or towards non-human nature. In a deliberative forum participants can debate issues under optimum conditions. Experiments with citizens' juries in the USA and the UK, and with planning cells in Germany, as well as with other innovative democratic designs, may offer models for the development of such forums (Renn *et al.*, 1995; Stewart *et al.*, 1994). If the environmental movement wishes to create conditions suitable for genuine debate on matters of principle, it should seriously consider pressing for initiatives and institutional designs of this sort to be included in policy-making processes.

CASE STUDY: AIR POLLUTION IN THE UNITED STATES[11]

Having introduced both the formal problems of aggregating preferences and the broader problem of collective action, it might be helpful to see how they combine in a real-life example. This case study demonstrates the problem of collective action in a situation where different groups are forming and breaking *de facto* alliances with other groups in order to achieve their goals. It illustrates how a group can be frustrated in its purposes by trying to achieve too much and where to have aimed for less would have resulted in achieving more. The conclusion is that not only should groups be careful about which actors they form alliances with, but also that they should learn to appreciate and understand the logic of collective action.

The legislation

New Source Pollution Standards (NSPS) were rules introduced in the USA for emission control, following lobbying and legislation, that all new plants emitting effluents (especially power stations) had to meet. For *existing* plants the rules demanded that the total ambient level of sulphur dioxide pollution in the local atmosphere must not exceed a certain threshold. *New* plants were required to achieve a *reduction* in emissions.

The legislation was designed to reduce pollution. In fact the consequence of seeking reductions of emissions from new plants was to increase their cost and keep less efficient, dirtier plants in use for longer. Sulphur dioxide was to be 'scrubbed' from exhaust gases until they were as clean as those produced by power stations burning low-sulphur coal. But the fitting of scrubbers added up to 20 per cent to the capital cost of a new plant, while old plants could be kept running for forty years or longer. Where, then, was the incentive for a company to replace old equipment? There was none. On the contrary there was a disincentive, and the replacement of old equipment slowed down accordingly (Cairncross, 1991, p. 95). Thus the policy was both more expensive than alternatives and left air dirtier because old and dirty power stations remained in use. How did this happen? It emerged from the logic of a situation in which three broad groupings, environmentalists, coal producers and power station operators, were each seeking to achieve certain goals. The lobbying went in two stages, based on two related but separate issues. The first issue (in 1977) was how to achieve reductions in emissions, that is, whether to employ tradeable permits or green taxes, or to insist on the installation of a particular technology in power station chimneys (flue gas desulphurisers). The second issue (in 1979) was that of the level of emissions to be permitted, that is, how stringent or lenient should the legally enforced 'scrubbing' be. In the first instance a coalition of environmentalists and coal producers emerged as both were in favour of scrubbing. The environmentalists wanted strong and obvious measures taken to reduce pollution, and they thought that scrubbing rather than less obvious measures such as fiscal incentives provided that; emission control 'scrubbers' in power station chimneys was seen as a more visible gain than changing the behaviour of utilities through the use of fiscal incentives. The coal producers wanted their coal, including that with a high sulphur content, to continue to be burnt. For the producers of dirty coal, scrubbing enabled them to continue marketing coal which otherwise could not be sold because utilities would have purchased low-sulphur coal from elsewhere. In opposition to the coalition of coal producers and environmentalists were the power station operators, who simply wanted regulations imposing the least cost on their operations. Although both groups comprising the original coalition considered the achievement of compulsory scrubbing a gain, when it came to the question of the stringency of the scrubbing their paths diverged. At this point the environmentalists found themselves isolated as the coal producers had nothing further to gain from the alliance. A new coalition was born with the coal producers throwing in their lot with the power station operators, who wanted to keep costs of production to a minimum.

At this point it is worth considering the nature of the different organisations involved in this bargaining process. Both industrial groups were internally divided. The utilities which planned new power stations (typically the larger ones) would be very much affected by NSPS; those with no such plans were not. The power station operators belonged to a weak trade association (the Edison Electrical Institute), which was made weaker by free riding: for example, members would send inexpert delegates to its meetings. The large utilities decided to form a new organisation to lobby on the legislation: the Utility Air Regulatory Group (UARG). This was a 'privileged' group, as each member had a sufficiently large interest in the outcome of the political bargaining over NSPS to be willing to take a share of the burden of organising it, whatever the others did. Hence it was the UARG which sponsored the utilities' litigation over NSPS. The coal industry also had its own internal divisions. Coal producers whose coal was naturally low in sulphur (in the West) were not interested in scrubbers; those whose coal was high in sulphur (in the mid-West and East) wanted scrubbers since this would allow continued consumption of their coal. Because the National Coal Association represented both high- and low-sulphur producers it was caught in the middle and could do little more than fudge the issue. The United Mine Workers Union, on the other hand, which had most of its members in the high-sulphur coal-producing East, came out in favour of universal scrubbing; the UMWU was a strong union with political influence which could lobby for high benefits for its members cheaply. On this occasion it had a clear interest in lobbying for the introduction of scrubbing as its members' livelihoods were at stake. In addition, some of the coal producers in the East who stood to lose most if scrubbing was not enforced were sufficiently concerned to be willing to take on the costs of lobbying themselves. Thus both the utilities and the coal industry managed to solve their collective action problems and emerged as formidable lobbies in the political bargaining over the introduction of NSPS. One consequence of the bargaining over pollution control was more expensive electricity, yet no consumer lobby emerged. Once again this was because of a collective action problem: despite the collective benefits if everyone were to act in concert, the marginal utility to an individual of taking part in a consumer group lobby is infinitesimal and therefore consumers tend to remain a 'latent' group.[12] The contrast with the utilities is quite stark.

The environmentalists[13] confused the appearance of tough action on emission controls with the reality of effective action. They took the view that forced scrubbing on new plants was preferable to no forced scrubbing, and that more stringent scrubbing was better than less, but failed to realise that the effect of introducing strenuous rules applying only to new plants would be to keep older and dirtier plants in operation for longer and that this would not reduce pollution but rather increase it. A less strenuous policy on new plants would have been less polluting overall and hence a better outcome for them, but they were unable to see this at the time. In addition, they suffered from a voting paradox (of the sort illustrated earlier in Chapter 4) because the lobbying over NSPS went in two stages and the order in which votes was taken partly determined the outcome.

Of course, there was no formal voting as such, but with three main actors making and unmaking alliances the effect was the same. At any given moment the most powerful lobby was the alliance with two 'votes' as compared with their opponent's one vote. In 1977 the issue was whether to legally enforce scrubbing or to adopt another policy instead. Because they saw it as being in their interests (although in each case for very different reasons), the environmentalists and the coal industry joined forces to lobby for forced scrubbing on the utilities. At this time both got what they wanted. But two years later the issue had changed. What had to be decided now was the level of scrubbing and the coal industry joined the utilities in a 'dirty coal/dirty air' alliance to fight off plans for stringent emission control. The utilities wanted to minimise their costs and hence preferred lenient emission levels as it kept the costs of installing new technology down. The coal producers were concerned only that their coal continued to be burnt and this was more likely if the emission controls were less rather than more stringent. Thus, the outcome of this bargaining and alliance making, as each group sought to maximise its interests, was forced scrubbing at a lenient level. If the voting order had been different, or if there had been a single straight choice between legally enforced scrubbing at a stringent level and no forced scrubbing, then the original coalition of environmentalists and coal producers would have held firm and the outcome would have been different. Environmentally speaking, this would not have been the best solution, but it would have been superior to the actual outcome. The voting can be illustrated by Table 4.2, in which the preference orderings for each lobby are represented.

Table 4.2 The lobbies' preferences

Environmentalists	*Utilities*	*Coal producers*
stringent scrubbing	no forced scrubbing	lenient scrubbing
lenient scrubbing	lenient scrubbing	stringent scrubbing
no forced scrubbing	stringent scrubbing	no forced scrubbing

The first 'vote' was a choice between forced scrubbing and no forced scrubbing. The groups for whom no forced scrubbing was their last preference (the coal industry and the environmentalists) combined to beat the utilities, for whom it was their first. In the second round of voting the choice was between stringent scrubbing and lenient scrubbing. But here stringent scrubbing was bound to lose out to a new coalition formed by the coal industry and the utilities, who both preferred lenient scrubbing to stringent scrubbing.

Conclusion

It is clear that although the environmentalists at first appeared to get what they wanted (in that scrubbing became compulsory), what they eventually got was far from their original aspirations. They achieved an outcome which was worse than the alternatives which they had spurned, because forced scrubbing looked tougher, with the result that they helped to convert the legislation into 'a multibillion-dollar bail-out for high-sulphur coal producers' (Ackerman and Hassler, 1981). This was hardly their intention. What lessons can be learnt from this? Clearly, environmentalists need to be tactically aware of the background conditions to their actions; they need to watch carefully to avoid falling into procedural and other traps. They also need to be aware of their real interests, and not to confuse green appearance with green reality. A policy or decision is not necessarily effective just because it looks tough and uncompromising; on the contrary, as in this case, it might be just the opposite. It is not in their interest to achieve something which merely looks like an environmentally radical policy; that, after all, is what they usually accuse governments and business of doing. Thus they need to make judgements about both the tactics and the suitability of policies by looking at their likely consequences in a hard-headed manner. While they might themselves not be calculating self-interested, egoistical utility maximisers, to a certain extent they need to assume that their opponents probably are, that they are well versed and cunning in maximising their interests. That is, after all, how many environmentalists themselves portray industrial actors and governments. The message for environmentalists is therefore to watch for potential pitfalls. These may come in many shapes and sizes: some deliberate, some accidental, some procedural, some substantive, some well concealed, some obvious.

(Adapted from McLean, 1987, with permission)

SUGGESTIONS FOR FURTHER READING

Matthew Crenson, *The Un-Politics of Air Pollution* (1971) and John Gaventa, *Power and Powerlessness* (1982) are classic studies of the politics of power in the environmental arena. Iain McLean's *Public Choice* (1987) is an accessible introductory text to this area of politics, while *Global Challenges* (1997) by Todd Sandler is an extended application of these ideas to global environmental problems. Tim O'Riordan and Andrew Jordan's 'The Precautionary Principle in Contemporary Environmental Politics' (1995) highlights a number of problems facing decision makers.

5 Valuation of the environment

Appraisal in central government is concerned with the best use of the nation's resources, and the economic analysis of major decisions should in principle be wholly in terms of economic costs and benefits.

(HM Treasury, 1991, p. 10)

If, as we have consistently argued, environmental concerns need to take a central place both ethically and politically, then we are faced with a pressing practical problem of how to value environmental entities in decision-making processes. The issues we raised in Chapters 1 and 2 concerning our relations to the natural world need to be represented in decision-making procedures; otherwise we are bound to misrepresent and distort the human condition and its relationship with the non-human world. Two interrelated issues form the core of this chapter.

First, how are we to assess the environmental consequences of proposed interventions, be they projects or policies? Non-intervention in natural systems is clearly not an option for humanity in contemporary society, so we need methods by which we can weigh the environmental, social and economic costs of proposed developments and policy options. Initially the chapter will engage with the growing discipline of environmental economics and the monetary valuation of ecological resources and values. Through a discussion of cost–benefit analysis (CBA) we will investigate the limits of such valuation techniques and the assumptions embedded within environmental economics. Potential alternatives to economic decision making such as environmental impact assessment will then be discussed.

The second question that needs to be attended to concerns the measurement of sustainable development. Traditional economic practice tends to measure the growth of national economies. It will be argued that this is far from a suitable measure of environmental sustainability in that growth usually entails environmental and social degradation. A single accurate measure of such a complicated objective as sustainable development is unlikely to be forthcoming and perhaps the best way of responding to such concerns is to develop broad quality-of-life indicators to guide policy decisions and other interventions into the non-human world.

ECONOMIC VALUATION OF ENVIRONMENTAL INTERVENTIONS

Cost–benefit analysis

> The need to balance the costs of an action against its benefits is intuitively appealing, and provides an important discipline with which to approach decisions.
>
> (Winpenny, 1991, p. 42)

How are we to make reasoned decisions concerning policy options or large-scale projects such as roads and railways, industrial complexes and the like? Not only do such schemes and policies have large financial implications but also social and environmental consequences. In attempting to aid decision makers in what is necessarily a balancing of a number of positive and negative impacts, welfare economists developed a technique known as cost–benefit analysis.[1] The theory behind CBA is relatively simple and, at its core, utilitarian – the social costs and benefits of an intervention are expressed by aggregating the gains or losses to well-being (or utility) of all individuals affected. The increase or decrease in levels of individuals' utility is represented through a common measure – money. Since all these costs and benefits do not occur immediately, a discount rate is applied to take into account the point in time at which they accrue – it is argued that individuals are impatient and have a time preference for immediate gains in well-being over postponement to a future occasion. If the aggregated benefits outweigh the aggregated costs – expressed in terms of the net present value (NPV) – a policy or project is viewed as socially worthwhile. In principle, the impact of a project or policy should be economically efficient or 'pareto optimal' – the effect of an intervention should increase the welfare of all, without reducing any particular individual's utility. However, in practice there are always 'losers' and CBA actually operates in terms of potential pareto optimality – taking into account all costs and benefits, there should be an overall gain in social welfare. The criterion of potential pareto optimality is also known as the Kaldor–Hicks compensation test. If the total social welfare is increased, those negatively affected by the intervention could in principle be compensated by those who gain. The theoretical nature of the compensation indicates that conventional CBA tends not to be concerned with distributional factors.

This sort of economic analysis of government interventions has become central to liberal democratic decision making (HM Treasury, 1991; DoE, 1991a). There is a clear tendency towards the inclusion of all costs and benefits in an economic form, and this includes environmental effects. In the UK (and elsewhere), the work of David Pearce and his colleagues has been particularly influential in this move towards the economic valuation of environmental values, particularly since the publication of *Blueprint for a Green Economy* (1989),[2] originally a report commissioned by the then Minister for the Environment, Chris Patten. This directly influenced the Department of the Environment's *Policy Appraisal and the Environment* (1991), one of the central aims of which was to promote the monetary valuation of environmental effects of policy options within economic decision-making procedures such as CBA.[3]

Monetary valuation: internalising environmental costs and benefits

All human activity has an impact on the environment, either positively or negatively. However, the prices of goods bought and sold in markets tend not to include environmental costs and benefits, for instance the pollution costs of production. Where the market price fails to take into account such costs and benefits, they are termed 'externalities'.[4] A seminal article by Ronald Coase (1960) argued that externalities could be internalised through a strict system of property rights, although for complex environmental problems such as air and water pollution such an option seems far from practicable.[5] Hence either direct control through state regulation or indirect control through taxes and charges on environmental degradation have been promoted to rectify these market imperfections. The relative benefits of regulation and economic instruments will be discussed in the next chapter. In this chapter we shall focus on the attempt to provide monetary valuations of environmental impacts such that environmental externalities can be internalised into an extended CBA for project or policy evaluations.

Traditionally, the environmental costs and benefits of projects and policies have not appeared in CBA calculations and have had to be balanced against the net present value (NPV) at the point of judgement. Many commentators have noted, however, that decision makers tend to be swayed more by a positive NPV than by a description of potential environmental impacts. As the environmental economist Ian Bateman contends: 'In general planners may well be familiar with the monetary rather than the qualitative assessments and critics have seen this as promoting a bias against the latter' (Bateman, 1991, p. 19). Certain projects and policies may not have been taken forward if environmental values had been included within an extended CBA: the environmental impacts valued monetarily and entered into the cost and benefit streams. For instance, Jean-Phillipe Barde and David Pearce argue that had the CBA for Twyford Down included the economic valuation of the aesthetic worth of the area, the road cutting would never have been allowed to progress (Barde and Pearce, 1991, pp. 1–2).[6] The developing field of environmental economics bears witness to this drive to internalise environmental costs and benefits through, for instance, the derivation of individuals' willingness to pay (WTP) for environmental improvements or their willingness to accept (WTA) compensation for a loss in environmental quality. A number of the assumptions and practices of environmental economic valuation have proved controversial, but before we look at the cogency of the criticisms made of them, it is necessary to investigate the environmental values that economists aim to reveal and some of the techniques they use.

The economic value of the environment

As in other areas of environmental thinking, there is some disagreement over terminology within the field of environmental economics. For this discussion we shall be using the typology found in the work of David Pearce and his colleagues (Pearce *et al.*, 1989, Pearce and Turner, pp. 60–63; 1990, pp. 129–140), where:

Total Economic Value = Actual Use Value + Option Value + Existence Value
(Pearce and Turner, 1990, p. 131)

Actual use value is relatively obvious – the quantification of the benefits derived by those who make use of the environment directly, for instance farmers, industrialists, anglers and walkers. Option value includes a number of different aspects: first, it takes into account the willingness to pay for the preservation of an entity in the likelihood that the individual may make use of it in the future; second, it includes the preference to conserve the environment for future generations (often referred to as bequest value); third, it also incorporates the pleasure secured in the knowledge that others derive a value from the entity in question. Existence value includes 'concern for, sympathy with, respect for the rights or welfare of non-human beings', the values of which are unrelated to human welfare (ibid., p. 130).

Environmental valuation techniques

Techniques for valuation can be roughly divided into two approaches, direct and indirect.[7] Direct valuation techniques utilise either revealed or expressed preferences in market situations and aim to derive individuals' willingness to pay (WTP) or accept (WTA) compensation for particular environmental conditions. The revealed preference or surrogate market approach attempts to derive the monetary value of environmental benefits or costs through individual behaviour in actual markets; for instance, the influence that air quality or a beautiful landscape has on house prices; the premium employees will accept to work in an environmentally risky workplace; or the travel costs incurred in visiting environmental amenities. Expressed preference or experimental techniques aim to create hypothetical market conditions where the WTP or WTA for particular environmental conditions is elicited. Indirect techniques, as the name suggests, do not derive economic valuation directly from market conditions; rather there is a two-stage approach. Initially a 'dose–response' relationship between a form of pollution and some effect is scientifically calculated, for instance acid rain on forests and buildings or pollutants on human health; only then is the economic value of that effect assigned a value utilising the appropriate direct valuation technique.

Direct approaches

Hedonic pricing method

The property value approach aims to isolate the value of environmental amenities, such as landscape, noise or pollution levels, by comparing prices of similar properties in different locations. Environmental quality is only one variable involved in relative prices and the technique is statistically complex. A second approach focuses on wage differentials, where the premium paid to workers exposed to environmental risks can be used 'to estimate the implicit values that workers place on the risk of death from workplace accidents' (Winpenny, 1991, p. 53) and health risks from pollution. Both of these techniques share the contested assumption that both the property and labour markets function freely and individuals are fully informed and in an economic position to respond to environmental conditions.

Travel cost method

This technique is used predominantly to reveal the value of recreational sites that typically have no entrance fee, such as national parks and lakes. The value of the time spent and the cost of travelling to the site are taken as the willingness to pay for such an amenity. Complications include the possible pleasure of travel itself – it may not be viewed as a cost by those travelling – or the fact that trips may be multipurpose. Further, the value of the site to those individuals who have chosen to live close by because they value it highly will be understated in terms of travel cost. For those individuals who do not or cannot visit the amenity but still value its existence, their valuations will be ignored.

Contingent valuation method (CVM)

The revealed preference techniques discussed thus far derive preferences from individuals' existing behaviour in markets. However, in many cases economists have noted that no market information exists and so hypothetical markets have been created through questioning the constituency involved. By making 'bids', individuals express their willingness to pay for environmental improvement or willingness to accept compensation for a loss of environmental quality. CVM is receiving a great deal of attention within environmental economics, both because it has potentially wide applicability over many areas of environmental concern and because it is the only technique available that enables economists to distinguish between aspects of the total economic value of environmental entities (use, option and existence values). However, there are concerns as to the values derived from such surveys since much will depend on, for instance, the structure of questions, how many issues are raised and the information provided. The accuracy of CVM depends crucially on the ability of economists to eliminate these practical and methodological biases.[8]

A familiar problem for economic analysis that appears in CVM is 'strategic bias', the temptation to free ride. Particularly in the case of public goods, into which category many environmental problems facing decision makers fall, there may be a temptation to bid a lower WTP in the expectation that others are likely to pay more. The methodology of welfare economics focuses simply on the private preferences of individuals, treating the collective as merely the aggregate of these preferences. But, as we argued in the previous chapter, the provision of public

---

Sources of bias within CVM

Strategic	Incentive to 'free ride'.
Design	(a) Starting point bias – any example of possible 'bids' affects the individual's response.
	(b) Vehicle bias – instruments of payment, such as taxation or entrance fees, affects responses.
	(c) Informational bias – amount and quality of information is important.
Hypothetical	Are bids in hypothetical markets different to actual market bids? Why should they be?
Operational	Are hypothetical markets genuinely comparable with existing markets in which actual choices are made?

(Expanded from Pearce and Turner, 1990, p. 149)

---

goods, by its very nature, requires us to think beyond purely private self-interest and towards a political, collective response.

Some of the most striking problems that CVM faces surround the question of the design of any survey: when, how much and what sort of information is provided to the respondents? In most surveys it is the interviewer who offers the initial 'bid' to which individuals respond. 'Starting point bias' has been frequently documented in which this initial bid affects the respondent's final choice. Further, there is a 'vehicle bias' with respect to the instrument of payment, for instance taxation, entrance fee, surcharge, higher prices or whatever. Respondents are far from neutral in respect of these payment strategies. Both of these biases could be included within a wider 'information bias', which takes into account the type of information offered during the decision-making process. Which information is relevant and in what form should it be presented?

The hypothetical nature of the exercise would also seem to offer problems. What is the relation between the hypothetical nature of the transactions of a CVM survey and actual market conditions? A 'hypothetical bias' can result from the difference between the nature of the survey and actual markets. 'Operational bias' may result from unfamiliarity with the good in question. Why should we assume that bids in a hypothetical market accurately represent actual market conditions? After all, most of the respondents will have no experience of paying for the environment in these terms.

It has been found that WTA compensation is consistently several times higher than WTP for environmental improvement. A number of explanations have been forthcoming. It is often argued, for example, that individuals place a higher value on those things with which they are familiar than on those of which they have no experience; or, again, that the discrepancy could also be explained by 'the fact that willingness to pay is constrained by ability to pay, while willingness to accept compensation is unconstrained' (Adams, 1995, p. 5). Alternatively, the higher WTA 'may be ... the only way non-monetary, non-preference based valuations can be expressed within the confines of the exercise' (Jacobs, 1994, p. 80); it is an expression of a moral dimension to our valuation of public goods. This differential can have a significant effect on policy decisions since economic theory assumes that WTP and WTA are equivalent and techniques for deriving environmental values tend to be based on WTP – consistently the lower of the two valuations. As Jack Knetsch argues:

> it is likely that, among other implications, losses are understated, standards are set at inappropriate levels, policy selections are biased, too many environmentally degrading activities are encouraged, and too few mitigation efforts are undertaken. ... The conventional assertion that values attached to gains and commensurate losses are equivalent, and the advice that 'practically speaking' it does not appear to make much difference which definition is accepted, seem now to be incorrect for a large class of environmental and other values. ... the continued reluctance to modify the assertion of symmetry appears to be increasingly costly.
>
> (Knetsch, 1990, pp. 227, 236)

Aside from this discrepancy, it is often the case that respondents lodge high protest bids or refuse to take part in the valuation exercise. Frequently economists will overlook such responses, treating them as 'errors'. For some commentators, however, such a reaction is illuminating since it may show that people balk at the idea of the 'commodification' of aspects of the environment. As O'Neill argues:

> The existence of protest bids shows individuals to have a healthy commitment to certain goods and an understanding of the limits of markets. Protests reveal neither irrationality nor strategic rationality, but decent ethical commitments.
>
> (O'Neill, 1993, p. 120)

Indirect approaches

We do not need to give too much attention to indirect techniques, since after the initial stage of scientific investigation of a particular environmental effect the actual monetary valuation proceeds using one of the direct techniques discussed above.

Indirect methods not only suffer from the monetary valuation problems associated with direct valuation techniques but also from the scientific uncertainties inescapable in the early stages of isolating the particular effect in question. For instance, with respect to the effect on human health of air pollution, it can be extremely difficult to isolate the specific impact of, say, traffic exhaust fumes. Other pollutants from other sources may be present; there may be reactions between pollutants from alternative sources; or something else may prove to be the trigger for respiratory problems with exhaust fumes simply exacerbating the situation.

Examples of indirect valuation techniques

- *Effect on production*: Physical effects on the environment are scientifically determined and then the monetary value of the impact is estimated, e.g. effect of over-fishing on fish stocks; air pollution on vegetation.

- *Human capital*: This method focuses on the link between environmental pollution and health problems and calculates loss of productive time and health-care costs.

- *Replacement cost*: The cost of replacing or restoring environment to its original condition is estimated, e.g. cost of cleaning building soiled by acid rain; achieving bathing water objectives.

- *Preventive expenditure*: This method relates to the money spent by individuals to mitigate the effect of environmental impacts, e.g. insulation to mitigate noise pollution.

Criticisms of economic decision-making procedures

As Pearce states in an introductory text on CBA, the procedure has the 'fundamental attraction of reducing a complex problem to something less complex and more manageable' (Pearce, 1983, p. 21). This is undoubtedly the case in that the various costs and benefits of a project or policy are weighed in terms of a single criterion, namely monetary value. Eventually a single figure, the net present value (NPV) of the proposed intervention, is produced. But what is lost in this reduction of complexity? What does that net present value represent, particularly if environmental valuations are incorporated? We have already discussed some of the limitations and biases inherent within particular valuation techniques such as CVM and hedonic pricing, but the central question at issue here is whether economic analysis *per se* distorts the values it claims to represent, particularly those we associate with the non-human world. In this section we shall briefly introduce a range of criticisms that are frequently aimed at such economic decision-making procedures, which range from the use of individual preferences through to the potential political misuse of economic figures.

Individual preferences, commensurability and environmental values

In welfare economic theory, individuals are taken to be calculating, utility maximisers with given and immutable preferences. It is assumed that individuals have both full information and are rational – rational in the sense that given full information about a state of affairs they will calculate and choose that option which will maximise their utility function. According to welfare economists, the welfare function of an individual can be discovered through their behaviour in market situations, through revealed preferences. As we noted earlier, where revealed preference techniques (hedonic pricing and travel cost) have had limited application, environmental economists have turned to contingent valuation methods (CVM) – the use of direct interview techniques to create hypothetical markets from which values can be derived. But are individuals best understood as utility maximisers? Does this correspond to the ways in which we value the non-human world? There are at least two problems with this account of individual choice and decision making: first, the availability of information and our sense of what is possible, and second, the impact of values aside from utility.

With respect to the use of CBA in policy decisions we are dealing with the practical world, where information is scarce. But if individuals are not fully informed, in what way can their behaviour be taken to be rational in the economic sense? We have already shown that there is an information bias in contingent valuation techniques and similarly, with respect to revealed preference techniques, the preferences derived will be affected by the knowledge of the particular individual in question and the information available to them. Further, and in many ways associated with this problem of information deficit, social and economic constraints would appear to affect decisions. An individual may not be in an economic or social position to act on information (such situations were raised earlier with respect to the limitations of hedonic pricing techniques) or their sense of what is possible may be restricted. As Williams argues:

> What one wants, or is capable of wanting, is itself the function of numerous social forces, and importantly rests on a sense of what is possible. Many a potential desire fails to become an express preference because the thought is absent that it would ever be possible to achieve.
>
> (Williams, 1973, p. 147)

Along similar lines, Cass Sunstein contends that taking market behaviour as a guide to preferences is highly problematic since people will adapt themselves 'to undue limitations in current practices and opportunities' (Sunstein, 1991, p. 21). He emphasises that: 'Poverty itself is perhaps the most severe obstacle to the free development of preferences and beliefs' (ibid., p. 23).

Information deficit and the sense of what is possible are two aspects of the world that raise uncomfortable questions for economic analysis. But the relationship between revealed preference and welfare can be further challenged if we take into account other values aside from utility that may be appealed to in individual decisions. As Amartya Sen argues, 'choice may reflect a compromise among a variety of considerations of which personal welfare may be just one' (Sen, 1977, p. 324). The preference schedule derived from revealed preference techniques in many situations is likely to be affected by our commitments, goals and values, many of which are associated with the non-human world. This can affect results in two ways: first, commitments can reduce utility functions – my behaviour in choosing not to visit a particular environmentally sensitive area because I believe it should be preserved rather than opened to tourists would not be recorded in travel cost assessments;

and second, behavioural analysis may overlook and disregard commitments and other values. An example of this latter occurrence can be seen in the Department of Transport's quantification of travel cost savings in its CBA for potential road developments. It is assumed that all road users have a preference for quicker journeys. The fact that specific individuals may 'prefer' environmental protection over a new road scheme is not regarded as relevant. As Sen argues: 'Commitment ... drives a wedge between personal choice and personal welfare' (1977, p. 329).

Contingent valuation methods have been used and supported because, unlike revealed preference techniques, they aim to isolate such commitments and include them in valuations. However, this raises a further question of whether the plurality of values that we associate with the environment can be represented by a single measure, money. Such an assumption is fundamental to welfare and environmental economics. As the DoE, for instance, states: 'a monetary standard is a convenient means of expressing the relative values which society places on different uses of resources' (1991a, p. 23). A monetary standard may be 'convenient', but does the view that there can be a single standard against which the relative worth of all other values can be judged stand up to critical scrutiny? Advocates of CVM argue that they can isolate and compare the different aspects of the total economic value of the environment. The actual use value of the environment may seem relatively uncontroversial, although even here questions of information and the sense of what is possible can be raised, as can problems associated with the valuation of public goods. But where environmental economists seek to determine a monetary value for option and existence values there would seem to be even more scope for dispute. The purpose of seeking these valuations is to decide on our duties to future generations and to non-human nature 'unrelated to human use' (Pearce and Turner, 1990, p. 130). Is it acceptable to attempt to value such commitments using the same criterion that we use for the comprehension of economic preferences? Are they not qualitatively different things? Here we might reflect on what the economic value of a duty to future generations or of the commitment to the preservation of aspects of the non-human world actually means. That economists have generated a monetary value is unquestionable; what precisely that value represents is another matter. Obligations, duties and commitments are understood and judged in terms of criteria other than utility. They refer to different aspects of the human condition and as such are not necessarily reducible to one another. They are probably best understood as incommensurable in the sense that when we reason about the environment we do so with respect to a range of criteria which may be neither reducible to one another nor clearly rankable in a scale of relative worth.[9]

At this point it would appear that economists are straying into an area where their methodology becomes meaningless. Either they need to make the strong claim that all values, commitments and beliefs are ultimately reducible to the single value of utility maximisation or they should recognise that there are values which cannot be adequately represented by CBA valuation techniques and that therefore their calculations are an extremely partial representation of our relations with the non-human world. The reduction of all environmental values to commodity values and the focus on individual preference satisfaction necessarily fails to account for many of the features of our relations with the non-human world. As Hayward comments, 'environmental economists can by definition recognise no sources of value in nature other than those which assume the form of human preferences' (Hayward, 1995, p. 104). Representing the aesthetic and ethical dimensions of environmental values in terms of individual preferences distorts the significance of such values. For Sagoff, there is a 'category mistake' in employing economic techniques (Sagoff, 1988, pp. 92–4). Environmental goods such as beautiful landscapes and rare species 'are not "commodities", since they are not traded in markets, and they are not consumed individually – their value is appreciated collectively' (Jacobs, 1991, p. 212). Questions concerning these goods ought to be the subject of deliberation amongst citizens and not reduced to a simple aggregate of consumer preferences.

Aggregation and discounting

A central issue for any technique that claims to aid decision making concerns the question of whose values count and by how much. Thus, two further features of CBA are open to criticism: the procedure of aggregation and the discounting of future values. Whose values are to be included in the decision-making process? Who is the constituency for a decision? For instance, with respect to the loss of an area such as Twyford Down, whose preferences should count? The drivers who will have a faster route? The local community, which may have less traffic passing through its town or may lose an important cultural landscape? Or wider still, to all those who value such areas? And what of the values of future generations? This is where the recognition of values beyond pure 'use' or 'resource' values begins to raise distinct problems for the analyst and the decision maker.

With respect to other values associated with the non-human world, it is far from clear that the community of concern is, or should be, a particular geographical location. Our emotions, attitudes and preferences can be shaped and transformed by aspects of the environment close to us in the sense that they constitute a significant aspect of our thoughts and actions, but physically distant. Perhaps the most obvious example is the values that people associate with the rain forests of Borneo, Brazil and the like. Where is the 'cut-off point' for the inclusion of such values in any decision-making process that affects such aspects of the environment? Even where environmental economists tend to recognise such values we have argued that their attempts to quantify them misrepresent and disrupt their significance.

Related to both the 'who' and 'by how much' questions is the practice of discounting – how are we to deal with future costs and benefits? Discounting is a familiar practice within resource management where we are 'simply' dealing with purely economic values. However, even here there is a serious debate concerning the level of the discount rate. A high rate often militates against environmental projects with a long-term return, for instance sustainable forestry, and can result in an economic argument for resource depletion. In the literature we find calls for lower or even negative discount rates for particular types of policies and projects as well as concerns as to what differential rates might mean for comparison between options (Pearce and Turner, 1990, pp. 211ff). The DoE is itself well aware of such problems:

> where there is a risk of losing as environmental benefit for all time, the appraisal should be sure to recognise both present and future perceptions of environmental values. Rising expectations about environmental quality, coupled with a diminishing stock of relatively untouched environmental assets, may mean that the value to society of certain resources will increase over time. Therefore, even though the loss of an environmental amenity may not seem to be of major importance now, that same amenity may be more highly valued in the future.
>
> (DoE, 1991a, p. 6)

Rather than tampering with the discount rate, however, the DoE, in line with the practice of most environmental economists, argues that the values incorporated into the CBA should be adjusted prior to discounting and that option values are the quantification of this future worth (ibid., p. 32). The interests, preferences and beliefs of future persons are therefore dependent on each currently existing individual's awareness of such values: the welfare and agency of future peoples is reliant upon the recognition of present individuals in their economic behaviour. Such problems have led to the proposal of introducing 'sustainability constraints', which would stop non-sustainable depletion of 'critical natural capital'. We shall consider the question of such constraints, and interpretations of weak and strong sustainability from which they are derived, in the case study at the end of the chapter. For the time being though, the recognition that such constraints are necessary is a further recognition of the limits of the economic paradigm.

> The view implicit in conventional CBA is that future generations are provided for by maximising the productivity of present investments so far as to bequeath them the largest possible stock of economic and financial wealth. However, this attitude will not safeguard the future if it is accompanied by the loss of vital natural capital which cannot be replaced or substituted.
>
> (Winpenny, 1991, p. 67)

Relating back to the question of commensurability, there is an assumption that all the values derived by economists are related to the future in the same manner, a manner similar to commodities in a market. But is this how we understand the aesthetic, moral, cultural or scientific values that economic techniques claim to distinguish? Does our aesthetic or moral sensibility relate to the future in the same way as an economic valuation of a natural resource? Are we impatient aesthetically and morally for immediate gratification and what would 'gratification' mean in these terms? Different values and modes of association with the non-human world have different temporal features. There are grounds for challenging not only the assumption that qualitatively different values can be represented by a monetary value but also that they then should be treated in the same manner as economic commodities when compared over time.

Finally, there is a range of criticisms that relate to the practice of aggregation and specifically to the Kaldor–Hicks compensation test. If, as we have argued, the economic assumption that differing values are commensurable is questioned, any simple aggregation becomes problematic. However, even if we overlook this issue there is still the standing of potential Pareto optimality to consider. Amartya Sen argues that the compensation criteria within potential Pareto optimality 'are either *unconvincing* or *redundant*': redundant if compensation is in fact paid, since the decision can then be said to be Pareto efficient; unconvincing if not paid, since this would be ethically questionable – the losers in CBA calculations, Sen argues, are frequently 'the most miserable in society, and it is little consolation to be told that it is possible to compensate them fully, but ("good God!") no actual plan exists to do so' (Sen, 1987, p. 33). This raises the issue of exactly who the losers and the gainers are – the distribution of costs and benefits. It raises questions of social justice. Pareto optimality is a criterion of economic or allocational efficiency; it does not consider, for instance, the distribution of effects. But why should we give priority to economic efficiency when we are considering environmental effects?

Uncertainty, risk and irreversibility

Most of our interventions in the natural world are unfortunately shrouded in a high level of uncertainty as to their outcome. To a large extent we are ignorant with respect to many of the ecological functions of environmental entities. For instance, what is the climatic function of the rain forest? How long can the oceans operate as a sink for carbon dioxide? What role in the local ecosystem does a threatened species of butterfly have? Once an ecosystem is destroyed it is difficult, if not impossible, to regenerate or replace. The extinction of a species is clearly irreversible. Can we really judge the risk of environmental damage? Is it meaningful to talk about the risk of nuclear leakage from a depository that is supposed to act as a safe for centuries? Could plants that will be lost in rain forest clearance hold the key to medical breakthrough or the development of new agriculturally valuable strains? Questions of uncertainty, risk and irreversibility with respect to the natural world are particularly problematic when judging between competing policy options where there is a much higher level of abstraction than for, say, local projects and developments – our ability to assess all possible outcomes and effects is diminished. Further, there is a risk of losing wild places, species and important ecosystems because of our ignorance of natural systems. Such losses may in themselves lead to a drastic impoverishment of human possibilities. These sort of issues raise further questions as to the 'accuracy' of any particular monetary valuation in that they incorporate a particular perspective on risk and uncertainty – one that may not be shared by decision makers or the wider public. Many environmental economists are sensitive to some of these problems and, for instance, have argued that CBA needs to be modified through the inclusion of sustainability constraints in order to ensure that critical aspects of the non-human world are maintained at sustainable levels. This theme is taken up in the case study at the end of the chapter.

Political misuse

The criticisms of CBA thus far have focused on its internal logic. Independent of this are questions concerning the way that it is used in decision-making processes. First, it is often argued that decision makers are more familiar with, and give more attention and priority to, the NPV generated by CBA over the environmental impacts that are not within the economic analysis. As Atkins argues:

> Recent public policy has been dominated by concerns over 'value for money' in public expenditure. In this context a measure that purports to show cash returns from public investment has a greater influence on decision-makers.
>
> (Atkins, 1990, p. 7)

This is the basis of the argument that a monetary valuation of environmental goods should be included within existing decision-making procedures. In response it can be argued that rather than misrepresenting environmental impacts in an extended CBA, it is the priority that decision makers give to financial return over environmental factors that needs to change. Another cause for concern is the inaccessibility of information in a CBA: monetary valuations can hide politically sensitive assumptions, including those made by economists themselves, which could not be defended in open debate. It often requires a training in economics to be in any position to expose these issues.

What future for environmental valuation and extended CBA?

What are we to make of the practice of economic analysis of policy and projects where those assessments attempt to incorporate environmental valuations? We have already exposed a number of the limitations in the use of such techniques and argued that economic assumptions are based on a misrepresentation of the human condition and the values associated with the non-human world. However, many environmentalists do support the use of extended CBA on what they term 'pragmatic' grounds – it is better to have some values in the primary decision-making procedure, even recognising that they are partial valuations.

> economic (monetary) valuation of non-market environmental assets may be more or less imperfect given the particular asset together with its environmental and valuation contexts; but, invariably, some valuation explicitly laid out for scrutiny by policy-makers and the public, is better than none, because none can mean some implicit valuation shrouded from public scrutiny.
>
> (Turner *et al.*, 1994, p. 109)

However, such a position is problematic on a number of counts. It may be the case that specific projects, such as the cutting through Twyford Down, may not have progressed, but this will not always be the case. If support has been given to the procedure of extended CBA and the decision favours an environmentally destructive option, the legitimacy of challenge is reduced. Environmentalists are implicated in a distorted decision-making process. Further, contrary to the views of Turner and his colleagues, valuation is far from 'explicitly laid out' in CBA. All that normally faces the decision maker is a row of figures representing the valuation of environmental and other impacts. The judgement of their worth has already been made by the economist. CBA leads to values and assumptions being shrouded from public scrutiny, with only the economist being granted privileged access.

There is clearly intuitive appeal in thinking about and weighing the costs and benefits of proposed interventions, but the idea that it this can be achieved in a quasi-scientific manner appears to be overstretching the intuition. Economic evaluation of environmental values over-extends economists' area of competence and brings the apparent 'expert' authority and status of economists into question. Behind the shroud of expertise, environmental economists are offering advice on the basis of valuation techniques which distort the very values they aim to weigh. Simplification leads to misrepresentation. Political conflict is reduced to questions of aggregating preference intensities.

ENVIRONMENTAL IMPACT ASSESSMENT

Environmental impacts do need to be weighed against other forms of costs and benefits. If we accept that monetary valuation of environmental entities is in some way mistaken, then how are environmental aspects of development to be taken into account? How are they to be presented in such a way as to be accessible to decision makers? In this section it is argued that environmental impact assessment (EIA) may offer an alternative, although it clearly places more emphasis on the role of sound political judgement. Decision makers are not faced simply with the numerical result of an economic calculation, the net present value of an intervention, but rather need to balance a range of qualitatively different economic, social and environmental factors.

> EIA can be described as a process for identifying the likely consequences for the biogeophysical environment and for man's health and welfare of implementing particular activities and for conveying this information, at a stage when it can materially affect their decision, to those responsible for sanctioning the proposals.
>
> (Wathern, 1988, p. 6)

Since the 1970s, environmental impact assessment has been increasingly turned to as a method of collating and presenting the significant environmental and social impacts of proposed projects. In June 1985, EC Directive 85/337/EEC instructed all member states to enact legislation within three years that would require an EIA for certain large-scale and potentially damaging projects.[10]

The aim of the EIA process is to present, in as bias-free a manner as possible, a systematic analysis of the significant impacts of a proposed development as an aid to decision makers. Consultation with statutory agencies (such as government departments or pollution control agencies) and non-statutory groups (such as voluntary conservation organisations) is seen as central to the process of information gathering, as is a period of consultation with agencies and the public after the environmental impact statement is published. Such consultation should mean that the best sources of information are accessed and can often lead to project redesign and mitigation of impacts. These comments, along with the environmental impact statement, feed into the decision-making process for authorisation, where they are balanced against other material considerations.

Minimum content of environmental impact statements (to conform with EC Directive 85/337/EEC)

1 An outline of the main alternatives to the chosen project which have been investigated by the developer and the main reasons for the preferred choice, taking their respective likely environmental effects into consideration;

2 A description of the main features of the chosen project which may cause significant impacts, including estimates of the residues and wastes it may create;

3 A description of the base-line condition of those aspects of the environment likely to be significantly affected by the chosen project;

4 An assessment of the likely significant impacts of a project, including its likely compatibility with existing and proposed environmental regulations and land-use plans;

5 A description of any ameliorating measures which are proposed (or which have already been incorporated into the project design) to reduce the potentially harmful effects of the project on the environment;

6 A non-technical summary of the total assessment.

(Lee, 1989, p. 19)

The EIA study should incorporate all significant effects, both positive and negative, direct and indirect, on:

• human beings, buildings, and man-made features;
• flora, fauna and geology;

- land;
- water;
- air and climate;
- other indirect and secondary effects associated with the project.

(DoE, 1989, pp. 39–40)

A number of problems have arisen, most specifically concerning the definition of 'significant impact'. It is the developer who is generally charged with producing the environmental impact statement and it may well be in their best interest to downplay the significance of potential environmental effects. For this reason the quality of many environmental impact statements in the UK has been questioned, resulting in calls for an independent body to review practice. Consultation and participation are seen as essential if the EIA process is to work well, and for many commentators and practitioners the earlier consultation occurs the more likely agreement over the impact of a development is achieved. EIA is still in its relative infancy but already its potential as an aid to decision makers is being widely recognised.

Further questions have been raised as to the timing of any EIA. Although EIA does provide a method of bringing environmental considerations into authorisation processes for developments and projects, it may be that in many cases it is too late in the decision-making process to have any profound effect. Focus on the environmental impact of projects does not entail analysis of the policy, plan or programme from which the project was developed. This has the effect of limiting the possible alternatives at the project stage. For instance, 'the use of an alternative transportation mode will not be considered in the EIA of a road link, because the alternative is no longer realistic' (Wood and Dejeddour, 1992, p. 6). Further, EIAs of projects tend to focus on the impact of the specific development and not on the cumulative impacts that are produced in combination with existing and future schemes. If environmental considerations are to substantially alter our practices, as environmentalists advocate, assessments need to be carried out at the earliest possible opportunity – hence the development of strategic environmental assessment (SEA).

Strategic environmental assessment

> Alternative approaches, cumulative impacts and synergistic impacts (which may be cross-sectorial in nature), ancillary impacts, regional or global impacts and non-project impacts may be better assessed initially at the policy, plan or programme level, rather than at the project level.
>
> (Wood and Dejeddour, 1992, p. 3)

Compared with project-based EIA, SEA has had an even shorter history. SEA follows the same basic methodology as EIA, although it focuses on policies, plans and programmes rather than on individual projects. A number of countries utilise strategic environmental assessment to a limited extent, particularly on land-use plans, and the 'European Commission has signalled its intention, in its latest

Environmental Programme, to propose a new Directive for the application of environmental assessment to certain policies, plans and programmes in Member States' (Lee and Walsh, 1992, p. 127). Perhaps the most interesting development, however, is the commitment in Canada for all cabinet policy decisions to undergo environmental assessment (ibid., p. 128).

SEA appears to offer the possibility of overcoming the deficiencies of project-specific EIA and offers the kind of analysis advocated by those who promote sustainable development – the integration of environmental concerns at all levels of decision making. Clearly the accuracy and detail of strategic environmental assessments will differ from EIAs, as will the time-scales involved. This, however, is simply a feature of any policy assessment when compared with project assessments.

EIA or extended CBA?

What is the best way of proceeding with the assessment of the environmental effects of interventions, from policy level through to project level? Is it a straight choice between cost–benefit analysis and environmental impact assessment? Could we not use both? If the EIA procedure is thought to have merit, then it follows that monetary valuations of environmental costs and benefits should not form part of an extended CBA for the same project or policy; otherwise we would be in the awkward position of double counting these environmental effects. This in turn would bias any decision made. Perhaps, in the end, the question needs to be recast in terms of the openness of any decision and the view that is taken as to the accuracy and commensurability of monetary valuation. Any detailed monetary valuation will actually require a full-scale EIA or SEA. The question then is whether political judgement is better served by the economic valuation of environmental and social impacts or through a more explicit process of weighing the significant effects of any intervention. We have argued that the move from a description of the environmental effects to a monetary valuation may alter the character of any decision. Further, there are numerous contested assumptions implicit within monetary valuations which are 'hidden' once the calculations enter the cost–benefit streams. Accountable political judgements require such assumptions to be as open to scrutiny, deliberation and challenge as the policy or project under assessment. If not, then it may appear that political questions are being surrendered to the authority of economic analysis and the values we associate with the non-human world will be distorted.

MEASURING SUSTAINABLE DEVELOPMENT

Re-evaluating economic growth

In Chapter 2, we discussed the relationship between the environment, society and the economy centred around the concept of sustainable development. The idea that there may be ecological and social limits to growth is seen as a fundamental critical standpoint for environmentalists – if the Earth is a finite planet, economies cannot continue to grow exponentially without permanent ecological damage and social disintegration. In this section we shall continue this discussion by focusing on the measurement of economic growth. The popular view, perpetrated particularly by economists and politicians, is that economic growth is basically 'a good thing', more growth is better, and a continued increase in economic performance can be directly translated to an increase in human welfare. It is this widely assumed correlation between economic growth and human development that critics of a growth-centred orientation reject. In recent years an increasing amount of work has focused on the inadequacies and inconsistencies of government economic statistics that incorporate such a correlation.[11] Initially we shall focus on the environmental and social critique of national income accounting used by states and international economic institutions and then turn our attention to possible alternatives.

National income accounting

National income accounting (NIA) produces statistics such as gross national product (GNP) and gross domestic product (GDP), consistently used by economists and politicians to indicate the state of national economies and the well-being of its citizens. It is in light of such statistics that comparative analysis of the standing of nations is made and in terms of which national and international agencies make investment decisions. For instance, the success or failure of development projects or economic restructuring instigated by the World Bank or the International Monetary Fund (IMF) is frequently measured in terms of changes in GNP or GDP. If these do not adequately reflect the environmental or social impacts, then the wisdom of such interventions may be challenged.

National income accounting

Gross domestic product (GDP) is the total monetary value of goods and services produced within a country.

Gross national product (GNP) is the total income of all residents of a country.

GNP is GDP plus rents and dividends flowing into a country from abroad, minus rents, interests, profits and dividends paid out to people in other countries. GNP depends on where the owners are located; GDP depends on where the economic activity is located.

GDP or *GNP per capita* is often referred to as the 'average standard of living'.

So what is wrong with such statistics? Critics argue that national income accounting takes into account only a limited set of economic factors, which tell us nothing about the social and environmental conditions central to an adequate conception of well-being. This mirrors the earlier criticism that economic analysis has an impoverished conception of well-being as utility maximisation. Even if GNP per capita is an accurate measure of economic welfare, it is only a partial representation of total well-being. It is conceivable that an increase in economic welfare so measured could be associated with a corresponding decrease in environmental and social conditions. NIA fails to account for a wide variety of environmental and social issues and incorporates a number of contradictions.

What is wrong with national income accounting?

NIA does not take into account:

- *unpaid domestic labour* (usually carried out by women), non-monetary transactions and voluntary work;

- the *distribution of income* across society and the marginal utility of money – an increase in income is worth relatively more to the poor than the rich;

- *defensive expenditure* – purchases to offset worsening social and environmental conditions. Rather this is counted as a benefit to the economy;

- unstable *exchange rates* used for international comparisons;

- the *benefits of conservation* over exploitation of resources – rapid throughput of transactions shows up more favourably than durability and reuse;

- *long-term environmental damage*, particularly to critical natural assets.
    (Adapted from Anderson, 1991; Daly and Cobb, 1990; Ekins, 1986)

Taking these different factors into consideration, the conventional view that there is a direct correlation between per capita GNP and economic welfare begins to look rather suspect. GNP appears to provide an inaccurate and misleading approximation of our quality of life and the state of the environment. So what alternatives have critics proposed?

The Index of Sustainable Economic Welfare

In response to the perceived weaknesses of national income accounting, Herman Daly and John Cobb developed the Index of Sustainable Economic Welfare (Daly and Cobb, 1990, pp. 401–56). The index adjusts GNP to take into account the contradictions inherent within conventional economic measures. An index of this sort is based on the recognition that a single figure can be useful in making broad comparisons of welfare over time. The index has been applied to both the US (ibid.) and the UK economy (Mayo, 1994, pp. 6–7) over the period 1950 to 1986. In both cases sustainable economic welfare rose broadly in line with GNP up until the mid-1970s. However, this was purely a contingent relationship because since then the measure of sustainable welfare has levelled off and begun to decline, most strikingly in the UK. Both studies highlight three interconnected factors which have caused this drop: the deepening of economic inequality within society; the exhaustion of natural resources; and the failure to invest in sustainable future practices.

Although the index apparently provides a critical standpoint from which to analyse the cogency of national income accounting, questions again need to be raised as to the accuracy of the monetary valuations of environmental and social factors used in the index, in particular with respect to long-term environmental damage. Equally, the political assumptions concerning the weighting of income distribution factors will have many critics. But, even given these methodological problems, the Index provides additional evidence that conventional measurements of economic growth are poor measures of the quality of life within a particular society.

Alternative economic indicators

GNP focuses attention on one particular form of progress, which even in its own terms appears to be a miscalculation. The Index of Sustainable Economic Welfare attempts to take into account the wider social and environmental context that GNP ignores, although it still depends on the economic valuations of such aspects of well-being. If the accuracy of these valuations is questionable, what other options are left? Perhaps one of the most interesting developments in recent years has been in the area of alternative economic indicators.

Victor Anderson has been at the forefront of arguing for the need to develop a range of indicators that take into account a wider understanding of well-being and correspond to our social and environmental situations. He isolates three aspects of welfare where indicators are necessary – financial, social and the relationship with the natural world (Anderson, 1991, pp. 42–7). Clearly it is the social and environmental aspects that have been predominantly overlooked in contemporary society. Anderson argues that social indicators need to be developed that take into account such factors as education and literacy; work and unemployment; consumption; distribution of income and wealth; and health. Similarly, environmental indicators need to take into account significant and critical factors such as deforestation, global warming, population pressures, nuclear threats and energy consumption. Various criteria for a good indicator are offered, particularly the need for readily accessible information and ease of understanding. Further, they should allow comparison between regions and nations although at the same time allowing for cultural specificity. With both social and environmental issues it is important that they are easily measurable and understandable and that only a small number of significant factors are measured for ease of comparison.

Using these indicators, a comparative analysis of a number of nations indicates that GNP obscures a number of important differences in well-being and the standard of living.[12] What is most striking, although perhaps unsurprising, is the gap between the nations of the North and South. The division occurs in terms of

---

Alternative social and environmental indicators

A. Human and social indicators
1 Net primary school enrolment ratio for girls.
2 Net primary school enrolment ratio for boys.
3 Female illiteracy rate.
4 Male illiteracy rate.
5 The rate of unemployment.
6 Average calorie supply as a percentage of requirements.
7 Percentage of population with access to safe drinking water.
8 Telephones per thousand people.
9 Household income received by the top 20 per cent of households divided by that received by the bottom 20 per cent.
10 Infant mortality rate.
11 Under-five mortality rate.

B. Environmental indicators
12 Deforestation in square kilometres per year.
13 Carbon dioxide emissions from fossil fuel use, in millions of metric tons per year.
14 Average annual percentage rate of increase in population.
15 Number of operable nuclear reactors.
16 Energy consumption (in tons of oil equivalent) per million dollars of GDP.

(In addition, there is an urgent need for more comprehensive data both on rates of species loss and rates of desertification.)

(Adapted from Anderson, 1991, pp. 55–74)

---

almost all the factors represented by each indicator. From his survey, Anderson draws the following conclusions:

1   Social conditions are generally improving, and in the short term, this is likely to continue.
2   In the medium term, environmental deterioration threatens to put these social improvements into reverse. For example, growing desertification threatens current improvements in calorie supply: pollution will threaten current improvements in health.
3   In the long term, the outcome depends on whether the current improvements in environmental 'cause indicators' (such as energy intensity and rate of population growth) continue and are sufficiently big scale to put the environmental 'effects indicators' into reverse. This would allow the social indicators to resume their past trend of general improvement.

(Anderson, 1991, p. 91)

There is growing recognition that such indicators provide a broader understanding of the relationship between the economy, society and the natural world
in terms of which more efficacious decisions might be forthcoming. This recognition has led a number of organisations to develop similar quality-of-life indic-
tors. For instance, the Environmental Challenge Group, an initiative supported
by a group of British non-governmental organisations, has developed a range of
environmental indicators in order to push its case for higher levels of environmental protection in Whitehall. The study seems to indicate that the UK's environment is deteriorating. Perhaps some of the most interesting work in this area
is taking place at the local level. In Seattle, for instance, a community-based
initiative – Sustainable Seattle – has achieved widespread local support in a
process of generating economic, social and environmental indicators for the city.
Only when such information is fully available will citizens be able to judge how
sustainable Seattle actually is and to generate initiatives to alter environmentally
and socially destructive practices (Lawrence, 1994; Sustainable Seattle, 1993).
Inspired by the success of Seattle and other enlightened localities, many UK
local authorities have been working on similar projects (LGMB, 1995b). We shall
return to these initiatives in Chapter 10.

Although such indicators do not offer a single figure such as in national income
accounting, they do make the trade-offs inherent in decisions explicit. They also
lead to a recognition that financial factors are but one aspect of political judg-
ments. Political decisions may be more difficult to make with respect to such a
range of information, but at least they will be made with a recognition of the range
of significant factors involved. After all, what is the economy there to achieve – the
creation of more economic wealth or the development of the quality of life, in the
broadest sense?

CONCLUSION

We can perhaps draw two conclusions from our discussion of the economic
analysis of environmental values and goods. First, decision makers appear to be
seduced by the apparent technical simplicity of quasi-scientific economic calculations. Both CBA and GNP provide a single figure with which simple comparisons can be made between alternative projects, policies or even national economies.
Our investigations have shown that such figures may well conceal a range of
assumptions and simplifications which misrepresent the human condition and
specifically its relationship with the non-human world. To what extent should we
accept political decisions based on such simplification and distortion? Second, it
is perhaps not surprising that such measures underpin the logic of capitalist
patterns of economic growth. Individuals are taken to be utility maximisers and
their economic preferences the only aspect of the human condition that is of
interest. Rethinking the way we assess interventions and economies as a whole
requires us to reassess what we believe is important about humanity and the
natural world. Closing off such a critical endeavour by shrouding politically

sensitive assumptions in economic analysis will simply mean more of the same, including continued environmental and social degradation. The relationship between the economy, society and the natural world needs to be articulated in all decisions.

CASE STUDY: WEAK AND STRONG SUSTAINABILITY

Cost–benefit analysis can only provide information about the relative economic value of different policy or project options – it cannot tell us whether a policy or project is sustainable. A commitment to sustainable development, with its requirement to take into account the needs of present and future generations, would appear to place certain requirements, if not constraints, on development projects. Questions concerning the optimal size of the economy or the minimum physical levels of certain stocks of environmental goods are such that conventional economic analytical tools are often far from useful; they can help with optimal allocation but not with optimal size or distribution.

Where environmental economists have attempted to respond to the obligations implicit within sustainable development, they have taken it to entail a duty to pass on to future generations the equivalent 'stock of wealth' (Pearce *et al.*, 1989, pp. 34ff). But, is this constant stock of wealth to be a mix of man-made and natural capital? Can manufactured goods be seen as substitutable for natural entities? Further, how is such a stock of wealth to be calculated? It is on such questions of the relationship between different forms of capital stock that distinctions in the interpretation of sustainable development can be made, specifically between weak and strong sustainability.

Three types of capital are commonly distinguished:

- Human-made: consumer goods, buildings, machinery.
- Human: labour, skills, knowledge, creativity.
- Natural: natural resources.

Advocates of weak sustainability hold that the three different types of capital are substitutable; the loss of a particular aspect of the environment can be substituted by the equivalent value of human-made or human capital. What we bequeath to future generations should be the equivalent total stock of all three types of capital. Clearly, holding such a position would sanction any level of environmental degradation, resource depletion or species loss, so long as the equivalent value of human or human-made capital is substituted in its place. The monetary valuation of environmental entities becomes central to the weak sustainability argument, since substitution requires a common measure in order that equivalent amounts of what are qualitatively different entities can be weighed against one another. In this sense, it is the economic value of human-made, human and natural capital that is to remain constant. To advocate weak sustainability requires the acceptance of the principles of economic valuation discussed earlier.

On the other hand, advocates of strong sustainability deny the direct substitutability of different types of capital, arguing that there is a common misinterpretation amongst economists as to the nature of natural capital. Paul Ekins (1995, p. 183) highlights three different functions of natural capital:

- Provision of resources for human activity.
- Absorption of wastes from human activity.
- Provision of environmental services independently of or interdependently with human activity.

The first two functions, although frequently neglected (particularly the waste assimilation function), can be incorporated in traditional economic modelling. It is the third function that is perhaps the most important and is neglected by advocates of weak sustainability. Not only does the environment provide the basic materials for production and the assimilation of humanity's waste products, but it is also the milieu in which human activity takes place. The natural world provides fundamental survival and amenity services (ibid., p. 185) that appear to be far from substitutable. These include such examples as the ozone layer, the climate-regulating functions of the oceans and rain forests, and the stability of ecosystems, as well as more aesthetic properties associated with, for instance, wilderness or other beautiful landscapes. Not only do such functions appear to be non-substitutable, but there is uncertainty concerning the consequences of depleting or degrading certain natural entities and losing the apparent resilience of diverse ecological systems; degradation is frequently irreversible and unjust in respect of the distribution of effects (Beder, 1996, pp. 145–52).

In response to the assertion that forms of capital are substitutable, strong sustainability holds that human-made/human capital and natural capital are better viewed as complements (Daly, 1995, p. 49; Jacobs, 1995c, p. 59). In the contemporary world, natural capital needs to be understood as the limiting factor for development, and constraints must be placed on certain environmentally destructive types of activity. Sustainable development requires the recognition of certain duties to future generations. These can be fulfilled to a certain extent by the preservation of a constant stock of natural capital.

Strong sustainability as a constraint is a way of implicitly providing property rights in the resource base to future generations. It says that they have ownership claims to as much natural capital as the present – i.e. the rule is to keep natural capital intact.

(Daly, 1995, p. 53)

Generally, advocates of strong sustainability are critical of the idea of ecological modernisation, in which economic growth and environmental protection are taken to be complementary (see Chapter 2). For instance Herman Daly (1991) has consistently argued that we require a 'steady-state' economy,[13] one where there is not only an unaltered reserve of natural wealth (strong sustainability) but also that this is also tied to a constant population, and zero economic and population growth. The Earth and its finite resources cannot provide the panacea of constant growth; rather humanity must concentrate its efforts and creativity on alternative forms of human development. Far more radical than Daly is the group of bioeconomists, including Nicholas Georgescu-Roegen and Juan Martinez-Alier, who share his view that processes of economic growth and accumulation degrade the natural system, returning waste products at a higher level of entropy and unfit for human use.[14] In their view, conventional economics pays little attention to the moral and physical aspects of the economy, focusing mainly on added value as if the current economic system were the end of the historical process of development. The contemporary capitalist economic system is open and linear rather than closed and circular and the dissipation of energy is irreversible. Such a situation requires not zero growth but a reduction in the scale of the economy that will have regard to the physical and moral aspects of development.

More conventional economists, who accept the distinction between the different types of capital, tend to accept the substitutability thesis whilst recognising that there clearly are some forms of critical natural capital that cannot be substituted. Such a position is somewhere between the two poles of weak and strong sustainability. It accepts the argument that the natural world provides certain types of capital which we cannot replace (such as that of the ozone layer, oceans, etc.) but that other types of natural capital can be replaced by human-made substitutes. Within environmental economics this is perhaps the dominant interpretation of sustainable development and tends to form part of the ecological modernisation stream of thought. It would be wrong, however, to claim that there is consensus within neo-liberal welfare economics as to the usefulness of the concept of sustainable development; Wilfred Beckerman, for instance, argues that unless we hold the strong interpretation, which he finds 'morally unacceptable and totally impracticable', the weak interpretation is nothing more than welfare maximisation and the principle of optimality. The concept of sustainable development cannot generate measurable criteria and is therefore redundant. The power of human creativity to discover and introduce substitutes and alternatives to natural resources should not be hampered by restricting market transactions and constraining economic analysis techniques such as CBA (Beckerman, 1994, pp. 191ff).[15] Within this debate there is a mirroring of some of the divisions in green thinking discussed in Part I of this book. Advocates of strong anthropocentrism or technical optimism tend to support a version of weak sustainability; those who subscribe to a weak or enlightened anthropocentrism tend towards a strong interpretation of sustainability.

Whichever position one takes on this (unless of course one does not accept the need to constrain policies in the name of sustainable development at all) there still remains the issue of how the level of natural capital is to be calculated. Is it the physical amount or a financial valuation of natural capital that needs to be taken into account? For environmental economists the answer is invariably the latter and this brings in the whole question of the economic valuation of environmental entities with which the above chapter engaged.

> It is ... a moot point whether we should be concerned with passing on a constant physical level of capital, or one that preserves its value on economic terms. As resources become scarce they become more economically valuable. The last piece of coal mined on earth will no doubt have a high rarity value, but that is no consolation to people dependent on burning coal.
>
> (Winpenny, 1991, p. 3)

Taking sustainability into account has certain implications for the development of projects and policies. First, it places a restriction on policies that impact on critical natural assets. Second, it points towards the inclusion of shadow projects or at least financial compensation within developments. For instance, the destruction of woodlands for housing might require the developer to plant the equivalent tree coverage elsewhere. Third, renewable natural capital such as fisheries or woodlands should be exploited only up to sustainable levels, that is, not beyond the point at which they are no longer able to regenerate. Clearly, however, many environmental assets are neither critical nor renewable and can be used only once, for instance oil and coal reserves. Sustainable development points towards the use of such resource in a prudent manner with perhaps emphasis being put on the search for alternatives. We cannot stop intervening in the environment for our own sustenance – it is quite simply a question of what form of development we aim to achieve and how we are to utilise the natural world in its fulfilment.

SUGGESTIONS FOR FURTHER READING

The seminal text defending the approach of environmental economics is David Pearce *et al.*, *Blueprint for a Green Economy* (1989), originally commissioned by the Department of the Environment. *Environmental Economics* (1994) by R. Kerry Turner *et al.* is an accessible introduction to the subject. Michael Jacobs in *The Green Economy* (1991) offers a number of critical reflections on this neo-classical approach. Peter Wathern (ed.), *Environmental Impact Assessment* (1988), is a useful collection by practitioners and academics. Victor Anderson's *Alternative Economic Indicators* (1991) raised the profile of the debate on the limits of national accounting.

6 Choosing the means

Taxation is in many cases an appropriate, efficient and effective way to protect the environment. It is not the only way; it will not be suitable or acceptable in all cases, and it will almost always work best in combination with regulations and educational campaigns. But taxation to make prices reflect the full social and environmental cost of particular activities is a necessary part of a transition to a sustainable society.

(Tindale and Holtham, 1996, p. 14)

Having identified the nature of environmental problems, it is necessary to turn to a discussion of the appropriate means for solving them. There is no single or simple answer to the question of means: it depends on the nature of the issue being addressed and on the responses of industry, consumers and pressure groups. Different problems may require different solutions. These can take the form of a tax, setting targets and limits, a ban, or an appropriate mixture of policy responses. As discussed in Chapter 4, the nature of environmental problems is such that collective action problems tend to lie at their heart. Thus, policy responses are all, in their various ways, attempts to solve collective action problems. Industry pollutes because it is a cheap method of waste disposal; resources are depleted because it is to the advantage of each to take what they can. If environmental resources are be used in a sustainable manner, then environmental policy has to find ways of ensuring that the actions of individuals, businesses and government are themselves sustainable. In this chapter we will address a number of policy responses: voluntary, regulation and standards, and economic instruments. The case study at the end of the chapter shows how these approaches might be used in different situations by focusing on the policy problems of global warming and traffic congestion in cities.

VOLUNTARY MEANS

Individuals and industry, producers and consumers, can adopt voluntary means of solving environmental problems. Individuals can recycle paper and bottles, and refrain from car use; businesses can voluntarily (perhaps under pressure from their employees and public opinion) clean up their processes. People can adapt to different patterns of consumption and change their lifestyles, seeking individually or collectively to develop sustainable practices.

Although business is often subject to legal requirements concerning waste products and so on, there are other voluntary approaches which have been adopted. For example, government departments now frequently run conferences for business and industry seeking to persuade companies of the benefits to be gained by an enhanced environmental awareness. More formally, the recently introduced International Standards Organisation ISO 14001 is a new environmental management systems (EMS) standard. This provides certification for those meeting its standards. To qualify, an EMS must satisfy a number of criteria by installing systems and procedures which allow the company to properly evaluate the effect of its activities on the environment and to ascertain how best to improve its environmental performance. Participation is voluntary, and participants may seek certification for a variety of reasons. One important reason is likely to be environmental credibility and the possibility of being at a commercial disadvantage if they do not participate. We can see voluntary action elsewhere. The Local Government Management Board (LGMB) disseminates information on good practice between local authorities. Many have undertaken state of the environment reports and developed green strategies for their localities. None of this is a statutory requirement. A further example is the citizens' environment initiative, 'Going for Green', which was launched as part of the UK government's response to the Rio Earth Summit. 'Going for Green' does not introduce any new legislation but rather aims to persuade individuals to lead a more environmentally sensitive lifestyle. We shall return to these initiatives in later chapters.

These voluntary responses are all valuable, and it is undeniable that there has been a shift in environmental consciousness. No rules or regulations or government direction will ultimately work unless people are prepared to modify their own behaviour. However, the problem with relying on voluntary action alone, important as it is, is that it cannot guarantee a particular outcome and is also likely to fall short of what is required. We have already looked in Chapter 4 at some of the reasons why this should be so. The environment is a public good and therefore collective action problems are likely to arise. Voluntary action alone is unlikely to be enough, because there is no guarantee that the sum of individual actions will be adequate, and every reason to believe that it will be inadequate. Thus, governments intervene because without intervention certain environmental goods will not be provided.

REGULATIONS AND ENFORCEMENT

What sort of governmental interventions are possible? The first and most easily understood is straightforward regulation and control through an appropriate regulatory body, such as the Environment Agency in the UK or the Environmental Protection Agency in the USA. Command and control (as the standard regulatory approach is often known) typically takes the form of legislation, the issuing of orders to industry and other actors. Although it tends to be thought of as related primarily to industry, it could in fact comprise anything from a ban on the use of cars in a city centre, to controls over the emission of effluent from a factory, to an outright ban on a particular pollutant. Regulations define acceptable processes, establish emissions standards and specify quality objectives. Traditionally, regulation requires the relevant agency to concern itself with the activities of an industry or plant and it can take many forms, from complete control over every aspect of a firm's activity to a more hands-off approach which assumes that firms are doing what they should unless it can be proved that they are not. Acceptable levels of emissions can be determined and companies punished where they fail to meet them. These standards may be uniform quantitative standards, identical for all firms (as is typically the case in German and EC policy) or take the form of a more flexible response, negotiating with individual companies to determine their acceptable levels of emissions.

Standards can be set by looking at what are known as ambient levels of pollution. Here the local carrying capacity of a particular environment is ascertained by determining that it can assimilate pollutants up to, but not beyond, a certain level; standards would be set accordingly. Companies which exceed the standard will then be punished in some way. One problem with this is that punishment, by definition, follows the crime, and hence emerges only after the environmental damage has already been done. Further, the level of fines may be inadequate to act as a deterrent: it may be cheaper for a company to pay the fines than to change its production processes. At this point draconian measures may be needed, such as preventing the company from producing or trading either permanently or until it has changed its processes. Another problem, and one which is of central importance to the arguments for economic incentives, is that setting a standard and punishing a firm for exceeding that level creates no incentive for it to seek to reduce its emissions beyond the standard. It receives nothing for doing so.

Standards are often set not at ambient levels but based instead on the use of particular types of pollution-control technology. For example, firms may simply be required to install the best available technology (BAT). What matters here is less their actual level of emissions and its effect on the environment than whether they are using the appropriate technology. There are problems with this approach. For example, if production increases, emissions will increase. As long as the approved technology is still being used there is little that can be done about this unless there is a separately stipulated emissions ceiling. What counts as the best available technology is also a matter of dispute; and even where it is not, it may be extremely expensive for some companies to install the best technology available. Requiring them to do so might simply put them out of business – although this may sometimes be the right thing to do. Hence, regulatory systems have evolved in countries such as the UK and Australia in which firms seeking authorisation for their manufacturing processes are required to install the best available technology not entailing excessive cost (BATNEEC) or the best practicable method (BPM). In addition, where discharge is to more than one environmental medium, authorisation of the industrial process concerned is subject to the condition that it meets the requirement of best practicable environmental option (BPEO).[1] This requires a lot of expensive, labour-intensive and time-consuming negotiation between the regulator and the regulated and there is also a danger of compromise. Inspectors and companies will inevitably find themselves in protracted discussion about what constitutes 'excessive cost' and what the 'best available technology' is at any given time. BATNEEC attempts to match the cut in pollution required of each firm to its cost structure. However, given an understandable reluctance on the part of inspectors to close down a firm which cannot afford to install the best available technology, there is a danger that companies will continue to use inferior technology on grounds of cost and hence to continue polluting at too high a level. A stringent uniform quantitative approach, such as that typical of Germany and increasingly advocated by the European Union, avoids this problem, but perhaps at the expense of a loss of flexibility in responding to individual companies' needs and to the peculiarities of a local environment.

The use of regulations is in many ways straightforward and uncomplicated; it is readily understood by governments and by the public. But, as Jacobs argues, for it to work effectively certain conditions have to be met:

> To the firm or consumer, regulations offer no legal choice. Pollution or resource use above the consented level or through use of unsanctioned technology ... is simply forbidden. The cost of non-compliance is judicial punishment: a fine or sometimes imprisonment. This means that enforcement and punishment are crucial. When enforcement is difficult, or where the level of punishment is too low, the environmental target may not be achieved.
>
> (Jacobs, 1991, p. 136)

There are some advantages to command and control, especially where a pollutant or a process requires an outright ban. In the case of some pollutants, for example heavy metals, the only acceptable level of emission is zero. If a monitoring regime and appropriate deterrents are in place, simple prohibition through regulation is a sound option. Further, it is possible to act quickly: the regulator can step in and ban or reduce an emission where serious environmental damage is occurring or likely to occur. Other means of doing this may be subject to appreciable time lags. The disadvantages are, however, well documented. Command and control, if it is to be fully comprehensive, requires an enormous amount of knowledge on the part of the regulator of the activities concerned. It is thus time-consuming and expensive. Since firms know what their productive activities entail, it may be better to set up a system in which they establish self-monitoring processes and are given incentives to reduce their polluting activities and then left to choose the best method of doing so. As we have already mentioned, command and control provides no incentive for firms to do better than the standard. Thus it is poor at reducing polluting activity below a fixed level, and in some cases it may allow increases as long as the appropriate technology is being employed. Further, under a regime such as in the UK, a flexible and responsive arrangement between regulator and regulated can degenerate into a cosy relationship whereby the regulator is 'captured' by those it is regulating. A regulator is said to be captured when the relationship with the industry being regulated becomes too close. This may be revealed by a circulation of personnel between the two, together with too great a willingness to listen sympathetically to the regulated industry at the expense of the public interest, consumers or the environment. Ultimately it leads to a bias in favour of the regulated industry characterised by an acceptance of its terms and agenda.

Given these problems with command and control regulation, might there not be other solutions which are both more flexible and more likely to achieve the desired ends? Moran argues that there are:

> The command and control solution, in opting for particular means of abatement, faces an impossible task of achieving abatement efficiently. Firms have a vast number of options in terms of their abatement equipment, its maintenance, the inputs they use and the quantity, quality and mix of their outputs. With direct controls, the regulatory authority needs to know the technological and other adjustment alternatives open to individual emitting firms in order to specify individual emission levels and technologies. Far less information is required for the implementation of taxes or marketable permits because individual emitters make their own decisions about output and emissions.
>
> (Moran, 1995, p. 77)

It is to such taxes and permits that we now turn.

ECONOMIC INSTRUMENTS

Command and control systems have their merits, but a key disadvantage is simply that they punish transgressors for doing wrong where what is needed in environmental policy is to encourage potential polluters to do right. One way of doing this is to establish a system within which polluters have an incentive not only to avoid polluting but also to reduce their polluting activities and in so doing gain a fiscal advantage. There are two main sources of inefficiency in the command and control approach. First, it requires the regulator to use resources in acquiring information the polluter already possesses. Second, polluters vary in the extent to which they can abate pollution. Under command and control each polluter has to meet a given standard or use a particular technology. However, some polluters find it easier or cheaper than others to reduce their polluting activities. Perhaps, then, control should be concentrated on where it is cheapest to abate pollution because then the overall costs of compliance would be minimised. Economic incentives enable a polluter to choose how to adjust to the required environmental standard. Some will prefer to pay while others will prefer to install new or modified equipment. Hence there is an incentive, not found under a direct regulatory system, to reduce levels of pollution.

Recalling the economic view of the person discussed in the previous two chapters, we could conceive of firms as self-interested rational utility maximisers. Whether the motives and behaviour of individual people are best understood in this way or not, there is little doubt that the description fits profit-making companies accurately and that, at least some of the time, it is an accurate description of people's behaviour. If this is a fair assumption, would it not be possible to recognise and possibly utilise such self-interested behaviour in the formulation of environmental policy? In Chapter 4 we saw that collective action problems arise out of the aggregation of the actions of rational self-interested actors where there is an incentive to free ride, and that it leads to an outcome which is the worst outcome for all. But must the outcome of self-interested actions necessarily be for the worst? Economists argue that the operation of the market provides a mechanism which harnesses individually self-interested actions to the good of all. In economic theory a properly working free market should produce an outcome which, although not intended by any single company or person (each of whom is assumed to behave according to their own self-interest), is nevertheless to everyone's advantage. Thus, through the operation of 'the invisible hand', self-interested individual actions lead to a collective outcome of benefit to all. It is the possibility of utilising self-interested behaviour in this way which lies behind proposals for the use of economic instruments in environmental policy. Intervention in the market is required to adjust the overall structure of incentives and disincentives and thereby modify the behaviour of producers and consumers in ways which benefit the environment.

But modifying the market in this way has a further objective. The use of economic instruments is not only concerned with providing internal incentives to polluters and resource users to reduce their emissions or to reduce their inputs. It also seeks to internalise the external costs of pollution and resource depletion. As we saw in Chapter 5, the prices of goods bought and sold in markets prior to this form of intervention tend not to include the environmental costs of production, consumption and disposal. These costs are known as 'externalities': they are external consequences of the activities of producers and consumers, who do not have to pay for them or take them into account. The attempt to remedy this links these forms of economic incentive directly to the polluter-pays principle (PPP). Although it is possible, in principle, to achieve PPP through direct regulatory means (if the costs to a polluter of polluting are sufficiently high, this is equivalent to forcing them to accept responsibility for the environmental damage they cause, and to pay for it), economic incentives offer a more flexible and efficient way of achieving this end:

> The lack of proper prices for, and the open access characteristic of many environmental resources means that there is a severe risk that over exploitation leading to eventual complete destruction will occur. The PPP seeks to rectify this market failure by making polluters internalize the costs of use or degradation of environmental resources.
>
> (Turner *et al.*, 1994, p. 45)

As with so many key terms in environmental politics and economics, it is possible to interpret what PPP requires in a variety of different ways. At a minimum it can be understood as merely the requirement that polluters should pay for their excess pollution. This would be seen as granting them the right to discharge their emissions up to the acceptable level free of charge. On the other hand, a stricter interpretation would require polluters to pay for all of their discharges to the environment, not merely those deemed to be in excess of some particular limit. This stricter interpretation, if implemented, means that polluters have an economic incentive to reduce their pollution across the board. It creates the necessary conditions for the use of economic incentives in environmental policy. Providing a continuing incentive to pollute less through internalising externalities can be a rigorous way of meeting PPP. Although direct regulation can force some internalisation of external costs, the use of economic instruments can do this while at the same time offering other advantages in pollution control. Where environmental goods are regarded as free, the cost of the production of a good is a combination of priced inputs (including labour, capital and technology) and unpriced inputs (environmental services). In such a case the market price does not reflect the true value of the resources used to produce goods and services and the market fails to allocate resources efficiently because there is a divergence between private and social cost; that is, a divergence between the cost to the individual or company and the cost to wider society. Many environmental resources are regarded in this manner and are not currently represented in the price mechanism. As such they tend to be over-consumed and the environment degraded. Giving them a positive price signals that they are not free and that consumption entails a cost. It means that the environmental costs of production, consumption and waste disposal are reflected in the costs of economic goods and services. The costs of production are altered and the price level reflects the environmental impact of the goods produced and consumed. The new, environmentally sensitive price indicates to consumers the full cost of producing a product. In such a system, assuming that environmental goods can be priced properly, PPP would deter over-consumption and environmental degradation.

Most economists argue that the market-based approach is more efficient and effective than command and control. The proper price for a good is (or should be) that which reflects the full social and environmental costs of production. In a competitive market a firm will increase production until the point where it would cost as much to produce an extra unit as would be gained from selling it. Economists then say that marginal cost equals marginal revenue and at this point production stabilises as there is no advantage to be gained by producing greater quantities. However, if production does not take proper account of the full social and environmental costs, marginal cost will be too low and, because the firm will be able to maximise profit at the higher level of production, it will produce (and consumers will consume) beyond the point at which excessive environmental and social damage is caused. Here the firm has not internalised the external cost of production. If, however, the firm is forced to include these external costs of its production process, overall costs will rise, prices will rise and demand will fall. The firm will therefore produce less and reduce its use of resources and its level of polluting emissions. Of course, matters are never quite so simple in reality. For some goods (typically necessities such as bread or fuel) consumers cannot easily find acceptable substitutes or reduce their consumption and will therefore tend to continue to buy them despite price rises. Demand will vary little with price. Economists describe goods of this type as 'price-inelastic'. In these cases the firm will be able to pass on increased costs to the consumer. Thus, if we are considering imposing a tax, the impact that it will have will depend on the type of goods concerned. In principle, however, the environment should benefit either way. On the one hand, if production falls, emissions and resource use fall with it; on the other, if production remains high, the higher level of tax revenues can be used to remedy environmental damage or to engage in research on improving the environmental impact of manufacturing processes.[2]

PPP states that the polluter should pay: but who is the polluter? Is it the company or is it the consumer? We perhaps have an image of firms producing goods while remaining complacently indifferent to the pollution caused, and we think they should be punished. However, as we have already seen, companies which face increased costs may in some cases simply pass on those extra costs to the consumer. In this case the phrase 'making the polluter pay' equates to 'making the consumer pay'. Is this fair? Are the public the innocent victims of a double bind in which they suffer at the hands of the polluter and are also asked to pay for the cost of putting matters right? Before we conclude that PPP is a capitalist fraud we need to look at the issue a little closer. Who is the polluter? Who should pay? There are a number of important considerations here.

Is there a valid objection to consumers paying higher prices for environmentally damaging products? Presumably the goods concerned are produced because there is consumer demand. But up to this point they have not been paying the proper price, which reflects the full environmental cost. Why should they escape their share of the extra cost? Both the producer and the consumer are 'the polluter'. Our overall pattern of consumption has a detrimental environmental effect. It would be hypocrisy to blame a firm as if it operated utterly independent of consumer demand. We are all to some extent complicit in the environmental degradation caused by the production of the goods and services we demand. However, despite these strictures, it should be remembered that existing markets do not function perfectly and that consumers have little or no knowledge or control over the processes and raw materials that firms employ. If they were fully informed about all aspects of production they might disapprove of, and object to, much that companies do. In practice, however, information is often limited, and even where it is available, consumers may be powerless if alternative products do not exist. Only in economists' models are consumers able to directly influence the mode and manner of production. In principle, the idea of consumers paying for environmental damage is fair, but in practice markets do not operate perfectly and the wishes of consumers tend not to influence the behaviour of companies to any great extent.

So far we have examined the basic principles lying behind the advocacy of economic instruments as an alternative to command and control and discussed their use in meeting the polluter pays principle. We now need to look at possible mechanisms in a little more detail. All economic mechanisms use markets, but some modify existing markets and others create new markets. Price-based mechanisms are so called because they affect prices in existing markets through the imposition of taxes. The incentives they provide can take different forms such as the direct alteration of price or cost levels through product charges, emissions charges or input charges; indirect alteration through financial or fiscal means such as subsidies or loans for good environmental practice; or market support where government agencies stabilise prices by, for example, guaranteeing a price for recycled paper, glass or metal. Rights-based mechanisms, on the other hand, create new markets by allocating to people or firms the right to use environmental resources in the form of quotas or permits and allowing these to be traded at a price determined by the market thus created (Beder, 1996, p. 105).

Price-based mechanisms: green taxes[3]

Support for the idea of green taxes is increasing. They are seen as a flexible and efficient alternative to traditional command and control techniques. In principle they reduce compliance costs (the costs that polluters bear in meeting the standard) and they allow polluters to choose how best to adjust to the environmental quality standard. Polluters facing high pollution abatement costs will prefer to pay the tax; those with low costs will instal equipment to avoid paying.

Taxes can be imposed in different ways and upon different things. For example, emissions charges are levied on the discharge of pollutants into the air, water or soil; user charges are related to treatment or disposal cost; product charges are levied on products that are harmful to the environment when used in production processes or when consumed. Although charges of these sort are the most commonly used economic instrument, their application has hitherto tended to be economically sub-optimal, that is, they have been set at too low a rate to achieve the environmental objectives. They have tended to be used merely as a way of raising revenue and have therefore not had a significant incentive effect (Cairncross, 1991, p. 97). However, recent proposals for green taxes require them to be more than mere revenue earners. The idea is that polluters should pay according to the estimated damage caused by their emissions and that the imposition of the tax should also change their behaviour. For example, the introduction of a landfill tax in the UK has forced local authorities to rethink their waste disposal strategies by making other processes more economically viable. But it is important to remember that green taxes should not be seen in isolation from taxation and economic policy as a whole. They can form part of a wider strategy which seeks to change the tax dynamics as a whole economy by shifting the tax burden away from taxes on income and labour. Taxes whose rationale is merely to raise revenue are becoming increasingly unpopular. They can be replaced by green taxes, which both raise revenue and have a direct positive environmental impact.[4]

From the point of view of administration, a green tax has several advantages over the traditional UK approach of quantitative emissions standards backed by low fines. The first is that they can be administered through the existing tax framework, and therefore there is a lower risk of evasion compared with fixed emissions standards policed through irregular on-site inspections. Second, taxes provide an incentive for further reductions in emissions, because reducing the amount of emissions reduces the amount of tax for which the firm is liable. Third, there is therefore an incentive to commit funds to research into new, less polluting forms of technology. Finally, taxes on one pollutant may have the related effect of reducing emissions of associated pollutants: for example, a tax on carbon emissions from fossil fuels may lead producers to switch to non-fossil fuels and thus simultaneously reduce the emissions of sulphur dioxide.

Green taxes are popular, in theory, because they enable government to intervene in the economy with the minimum of direct interference with the actions of firms or individuals. In principle the idea is simple: government sets a tax at a level which discourages people from buying environmentally unsound products. If people buy products in smaller quantities the tax has done its work; if, on the other hand, they continue to buy products in significant quantities the revenue raised can be used for environmental protection purposes. Where they work best, taxes of this sort, such as a carbon tax on fuel, succeed by significantly changing the behaviour of individuals and companies. But behaviour will only be changed if the tax is set at a sufficiently high rate. Measures such as increased taxes on road use and fuel will not measurably reduce vehicle if the alteration is only at the margins. But even marginal changes in tax provide revenue which can be used for ameliorative purposes such as environmental enhancement projects, funding emergency services and hospitals, and research and development. However, for taxes to change behaviour as well as provide welcome extra revenue they need to be set at a rate which makes the cost of motoring so high it borders on the prohibitive.

There are, however, problems with green taxes. One is that they are often regressive in impact. For example, a carbon tax levied on domestic or motor fuel has a high impact on low-income groups, whereas the better-off can afford to pay the higher costs because fuel makes up a much smaller proportion of their total income. These regressive impacts can be offset in various ways, such as through the provision of grants or aid to those directly affected by them. The point is that their regressive nature needs to be recognised and green taxes should be thought of as part of an overall shift in taxation strategy rather than as a separate solution to a separate problem. Another technical problem with setting a tax is that it is intrinsically difficult to set it at precisely that level at which people are sufficiently discouraged from using that product to have the desired environmental effect.[5] If it is set too low the environment will suffer; if it is set too high people and industry will protest. The problem is that one is trying to achieve a certain target in actual use and in order to do this one has to make a number of assumptions about elasticity of demand, about the relative value of goods and about the value of money. Taxes will need to be readjusted frequently to ensure that they maintain the same effects against a background of changing relative costs, currency fluctuations, innovations in research and development, entry into and out of an industry, and shifting patterns of consumer demand. It is possible to adjust tax rates year by year: but this is fraught with technical difficulties if the objective is to ensure consistent environmental protection, and also with political difficulties because it is highly unpopular with industry since it hinders its long-term investment plans.

Rights-based mechanisms: tradeable permits and quotas

Price-based instruments, such as taxes, rely on the workings of already existing markets and seek to achieve their objective by altering the relative prices of goods so as to influence behaviour. Rights-based responses, on the other hand, start from the view that new markets can be created or existing markets can be modified or extended. For example, markets can be created in previously free services: entrance fees to natural amenities could be charged or coastal zones could be privately owned with their owners charging for the use of waters as sewage dumps. An amenity or environmental asset which is privately owned would not be vulnerable, it is argued, to the problem of open access which we examined in Chapter 4. The owner of such an amenity has a direct financial incentive to preserve it and ensure its profitability over a period of time.[6] Other schemes establish rights to pollute or rights to exploit resources and combine this with the establishment of a market in these rights. Rights-based approaches, such as tradeable quotas and permits, start with the end to be achieved and work backwards. Industries are given the right to consume environmental resources and to trade any surplus they do not need. A market is created in the right to pollute or to consume resources: the overall level of emissions or resource use is determined in advance and the quotas or permits are left to find their own price. This avoids the need to adjust the tax rates continually and is well suited to situations in which the carrying capacity of the environment can be accurately specified and in which the optimum number of firms exists to generate a working market.

> Instead of setting a pollution target in terms of price, as a tax does, this sets it in terms of quantity. ... Under such schemes, governments set a standard in terms of, say, tons of sulphur dioxide a year. That total is then shared out among companies or power stations. Each polluter thus has a quota of gas that it can emit. If it introduces new, cleaner technology so that its emissions fall below its permitted level, it can sell its unneeded share to other polluters, or to new companies that may want to set up in the same business. Companies for whom cleaning up is relatively cheap thus have an incentive to be as clean as possible. But the dirty can also stay in business, though carrying the cost of buying more pollution credits.
>
> (Cairncross, 1991, pp. 100–1)

Those who find it expensive and difficult to reduce their pollution costs, or who want to continue using resources, will prefer to buy permits; those with low abatement costs, or who are not tied to the use of a particular resource, will be willing and able to sell their permits. Tradeable permits have a number of advantages:

they are flexible; they encourage efficiency; they do not discourage polluters from emitting at levels below the maximum permitted. Where a permit scheme is set up for air pollution, what matters is the total ambient level of pollution, not how much each individual polluter pollutes. For fisheries, what matters is whether the catch or yield is sustainable, not how much each individual boat catches. Tradeable permit schemes have been put into practice in various parts of the world, most success-fully in the USA, where a system was set up under the Clean Air Acts of the 1970s and expanded by the Clean Air Act of 1991.

Permits are seen as attractive because they avoid some of the problems associ-ated with taxes while at the same time retaining the flexibility associated with the use of economic incentives and avoiding the perceived defects of command and control. With taxes there is always the problem of the correct estimation of the tax to achieve the desired effect. Permits, on the other hand, have the advantage that they can 'guarantee the achievement of particular pollution targets, because the authorities control the number of available permits. Moreover, if permits are leased rather than sold, the authorities are able to tighten the ambient targets by cutting the number of permits available' (Jacobs, 1991, p. 142).

There is thus an incentive to benefit the environment rather than simply (as in command and control systems) a punishment for harming the environment. By starting from the premise that the target is being met (although the target can be adjusted if necessary) and allowing companies to decide for themselves how to meet their share of the target, standards can be varied to reflect the conditions of the day. The authority would then act like a central bank in buying and selling securities to influence their price (Pearce and Turner, 1990, pp. 113–14).

Tradeable permit systems have the advantage that there is no need, as there is with the imposition of environmental taxes, to ascertain both the required stand-ard and the appropriate tax rate. All that is needed is for the proper environmental standard to be identified and for permits to be distributed through a fair and acceptable procedure. The price of the permits is determined by market transac-tions and this removes the difficulty governments traditionally have in determining the appropriate price level. This is because a permit scheme starts from the conclu-sion and works backwards by setting the overall permissible levels of emissions and then allocating permits which in aggregate are equivalent to that level. Prices find their own level. Government does not therefore need to keep adjusting the tax so as to ensure that the target is being met. Permits are thus much more flexible (and in principle cheaper to administer) than command and control and often more appropriate than a system of taxes.

There are, however, two important conditions that have to be met for a permit system to work properly. First, it has to be possible to determine the permissible overall level of emissions, and this can be difficult because it requires the ability to be able to judge the carrying capacity of the affected environment. Second, it has to be possible to set up a market in which genuine trading can and will take place and where emissions can be monitored. This in itself is a strong reason for resisting the idea that permit schemes are some sort of environmental panacea. As with other approaches they should be used with caution and in an appropriate manner. There are problems both with too many permit holders in a market and with too few:

> Under a tradeable permits scheme, the administrative costs could be very high if there are a great many polluters. Where there are comparatively few, the costs of administration are low, but a new problem arises in that one or two polluters may corner the market in permits and refuse to trade them. This would act like a barrier to entry for new firms and the permits could therefore contribute to non-competitive behaviour.
>
> (Turner *et al.*, 1994, p. 187)

Thus a permits scheme is unsuitable in cases both where there is a very high number of emissions sources (for example, exhaust emissions from motor cars) and where the number of sources is so low that a few operators dominate the market. Where the appropriate conditions are not met it is better to turn to taxation, or command and control solutions.

There are also practical drawbacks to permit schemes which need to be borne in mind. For example, the unrestricted use of permits could easily lead to a situation in which a particular locality suffers excess pollution or resource use, simply because the focus is on the overall condition of the environment in a region, irrespective of localised 'hot spots'. Regulation in addition to a permit scheme may very well be necessary. As Jacobs argues:

> tradeable permits have the disadvantage that they may allow very high discharges in some places, compensated by very low emissions elsewhere. This will often be unacceptable: they therefore usually have to operate with 'backstop' regulations setting maximum discharge rates.
>
> (Jacobs, 1991, p. 142)

Although tradeable permits have (to date) mostly been employed in respect of air pollution, the principle can be extended to many different forms of pollution and also, as we have already seen, to the achieving of sustainable levels of resource extraction. Take for example, over-fishing in the world's oceans. New Zealand has introduced a system of giving fishermen quotas which they can either take up or sell. This gives them a predictable income and removes the incentive to catch as many fish as quickly as they can. It also encourages them to fish at the times when they will get the best price. This system has proved popular with fishermen themselves. By contrast, the European Union's Common Fisheries Policy is both unpopular and ineffective. Quotas are allocated each year but tend to be set by fisheries ministers at far higher levels than official scientists recommend.

In addition to the questions relating to the effective environmental and economic workings of permit schemes, there is another issue which has to be addressed, and this is how the initial allocation of permits is determined. It is not enough merely to determine the aggregate level of permitted emissions: decisions have to be made as to who is to receive the permits and why. One method is to allocate permits according to past emissions levels. This can be both inequitable and environmentally inefficient: inequitable because it is granting further pollution rights to companies in direct proportion to their previous polluting activities and inefficient unless the overall level of permits issued is for less than the current volume of emissions and the initial allocation is reduced over time. The system of allocating according to previous emissions levels is known as 'grandfathering'. The problems with this approach can be seen clearly if we look at global emissions of carbon dioxide country by country. Should we give permits to those which already are, and for many years have been, emitting large quantities of carbon dioxide? This might be objected to on the grounds both that it is rewarding those who caused the problem in the first place and that it denies to Southern nations their opportunity to achieve the higher standard of living which they see industrial nations enjoying. An alternative would be to allocate permits on the basis of population; but this is problematic in that it might be construed as an encouragement to achieve a higher birth rate. Further, it is obvious that, whatever the problems of equitable distribution of global environmental resources, we cannot afford the continued emission of carbon dioxide at anything like the levels previously achieved by the industrialised nations.[7] This theme is taken up further in Chapter 7 on international politics.

How have tradeable permits worked in practice? Not surprisingly the picture is complicated: experience has varied and the details of the schemes adopted are arcane. However, from the experience in the USA, it is possible to report that most trading has been internal, that is between the plants owned by a single company. There has been some trading between firms under the offset system, which requires new or expanding sources in 'non-attainment areas' (where air quality does not meet standards) to secure permits from existing firms so that the air is as clean (or cleaner) afterwards as before. This policy allows new industry to move into an area. Cost savings have been considerable, although it is difficult to give a precise figure – estimates range from $1 billion to $13 billion. Netting, which allows new, modified or expanding sources to emit within an established threshold so long as there is a transfer from elsewhere within the plant or firm, has also been used extensively. New sources are subject to stricter regulations than existing ones, and firms are therefore keen to adopt offsetting procedures when a new source starts up.[8]

REGULATION OR MARKET-BASED INSTRUMENTS?

Regulation and market-based instruments are often compared as though there was a closed set of options in which we have to choose either one or the other. This is seriously misleading. What we are looking for is the most appropriate policies, and this does not mean that a single policy instrument or type of policy necessarily has to dominate. An appropriate response is far more likely to require a mix of policy styles, each component being that best suited to achieving a given end in a certain set of circumstances. However, to determine which policy approach is appropriate to which circumstances, it is necessary to compare and contrast them with a keen eye to their merits and weaknesses. In comparing their merits it is vital to make genuine comparisons. This is not always done. Thus, for example, the proper comparison is not that between the pollution abatement secured by economic instruments and zero pollution (as though regulation achieved that), but between a specific economic instrument and what command and control achieves in practice. Again, it is important to compare command and control in practice with the practice of economic instruments rather than their theory. There is a tendency to compare practice in the one with theory in the other and this is seriously misleading. In addition, given the variety of policy approaches, it is also important to distinguish between the relative merits of different types falling under the broad headings of 'regulation', 'command and control', 'economic instruments' and 'market-based instruments'.

To takes some examples. With a tradeable permits scheme, it is hard to attain reductions in emissions levels by reducing the number of permits in the system. If this is done the incentive to trade is lessened. In practice a tax might be better. Again, where there are a large number of polluters a permit system is inoperable as the conditions for effective trading and monitoring do not exist. A tax is likely to be the best solution where there are a large number of purchasers, each relatively insignificant compared with the whole; a permit system is the best solution where there are enough relatively large operators to allow a market to operate but not so many as to make monitoring impossible. It follows that sensible policy in respect of the environment will therefore rely not on one or other mechanism to the exclusion of all others, but on a mixture depending on the conditions facing it. And the choice, it should be remembered, is not simply between types of economic instrument; it is also between economic instruments and other forms of regulation and control. For example, where the target for a damaging emission is zero only legal prohibition backed by strong sanctions can ensure that it will be met. Merely taxing heavy metals such as cadmium, for instance, would allow some level of pollution, however low – and this is unacceptable. In other cases, where the environment can absorb a certain level of pollution or resources use, a method based on economic incentives might be suitable.

Because economic instruments are typically advocated by economists who have a high regard for the operations of the free market, it is sometimes assumed that their introduction eliminates the need for government monitoring and intervention. This is false.

> A tradeable permit system does not do away with the need for accompanying regulatory activity. In particular, somebody would have to oversee the trades and make sure that emissions were being kept within specified limits.
>
> (DoE, 1990, Annex A, A24)

This applies equally to green taxes. Even though the intervention is relatively indirect, it is still there, and governments have to set the tax rates, ensure their collection and arrange for monitoring. So the use of economic instruments does not offer a miraculous escape from government regulation, it merely alters its character and in practice permits and taxes would seldom, if ever, be used as the sole instruments of policy. There will often be a need to bolster the use of economic instruments with 'backstop' command and control measures to act as security against excess or abuse. There are limits to the carrying capacity of a local environment such that, even though a firm might be operating within its overall emissions ceiling, a heavy or sudden discharge might be environmentally deleterious and thus require government-backed sanctions to prevent its occurrence. In such cases green taxes alone are not appropriate. As Cairncross contends:

> They work best when the market works best. Where one dirty company has a monopoly ... it may be better to regulate it than to tax: if taxed it will simply pass the whole bill to the consumer and stay dirty. Green taxes may also be less helpful than regulation when what matters is the concentration of filth: when a river can tolerate a given concentration of effluent through the day, say, but not a sudden flood jammed into a brief half hour. A tax per unit of muck would not discourage sudden discharges. Where what matters most is the capacity of the environment to absorb pollution, regulation may sometimes be the wisest course.
>
> (Cairncross, 1991, p. 99)

Jacobs suggests (1991, p. 152) that there are six criteria which should be employed in comparing different methods. These are outlined below.

1   *Effectiveness.* Each method can be effective if used appropriately. However, it is worth noting that if the goal is to reduce a damaging activity quickly, it is often better to use regulations as incentives take time to introduce and to become effective.
2   *Motivation.* Taxes and permits provide a motive to constantly improve environmental performance; command and control does not.
3   *Administrative cost.* Command and control tends to have high administrative costs; taxes and permits generally reduce these costs.
4   *Efficiency.* The efficiency of each type of measure is a function of effectiveness, motivation and cost: the method which maximises effectiveness whilst minimising costs and providing a motive to avoid environmentally harmful acts in each particular sphere is the one which should be chosen.
5   *Political acceptability.* Some solutions might be theoretically sound but hard to implement because they are, for example, seen as 'giving a licence to pollute'. Irrespective of the truth of this claim, or the claimed effectiveness of the policy, political sensitivities might lead to a reluctance to employ certain approaches.
6   *Distributional impact.* Methods affect different groups differentially. For example, taxes tend to be regressive in that they have a greater impact on the poor. Thus they might be politically or morally sensitive and best avoided in

some cases, or, where they are deemed appropriate, they may require additional measures to be taken to offset the impact on those most affected by them.

CONCLUSION

This chapter has taken a broad look at the variety of policy options available in dealing with environmental problems. We have seen that there are many considerations which have to be taken into account, ranging from political acceptability to technical efficiency. There is no single approach or policy which will work best for all occasions or will solve every possible problem, and we should be suspicious of anyone who says that there is. And there are also wider considerations. Environmental policy does not exist in a vacuum unrelated to other welfare and policy issues. For example, consideration of different types of policy instrument provides an opportunity to examine not only the immediate impact or effectiveness of a particular policy but also to refocus the economy and the tax system. To properly evaluate the merits and demerits of different policy approaches it is necessary to take a comprehensive view which incorporates the relevant dimensions both of the problem to be addressed and of proposed solutions. Table 6.1 summarises some of these dimensions.

Table 6.1 Regulation versus economic instruments

Regulations	*Economic instruments*
Advantages	
Objectives and means are determined independently of market forces and economic factors.	Allow each polluter to choose the most efficient way of reducing pollution.
Best means of preventing irreversible damage or unacceptable levels of pollution.	Provide an incentive to continue reducing pollution.
They are widely understood.	Minimise the cost of achieving pollution reductions.
	Provide finance for the restoration of damage.
	Taxes may be more effective where consumers' behaviour needs to be controlled.
Disadvantages	
May not be the most cost-effective way of ensuring that standards are met.	Depend on trial and error to set tax/charge at the right level.
Provide no incentive for polluters to do better than the standard.	Initial allocation of permits difficult to set.
Difficult to administer, and enforcement depends on resources available to the regulatory authority.	Limited applicability to more than one pollutant.
	Work well only in certain well-defined circumstances.
	Give a 'licence to pollute'.

Source: Adapted from Beder, 1996, p. 119; Turner *et al.*, 1994, pp. 161–63.

CASE STUDY: POLICY INSTRUMENTS

As a way of considering the respective merits of the different policy means and instruments available, and how they might each be best suited to different purposes, we shall focus on two policy areas: global warming and pollution and traffic congestion. These examples also show how different policies and approaches might complement one another .

Global warming

Global warming results from emissions of carbon dioxide from the burning of fossil fuels in industrial plant and motor vehicle use, from CFCs (which are both ozone-depleting gases and powerful greenhouse gases) and from methane from the agricultural sector. It raises questions of individual responsibility. For example, cars produce up to four tons of carbon dioxide per annum, and fossil fuels are burned to produce domestic heating. It raises questions of corporate responsibility: industrial processes produce vast quantities of carbon dioxide. And it also raises questions of governmental responsibility. It generates collective action problems in relation to the actions of individuals, companies and governments and it also raises issues of equity and global distribution. If growth and industrialisation are to be limited in the future, is it fair that the South loses out on the benefits that the industrialised nations have gained? Might it not be fairer for the industrialised world to take on the burden of reduction?[9]

Bans

For an industrialised country it is impracticable to consider banning most greenhouse gases. Some, such as CFCs, have been banned for different reasons; but an outright ban on carbon dioxide or methane emissions is impossible. However, some activities could be banned: for example, the use of private cars in particular areas or certain highly polluting industrial processes.

Restructuring the energy market

If the aim of energy policy is to reduce the production of carbon dioxide, it makes sense to move away from fossil fuels and towards solar energy, wind power and even nuclear energy.[10] It also makes sense to encourage a switch away from fuels with a high carbon content – for instance, through burning natural gas instead of coal. Clearly the most environmentally beneficial response is to reduce fuel consumption, and to look towards greater energy efficiency. By introducing different tax regimes and regulations it is possible to set up energy markets so that the promotion of fuel efficiency is more profitable for energy producers and suppliers than increasing capacity and building new plant. Two methods available for altering the market are the introduction of a requirement to generate energy from renewable resources and a carbon tax.

The non-fossil fuel obligation

Energy providers could be required by law to produce a certain percentage of energy from renewable or non-fossil fuel sources. The production of renewable energy is at present far more expensive than conventional processes. It requires intervention of this sort to create market opportunities for more environmentally sound energy production.

Carbon taxes

A tax on carbon dioxide emitting activity would alter consumer behaviour by increasing the price of fuels or processes emitting carbon dioxide. A genuine carbon tax would be graded according to relative carbon content. The drawback is that such a tax is likely to be regressive in that it will hit the poor, for whom fuel comprises a relatively high proportion of their disposable income, more than it will hit the rich. This has political implications although the effects can to some extent be ameliorated by combining a tax with other policy measures such as grants for improved domestic insulation and fuel efficiency.

Permits

For industrial users it might be possible to introduce carbon dioxide emissions quotas to encourage reductions through incentives and trading. Globally countries could be given carbon dioxide emissions quotas and then left to determine the best means of achieving them. As discussed in this chapter, there would be serious problems with the initial allocation of quotas.

Traffic congestion and pollution in cities

Road transport is a significant source of air pollution, in the UK producing 89 per cent of the carbon monoxide, 51 per cent of the nitrogen oxides, 36 per cent of the volatile organic compounds and 42 per cent of the black smoke in the air we breathe. It is also the most rapidly growing source of the greenhouse gas carbon dioxide – around 20 per cent and rising. Private and commercial vehicle usage is particularly a problem in urban areas, where emissions contribute to ill health, particularly breathing problems among children and the elderly, as well as the corrosion of buildings and vegetation. Exhaust fumes are particularly concentrated in towns and cities, where the volume of motor vehicles is high and where traffic speeds are low because of congestion. Slow or non-moving vehicles release higher levels of emissions than vehicles running relatively efficiently at optimum speeds. Finally, the cost of road accidents is high, not only in personal terms, but also in social terms – the cost of emergency services and hospital treatment is increasing. The increased use of cars has meant that many people no longer feel safe and find cities unappealing.

Bans

Motor cars can simply be banned from town centres with access allowed only for deliveries and other specified uses. Traffic congestion can also be reduced by stipulating that private cars are allowed access to city centres only on alternate days. A simple way of doing this is to allow access one day to cars with even-numbered licence plates and the next day to those with odd-numbered plates. In principle this encourages people to look for and demand alternative means of transport. However, in practice it may be less effective as many people already have two cars, and in some cases they purchase another car with different number plates in order to bypass the system.

Pedestrianisation

This is a good way of freeing up city centres to pedestrians, who are no longer hampered by congested and dangerous roads. Shop keepers sometimes complain that pedestrianisation reduces their trade, but the evidence indicates that perhaps the contrary is the case. Trade can increase as people find it more pleasant to shop without traffic-induced hassle.

Charges

Charges can be levied on access to city centres, thus restricting entry to those prepared to pay for it. One drawback is that this solution is regressive in that the rich will probably be prepared to pay the charge and continue to drive into city centres. However, it does raise revenue that can be ploughed back into developing alternative means of transport.

Public transport

Even when a quarter full, a bus is more than twice as fuel-efficient as a family car. It is also safer – the risk of being killed or seriously hurt while travelling on public transport is about thirteen times less than in a car. Buses and trains can efficiently convey proportionately many more people than cars. Given that cars are rarely filled to capacity the disparity is even greater. Hence moves towards the greater use of buses, trams and trains could significantly reduce city centre road traffic. Enhanced public transport would include regular and frequent bus services combined with park-and-ride schemes; trams or light rail systems; and a efficient train service. Such provisions will not in themselves free city centres from all committed car users. Good public transport together with positive discouragement of the private car is probably required for a successful overall policy.

Bus lanes

Bus lanes give priority to buses and thereby allow them to run efficiently and on time. It thus enhances the bus service by ensuring reliability and it sends a signal to those in cars that they could reach their destination quicker by switching modes of transport.

Cycle lanes

Cyclists find town centres unpleasant and dangerous because of cars and their exhaust emissions. The provision of cycle lanes helps switch priority away from motor vehicles, although cycling will remain unpopular unless car use is also reduced.

Traffic lights

Experiments have been conducted in which cars are kept waiting at traffic lights while the lights give priority to bicycles, buses and pedestrians. This is a reversal of the traditional approach, which has always tended to give priority to road users. The idea is simple: it is to make city centres as difficult for motorists as they have always been for pedestrians and cyclists. Motorists may still use the city centre, but the price of doing so is considerable inconvenience.

Conclusion

The example of global warming shows that a mixture of policy instruments is necessary if energy provision and usage is to be dramatically changed to reduce carbon dioxide emission. The whole structure of the energy market needs to be reconsidered. A mixture of bans, incentives and new tax regimes ought to be promoted. The problem of urban traffic congestion and air pollution requires a similar 'package' approach, combining a number of different elements aimed at encouraging people out of their cars and on to public transport, bicycles and their feet. We should not dogmatically insist on using only one type of policy instrument. Rather we must be pragmatic in searching for the most appropriate means of solving the problems we face.

SUGGESTIONS FOR FURTHER READING

For a collection of essays on the relative merits of different policy approaches, see Robyn Eckersley (ed.), *Markets, the State and the Environment* (1995a). Stephen Tindale and Gerald Holtham develop an accessible argument in favour of reorientating the tax system to protect the environment in *Green Tax Reform* (1996). Albert Weale's *The New Politics of Pollution* (1992) considers pollution control policy options within the framework of ecological modernisation.

Part III

Environmental policy: global to local

7 International dimensions

Can a fragmented and often highly conflictual political system made up of over 170 sovereign states and numerous other actors achieve the high (and historically unprecedented) levels of cooperation and policy coordination needed to manage environmental problems on a global scale?

(Hurrell and Kingsbury, 1992, p. 1)

Since the early 1970s there has been a growing recognition that many environmental problems, in particular those of a transboundary nature, could not be successfully tackled solely at the national level. A nation state can no longer act alone to solve many of the environmental problems that it faces. States have responded by creating international 'regimes' in an attempt to tackle problems ranging from ozone depletion and global warming to biodiversity loss and toxic waste export. A regime is typically defined as a set of 'implicit or explicit principles, norms, rules and decision-making procedures around which actors' expectations converge in a given area of international relations' (Krasner, 1983, p. 2).[1] However, some regimes are stronger than others and one of the aims of this chapter is to analyse why that should be so. For example, the ozone-depletion regime is taken to be one of the most effective, with the 1990 amendment to the Montreal Protocol requiring the phasing out of CFCs and other ozone-depleting chemicals by 2000. By comparison, the forestry regime is only held together by a weak set of principles agreed in 1992 at the Rio Earth Summit. In the development of regimes difficulties arise from all sorts of directions. These include the basic definition of the environmental problem; disagreements over scientific and economic impacts; the actions of states which are willing to veto agreements that appear to conflict with their perceived interests; the vagueness of commitments and soft obligations embodied in many agreements; and problems with implementation and compliance. It is simply not possible to discuss here the development of each environmental regime and all the different factors alluded to above.[2] Instead, the chapter will initially look at two factors which seem to militate against the creation of effective environmental regimes: the nature of the international political and economic systems. Sovereignty and the logic of capital accumulation are often seen as inimical to the development of adequate responses to global environmental problems.

However, there have been over sixty multilateral environmental treaties signed in the last three decades and, in some areas, regimes are proving to be effective. To begin to understand why this might be the case it is necessary to focus on the activities of two different types of international actors and the role they play in global environmental politics: international organisations (IOs) such as the United Nations Environment Programme (UNEP) and international non-governmental organisations (NGOs). In seeking to understand the nature of international environmental politics, it is not enough to simply focus on the actions of states and the multilateral agreements they sign.

In the final section of this chapter, the discussion will turn from the generation of regimes in response to isolated environmental problems to the international response to sustainable development. The growing recognition that patterns of development and environmental degradation are linked achieved its greatest political expression to date at the United Nations Conference on Environment and Development (UNCED), held in Rio in June 1992. The genesis of the 'Earth Summit' can be located in two earlier events. The first is the United Nation Conference on the Human Environment held in Stockholm in 1972, where the global nature of environmental degradation achieved initial recognition. The second is the publication in 1987 of *Our Common Future*, the report of the World Commission on Environment and Development (the Brundtland Report) (WCED, 1987), which capitalised on the political space created as the Cold War came to an end. The principles and implications of sustainable development can challenge the very structures of the global political and economic systems far more than the environmental regimes developing in response to separate problems. It is not surprising, then, that the agreements produced at Rio fell far short of what many environmentalists desired. It is a hotly debated question as to whether the Earth Summit can be described as a success and it is with an analysis of the outcomes of UNCED that this chapter will end. What is clear is that environmental politics and the principles of sustainable development challenge some of the fundamental assumptions of international relations.

THE INTERNATIONAL POLITICAL AND ECONOMIC SYSTEMS

The international politics of the environment is marked by a series of related conflicts and tensions between Northern and Southern nations around issues such as the nature of the global economy, population and resource consumption and the significance of sovereignty. These disagreements in many ways structure the debates during the creation and evolution of regimes and will be continuing themes that resurface throughout this chapter. The manner in which environmental problems are understood has implications for questions of responsibility and international justice.

One of the fundamental disputes surrounds the nature of the economic system. Typically, Northern nations which benefit from existing economic arrangements tend to conceive of environmental problems as separate from the nature of economic relations. Environmental problems are viewed as technical issues which can be tackled without altering the structures of the global economic system; without challenging free-market principles and the logic of capital accumulation. For most Southern states economic reform is taken as essential, but typically the language of capital accumulation is not challenged. Rather, trade rules need to be restructured so that the South can enjoy the development opportunities that the North has achieved. States in the North and the South share the view that economic growth and environmental protection are reconcilable, that is, they both share a conception of sustainable development as ecological modernisation (Weale, 1992). For many greens such analyses are flawed in that the global environment cannot sustain ever-increasing economic development. In their view both the North and the South will have to radically restructure their economies, with the North reducing its levels of consumption and the South developing in a manner which is both sustainable and provides for the needs of its populations. Greens are also aware that the focus on national development and the North–South dynamic of much of the international debate fails to acknowledge the effect of Western-style development on local communities and traditional practices and forms of knowledge. The discourse of ecological modernisation is often charged with being a discourse that supports the interests of political and economic elites in both the North and the South, with little regard for other communities. An adequate response to environmental problems means a radical reappraisal of what is understood by 'development'.

A related area of contention is the relative impact on the global environment of resource consumption and increasing population levels. Northern countries tend to emphasise the increase in sheer numbers in the South, pointing to the impact that existing levels have on resources and asking what the global effect of an increased population might be. The world's population stands at just over 5.7 billion and although earlier estimates that it will double by 2050 have recently been brought into question, levels in the South are still increasing, putting further pressure on resources (Brown *et al.*, 1996, p. 88). Projections of increased population growth have fuelled recent resurgences in neo-Malthusian theories, many influenced by the Club of Rome's *The Limits to Growth* (see Chapter 2). Concerns are frequently aired as to the pressures that such numbers will have on resources such as agricultural land, water supplies and the like. Organisations such as the World Health Organisation argue that the sheer pressure of numbers leads to millions of deaths each year 'largely owing to their own contamination of water, soil and air' (Thomas 1993, p. 22). However, studies of the impact of sheer numbers on natural resources are often seen by Southern states as an attempt to deflect attention away from the North's consumption rates and its responsibility for the creation of many contemporary environmental problems. Take for example the issue of use of fossil fuels: 'There are great disparities in fossil carbon per capita emissions. The US emits approximately 5.7 tonnes of carbon per person per year, while India (for example) emits approximately 0.4 tonnes' (Paterson, 1996, p. 14). In a similar manner, Richard Falk highlights the fact that 85 per cent of the world's income is enjoyed by only 23 per cent of the world's population living in the North, whereas the other 77 per cent of the population in the South is left with only 23 per cent of the wealth (Falk, 1995, pp. 57–8).[3] Focusing on the question of consumption levels emphasises the role that the North has played and is still playing in global environmental degradation.

A final area of conflict is over the issue of sovereignty. For example, Southern states view population issues as a matter of domestic concern and see attempts by Northern countries to establish demographic regimes as attempts to override their sovereignty. Equally, they see pressure put on them to stem their development and to take the environment into account as further attempts to undermine their sovereignty; a form of 'ecocolonialism' (Salih, 1997, p. 124ff). Environmental concern is taken to be an obstacle erected to halt development in the South. One of the reasons that the regime on forests is so weak is that there is a fundamental disagreement as to the status of tropical forests. Attempts to view forests as global commons or the 'common heritage of mankind' are seen by many Southern nations as legitimising the North's right to interfere with their management of their own resources. A similar disagreement can be seen over the issue of biodiversity. It is with this question of sovereignty that we begin our analysis of the international political system.

Sovereignty and the international political system

Sovereignty is at the heart of what can be termed the 'settled norms' of the contemporary international order: 'national self-determination, non-aggression and respect for international law combined with support for the principles of sovereignty' (Brown, 1997, p. 31). Take, for example, the second principle of the Rio Declaration (emphasis added):

> States have, in accordance with the Charter of the United Nations and the principles of international law, *the sovereign right to exploit their own resources pursuant to their own environmental and developmental policies*, and the responsibility to ensure that activities within their jurisdiction or control do not cause damage to the environment of other States or of areas beyond the limits of jurisdiction.

As has already been intimated, environmental problems can be seen as a challenge to this principle of sovereignty, particularly as it embodies the idea of complete dominion over the resources within a state's territory rather than the idea of stewardship so central to green thinking (see Chapter 1). However, Southern states are far from happy with any weakening of the principle given that they see this as an attempt by Northern nations to control their development patterns.

The idea of sovereignty is central to much international relations theory, as is the state of anarchy that is said to exist at the international level – there is no formal system of government or authority above the level of the state.[4] The state is taken to have sovereign authority over its territory and its legitimacy rests on its ability to achieve internal and external security and to provide for the well-being of its citizens. How then are states with apparently divergent interests expected to cooperate in a manner that is effective in responding to international environmental problems? Typically, the development of international environmental regimes is taken to provide an excellent example of the problem of collective action which we discussed in some depth in Chapter 4. The two dominant theories of international relations, neo-realism and neo-institutionalism, can be understood as competing variants on rational choice theory.[5]

Neo-realism stresses that states should be understood as self-interested egoists whose actions are determined by attempts to maximise their welfare relative to other states. Under such conditions it is no surprise that there is difficulty in achieving international cooperation as the actions of states are always to be interpreted as an attempt to exercise power over others; to gain an advantage over other states. We are left with collective action problems writ large – with no 'supranational' organisation that can claim authority over states, any attempt to develop environmental regimes flounders in the face of the logic of the 'tragedy of the commons' – free riding and non-cooperation would be rife. However, international cooperation does occur and needs to be explained.

Neo-liberal institutionalists argue that it is possible to overcome such collective action problems and to develop stable regimes. The basic realist assumptions of international anarchy and rational egoism are accepted, but it is argued that particularly strong states – hegemons – are willing to accept the costs of establishing regimes. Such hegemonic states recognise that it is in their own interests that cooperation occurs, their interests being defined in terms of absolute improvements in the state's welfare rather than improvements relative to other states. Typically, the hegemonic power on the international stage has been taken to be the United States and this goes some way to explaining why environmental problems have been cast in language that does not bring into question free-market assumptions and why the environmental problems seen as affecting the interests of the Northern, more industrialised nations have been the most effectively tackled. However, in the environmental arena, the USA appears to be a declining influence as a hegemon. Whether this is because of a lack of willingness or ability (read power) on the part of the USA is not always clear. However, as Porter and Brown argue:

> When the United States has taken the lead, as it did in the Montreal Protocol on ozone depletion, whaling, or the African elephant, the result has been a stronger regime than would otherwise have been established. But when it has been a veto state, as in the sulfur dioxide protocol to the acid rain convention, the hazardous waste trade convention, and the climate convention, the result has been a significantly weaker regime.
>
> (Porter and Brown, 1996, p. 106)

But, liberal institutionalists argue that even with the decline of a hegemon, cooperation can still occur, although normally at a sub-optimal level: formalised agreements and an environment that affords the possibility of the exchange of

knowledge and information increase the likelihood of stable regimes. Cooperation is fostered through the development of institutions; sets of norms which guide
behaviour and provide an incentive for states to cooperate.

The analysis of international politics as the politics of collective action does
offer certain insights into some of the problems facing the development of international environmental regimes. However, the basic assumptions of such an analysis
are somewhat limited, specifically the accounts of sovereignty and international
anarchy. With respect to sovereignty, it is important to recognise that the term can
be understood in different ways. Perhaps the most important differentiation here is
between the understanding of sovereignty as a judicial status and as a political
concept (Brown, 1997, pp. 125–7). The identification of the state system as one of
'anarchy' implies that under international law, states have judicial sovereignty. This
is unqualified – there is no legal authority above the state. However, the second
aspect of sovereignty, understood as a political concept, is far from unqualified.
The political understanding of sovereignty highlights the fact that states have differential powers and capacities. What follows from this?

First, for states to retain their legitimacy in terms of the provision of welfare for
their citizens, *to protect them from environmental degradation which reduces their quality of life*,
it may be necessary for states to cooperate; to 'pool' their sovereignty and as such
increase their (collective) capacities and powers. For instance, no single state has it
in its powers to protect its citizens from the effects of hazardous ultraviolet radiation caused by the degradation of the ozone layer. Only the pooling of sovereignty,
the institutionalisation of a ban on production of CFCs, could achieve that. As
Chris Brown notes: 'The bundle of powers that a state possesses as a "sovereign"
body is thereby simultaneously diminished *and* enhanced' (ibid., p. 126) – each
state is able to protect itself from certain forms of ultraviolet radiation, but only by
giving up certain capacities in agreeing to abide by the rules of the ozone regime.
As Brown reflects, 'although the world lacks government, because states have been
unwilling to surrender their judicial status as sovereign, their attempts to rule effectively and exercise their political sovereignty have created extensive networks of
global "governance" ' (ibid., 1997, p. 128). Environmental regimes are an aspect
of these networks of governance.

Second, it is important to recognise the differing abilities of states to realise their
desired ends and to influence other states. Legal authority over a given territory
does not necessarily mean that states are immune from the actions and behaviour
of others; neither does it mean that a state will confine its power and influence
within its own borders. Reflecting on the dimensions of power discussed in Chapter 4, we can understand how states such as the USA can exercise power over other
states in a number of ways: overtly by simply threatening military action or trade
sanctions; covertly by keeping certain issues off the political agenda (non-decision
making); or perhaps even structurally in that the legitimacy of states is taken to rest
on capital accumulation. As we shall see below, the structure of the international
economy is most definitely in the interests of certain nations over others. What is
interesting about international environmental politics is that the capacity for some
Southern nations to exercise power is likely to increase as the global reach of

environmental problems is further recognised. States such as India, Brazil and China have threatened to veto agreements in areas such as ozone depletion if issues of technology transfer and financial assistance are not strengthened. More fundamentally, it is important to recognise that environmental politics can be seen as fundamentally challenging dominant understandings of sovereignty as the legitimacy of states understood in terms of capital accumulation is itself challenged. Such accumulation does not necessarily defend citizens from the harms of global environmental degradation.

The collective action assumptions of neo-realism and neo-institutionalism can be further challenged along the lines of arguments raised at the end of Chapter 4 and in Chapter 5 concerning preference and interest formation: to what extent should the preferences and interests of states be taken as given and immutable? We have already begun to suggest that stable regimes may provide the conditions for actors to exchange information and understandings of environmental problems. As such, social learning is promoted. We must be alive to the way in which preferences and interests are formed. Preferences and interests are not simply given, but can be transformed. Environmental regimes and forms of governance need therefore to attend to the process of formation of preferences. Stable regimes can promote trust, mutual learning and the transformation of preferences when states are exposed to alternative interpretations of environmental problems, and can pool their knowledge and information. It is thus necessary to begin to look beyond the actions of states alone and to analyse the roles played by other international actors. It should not be surprising that the central focus of international relations is the actions of states, but this downplays and disregards the importance of other actors. For instance, the existence of the United Nations system, although not having any legal priority over state sovereignty, has helped to accelerate the institutionalisation of functional cooperation, particularly in the environmental arena. Here we can point to actors such as the United Nations Environment Programme (UNEP) and more recently the Commission on Sustainable Development (CSD) which have been crucial in bringing together states and creating the conditions for the development of stable expectations and relations of trust so essential for mutual understanding that underpins the development of successful regimes. Of course, not all actors have such a positive impact, and we have only to reflect on the impact of the business lobby in watering down the global climate agreements in Kyoto at the end of 1997 to see the power of 'anti-environmental' actors. These different actors will be returned to later in the chapter, but for now it is enough to recognise that the conception of international politics based on the anarchical nature of inter-state relations is too restricted. As Brown argues: 'The *anarchy problematic* ... does not simply serve the interests of rich and powerful states by legitimising certain ways of exercising power, it also sets in place a particular conception of politics which privileges *all* states' (Brown, 1997, p. 120). We must be alive to the role that other non-state actors play in the development of environmental regimes.

What is clear is that environmental politics challenges the position of certain dominant interests. In the next section we shall focus on the actors and interests in the economic arena, but to conclude this discussion of the manner in which environmental politics challenges standard notions of sovereignty it is worth returning to the question of security. National security has been seen as the fundamental concern of states, built into the very logic of the anarchical nature of the global system. It is well understood that this creates a 'security dilemma' in that increasing the military capacity to defend national security causes insecurity in other states, which then increase their own military capacity, thus ironically creating further instability in the system. This dilemma results in incredibly powerful political–military interests, particularly in the USA. Reflecting on the nature of contemporary global environmental problems offers an alternative interpretation of international security, one that challenges this allocation of resources and established interests. The end of the Cold War has opened the space for the development of new understandings of security beyond traditional military interpretations. Here the common nature of global threats is emphasised, in particular the possibility of environmental and nuclear catastrophe. This 'comprehensive' or 'common security' agenda was vociferously championed by Mikhail Gorbachev, former leader of the USSR, and Boutros Boutros-Ghali, former Secretary-General of the UN (Thomas 1993, pp. 6–9; Boutros-Ghali, 1992, Brown, 1997, pp. 231ff). The new security agenda is highly critical of global militarism and the traditional security view based almost solely on the protection of national territory. Obviously though, such a position finds strong resistance from powerful vested political–military interests. Moves by the UN to link militarism with environmental degradation have been vehemently opposed by the USA, the UK and France (Porter and Brown, 1996, p. 29). Again, though, we can see that environmental politics challenges traditional interpretations of the nature of international politics.

The global economy

The global economic system is built on neo-liberal free-market principles. The dominant capitalist economic paradigm holds that the well-being of states is increased as the sphere of free trade is increased and as such is sceptical of any environmental regulation which might inhibit the free movement of goods and services. However, just as the nature of the international political system and international security is challenged by environmental politics, so also is the dominant economic paradigm. Typically, it is those economically powerful nations that support the present structures: their political power stems in large part from their economic dominance.[6] At the same time we are witnessing the rise of powerful transnational corporations (TNCs),[7] which have become the target of much green analysis and rhetoric. The activities of these new economic actors and the nature of the economic system will provide further insights into the barriers facing the development of effective environmental regimes.

The current global economic system has its roots in the Bretton Woods Conference held in the United States in 1944. As the end of the Second World War approached, the USA and other nations, including the UK, looked towards the development of a new world economic order based on free-market principles. The Bretton Woods system was to be regulated by three institutions: the World Trade Organisation (WTO), the International Monetary Fund (IMF) and the World Bank.

The Bretton Woods institutions

The *World Trade Organisation* (*WTO*) was established only as recently as 1995 to administer global trade rules agreed in the Uruguay Round[8] – seven years of international negotiations dominated by the major economically developed nations. The new rules have increased world competition in areas such as service industries (for instance, banking and insurance), which is seen to favour highly efficient Northern industries able to capitalise on improved access to the markets of developing nations. It has been criticised by many NGOs for lacking any environmental or labour standards, although future negotiations under the auspices of the WTO may attend to such standards as well as the further lowering of trade barriers.

The *IMF* is the central organisation that deals with balance-of-payments crises. Its long-term loans to low-GDP countries are almost always conditional upon the recipient applying structural adjustment programmes (SAPs). 'SAPs include exchange rate devaluation, restraints on government spending, controls on wage increases to public and private sector workers, improved regulatory environments for private-sector economic actors, liberalisation of trade and encouragement for export-orientated economic activities' (Devlin and Yap, 1993, p. 67). SAPs do not have an environmental component and their limited government/free trade agenda is seen as exacerbating poverty and environmental degradation.

The *World Bank* provides loans to Southern states for specific development projects in such areas as agriculture, energy and transport infrastructure. In recent years, following growing pressure by NGOs, the World Bank has begun to alter its lending principles through the introduction of environmental impact assessments on all large-scale development projects. The bank is still criticised for a lack of transparency and democratic accountability and its failure to consult with local communities affected by development proposals (Thomas, 1992, pp. 79–91).

The ability of nation states to influence these global economic institutions is tied directly to economic power – unlike the UN General Assembly it is not 'one member, one vote'; rather, the boards are appointed according to the relative economic strength of states. This immediately raises questions as to their neutrality in regulation and their democratic legitimacy and accountability, a theme that appears in much green writing on international institutions. Hence there have been major disagreements recently over the location of the Global Environment Facility. Southern nations were far from happy that a fund to assist the development of environmentally sensitive practices should be located in the World Bank, an institution whose practices are seen as biased against their interests and lacking in any transparency (Paterson, 1996, p. 76).[9] The central role envisioned for the Bretton Woods institutions after the war was thrown into question in the 1970s when the international system of fixed exchange rates was abandoned. The late 1990s sees a completely different global economic climate and context and although the Bretton Woods institutions still have an important role to play, it is now also necessary to take into account the activities of TNCs and global financial markets.[10]

A question mark hangs over the Bretton Woods institutions' ability to respond to the growing recognition of links between trade, development and environmental degradation. Any changes seem to be on the periphery of the structure of the world trade system, which continues to produce unsustainable patterns of production and consumption in the North and the adoption of unsuitable development patterns in the South. The logic of free-market economics permeates the trade rules and the lending policies of these institutions. The system has provided enormous economic growth in the Northern nations, but the supposed 'trickle down' of wealth to the South has not always been apparent. Crippled by the debt crisis of the 1980s, repayment conditions and structural adjustment policies, the gap between the rich and the poor nations has grown dramatically.[11] As such, natural resources in the South have been consistently exploited to aid balance-of-payments deficits. The gap between the rich and the poor is growing: looking at incomes, the gap between the richest and poorest 20 per cent of the world's population has more than doubled in the last thirty years. It is too simplistic to say that this is just a gap between the North and the South – there are elites in the South who benefit to a great degree from the structure of the present economic system, just as there are many who suffer in the more industrialised nations. Such figures need to be treated with some caution – they do not expose the growing differentiations within the North and the South (Thomas, 1997, pp. 2–4).[12] Any discussion of global distributive justice must thus not only be seen as justice between states but also within states, hence the growing concern in green writings about the impact of the global economic system on local communities and practices.

The economic system is subject to a wide range of green criticisms and we can only hope to touch on some of these. One that we have already discussed and which takes us back to the concept of power is the differential influence that states have on the institutions that 'police' the economic system. We have already pointed out that representation of states in the Bretton Woods institutions is in proportion to economic strength. This raises a question about the 'neutrality' of these institutions in regulating the free-market system; it raises a shadow over whether the system can be understood as 'free' at all. For instance, it has been argued that the conditions of trade which are the outcome of the Uruguay Round of negotiations have been designed to open up markets in those areas where the North is most competitive and where it has most to gain; and that the WTO presides over an elaborate set of rules which protects Northern economies, while removing trade barriers in the South. For example, the South unsuccessfully opposed the inclusion of trade-related investment measures (TRIMS) and trade-related property rights (TRIPS). TRIMS open up the world's financial and insurance sectors, sensitive economic sectors where Northern companies are in a position to dominate; whereas TRIPS allow companies to take out patents on various biological materials. As Peter Wilkin argues: 'TRIPS enabled Northern transnational corporations (TNCs) to take out patents on a range of genetic, agricultural and pharmaceutical materials that have their origins in the historical practices of Southern farmers, communities, and so on. Having secured the patent, Northern-based TNCs will then be free to sell these commodities back to Southern states at profitable prices' (Wilkin, 1997, p. 30). Not surprisingly, environmentalists have seen such moves as attempts by the North to exert even more control over the South.

A further aspect of the free-trade rhetoric which greens challenge is the theory of competitive advantage upon which such trade is supposed to be based. The theory of competitive advantage basically holds that under a system of free trade it is economically more effective for nations to develop and specialise in the production of particular goods. To a certain degree, we can see such patterns of specialisation in national economies. However, critics are quick to point out two basic problems. The first challenges the underlying theory of competitive advantage, the argument being that the theory relates to a period of time when capital movements were bound to a greater extent by national borders. Deregulation and the globalisation of capital movements means that these assumptions are no longer relevant (Lang and Hines, 1993, p. 20–3; Daly and Cobb, 1990, pp. 209ff). Second, it is argued that even if we accept the basic thrust of the theory, we need to look at the kind of goods that states have specialised in. Typically, the economies of the South are based on primary products – food and raw materials. For example, the economy of Uganda is almost entirely dependent on coffee production; Nigeria on crude petroleum. It is argued that, first, the demand for such goods is limited compared with the demand for manufactured goods mainly produced in the North; and second that an economy based to such an extent on a single primary product has few defences against the vagaries of the market (Brown, 1997, pp. 189–90). Falls in commodity prices put pressure on resources and the environment as Southern states are forced to increase production and exports as they struggle to repay debt. As Porter and Brown state:

> Falling commodity prices devastated the economies of those countries that were heavily dependent on commodity exports. Between 1980 and 1991, the weighted index for thirty-three primary commodities exported by developing countries ... declined by 46 per cent. And heavy debt burdens, taken on at a time when commodity prices were high and Northern banks were freely lending dollars from Arab oil revenues, siphoned off much of the foreign exchange of many developing countries. At the beginning of the 1990s, no less than forty severely indebted countries were spending the equivalent of 30 per cent or more of their export income on debt repayments – well beyond what capital markets normally regard as the threshold of a financial crisis.
>
> (Porter and Brown, 1996, p. 109)

Tied in with criticisms of the logic of the capitalist system is the attention given to the activities of TNCs. The relative wealth of TNCs brings into question the ability of states to control world capital flows. As Thomas argues:

> Their influence is clear when we consider that the largest 500 (which incidently generate more than half the greenhouse gas produced annually) control about 70 per cent of world trade, 80 per cent of foreign investment, and 30 per cent of world GDP (about US $300 billion per annum).
>
> (Thomas 1993, p. 19)

The United Nations Conference on Trade and Development (UNCTAD) in its *World Investment Report 1995* highlights the growing influence of TNCs, with over two-thirds of global transactions in goods and services taking place either within or between TNCs. This means, as Chakravarthi Raghavan argues, 'only one-third of world trade in goods and services operates according to free-market–free-trade theories of arms-length transactions' (Raghavan 1996, p. 31), leading to an enormous potential for TNCs to manipulate markets. There is some contention as to how much control states have on the activities of TNCs and the level of political influence these firms enjoy. There is also some disagreement as to how mobile their activities actually are. In the case of raw materials such as oil, TNCs have little choice about location and there is evidence of corporations such as Shell helping to prop up the military dictatorship in Nigeria in order to access resources. In the sphere of manufacturing, by comparison, TNCs are able to be more selective about their location and have been frequently charged with locating where there is weak or non-existent environmental legislation and where the state in question is desperate for any form of investment.

The financial muscle of TNCs is clearly converted into political power: the only UN agency formally charged to investigate their activities, the United Nations Commission on Transnational Corporations (UNCTC), has recently been disbanded; at Rio, TNCs financed the Summit and were able to use their influence such that the only mention of TNCs in Agenda 21 is that they should be self-monitoring; and at the recent Kyoto negotiations on climate change the Global Climate Coalition, an industrial lobby group led by most of the major oil companies, was able to obstruct the development of more effective targets. UNCTC's final report stressed the ability of TNCs to influence and at times control the economic and social performances of many countries, but its calls for regulation went unheeded.

The 'myth' of the free market thus needs to be challenged. Industrialised nations impose protectionist measures in areas where the South is competitive to defend their economic advantage while pushing for those nations to open up their own domestic markets to international competition. The role that protectionism actually plays in the so-called free market needs to be recognised. We only have to look at the rise of the 'tiger' economies in East Asia to see the role that protectionist measures and state intervention can play in development. This runs completely counter to the rhetoric of free trade and economic liberalisation

(Thomas, 1997, p. 11). Similarly, we need to be aware that according to certain accounts of globalisation, economic liberalisation is taken as the only possible mode of development – the state has been marginalised as a major actor and can do little in the face of the power of global financial markets and movements of goods and services.[13] Greens need to be wary of such rhetoric as it acts as an apology for current distributions of production and consumption. As Wilkin rightly contends: 'The idea that all governments are necessarily powerless to control the forces of capitalism serves only to mystify and mythologise the workings of the capitalist world-system and to reify the restructuring that has taken place. As is well recognised, it is the people of the South that have suffered most severely from this global discipline' (Wilkin, 1997, pp. 24–5). The role of the state has changed in the contemporary capitalist system, but there is political space to act, to restructure the system: the question is whether states, and particularly those in the North, are willing to act to change a system that without doubt is of benefit (in economic terms) to themselves. Calls by greens for new forms of protectionism (Lang and Hines, 1993) and the restructuring of existing forms of property rights and ownership (*The Ecologist*, 1993) are a clear challenge to existing economic relations.

What should be clear from this discussion of the global economic system is that the logic of global capitalism is having a detrimental effect on those living in poverty and on the environment. But the logic is deeply ingrained. Capital accumulation is seen as the fundamental goal of the state. As Paterson contends, global capitalism operates at a deep level, 'structuring states in certain ways – in particular by making promotion of capital accumulation central to their identity, something which they cannot avoid in decisions and still maintain their legitimacy either domestically (to electorates) or internationally (with international financial institutions)' (Paterson, 1996, pp. 180–1). If global environmental concerns are to be taken seriously, the actions needed will often conflict with the accumulative logic of capitalism. Increased growth in GDP can no longer be an indicator of success. The logic of sustainable development is based on different values from capitalist models of development. Green values of self-reliance and local self-determination are in conflict with the logic of global capitalism and capital accumulation. However, although the Western model of economic development cannot be universalised – the global environment could simply not cope with the impact of such a level of industrialisation – this must not be taken as an excuse to abandon those in the South to ever more disastrous levels of poverty and environmental degradation. Global environmental politics must not become a form of protectionism that allows the North to continue to enjoy lifestyles which are based on the subjection of the South. Global justice and security demands a more effective international response. Later in the chapter we shall look at how far international politics has responded to the need to develop new patterns of sustainable development, patterns that are sensitive to the uneven development of the contemporary economic system. Before we move on to such issues, however, it is necessary to turn our attention to other international actors that have been central to the development of environmental regimes.

AGENTS OF CHANGE: INTERNATIONAL ORGANISATIONS AND NON-GOVERNMENTAL ORGANISATIONS

So far, much of our discussion of the international political and economic systems has, from an environmentalist's perspective, looked fairly bleak. The 'logics' of sovereignty and of capital accumulation would appear to structure international relations so as to ensure that environmental problems are both marginalised and ineffectively responded to. To a certain degree such a pessimistic attitude is not misplaced in that, by and large, there has been an insufficient response to contemporary environmental problems. But none the less there has been a response, as the number of treaties and agreements forged in the last two decades indicates. But given the emphasis on sovereignty and the 'settled norms' of international relations, how are we to explain the emergence of environmental regimes? As we have already intimated, the traditional 'state-centric' approaches to international relations tend to ignore or misrepresent the impact of other actors. In the discussion of the international economy, for instance, it was shown that any meaningful understanding of the system must have regard to international organisations such as the World Bank, IMF and WTO and to other actors such as TNCs. This is not to say that the role of the state is meaningless, but rather that any analysis must be tempered by a recognition that other actors besides states affect international politics. In this vein, this section will focus on two types of actors that have a central role in the development and success of environmental regimes. The first is international organisations (IOs), which facilitate the generation of environmental regimes. After a brief discussion of the roles that such organisations play, the work of one particular institution, the United Nations Environment Programme, will be highlighted.[14] The second agent of change will be taken to be international environment and development non-governmental organisations (NGOs), whose emergence and influence have been relatively recent. Both environmental IOs and NGOs have been fundamental in creating the conditions where the 'implicit or explicit principles, norms, rules and decision-making procedures around which actors' expectations converge' (Krasner, 1983, p. 2) have emerged in response to environmental problems.

International organisations

Is it possible to mitigate environmental problems without abrogating state sovereignty? ... If judging by standards of budgets and authority, intergovernmental organisations and rules are extremely weak. The impact of international institutions lies in their performance of three catalytic functions: increasing governmental concern, enhancing the contractual environment, and increasing national political and administrative capacity.

(Levy *et al.*, 1993, p. 424)

If states are going to cooperate in response to environmental problems, international organisations such as UNEP have an essential role to play in creating the conditions for that cooperation. In the first instance, they play a central function in building scientific consensus. For instance, UNEP, along with the World Meteorological Convention (WMO), was pivotal in setting up the Intergovernmental Panel on Climate Change (IPCC). The IPCC's first report produced in 1990 was essential in setting the agenda for future climate negotiations.[15] Such scientific consensus is important to provide the cognitive basis upon which political negotiations take place. A number of commentators have pointed to the emergence of 'epistemic communities' (Haas, 1989) as the basic reason why there has been collective action on particular environmental issues. The emergence of scientific consensus, a dominant interpretation of the cause of environmental degradation, is seen as a central condition for establishing effective environmental regimes.[16]

It is clear that scientific consensus can have a definite impact. Take for instance the issue of ozone depletion. In November 1987, under the Montreal Protocol, industrialised countries pledged to reduce the production of CFCs by 50 per cent by 1990. A complete ban on production had been vetoed by the EC, which claimed that there was not enough scientific evidence to warrant a total ban. Within months its opposition had crumbled with the discovery of the infamous 'ozone hole' by the British Antarctica Expedition. In the follow-up meeting in London, an agreement to completely phase out CFC production by 2000 was signed.

But it is not enough simply to produce scientific evidence, and international organisations involved in environmental regime building play an important role in creating the conditions in which states and other actors are able to develop relations of trust and to increase their knowledge of environmental problems. We have already argued that traditional models of international relations typically assume that states' interests are given and immutable. This has been challenged and international organisations can be seen as providing the conditions for states to transform their preferences and interests and to develop institutional arrangements through which resources – whether knowledge, technology or financial assistance – can be shared or transferred. This is not to say that this is in any way easy, as any analysis of technological and financial transfer would highlight, only that international organisations provide stability in negotiations such that cooperation and mutual learning is more likely. As this analysis highlights, it is as much the process and informal aspects of regime building that is important in effective responses to international environmental problems, not simply the documentation and agreements produced.

United Nations Environment Programme (UNEP)

> In two decades, UNEP has come to play an international role and exercise influence out of all proportion to the very limited means at its disposal.
>
> (Thomas, 1992, p. 38)

UNEP was established in the follow-up to the United Nations Conference on the Human Environment by the UN General Assembly on 15 December 1972. It was set up specifically to address environmental issues although not as a large-scale direct operational agency. It plays a vital role in monitoring and coordinating international action and its role is often described as that of a 'catalyst' – in almost every area of global environmental concern UNEP has played a consciousness-raising role, often cooperating with other organisations to define issues and promote conferences, research and negotiations. Returning to the issue of ozone depletion, for example, it was UNEP which was instrumental in establishing expert scientific, technological, environmental effects and economics panels (Parson, 1993, p. 47) and acting as a secretariat for the negotiations. The then Executive Director, Dr Mostafa Tolba, exploited UNEP's position to push aggressively for an effective treaty (ibid., p. 65). Much of this work in regime building goes unnoticed, but it is quite incredible how much influence UNEP has asserted when taking into account the meagre and unreliable funding it has been provided with: in comparison with UNEP's annual budget of only $60 million and a professional staff of 240, the World Bank has a staff of over 6,000, lending billions of dollars annually (Porter and Brown, 1996, p. 41).

UNEP has its headquarters in Nairobi and although this can prove isolating – the majority of UN organisations are located in Europe and North America – it has at times been useful in relations with Southern nations, which often feel removed from the agenda-setting process. Fifty-eight states have places on UNEP's principle decision-making body, the General Council, which reports through the Economic and Social Council (ECOSOC) to the UN General Assembly. Its annual budget is based mainly on voluntary donations, which can make planning very difficult. UNEP has had only four directors: Maurice Strong from Canada (1973–75),[17] Dr Mostafa Tolba from Egypt (1976–93), Elizabeth Dowdeswell, also from Canada (1993–98), and now Dr Klaus Töpfer from Germany.[18] It was the charismatic Tolba who tried to champion the causes of the South, although he was often forced to compromise his position because of the influence of the Group of Seven (G7) – the seven leading industrialised nations – whose funding is essential to UNEP's work. Although the General Council officially holds a broad holistic view of the environmental crisis, most attention has been focused on issues affecting the North such as ozone depletion, climate change and biological diversity. UNEP has attempted to raise issues such as desertification and fresh water supply, but since these problems mainly affect the South, little attention has been given to them by the Northern industrialised nations.

The work of UNEP has been widely praised, in particular in the Brundtland Report, and in the late 1980s the UN General Assembly raised the profile of UNEP. Its contemporary role, however, has become slightly ambiguous since the Rio Earth Summit and the establishment of new international organisations such as the Commission on Sustainable Development (CSD)[19] in areas where UNEP had previously taken the lead. On the positive side, the CSD has taken over the coordinating role that UNEP had played within the UN. Given its lack of funding and staff, the removal of this burdensome function should allow UNEP to target its limited resources to awareness raising, monitoring and improving its links with financially more robust organisations such as the United Nations Development Programme (UNDP). However, the loss of this responsibility and others such as the secretariat of climate change negotiations to the Intergovernmental Negotiating Committee for a Framework Convention on Climate Change (INC) may have the effect of further marginalising UNEP. With the current restructuring of the United Nations in process, the future role of UNEP is far from clear.

International non-governmental organisations

Without doubt, the part played by international NGOs has increased in the last two decades –the number of NGOs has increased significantly as has their access to, and affect on, international negotiations. The international arena offers an alternative dimension for NGOs, beyond simply lobbying national governments before negotiations. NGOs play key roles as independent bargainers and as agents of social learning (Princen and Finger, 1994, p. 217). Many NGOs have access to sophisticated information and knowledge and can claim to be an expression of citizen concern. At times this can promote radical changes in the positions of states. NGOs have a freedom to manoeuvre that states clearly do not have and play an increasingly important role in setting the international agenda.

There are a variety of NGOs with different capabilities and perspectives on environmental problems. Different organisations will have differing aims and strategies, from the more high-profile, mass-membership groups such as Greenpeace International, which could well be described as a multi-national, multi-million dollar institution, to expert think-tanks such as the World Resources Institute (WRI). Southern NGOs may not be as well financed as their Northern counterparts but play an important part in radicalising the international environmental agenda.[20]

A whole range of tactics and actions are employed by NGOs. Most people are aware of the visually stunning actions of Greenpeace activists, which are often timed to coincide with important negotiations. Again, much influence has been gained through publicity and consumer boycotts. For instance, the global CFC boycott launched by Friends of the Earth International (FoEI) helped to persuade many industries to stop the use of ozone depleters in production processes and influenced governments to support stronger agreements. Similarly the boycott of Icelandic fish products, coordinated by a coalition of environmental and animal welfare groups in 1988, helped force Iceland to halt its violation of the global moratorium on whaling (Porter and Brown, 1996, p. 79).

Perhaps the most interesting development has been the activities of NGOs at international conferences and negotiations. Often NGOs will run parallel events, which can at times generate as much interest as the official negotiations. The Global Forum in Rio was attended by some 30,000 NGO representatives; The Other Economic Summit (TOES) organised by a network of environmental and social groups accompanies the major G7 meetings. But it is the activities of NGOs within the negotiations that is changing most rapidly. NGOs have stepped up their lobbying at major conferences and preparatory negotiations and are generally afforded official observer status. Their influence has increased dramatically as NGOs such as Greenpeace and Oxfam have included scientists, economists and legal experts in their delegations. Often their research and information is much more accurate and up to date and they have been able to hold states to account over their environment and development policies and practices and also supply them with precious data that can influence the outcome of negotiations. The Commission on Sustainable Development (CSD), created in the wake of Rio, has raised the profile of NGOs further. As well as reviewing nation states' progress towards sustainable development, the Commission will also accept reports from NGOs (see case study). Again, NGOs are often deeply involved in the drafting of agreements and proposals and, as in the case of the International Tropical Timber Organisation's (ITTO) 1990 Action Plan, are 'frequently cited as key actors for implementation' (Princen and Finger, 1994, p. 5).

The increasing success of NGOs at the international level has brought with it a number of problems.[21] The first is a set of tensions that exist between the different types of organisations – they will not all have interests and aims that are in harmony. Southern NGOs are often suspicious of some of the proposals for environmental standards and regulations put forward by Northern-based NGOs, which are often viewed as further mechanisms for denying domestic industries and local economies access to world markets, hence slowing development and exacerbating poverty. Second, there are problems associated with 'cooption' – if NGOs are party to agreements they may well lose their critical edge; their ability to challenge future developments. A tension often exists between internationally focused NGOs, which are willing to engage in international negotiations, and more radical grassroots, community-based organisations. What is clear, however, is that the impact of NGOs on international politics is increasing and that they have a unique role to play in creating meaningful regimes, particularly in holding states and other international organisations to account.

RIO AND BEYOND: SUSTAINABLE DEVELOPMENT AND INTERNATIONAL POLITICS

So far in this chapter, discussion of environmental regimes has tended to focus on the development of formal and informal relations around a single issue, be it ozone depletion, climate change or forestry. However, as we have made clear in earlier chapters, focusing on single environmental problems may not provide an effective enough response to environmental degradation: responding to environmental problems requires a consideration of the connections between the economy, society and the environment. Since the late 1980s, there has been growing international attention given to the idea of sustainable development and this manifested itself most prominently in 1992 at the United Nations Conference on Environment and Development (UNCED), also known as the Rio 'Earth Summit'. Sustainable development requires states to negotiate the difficult terrain around increasing Northern consumption levels, the South's desire for industrial development and the environmental and social impact of these two trends. But, as has been made clear in Chapter 2 and elsewhere in this book, sustainable development is an 'essentially contested concept' and, as such, a number of different interpretations are given as to what it entails in practice. These range from proposals for ecological modernisation, a largely technical response to environmental problems and the inclusion of environmental costs in economic decision making (Weale, 1992), through to calls for radical changes in economic and political structures that would leave control of resources in the hands of local communities (Sachs, 1993; *The Ecologist*, 1993). At one end there is a defence of the existing economic order, at the other a radical restructuring of political and economic arrangements and organisations. Given the primacy of states in the international arena, it should be no surprise that radical proposals that suggest a diminution of state influence tend to have little effect on the agenda of international relations. Where Southern states challenge the dominant economic system, it is typically on the grounds that they do not enjoy the same levels of economic development as the North. The logic of capital accumulation is rarely challenged, rather the injustice of present uneven development patterns. That this would require a reform of the present system is undeniable; whether it is anything close to a 'sustainable' response is a moot question. Thus, even the interpretation of sustainable development appealed to by Southern states can be understood as one of ecological modernisation – more radical challenges are marginalised.

1972 – The birth of a new agenda?

The year 1972 has been highlighted already as an important date for environmental politics with the publication of *The Limits to Growth*. As we saw in Chapter 2, this report argued that the post-war rate of economic expansion and population growth cannot be sustained without exhaustion of global natural resources, irreparable environmental damage and an increase in poverty and malnutrition.

In the same year, the United Nations Conference on the Human Environment, held in Stockholm, provided the first major international opportunity for the South to highlight the links between the prevailing international economic system, environmental degradation and poverty. Not surprisingly, there was a lack of consensus on the way forward – Stockholm witnessed major disagreements between the North and South on the causes of global environmental degradation and poverty. Conflicts over the relative impact of population levels and consumption that emerged at this conference have raged on ever since. Only a broad set of sometimes contradictory principles were forthcoming. However, the Stockholm conference allowed the issues to be aired for the first time in an international context and it opened possibilities for further developments, in particular the emergence of UNEP and the legitimising of environment and development NGOs.

The Brundtland Report

During the 1970s and 1980s, the focus of the international community was very much on the international security concerns generated by the Cold War. Where the South had looked as if it was beginning to gain increased influence in global politics in the 1970s, the 1980s saw many of these nations plunged into financial crisis as commodity prices fell and debt levels increased. The majority of national economies, particularly in the South, found themselves in recession, resulting in widespread environmental damage and a worsening of the plight of a large percentage of the world's population.

In 1983, against this background of a growing security dilemma and increased environmental degradation and poverty, the UN Secretary-General called upon Gro Harlem Brundtland, former Prime Minister of Norway, to set up and chair an independent commission to assess and address environment and development pressures. The World Commission on Environment and Development (WCED) presented its highly influential report, *Our Common Future*, to the UN General Assembly in 1987. The significance of the Brundtland Report cannot be understated in that it introduced the concept of sustainable development into common usage. The report advocated a now widely accepted interpretation of sustainable development: 'development that meets the needs of the present without compromising the ability of future generations to meet their own needs' (WCED, 1987, p. 43). Brundtland's interpretation of sustainable development emphasises the links between environmental degradation and patterns of economic development and argues that environment and development policies must be integrated in all countries. However, the report's prescription for sustainable development emphasises the centrality of continued economic growth for environmental protection and as such the language of ecological modernisation became common currency at the international level.

In February 1987 the final meeting of the Commission was held in Tokyo. The members called upon 'all nations of the World, both jointly and individually, to integrate sustainable development into their goals and to adopt the following principles to guide their policy actions':

- revive growth;
- change the quality of growth;
- conserve and enhance the resource base;
- ensure a sustainable level of population;
- reorientate technology and manage risk;
- integrate environment and economics in decision making;
- reform international economic relations;
- strengthen international cooperation.

(WCED, 1987, pp. 4–5)

The Brundtland Report emphasised the mutual reinforcing of economic growth, social development and environmental protection, putting a forceful case forward for a higher level of multilateral cooperation and the need to reform economic practices such as trade, finance and aid. These recommendations found widespread support among many states and international economic organisations since the case for continued economic growth was understood as reaffirming their legitimacy. The report was also generally well received by NGOs – those campaigners who did not accept the primacy given to economic growth and believed the development patterns outlined by Brundtland would result in the loss of traditionally sustainable practices were further marginalised (de la Court, 1990). Although the Brundtland Report raised the profile of the environment in international politics, at the same time it ensured that future deliberations would be structured by the discourse of ecological modernisation; interpretations of sustainable development that centred on a more locally sensitive and pluralistic understanding of sustainability could find no voice on the international stage. However, although the Brundtland Report can be seen as marginalising more radical accounts of sustainable development, it must be recognised that if the policies it suggested were to be implemented, the world would most definitely be a more just and sustainable place – in itself it would have a quite radical and far-reaching impact.

The United Nations Conference on Environment and Development

The Brundtland Report galvanised international support around the idea of sustainable development and was instrumental in the launch of the United Nations Conference on Environment and Development (UNCED) by the UN General Assembly in 1989. Maurice Strong, the first Executive Director of UNEP, was appointed Secretary-General of UNCED and a series of 'prep-coms' (preparatory committees) and conferences followed over the next two years as the agenda of UNCED was fought over. In some ways the debate appeared not to have moved on since Stockholm two decades earlier. The industrialised nations of the North were looking to focus on environmental degradation as a short-term, technically solvable issue; in response, the South argued that such an approach only tackled the symptoms of the crisis and avoided the background issues which they believed desperately needed tackling, namely the international economy, debt, SAPs, the role of TNCs, and financial and technological transfers.

UNCED, held in Rio in June 1992, was unprecedented for an international environmental event – 176 national delegations attended and the levels of media and public attention were quite staggering. A parallel event, the Global Forum, attracted some 30,000 NGO representatives from all over the world. Five agreements were signed, including Agenda 21.

- Rio Declaration
- Agenda 21
- Declaration on Forest Principles
- Convention on Climate Change
- Convention on Biological Diversity

Strictly speaking, the Conventions on Climate Change and Biological Diversity were not really part of the Rio process – they were negotiated through separate processes and opened for signature at the Summit. Again they are examples of international responses to individual environmental problems rather than an attempt to respond to the interconnectedness of environmental and developmental pressures. This interconnection was recognised within the Rio Declaration and, more importantly, Agenda 21.

The Rio Declaration on environment and development

This builds on a similar declaration that was produced two decades earlier in Stockholm. It is a set of guiding principles for national and international environmental behaviour. The declaration endorses the polluter-pays principle (PPP) and the precautionary principle as well as the need for access to environmental information, increased public participation, and environmental impact assessment of development schemes. The declaration also explicitly makes the link between poverty and environmental degradation: it is perhaps surprising that Principle 7 asserts that: 'States have common but differentiated responsibilities. The developed countries acknowledge the responsibility that they bear in the international pursuit of sustainable development in view of the pressures their societies place on the global environment and of the technologies and financial resources they command.' Although such principles have no legal status, Southern nations believe that it was an important step for the North to acknowledge its particular responsibility for present environmental conditions.

Agenda 21

Agenda 21 is probably the most significant outcome of the Earth Summit. It is perhaps the most thorough and ambitious attempt at the international level to specify what actions are necessary if development is to be reconciled with global environmental concerns. With its adoption by all the nations represented at UNCED, it is intended to guide all nations towards sustainable development into the twenty-first century.

The document is the result of long and protracted negotiations between virtually all political, social and economic interest groups in the run-up to UNCED and

---

Agenda 21

Agenda 21 consists of four sections:

1 *Social and economic dimensions*: highlights the interconnectedness of environmental problems with poverty, health, trade, debt, consumption and population.

2 *Conservation and management of resources for development*: emphasises the need to manage physical resources such as land, seas, energy and wastes to further sustainable development.

3 *Strengthening the role of major social groups*: stresses the need for partnership with women, indigenous populations, local authorities, NGOs, workers and trade unions, business and industry, scientists and farmers.

4 *Means of implementation*: discusses the role of governments and non-governmental agencies in funding and technological transfer.

at the conference itself. The text is often contradictory because of the need to find compromises acceptable to the different interests. Areas fought over included population control (offensive to the Vatican), reduction of fossil fuel usage (against the commercial interests of the oil-producing states) and the nature of North–South debt. It is not surprising that the final text did not appear until September 1992 – four months after the conference.

Criticisms of the Rio process

> I had low expectations, and all of them were met.
> (Jonathon Porritt, environmentalist and former director of FoE)

The significance of the Rio process divides greens – some argue that it should be seen as an important turning point in the move towards more sustainable practices, others that it was simply 'greenwash' and that the conference actually subverted the environmental movement and reinforced existing political and economic relations. Where does the truth lie? Certainly as time goes on it often seems that environmental concerns have dropped down the international political agenda. How are we to judge the impact of the Earth Summit?

Critics point to the fact that there were no firm commitments on important issues such as debt, SAPs, population, and financial and technological transfer, and that fundamental questions about the structure of the capitalist system, the role of TNCs and global militarism were completely ignored (Third World Network, 1992; Thomas, 1993; Chatterjee and Finger, 1994). Given that the logic of ecological modernisation underpinned much of the negotiations, this should not be so much of a surprise. There may have been reference to consumption levels in Agenda 21, but where are the targets and action plans to actually reduce these levels? One Third World diplomat famously remarked: 'What was unsaid at UNCED eclipsed what was said.'

Although the relationship between debt and poverty was recognised in Agenda 21, most of the text celebrated the free market; much of the debate and final documentation was based on free-market ideals. This highlights the continued international domination of the North and the Bretton Woods institutions. Visions of sustainable development were based on the 'ecological modernisation' model with the emphasis on the necessity of continued economic growth. Other visions of development were marginalised and any minor concessions made to alternative ideas will be swamped by the force of recent trade agreements. After all, how are the non-binding proposals in Agenda 21 going to fare against the WTO's trade regulations?

Many Southern states were looking to Rio as an opportunity to begin to 'rein in' the activities of TNCs. However, the international industrial and business lobby proved too powerful. In the run-up to the conference, many of the leading TNCs came together under the banner of the Business Council for Sustainable Development (BCSD), whose Chair, the Swiss billionaire Stephen Schmidheiny, became a prominent advisor to Maurice Strong. Compared with environment and development NGOs, such an alliance was well resourced and was able to put forward a unified and coherent position. At the same time, the TNCs basically 'bank-rolled' the conference and the Global Forum – much of the finance came from the business sector – and many of the world's business leaders were part of national delegations. It should be no surprise then that at the same time as the only UN agency that monitored the activities of TNCs – the United Nations Commission on Transnational Corporations (UNCTC) – was disbanded, TNCs were able to raise their profile as 'pro-environment' actors. Rather than the threatened limiting of operations, the business lobby successfully negotiated a self-monitoring role for itself. The only mention of TNCs in Agenda 21 is in a positive light, as a major social group whose role needs to be strengthened; as a 'partner'. For many environmentalists this was simply too much and exposed the Rio process as a sham (Chatterjee and Finger, 1994, pp. 109ff).

Another special interest group that managed to steer the negotiations away from a strict programme was the Vatican on the issue of population control. Much of the blame is put on the Holy See's attitude to contraception, but as noted earlier, the Northern states are happy to avoid the issue in order to keep per capita consumption off the agenda. Similarly, the South still views any programme as interference in domestic policies. The follow-up International Conference on Population and Development held in Cairo in September 1994 was fraught with similar tensions.

Questions also remain over the issue of funding and financial assistance for the South. It has been estimated by the UN that around $600 billion per annum would be needed for the developing countries if they are to begin the process of moving towards a more sustainable future. In the event only about 1 per cent of that total was forthcoming at UNCED – the largest pledges coming from Japan (Young, 1993, p. 46). Not only were donations thin on the ground, but the industrialised nations did not even agree to immediately provide the 0.7 per cent GNP that the UN had previously advised should be allocated to aid and development projects. All this even though Agenda 21 has a chapter dedicated specifically to the interconnections of debt and environmental degradation. At the same time, Southern nations were far from satisfied with the funding mechanism, the Global Environment Facility (GEF), which is attached to the World Bank. The bank has a poor reputation and the South wanted to see an independent fund established, separate from existing financial institutions that they believe to be heavily influenced by Northern economic interests. Since Rio, however, Southern nations have to a certain degree been successful in reforming the GEF.

The Global Environment Facility

The GEF is the primary institution through which financial assistance is provided to the South for sustainable development projects. It was established in 1991 by the leading industrialised nations (without the input of the G77[22]) as a three-year pilot project to support financial transfers within environmental regimes, such as climate change, biodiversity, etc. The GEF is housed within the World Bank, with UNEP and UNDP acting as advisory bodies. It is this relationship with the World Bank and the fact that control was relative to financial contributions that made Southern nations suspicious of the GEF. Their grievances were ignored at Rio when the South's alternative proposal for a new environment fund controlled on the more democratic basis of one-country-one-vote was rejected by the North which was only willing to recognise the GEF. At the time this seemed a substantial defeat for the South. Since Rio, however, the South has managed to win some important concessions. As the reputation of the World Bank continued to diminish with continued exposure of poor environmental lending practices and its lack of openness and accountability, the G77 collaborated with Northern NGOs to persuade the Clinton administration that the decision-making structures of the GEF needed to be reformed. The new council of the GEF is made up of sixteen developing nations, fourteen developed nations and two members from Central and Eastern Europe and the Soviet Union. Decisions are also no longer left purely to the World Bank: the council has the final approval on all projects. Although the funds available to the GEF are relatively meagre in global terms ($1.2 billion in the first three years; $2 billion for the next three), the concessions gained by the South are important, since 'the GEF represented the first major North–South battle over the governance of a global environmental institution'.

(Porter and Brown, 1996, p. 142)[23]

Two other aspects of the Rio process are often raised by critical commentators. The first is the manner in which the USA used its hegemonic status to defend the existing political and economic relations.

The Bush administration's strategy for UNCED negotiations, based on the assumption that UNCED represented a potential threat to US interests, was aimed at averting any initiatives that would limit US freedom of economic action worldwide. The United States was prepared to veto any initiative that could be viewed as redistributing economic power at the global level, that would create new institutions, or that would require additional budgetary resources, technology transfers, or changes in domestic US policies.

(Porter and Brown, 1996, pp. 117–18)

In many ways the actions of the USA seem to fulfil the prophecies of the realist account of international relations discussed earlier in the chapter. Its behaviour at the subsequent Kyoto climate change conference simply reinforces such a position. With the dominant world power viewing its interests as conflicting with global environmental protection, critics question just how far any moves toward sustainable development can go. It is an interesting question as to how far the emergence of the European Union as an international political actor will affect international environmental politics. It is certainly more sympathetic to environmental issues than the US government.

Finally, did Rio see the cooption of the green movement itself? Unquestionably, environment and development NGOs achieved previously unknown levels of access to negotiations. But, as Chatterjee and Finger rightly argue, access does not necessarily equate to influence.

> the mobilisation of peoples and NGOs to participate actively in the UNCED process, while not letting them influence the outcome, has led to an overall legitimation of a process that is ultimately destructive of the very forces that were mobilised.
>
> (Chatterjee and Finger, 1994, p. 103)

In their view, NGO participation could simply be viewed as a public relations exercise by the organisers of the conference and any democratic principles that Agenda 21 might embody will be subverted by national and international institutions. Few truly grassroots community groups were either willing or able to attend and influence the UNCED process, and the international NGOs that were involved have now been coopted into the international political processes that they are supposed to be challenging. There is simply no way that NGOs can compete in terms of lobbying or resources with the business and industrial community (ibid., p. 113). If this is an accurate analysis, then green politics at the international level is facing serious dilemmas.

Agenda 21 as a move towards sustainable practices?

Without wishing to discount or ignore these criticisms of the UNCED process, can a positive light be shed on the Earth Summit? Have some greens been too enthusiastic in damning UNCED? Certainly greens did not achieve all that they desired (although it must be remembered that greens have competing understandings of what sustainable development entails), but should we write off everything that happened?

It is true that generally UNCED reinforced many of the 'settled norms' of the international order – we have earlier noted that Principle 2 of the Rio Declaration defends a strong interpretation of sovereignty. But what else would we expect from a set of negotiations between states? The state is, and will for some time, remain a dominant actor in international politics – green thinking needs to recognise this fact. However, given the continued existence of the state, Agenda 21 and the Rio Declaration stress important themes that greens should support and reinforce: themes such as improved cooperation between states and other actors; the defence of equal rights, empowerment and education of individuals and communities; increasing the capacity of institutions to manage the changes that sustainable development requires; and the need for increased financial and technological assistance for the South. These are all fundamental principles within environmental politics and can all be found in Agenda 21. For instance, given the criticisms of the Earth Summit itself and the fact that the final version of Agenda 21 is the result of long and protracted negotiations, it is perhaps surprising that such a strong theme of democratic renewal runs through the document. At all levels of governance, local to inter-national, the development of new institutional forms that increase participation by all major groups is taken to be fundamental (Roddick and Dodds, 1993).

> Critical to the effective implementation of the objectives, policies and mecha-nisms agreed by Governments in all programme areas of Agenda 21 will be the commitment and genuine involvement of all social groups. ... *One of the fundamental prerequisites for the achievement of sustainable development is broad public participation in decision-making.* Furthermore, in the more specific context of en-vironment and development, *the need for new forms of participation has emerged.*
> (UNCED, 1992, Chapter 23: emphasis added)

The third section of the document, 'Strengthening the Role of Major Groups' argues the case for the involvement and participation of all social groups within decision-making processes. The theme of inclusiveness and participation is taken to be fundamental to the restructuring of political institutions and the creation of new forms of dialogue: 'The overall objective is to improve or restructure the decision-making process so that consideration of socio-economic and environ-mental issues is fully integrated and a broader range of public participation as-sured' (ibid., Chapter 8).

Agenda 21 does not simply promote the principle of basic rights to, for instance, health, shelter, clean food and a safe environment. Its reach is far more radical and participatory – all groups have the right to articulate their perspectives in decision-making processes.

> Its concern is more than charitable and welfare-related. It also sees disadvan-taged groups as having the same rights to a voice in decisions about the path that development should take, and as having their own contribution – of tra-ditional knowledge, values, life experience or place in a broader society or culture – to make to its achievement. Agenda 21 is thus profoundly demo-cratic and egalitarian in its outlook.
> (LGMB, 1992, pp. 4–5)

We have argued in Chapter 2 and elsewhere that new forms of democratic en-gagement are necessary for the development of sustainable practices and in many ways Agenda 21 embodies such ideals. The whole Rio process should not be dis-counted simply because conflicts remain: greens need to take what they can from the process and advocate those themes and principles which accord with their own vi-sions of a sustainable society. As we shall see in Chapter 10, at the local level many different groups have been inspired by the democratic principles of Agenda 21. It is too easy to be critical of the non-binding nature of much of the output of the Earth Summit – to focus solely on the documents is to neglect the impact of the event on public and governmental consciousness. The level of media coverage, the high level of the delegations and the tough negotiating stance of many nations bear testimony to the importance placed on environment and development issues, even if many states still view short-term domestic issues as a higher priority. Agenda 21 has emerged as a catalyst for national and local activity and, as we shall see in the case study below, the recently established Commission on Sustainable Development (CSD) may offer a model for international environment and development institutions. Along similar lines, the view that NGOs were coopted within the Rio process can be tempered somewhat by comments made by some of the NGO representatives themselves. For instance, Martin Khor of the Third World Network argued that although the documentation and commitments from the Earth Summit were disappointing, the activities of NGOs in and around the UNCED process have led to important contacts and opportunities for mutual learning:

> The UNCED process forged new and stronger links between Northern and Southern groups, between development and environmental activists. It would now be difficult for environmentalists to stick to wildlife issues or population, without simultaneously addressing international equity and global power structures. A major step forward has been the increasing involvement of Northern based environment groups like Greenpeace, WWF, and Friends of the Earth in economic issues such as trade, debt, and aid.
>
> (Khor, quoted in Chatterjee and Finger, 1994, p. 99)

CONCLUSION

The UN General Assembly Special Session to review the outcome of the Rio Summit – 'Earth Summit II' – was held in New York in June 1997. By all accounts it was a disappointment, with little in the way of notable progress (Bigg, 1997). It could be said that the Earth Summit II exposed the hypocrisy of the North in that few, if any, of the commitments made in Rio have been forthcoming. The South is right to be disappointed by the lack of international resolve. In an analysis of the current international situation, Martin Khor argues that the continuing globalisation of the world economy and the lack of willingness on the part of the North to restructure economic relations has undermined any positive results of the Rio process. The 'spirit of Rio' has been lost as the volume of aid has dropped further; no progress has occurred in technology transfer; environment and development concerns in the North have been downgraded, while the South continues to suffer from environmental degradation and development problems (Khor, 1997, pp. 5ff). Have the critics of the Rio process been proved right?

But, there was a 'spirit of Rio' and environmental regimes have developed quite considerably over the past two decades. Certainly, the agenda has been dominated by the interests of Northern states – particularly the G7 – and those international and domestic institutions that share similar short-term economic and political interests. This means that issues directly affecting the industrialised nations are normally given priority and that those of more concern to developing nations often lack international attention and funding. This Northern hegemony also means that environmental issues tend to be viewed both as isolated phenomena and as merely technical problems admitting of technical solutions. They are considered in an isolated fashion because it is not in the short-term interest of the North to tackle wider structural issues such as the international economy and political–military interests; they are considered as merely technical problems because this means that they can be controlled by the industrialised nations, which are also able to sidestep issues of justice and economic and social relations.

If this was all that could be said then it would seem that the North will continue its dominance of the international agenda and patterns of development and environmental degradation will continue to be at the expense of the South. However, this does not necessarily have to be the case. As the importance of successfully implementing environmental treaties is understood, the bargaining power of the South will increase. If it is fully appreciated that a more concerted approach to issues such as climate change is necessary and that global warming will affect all nations regardless of wealth or political status, Southern nations will be able to apply more pressure for technological and financial transfers and reassessment of the structure of the international political and economic system. Whether there is a will to challenge the hegemony of values associated with capital accumulation and free-market rhetoric is a moot point. Perhaps then we are left with two possible scenarios. The first is desperate, with continued deterioration of the planet and increasing economic, social and environmental differentials between the North and the South. Environmental issues and international policy forums are used to provide domestic publicity stunts for political leaders. Empty speeches and hollow promises are made.

An alternative scenario would see the embrace of the democratic and cooperative principles of Agenda 21 together with a recognition that sustainable development requires a reassessment of uneven patterns of development, consumption levels and poverty. Ecological modernisation could be seen as a first step – a stepping stone – to much more sustainable patterns of development and environmental protection. Whether states and other international actors are able to truly grasp this agenda is another question.

CASE STUDY: THE UNITED NATIONS COMMISSION ON SUSTAINABLE DEVELOPMENT

Thus far, the Commission has distinguished itself as the primary forum for review of the implementation of Agenda 21. The Commission has made it possible for the discussions to take place at the highest level, on issues involving the environment and development. In addition, the Commission has brought together different sectors concerned with the environment and development – namely NGOs, the other major groups, politicians, diplomats, and experts.

(Mensah, 1996, p. 36)

The United Nations Commission on Sustainable Development (CSD) was created in 1993 in the wake of UNCED. According to its mandate, the CSD's role is to act as a forum for international dialogue on sustainable development: 'To monitor progress on the implementation of Agenda 21 and activities related to the integration of environmental and developmental goals' (ibid., p. 28). The CSD is not itself a decision-making body – it can only provide advice and recommendations to the General Assembly through the Economic and Social Council (ECOSOC). The CSD's primary role is thus to act as an independent body monitoring the progress of nations in the implementation of Agenda 21 and, as such, it has developed a rolling programme to tackle all the issues raised within the action plan.[24] In its own right, the monitoring of states is a massive task, but the role of coordination inherited from UNEP could restrict the success of the CSD – the Commission is also required to oversee the environmental activities of 'all relevant organs, organisations, programmes and institutions of the UN dealing with various issues of environment and development, including those related to finance' (Hurrell, 1993, p. 277). Critics have argued that these coordination and facilitation functions may blunt its immediate effectiveness (Imber, 1993; Thomas, 1993, Henry, 1996). Much will depend upon the importance placed on its work by the UN Secretary-General, the General Assembly and the states that are required to provide national reports. The CSD appears as if it will function in the same way as the Commission on Human Rights in that it will have no legal powers over states to fulfil their obligations. However, it will be a 'much needed forum for publicising progress (or lack of it) of states towards sustainable development – if only through moral persuasion and public criticism' (Hurrell, 1993, p. 278).

The CSD as an innovative democratic design?

The CSD may offer a model for more democratic and deliberative international institutions. Non-governmental organisations (NGOs) and other non-governmental institutions and actors are given a role well beyond that afforded them in other official forums. The CSD mandate states that one of its functions should be:

> To receive and analyse relevant input from competent NGOs, including the scientific and private sector, in the context of the overall implementation of Agenda 21; to enhance the dialogue, within the framework of the United Nations with NGOs and the independent sector.
>
> (Mensah, 1996, p. 29)

What is innovative about the structure of the CSD is that not only are national governments expected to provide reports on their response to Agenda 21 but also the CSD allows other bodies to make representations, to participate in the ongoing dialogue on environment and development. As Tom Bigg and Felix Dodds argue:

> The Commission itself has come to be seen as a testing ground for new ways of involving non-governmental organisations in UN processes, and the involvement of organisations which work principally or exclusively at national level has had a major impact. In future, it may not be just governments that hold up their records for scrutiny in the CSD: increasingly, there is pressure to allow equivalent opportunities to major groups.
>
> (Bigg and Dodds, 1997, p. 17)

The inclusion of representatives other than state delegates leads to a democratic potential far beyond that of many existing international institutions. New forms of practice are developing. For instance: 'None of the sessions is now closed – even the small working groups are held open for major group representatives to attend and in many cases speak. Their increased involvement in implementing the UN Conference agreements has also meant increased involvement in framing them in the first place' (ibid., p. 31).

The response of national governments

There are some aspects of the CSD's actual functioning that raise problems. First, there is a lack of willingness on the part of many national delegations to speak candidly about their domestic actions. 'Delegates tend to speak more for the record and from prepared statements ... particularly when they know that they are being watched by groups outside the diplomatic community' (Mensah, 1996, p. 36). This is particularly the case in situations where the government representative does not have the political authority to engage in critical debate. Frequently, it is environment ministers that attend CSD sessions. As such, their authority to deliberate on issues outside their ministerial responsibilities is limited. Klaus Töpfer, the Chair of the CSD between 1994 and 1995, thus argues:

> The CSD must become the most important global forum not only for environment ministers, but also for ministers responsible for development, planning and finance as well. It is of vital importance to integrate

the concept of sustainability into all major policy areas, especially into trade, economic development and finance policies.

(Klaus Töpfer, quoted in UNED–UK, 1996, p. 9)

A positive trend, however, is recognised by Bigg and Dodds, who note that the nature of delegations 'is steadily changing as ministers from housing and urban development, overseas development, transport, forestry and even finance departments have put in appearances' (Bigg and Dodds, 1997, p. 16).

Even though, at times, the operations of the CSD have been compared to an 'international beauty contest', critics have admitted that it 'has acted as a spur for change' (Sandbrook, 1996, p. 5). For instance, the CSD has been successful in bringing issues such as forestry and Northern consumption levels back onto the political agenda; issues that had generally been kept out of the original UNCED agreements by powerful interest groups. Tom Bigg of UNED–UK sees the potential of the CSD lying in its 'ability to hold governments responsible to their peers, and to their citizens, for progress achieved.' But, as he continues: 'There are obvious problems with this, not least the difficulty of persuading governments to lay themselves open to such criticism and accountability. It also presupposes that the impetus for change is a good deal more forceful than at present' (Bigg, 1994, p. 18). National governments may not actually be prepared to engage in meaningful deliberations, particularly as they are stepping into an arena, unchartered in diplomatic terms, where other actors aside from states are in a position to respond. But, in itself, this situation may also have the potential to encourage meaningful exchanges. The presence of NGOs to corroborate or challenge national reports and positions may actually lead to more transparency and critical engagement with the agenda of sustainable development. As Bigg argues:

> The importance of having a political focus for international reviewing of Agenda 21 implementation should not be underestimated. It gives domestic relevance to many of the global issues which might otherwise fall outside the scope of national political life. It also gives a hook on which to hang many issues addressed in Agenda 21, but not adequately dealt with by their governments. ... The Commission's mandate ... makes it the only body to focus on the wide-ranging roles and rights assigned to the major groups in Agenda 21. This has considerable implications for organisations with a national or local focus, as governments can be called to account for their implementation of specific aspects of Agenda 21, including the degree to which they have incorpo-

rated its provisions for the roles of major groups into national and local decision-making processes.

(ibid., p. 22)

The activities of non-state actors

The role of NGOs and other non-governmental institutions and actors can therefore be seen as important in developing a culture of democratic deliberation at the international level. But here, perhaps, another problem emerges with respect to the legitimacy of the NGOs that attend. The availability of resources may affect the ability of parties to affect negotiations. Relatively small numbers of NGOs take part in the work of the CSD compared with those involved in the original UNCED process. Amongst the attributing factors to this low level of involvement by large sections of the NGO sector may be a lack of knowledge as to the remit of the CSD, a lack of funds and resources for participation in proceedings and a disillusionment with international processes in general (Bigg, 1994, p. 19). Questions have been raised as to whether involvement with the CSD diverts attention from 'more important arenas where key decisions are taken (G7, Bretton Woods, WTO, etc.)' (Bigg and Mucke, 1996, p. 5). Where there is participation, NGO involvement is dominated by environmental groups based in more industrialised nations; there is a clear under-representation of NGOs from Southern and Eastern regions. Martin Khor of the Third World Network quotes one Southern participant:

> 'It's very positive that issues like consumption and trade, that were forced off the agenda at Rio, have been put back on the table', said Maria Onestini of Argentina's Centre for Environmental Studies. But 'women, farmers and unions have fallen off the agenda', seriously placing in doubt the Commission's commitment to people-centred development.
> (Khor, 1994, p. 4)

That the CSD offers major groups a voice in international deliberations is not questioned; what needs to be the focus of some attention is the resourcing of organisations to attend and be fully involved in the process. The potential of the CSD to develop more democratically deliberative practices at the international level is high; whether it will be able to achieve this is another matter. As the 1996 United Nations Environment and Development UK Committee (UNED–UK) annual report states:

> A valid role for the Commission in future will be to act as the forum for political impetus in key areas where change is necessary. It should also

build on the unique links already established with the Major Groups of civil society and develop the concepts of partnership and co-operation which have underpinned its operations. These views were widely expressed by both government and NGO delegates. Translating this vision into reality is the challenge before both over the coming years.

(UNED–UK, 1996, p. 8)

SUGGESTIONS FOR FURTHER READING

Gareth Porter and Janet Walsh Brown, *Global Environmental Politics* (1996), is now in its second edition and provides an excellent survey of international regimes and institutions. Caroline Thomas (ed.), *Rio: Unravelling the Consequences* (1994), is a collection of essays investigating the impact of UNCED. For a comprehensive analysis of both the politics of climate change and the state of international relations theory, see Matthew Paterson, *Global Warming and Global Politics* (1996). *Environmental Politics* frequently contains articles relating to international environmental politics. It is also an important source of material on the European Union and national and local policy developments are covered in subsequent chapters of this book. Finally, *Third World Resurgence*, published monthly by the Third World Network, contains regular articles on environment and development issues from the perspective of Southern NGOs.

8 European integration

The EU is one of the most significant of the new international regimes and organizations that have been established to manage areas of transnational activity, including environmental policy. Its significance lies in the fact that its powers reach further than any other kind of international organization by virtue of its rights to make laws which can be imposed on member-states.

(Baker, 1996, p. 215)

The European Union (EU)[1] has emerged over the past two decades as a major source of environmental action and law making. On the global stage it enters into negotiations in its own right: for example, it is the only supranational organisation that is a signatory to the Earth Summit documents and recently took a strong stance in the Kyoto climate change negotiations. For an organisation whose original rationale was the creation of the conditions for sustained economic growth for its member states, the transformation into a leading promoter of environmental innovation and change needs some investigation. Despite the EU's emergence as an important policy maker and international actor in the environmental sphere, it has none the less attracted criticism. For example, it has been reproached for lacking an adequate monitoring and enforcement machinery, for depressing environmental standards to the lowest common denominator and for supposing that it can pursue an effective environmental policy while at the same time promoting economic growth and increased trade.

This chapter will examine how and why the EU adopted an environmental role. Initially, it is necessary to briefly describe the institutional arrangements of the EU, as a number of different institutions have an input into policy making. The development of comprehensive European environmental policy can be seen as an incremental process and the chapter will focus on the political and administrative aspects of its evolution. In the final section, the recent Fifth Environmental Action Programme (5EAP) will be analysed as it purports to be one of the most systematic attempts to move towards sustainable development, as its title, *Towards Sustainability*, suggests. The case study will focus on the creation and development of the European Environment Agency (EEA), an institution over which there has been much political disagreement. Does the EU require a supranational environmental inspectorate, or would that be an unaccepable infringement of national sovereignty? As we shall see, conflicts such as this are at the heart of the emerging European project and environmental policy is a creature of such tensions.

THE STRUCTURE AND OPERATION OF THE EUROPEAN UNION

The EU is a supranational organisation. This entails not only that member states are committed to work together, but that (in contrast to other international organisations) there are formal constraints on the actions of its members. The EU has a quite distinctive structure and set of practices. For example, it creates a body of law which takes precedence over national law (much of the British concern over 'loss of parliamentary sovereignty' arises from this) and its network of institutions, most of which are located in Brussels, comprises a political and administrative structure quite unlike any national arrangement. Its actions and judgements penetrate the politics of member states to an extent beyond that of any other international organisation.

The European Economic Community (EEC) was initially established, as its name indicates, to promote and secure the economic well-being of its member states. Article 2 of the 1957 Treaty of Rome originally defined its purpose:

> The Community shall have as its task, by establishing a common market and progressively approximating the economic policies of Member States, to promote throughout the Community a harmonious development of economic activities, a continuous and balanced expansion, an increase in stability, an accelerated raising of the standard of living and closer relations between the States belonging to it.

The primary rationale of the Community was, therefore, not only directly economic in intention, but also, it might be argued, anti-environmental in practice in the sense that it gave a clear priority to the promotion of economic growth. Subsequently the Treaty of Rome has been supplemented and modified in a number of ways, the most important being the 1987 Single European Act (SEA) and the 1993 Maastricht Treaty on European Union (TEU), which together enhanced the powers of the European Parliament, developed the principle of subsidiarity, moved the European Community towards an integrated European Union with enhanced powers, and established a firm legal basis for environmental policy. These moves have now been modified and confirmed by the Treaty of Amsterdam (1997), which states that one of the EU's main tasks is to promote 'balanced and sustainable development of economic activities' and 'a high level of protection and improvement of the quality of the environment' (ENDS, 1997a, p. 45). Since 1957, the Community has grown in size from the original six (France, West Germany, Italy, Luxembourg, Belgium, the Netherlands) in 1957, to nine in 1973 (with the accession of the UK, the Republic of Ireland and Denmark). Greece joined in 1981, Spain and Portugal in 1986, Austria, Finland and Sweden in 1995; hence the European Union currently comprises fifteen members. Further expansion through the incorporation of former East European communist bloc countries and Turkey is likely, but no timetable has yet been set.

The institutions

The EU comprises a number of bodies, such as the European Commission, the Council of Ministers and the European Parliament, which have varying powers and capabilities and which interact with one another in an often complicated and opaque manner. The key institutions are:

- European Commission
- Council of Ministers
- European Council
- European Parliament
- European Court of Justice

To describe the European Commission as the EU's equivalent of the 'civil service' would be to underestimate its degree of autonomy. Its role is not simply to administer, but also to initiate policy, and in particular to initiate policy that 'transcends' a limited notion of the national self-interest of its member states. As such it is an activist organisation and often finds itself in conflict with national governments and other institutions within the EU. The Commission consists of a number of commissioners appointed by each member state.[2] For example, at present the British European commissioners are Sir Leon Brittan (trade) and Neil Kinnock (transport), with the Dane Ritt Bjerregaard responsible for environmental matters. These commissioners are serviced by officials grouped into a number of directorates, each charged with specific responsibility for a particular policy area. Directorate General XI (DG XI) covers the environment, consumer protection and nuclear safety. The Commission initiates and drafts policy (including Environmental Action Programmes) and draws up proposals for the Council of Ministers to approve. It also has responsibility for implementing EU policies and for policing and enforcing EC law.

The Council of Ministers is the main decision-making body of the EU and is made up of one representative from each member state. It is an avowedly political body, unlike the Commission. Although formally the Council of Ministers comprises only foreign ministers, in practice representatives are usually the relevant ministers from each member state according to the nature of the decision being taken. Thus, for example, environmental ministers will decide on environmental policy, agricultural ministers on agricultural policy, and so on. These decisions are later formally ratified by a full Council meeting. Decisions are made in the Council of Ministers using different voting procedures. For some measures unanimity is required, but for an increasing number of decisions a qualified majority is sufficient.[3] Before the introduction of the SEA in 1987, all environmental policy required a unanimous decision; the SEA modified this. Following the Maastricht TEU in 1993, qualified majority voting was adopted for most (but not all) environmental policy. The removal of the *de facto* veto means that it is now easier to push through environmental legislation. The Council's area of competence also covers the work of The Committee of Permanent Representatives (COREPER), which comprises national officials from member states who discuss proposals emanating from the Commission and explore possible areas of agreement and conflict.

The European Council (at times referred to as the European Summit) typically meets twice a year and consists of heads of government from each member state. Its purpose is to resolve any issues which have proven intractable to the normal decision-making procedures of the EU. The introduction of European Council meetings to some extent represented a move away from supranational decision making and towards intergovernmental decision making. A supranational body is one which has powers over and above the powers of its members and which is (at least to some extent) an actor in its own right in international politics; an intergovernmental body is a forum for debate and common action between states, with no additional powers. The EU contains elements of both supranationalism and intergovernmentalism – whether it acts in one or the other way depends on circumstances and the issues concerned. In practice it often appears to be a hybrid of the two.

The EU as an independent international actor

It is important to recognise that the EU can act in its own right as an international actor. On these occasions it is more than an intergovernmental body; it is a supranational actor. This brings into question the 'settled norm' of national sovereignty at the international level (see Chapter 7). The EU is a signatory to the Geneva Convention on Long-range Transboundary Air Pollution (1981) and the Montreal Protocol on Ozone Depleting Substances (1987). In 1992 it was one of the signatories to the Framework Convention on Climate Change agreed at Rio, and in the recent negotiations on climate change in Kyoto it committed itself to an 8 per cent reduction in carbon dioxide emissions by the year 2010. In the negotiations it proposed the idea of a European 'bubble' in which it was the overall emissions of the EU which were to be measured.[4] Within this bubble individual member states could be permitted different emission levels. For example, Germany and the UK are committed to reductions while Portugal (as a less industrialised member) is to be allowed to increase its emissions for the immediate future.

The European Parliament is composed of directly elected representatives – Members of the European Parliament (MEPs) – from each member state. These representatives are not grouped by national origin but by political affinity, including the European Green Group (see later). Although the Parliament has gained powers in the course of the EU's development, it does not possess the extensive powers of the Council of Ministers or the European Commission. In large part it is a body limited to a consultation and advisory role, although following the introduction of direct elections in 1979, and the ratification of the SEA and the TEU, it is gradually acquiring new powers which perhaps go some way towards remedying the 'democratic deficit' which many have identified in the decision-making processes of the EU. The Parliament cannot, as such, reject a piece of legislation, but consultation with the assembly has always been a requirement without which a piece of EU legislation will be void. In addition, following the ratification of the SEA, the Parliament can delay matters by withholding its opinion on a piece of legislation, and in respect of legislation subject to qualified majority voting, it can reject or propose amendments. It also has the power to withhold its assent to some parts of the Union budget. This gives it some important powers and capabilities, which, given its general willingness to embrace environmental issues, mean that environmental policies continue to have a platform in the EU even when they may have dropped down the broader political agenda of other institutions and member states. Although the recent Treaty of Amsterdam continued the slow process of extending the Parliament's limited powers by granting it rights of co-decision over certain objectives of environmental policy, 'MEPs will have to work hard to ensure the greening of the European Union' (Duff, 1997, p. 77).

Other key institutions include the European Court of Justice (ECJ), which has supreme authority on matters relating to EU law. It is responsible for interpreting EU law and for ensuring that it is properly implemented. As such, its major concern is to ensure uniformity in application of the law across member states. Article 169 gives the Commission power to bring enforcement proceedings against a member state which has not properly transposed a directive into national law or ensured practical compliance with it. However, procedures are begun in only a very small proportion of breaches of environmental law. As Krämer remarks:

> it is increasingly recognised that the effective application of environmental measures is the most serious existing problem of environmental law. The numerous environmental provisions … are frequently either not transposed at all into national law, or not properly applied in practice.
>
> (Krämer, 1997, p. 300)[5]

Other notable European institutional arrangements include the Economic and Social Committee (ECOSOC), a consultative committee comprising members representing employers, trade unions and consumers. It produces opinions on policy proposals. Finally, the Committee of the Regions, created by the Maastricht Treaty in 1993, is likely to become increasingly important as the application of the principle of subsidiarity devolves decision-making power to regional and local level. Most countries in Europe (with the glaring exception of the UK) have a regional structure able to act on its own initiative and to take advantage of EU funding channelled through the Committee of the Regions.[6]

The instruments of EU legislation

The most important legislative instruments employed by the EU are regulations and directives. Other available instruments are decisions, recommendations and opinions. The bulk of EU environmental law is made in the form of directives.

European Union legislation

Regulations have general application. They are binding in their entirety and directly applicable in all member states. There are very few regulations in EU environmental policy.

Directives are binding as to the result to be achieved upon each member state to which they are addressed, but leave to the national authorities the choice of form and methods. Most EU environmental legislation takes the form of directives; they are well suited to this as they leave some flexibility in the choice of how best to implement policy to each member state. Increasingly *framework directives* are being used in EU environmental legislation. These are general directives laying down a strategic framework to achieve specified aims; later, more detailed directives deal with particular issues to achieve the aims. Framework directives currently exist for discharge of pollutants into water, waste, the restriction and use of chemicals, and for air pollution. Although sometimes criticised for diluting legislation, they have the advantage that they provide a clear strategic statement: 'definitions, adaptation procedures and other mechanisms are established in the basic or mother directive, to which other directives then refer' (Krämer, 1997, p. 121).

Decisions are not general but specific to the member state concerned. They are rare in EU environmental policy.

Recommendations and *Opinions* have recommendatory or persuasive force, but are not binding.

Regulations are directly applicable: once a regulation is adopted it automatically becomes part of the national legal system of all of the EU's member states without any need for further legislative or administrative implementation. Directives, on the other hand, are more flexible in that it is left to member states to chose the most appropriate method of implementation. Accordingly, member states vary in the ways they enact EU directives. They can be enacted through primary legislation (very often a composite bill such as the UK's 1990 Environmental Protection Act, which consisted largely of measures required under a whole range of EU directives); they can be enacted through statutory instruments[7]; they can also be implemented by means of administrative circulars. Given that directives explicitly admit of flexibility in their interpretation and execution (setting, as they do, the ends, but leaving the means to national discretion) there is sometimes a danger that member states will interpret them more liberally than the EU intended. However, it would be a mistake to suppose that the difference between regulations and directives is always sharp; very often it is a matter of degree, and as EU law has developed the difference has further eroded with the emergence of the principle of 'direct effect'. Legislation which has direct effect gives rights to citizens of member states on which they can rely in a national court in challenging lax implementation. All regulations are directly effective, and directives may also be directly effective in cases where they are clear, unambiguous and unconditional.

Monitoring and implementation

In complying with EU legislation, member states have both a positive and a negative duty. Positively they are required to implement a directive fully and within the specified time limit; negatively they are required to repeal any previous law incompatible with the directive. But EU environmental legislation suffers from one obvious drawback: monitoring is largely, and implementation is solely, in the hands of the member states themselves. Each member state is normally required to file a compliance letter with the Commission indicating the action or actions it has taken to implement the relevant legislation. In the past this procedure has been neither uniformly nor rigorously followed. Directive 91/692 on the Standardisation and Rationalisation of Implementation Reports for Environmental Directives seeks to remedy this unsatisfactory situation. Reports will be made through the use of questionnaires covering a policy sector, be it water, air, or waste. National reports by member states and an EU-wide report by the Commission will be presented every three years. It is hoped that this new procedure will avoid unnecessary infringement procedures against member states. Further, the European Environmental Agency (EEA) should also enhance the ability of the Commission to detect non-compliance on the part of member states (see case study). Where the Commission takes the view that an infringement has occurred, it will deliver a formal notice to the member state concerned. Following a formal reply it will issue a reasoned opinion setting out the grounds for its belief that the member state has not complied; this opinion must also set out the steps to be taken by the member state, together with a timetable for action. Ultimately, if the state still does not comply, the case will be taken to the ECJ, which, if it finds against the member state, may impose a penalty payment.

However, the Commission has no independent method for checking and monitoring implementation: its responses are largely based on information supplied by member states themselves. This means that very often the countries which are most assiduous in monitoring and issuing reports are the ones which are reprimanded by the Commission, simply because they are supplying the evidence on which it bases its judgement. Although it is a disadvantage for the EU to have no independent means of checking, the story does not end there, because the implementation of EU policy by any member state can be challenged by individuals and groups and reports made to the Commission. This possibility has been strengthened by the Fifth Environmental Action Programme (5EAP), which encourages citizens of member states to engage in 'shared responsibility' for the environment. Citizens can act as complainants, and in this they are aided by legislation such as Directive 90/313 on Free Access to Environmental Information, which came into force in 1992. This directive allows for any individual in any member state to request, without having to show an interest, environmental information covering the activities of any member state. This directive, especially if exploited by environmental groups, might have an important impact on environmental policy, especially in those countries which are relatively lax in monitoring and implementing environmental policy. There are, none the less, drawbacks. Although most enforcement proceedings are initiated in response to complaints made by citizens, the procedure under Article 169 is time-consuming and unwieldy. In addition, the dispute is regarded as being between the Commission and the defaulting state. The complainant is not a party and hence has no legal right to be informed of progress or to have access to copies of the formal notice or the reasoned opinion: this limits the ability of the complainant to force the issue and exert pressure (Kunzlik, 1994, pp. 115–16). Despite these limitations, there is clearly scope for action on the part of concerned groups and individuals, and this scope may be enhanced further by the current emphasis in the 5EAP on joint responsibility for the environment.

The role of active environmental groups in ensuring that states (particularly the UK) implement EU environmental legislation properly is well illustrated by Haigh and Lanigan:

> More and more information reached the Commission from British citizens and pressure groups as they became aware of the possibility that Commission action could challenge both past and present government policies which threatened the environment. By 1990, one third of individual complaints made to the Commission about breaches of environmental directives were coming from Britain, and pressure groups were setting up their own monitoring systems to provide the Commission with information on breaches they could otherwise never have known about. Given that DG XI was more accustomed to EC states providing too little monitoring data with which to identify offences to prosecute, it is hardly surprising that enthusiastic action against Britain should have resulted.
>
> (Haigh and Lanigan, 1995, p. 26)

The corollary is, of course, that member states without an active environmental movement may be (and often are) relatively lax in both their interpretation and their implementation of environmental policy. The UK stands third (behind Spain and France) in the table of suspected infringements of EU environmental policy. This gives some credence to the frequent characterisation of the UK as the 'dirty man of Europe'. But this is perhaps overstated and to some degree unfair. First, by comparison with the EU average, it has a better record than most in persuading the Commission that suspected infringements are not real and in correcting breaches when threatened with legal action (ENDS, 1996c, p. 39). Second, the UK was instrumental, for example, in the European push for lead-free petrol and has been a vociferous (and at times isolated) voice in debates on reform of the Common Agricultural Policy, animal welfare and over-consumption of fish stocks. None the less, it is certainly true that the UK has on occasion frustrated or delayed a number of European environmental initiatives. The Conservative administration refused for many years to accept the link between sulphur dioxide emissions, acid rain and the destruction of forests in Europe, and vociferously fought the directive on large combustion plants (88/609). At other times, the UK has been forced to implement directives on issues where it would have otherwise delayed or even neglected action. The content of the Wildlife and Countryside Act (1981) and the Environmental Protection Act (1990) is, for the most part, the necessary national implementation of relevant EU directives. Further, the ECJ has found the UK to be in breach of directives on two occasions. But the picture is a complex one and, ironically, one in which the UK is to some extent a victim of its own good practice. It has a good record of reporting on its compliance with directives[8] and it also has an active environmental movement. These two facts taken together mean that the UK is likely to be taken to task more quickly and more readily than other member states, whose environmental inactivity may be relatively invisible to the Commission. Countries whose environmental record is worse than the UK's may appear to have a better record simply because their reporting is poorer.

DEVELOPMENT OF AN ENVIRONMENTAL POLICY

The EEC was not originally set up with the intention of promoting environmental policy. Despite this, by 1967 the Community had begun to issue directives concerning environmental matters; and by 1973 it had developed environmental policy explicitly stated in the form of the First Environmental Action Programme. Subsequently there have been four other action programmes: the current Fifth Environmental Action Plan (5EAP), which we shall discuss later, runs from 1993 to 2000. Hence an organisation which originally emerged with a purely economic mandate has metamorphosed not only into the European Union but also into an organisation which is increasingly seen as an important agent of environmental protection. How did this come about?

The incidental nature of environmental policy

As the EC grew and developed, it became impossible in practice to separate environmental issues from the other issues to which it was dedicated. At the barest minimum (that is, leaving aside environmental concern for its own sake) the establishment of the common market, and later the single European market, required that standards within and between countries be comparable so as to ensure equality of competition. A framework was needed in which no member state was advantaged or disadvantaged by unfair competition arising from local conditions. In economic terms this is often referred to as the maintenance of a 'level playing field'. For instance, if environmental standards were lower in one country, firms operating there would have a competitive advantage because their costs of waste disposal or emission control would be lower. This would be an unfair advantage, which might also have the effect of encouraging firms to move their operations to locations where environmental standards were relatively lax.[9] Thus legislation in these matters was necessary, not directly for environmental protection *per se*, but to secure protection of the primary purpose of the community, that is, the achievement of an economic common market. Environmental concern was thus contingent on the primary rationale of the Community.

Despite its secondary or incidental origin, European environmental legislation began to take on a life of its own as environmental concern increasingly became a focus of governmental activity in general in the 1970s. The EC matched the mood of the times in formulating its first Environmental Action Programme in the wake of the publication of *The Limits to Growth* (Meadows *et al.*, 1972). Thus the EC became concerned with environmental issues, but faced the problem that there was no explicit provision for the making of environmental policy within the Treaty of Rome. All legislation at the European level has to be sanctioned by reference to specific articles in the treaty and its relevance justified in relation to the primary purpose of the EC. Environmental legislation had thus to be 'smuggled' into the Community's legislative processes on the back of non-environmental concerns, through a reinterpretation of Article 2 of the Treaty of Rome. Recalling Article 2, there was an emphasis on 'an accelerated raising of the standard of living'. Despite the context of the promotion of economic growth, such a statement could none the less be interpreted as including environmental protection as environmental quality was increasingly coming to be seen as an essential part of what constituted 'a good standard of living' (Marin, 1997, p. 575).

However, a comprehensive turn towards environmental protection ultimately required more than this: it required an independent legal basis. Prior to the SEA, environmental policy was given such a basis under Article 100 dealing with the approximation of laws and Article 235 relating to the EC's general powers. The wording of these articles indicated clearly that, first, the Council had to act unanimously in the making of environmental policy, and, second, that environmental policy had no independent status within the treaty. Hence, there were distinct practical problems as all states had the power of veto, thereby making it difficult to ensure high standards of environmental protection and maximising the chances that any unanimously agreed policy would operate at the level of the lowest common denominator. Despite these restrictions, the EC was none the less passing environmental legislation, and developing a positive environmental policy expressed through its environmental action programmes, e.g.:

- Bathing Waters (1975)
- Lead in Petrol (1978/1985)
- Sulphur Dioxide and Suspended Particulates (1980)
- Lead in Air (1982)
- Emission of Pollutants from Industrial Plants (1984)
- Environmental Impact Assessment (1985)

- Large Combustion Plants (1988)
- Framework Directive on Waste (1991)
- Integrated Pollution Prevention and Control (1996)

The third programme (1982–86) was succeeded in 1987 by the SEA, which revised the Treaty of Rome in a number of important respects, particularly in the creation of the unified internal market. The SEA was particularly important for European environmental policy making because it established for the first time the principle that environmental policy should be one of the direct concerns of the Community itself. To that end, a new title was inserted into the modified treaty and new articles were added which legitimised the position of environmental actions. In addition, DG XI of the Commission was given the explicit responsibility for environmental policy. Title VII of the treaty included the new Articles 130r, 130s and 130t, which introduced explicit powers for making environmental law. From this point on, environmental policy had a secure place within the structures and purposes of the Community, a place which was confirmed and strengthened by the Treaty of Maastricht in 1993. This treaty further integrated environmental concerns into the EU by further modifications to these articles. It recognised that 'a policy in the sphere of the environment' should be one of the EU's main activities and replaced the original Article 2 of the Treaty of Rome with a new version which referred to promoting 'a harmonious and balanced development of economic activities' and 'sustainable and non-inflationary growth respecting the environment'. Increasingly, decisions were being taken by qualified majority voting and policy promoted to a greater degree by the European Parliament, a body sympathetic to environmental issues. The treaty explicitly states that decisions should be taken by qualified majority voting, with the Parliament able to amend but not to veto.

The purpose of the environmental action programmes is to lay down basic principles of environmental policy and thereby to act as a framework within which specific legislation will be enacted. They also assert current priorities and commitments and plan future action. The first two action plans (1973–76 and 1977–81) focused on pollution control and remedial measures, and also stated the basic principles of emerging EC environmental policy. The third and fourth (1982–86 and 1987–92) emphasised preventive measures and the integration of environmental protection into other policies. The 5EAP (1993–2000) goes beyond these objectives through an explicit commitment to sustainable development (see later). EU environmental policy has been incremental in approach, each action programme building on its predecessors, although the principles enunciated in the first programme have been common to all later environmental policy making.

PRINCIPLES OF EU ENVIRONMENTAL POLICY

The principles of EU environmental policy are clearly stated in the first action programme. This indicates that although environmental policy still largely consisted of relatively *ad hoc* legislation responding to issues as they arose, there was none the less a desire to go further and to develop comprehensive and even holistic environmental policy. Although these principles have been modified by subsequent developments, they are largely still operative. They state that:

- Pollution and nuisance should be prevented at source.
- Decision making should take account of environmental effects as early as possible.
- Exploitation of natural resources which causes significant damage to the ecological balance should be avoided.
- Scientific knowledge should be improved and research encouraged.
- The cost of preventing and eliminating nuisances should be borne by the polluter.
- Activities carried out in one member state should not cause environmental deterioration in another.
- The effects of environmental policy should take account of the interests of developing countries.
- The Community and its member states should act together to promote international environmental policy.
- The public should be informed and educated about environmental protection.
- Action should be taken at the appropriate level.
- National environmental policies should be coordinated and harmonised.

                    (Summarised from Johnson and Corcelle, 1995, pp. 14–15)

Following the ratification of the SEA and TEU, some of these principles have been formally included in the Treaty of Rome. These include the polluter-pays principle, the preventive principle, the precautionary principle and the principle of integration. The treaty now states that:

> Community policy on the environment shall aim at a high level of protection taking into account the diversity of situations in the various regions of the Community. It shall be based on the precautionary principle and on the principles that preventative action should be taken, that environmental damage should as a priority be rectified at source and that the polluter should pay. Environmental protection requirements must be integrated into the definition and implementation of other Community policies.

                                                              (Article 130r)

The preventive principle

Rather than seeking only to remedy environmental damage after the event, EU policy is to be based in part on the principle that preventive action should be taken. Damage should, where possible, be avoided at source. The importance of this principle is reflected by the fact that it was listed as the first of eleven policy principles enunciated in the First Environmental Action Programme:

The best environmental policy consists in preventing the creation of nuisances at source, rather than subsequently trying to counteract their effects. To this end, technical progress must be conceived and devised so as to take into account the concern for protection of the environment and for the improvement of the quality of life at the lowest cost to the Community. ...

The First Action Programme conceived of the preventive principle as primarily concerned with the development of technological solutions to avoid or reduce pollution at source. The need to encourage the development of new 'clean technologies' remains an important part of EU policy, and one of the key functions of the EEA is to support research and development projects in this field (see case study).

The preventive principle can be activated in a number of ways: an example is the 1985 Directive on Environmental Impact Assessment (85/337), which provides common rules for the prior evaluation of the environmental effects of certain private and public projects (see Chapter 5). The information required includes a technical description of the project, details of likely significant effects on the environment; details of alternatives explored by the developer; and details of measures taken to avoid or reduce any negative effects on the environment. In addition, a non-technical summary has to be made available. All of these have to be provided to the relevant planning authority. Projects covered include oil refineries, power stations, radioactive waste storage and disposal facilities, iron and steel works, asbestos facilities, chemical installations, motorways, long-distance railway lines, large airports, ports, and toxic waste disposal installations.

Again, direct help and finance can be given to help enact the principle. For example, in 1984 a regulation on action by the Community relating to the environment (ACE) created a fund for financing environment projects (1872/84). The driving force behind this was the preventive principle. The rationale was to provide support to projects aimed at creating clean technologies, developing new techniques and methods for measuring and monitoring the quality of the natural environment, and maintaining or re-establishing the habitat of endangered species of birds. Later ACE was given a wider remit including recycling and locating and restoring sites contaminated by hazardous wastes. It was replaced in 1992 by Regulation 1973/92, which established a financial instrument for the environment (LIFE). Like its predecessor, this is used to finance projects which have as their objective the definition and implementation of environmental policies. LIFE is an integral part of the 5EAP.

The precautionary principle

The TEU amended article 130r by stating that environmental policy should be based on the precautionary principle (see Chapter 4). Although this appears similar to the preventive principle, it goes further in that it implies that action should be taken even before a definite causal link has been established between an activity and any consequent harm to the environment or human health; reasonable evidence of an environmental threat is enough. This approach is similar to that adopted by the US Clean Air Act in 1982.

The precautionary principle is not defined by either the treaty or by the 5EAP, but its meaning can be interpreted from international agreements to which the EU is a party. For example, the UN Framework Convention on Climate Change provides that the parties should:

> take precautionary measures to anticipate, prevent or minimise the causes of climate change and mitigate its adverse effects. Where there are threats of serious or irreversible damage, lack of full scientific certainty should not be used as a reason for postponing such measures.
>
> (Quoted in Kunzlik, 1994, p. 26)

Integration of environmental policy

If environmental policy is to be effective, environmental protection cannot be seen as a separate item or policy area among other discrete policy areas. Rather it must penetrate all areas of policy. The First Environmental Action Programme stated that effects on the environment should be taken into account at the earliest possible stage in all the technical planning and decision-making processes and that:

> The environment cannot be considered as external surroundings by which man is harassed and assailed; it must be considered as an essential factor in the organization and promotion of human progress. It is therefore necessary to evaluate the effects on the quality of life and on the natural environment of any measure that is adopted at national or Community level and is liable to affect these factors.

The SEA reinforces the principle of integration explicitly by stating in Article 130r that: 'Environmental protection requirements shall be a component of the Community's other policies.' This article was further modified by the TEU and now reads: 'Environmental protection requirements must be integrated into the definition and implementation of other Community policies.' This formulation is clearly stronger than the original in that it emphasises that environmental protection should not only be part of the framing of other policies but also of their implementation. It follows that integration is no longer merely a matter of the way policy is formulated within the EU itself: implementation of policy imposes direct responsibilities on member states.

Ensuring genuine integration of environmental policy is no easy matter. One problem is that it will almost inevitably require a shift in focus away from the environmentally active DG XI. This is inevitable if environmental policy is not to be seen as a mere add-on or separate policy area, but as integral to all policy areas. The problem is that DG XI is known to be assiduous in its environmental concern; it is less obvious that other DGs will be equally attentive, and even where they might intend to be, there is a danger that environmental policy will come second to their traditional primary priorities and remit. Proposals to make an initial step towards better integration include the setting up of an Integration Unit within DG XI, the appointment of an Integration Correspondent for each DG and sub-jecting all policy proposals with significant environmental effects to an environ-mental appraisal. In addition it is proposed that each DG carry out an annual evaluation of its environmental performance and that a code of conduct be drawn up for the Commission itself (Wilkinson, 1997, p. 160). These are all important proposals, but implementing them will be far from straightforward. The effects of trying to secure integration are potentially far-reaching and valuable, but there is an associated danger of a loss of focus and a dilution of corporate effort. The dilemma is brought out by Wilkinson:

> Successful integration entails a fundamental redefinition of the role of the environment departments, and some loss of control over environmental policy. The dilemma this poses is that the focus for advancing integration across the activities of government may consequently become less distinct.
>
> (ibid., p. 165)

Maintaining standards

Some EU members, in particular the environmental 'lead' nations of Germany, Scandinavia and the Netherlands, have consistently argued that they should not be prevented from going further than the minimum environmental standards agreed by the EU. Despite the common claim that EU environmental policy sets stand-ards at too low a level because of the need to secure agreement, Article 130s (SEA) states that protective measures adopted under its aegis 'shall not prevent any mem-ber state from maintaining or introducing more stringent protective measures com-patible with this Treaty.' Together with the move towards qualified majority voting on environmental legislation, extra pressure from new member states such as Swe-den and Finland should go some way towards revitalising EU environmental policy. However, there is clearly a danger on the horizon: when the EU is further enlarged to include countries from the former communist bloc there may be pressure for the dilution of environmental initiatives in favour of economic development (see later).

A related issue is the type of pollution standard adopted in EU environmental legislation. Although there are a variety of approaches and standards available for pollution control (see Chapters 6 and 9), debate at the European level has tended to centre on two approaches often seen as mutually exclusive: emission standards and environmental quality standards. There is a widespread impression that the Commission and countries such as Germany have a particular preference for uni-form emission standards, while the UK has an equal and opposite preference for setting emission standards individually in relation to environmental quality. This may be an accurate description of views expressed in the negotiations over Direc-tive 76/464 on dangerous substances in water, but it is an inaccurate and over-simplified view of national approaches to pollution control as such. In fact, for the most part, the two approaches are not necessarily opposed. Each has arguments in its favour, reflecting the best way to ensure administrative efficiency and whether it makes sense only to worry about a pollutant which is known to be actively causing harm, or to minimise emissions of anything with harmful potential even where no actual harm has or is likely to be incurred.

The argument for environmental quality standards is based on the assumption that the purpose of pollution control is for ambient pollution to remain below a certain level and therefore that it makes sense to monitor and control at the point of impact. However, it may be accepted that it is often more practicable to control and monitor nearer the point of emission. Emissions standards are thus viewed as a means to the end of achieving quality objectives designed to protect identified targets, and they do not need to be any more stringent than necessary to meet those objectives. It follows from this that emissions standards might therefore justifiably vary from place to place. The counter argument holds that the emission of polluting substances should be reduced as far as is technically possible, even if at a particular concentration they have no known effect. This could be seen as a strict interpretation of the principles of prevention and precaution. The best place to control and monitor is taken to be the point of emission, and controls should be as stringent as possible. Uniform, fixed emission standards are taken as the best way to proceed.

Haigh points out that these contrasting views are not always made explicit and applied uniformly. In the UK, for example, air pollution control has been based on the uniform standards view while water pollution control has been based on achieving defined quality objectives through the setting of local emission standards (Haigh, 1989, p. 21). There may be good reasons for these different approaches: the issue becomes that of acceptable levels of emissions and the most effective and efficient means of monitoring and controlling them. Should permitted emissions levels reflect the ability of the local environment to disperse or absorb the pollutant, with the corollary that what might be acceptable in one place is not necessarily acceptable elsewhere; or is it always best to insist on reducing emissions to the absolute minimum technically possible? The uniform emissions standards approach has the practical advantage that monitoring is relatively easy and it is easy to assess compliance; it also contains a built-in presumption of improvement in standards – the better the technology the further the reduction in emissions. Monitoring and control are more difficult where ambient environmental conditions have also to be taken into account. Emissions standards have the advantage of seeking to minimise within an overall acceptable level of emissions; but quality standards can allow flexibility according to local circumstances. For example, the UK has relatively short, fast-running rivers and is surrounded by sea. There is therefore an obvious argument against applying emissions standards for water set by reference to what is necessary to protect, say, the Rhine, which drains many industrial areas and which is used as an important source of drinking water by the Germans and the Dutch. Controls can and should be applied most stringently where the environment is most vulnerable (ibid., p. 22).

The challenge for the EU is to allow member states flexibility in implementation of policy without sacrificing local environments to the mercies of those governments whose approach to the environment perhaps reflects not a considered and reasonable preference for one policy approach over another, but an indifference to environment policy and issues as such.

CONTEMPORARY ISSUES IN EU ENVIRONMENTAL ACTION

The fact that the EU has adopted environmental policy making as one of its main activities should not lead to complacency. There are a number of reasons for this. The first is that although the EU has moved on from its primary concern being purely economic objectives, none the less these objectives still constitute a major thrust of its activities and therefore there is always likely to be conflict between environmental and economic considerations. The revised Article 2 may refer to environmental considerations, but at the same time it explicitly requires a balance to be struck between economic and environmental issues and this is likely to constrain radical environmental policy making in the EU. Second, there is always going to be a problem of enforcement. There is currently no effective enforcement machinery (see case study on the EEA). The implementation of policy is largely at the mercy of individual member states and therefore subject to their willingness (or otherwise) to implement and promote environmental policy. Third, there are clashes between environmental policy and other policy areas such as agriculture and fisheries: environmental policy can be negated by other EU policy areas, not only by economic objectives. Fourth, it is not clear that EU environmental policy will always improve standards; in many cases a levelling down may be required to ensure a level economic playing field. These are all pertinent concerns for the future development of environmental policy and have already been touched on in this chapter; we will now briefly attend to three other areas which impinge on the efficacy of European environmental policy: the principle of subsidiarity, the entry of new member states, and the impact of green parties in the European Parliament.

The impact of subsidiarity

Maastricht put subsidiarity at the top of the European political agenda. It is a concept which is interpreted in different ways. Some member states hope to use it to curb the power of the EU itself (the UK under the Conservative administration and Denmark); others see it as a way of safeguarding the power of their regions (Germany and Spain). Again, others, such as the Netherlands, support the principle of subsidiarity because it is seen as a way of preserving their different regulatory traditions. The principle of subsidiarity was stated in the First Environmental Action Programme and later incorporated into the Treaty of Rome through the SEA. When it was first introduced it referred solely to environmental policy. Article 130r states: 'The Community shall take action relating to the environment to the extent to which the objectives ... can be attained better at Community level than at the level of the individual Member States.' The political and legal meaning of the principle is still a matter of dispute, despite its more general application in the TEU, where the principle was extended to cover all the EU's activities. Whether it should act as a constraint on coordinated EU policy, as some member states suggest, is at the very least disputable. However, the principle of subsidiarity – sometimes expressed as 'do less but do it better' – in principle leaves the EU free to legislate principally for issues of a cross-border nature and at the same time to increase the enforcement of compliance.

In a positive environmental light, the principle of subsidiarity can be seen as lying at the heart of the green idea of appropriate action at the appropriate level, which we have argued is central to sustainable development (see Chapter 2). Subsidiarity, along with increased deregulation, could lead to a flexible approach to environmental protection that is sensitive to local environmental conditions – perhaps to an increase in the effective use of market-based instruments and genuine self-regulation. Again, if subsidiarity leads to decisions being taken as close to the citizens as possible and with their increased participation, this can only be seen as positive from a green perspective.

However, sceptics see the challenge to European-level environmental policy making in a different light. If individual governments are left to their own devices, not only might this compromise the idea of a single market, but also subsidiarity (and de-regulation) may become an excuse for not taking action and also raises issues of the enforcement of environmental directives. The unhappy truth is that many EU member states are unlikely to take environmental action in the absence of EU legislation, and that the concept of subsidiarity can be used as a justification for their inaction. The principle of subsidiarity can be exploited in the narrower interests of national sovereignty and the idea of deregulation can degenerate into unenforced self-regulation by industry and business. The various interpretations of subsidiarity makes environmental policy vulnerable, as not only do member states legitimately differ on their interpretation, but, given their reluctance to take environment action in the absence of EU legislation, perhaps deliberately use ambiguity as a cover for inaction (Collier, 1997, p. 3). Although the principle of subsidiarity can be used to legitimise EU environmental action on the one hand or to strengthen the role of sub-national actors on the other,[10] its effect in practice has tended to be a downgrading of environmental proposals in which a greater scope is left for national interpretations. It has led to repatriation of proposed measures and there has also been a move away from the use of directives towards weaker framework directives and recommendations.

New member states

The fourth enlargement of the EU occurred in 1995 when Sweden, Finland and Austria joined. This is generally expected to have a positive impact on the environmental policy of the EU as both Sweden and Finland have high domestic environmental standards and concerns and will now join the green lead states – the Netherlands, Germany and Denmark. Given the increasing amount of environmental policy being enacted through qualified majority voting, and the relative isolation of these lead states, the addition of the new members means that environmental policy should receive an easier passage; it also means that these countries can together form a 'blocking minority' and thereby act to prevent environmental policy being overridden, ignored or weakened. The new member states will also affect the type of policy instruments employed. For example, both Sweden and Finland are strong advocates of the use of economic instruments and this enthusiasm is likely to carry over into promoting a new direction in EU environmental policy.

However, what will be the effect of further enlargement? At present, ex-communist bloc countries such as Poland and Hungary are applying for EU membership. It is clear that the primary concern of these nations is economic regeneration and there is a belief that they will not be able to adhere to the relatively strict European standards on environmental protection. Equally, there is some concern that these nations could become part of a larger blocking vote which could hamper the further development of Europe-wide environmental policy. At present, this is simply speculation, but enlargement of the EU is a political priority and whatever else happens, this will undoubtably have some effect on environmental initiatives.

Green parties in Europe

Greens first entered the European Parliament after the 1984 European elections, when eleven were elected from three member states. In the 1989 elections, twenty-eight greens from six different countries were elected. Green MEPs sit as part of the Green Group in the EP (GGEP); following the 1994 elections the group had twenty-two members, and by 1998 this had increased to twenty-eight. However, given their commitments to democratic renewal and openness in decision making, membership of the Parliament is fraught with tensions for green MEPs: the EU itself is frequently charged with violating these basic principles. So, on the one hand, the EU allows access to influence on decision making, while on the other the institution is, in the eyes of many greens, basically flawed, characterised in their view by technocratic policy making, remote decision-making bodies and the dominance of intergovernmental influence and the politics of national self-interest.

Despite its misgivings about the democratic deficit in the EU, the Green Group has now largely adopted a policy of working within the institutions. For example, green MEPs are able to force environmental concerns on to the agenda by submitting written questions to the Council and Commission. These questions have to be answered in either written or oral form. They can also introduce new issues through 'urgency resolutions'. If the subject matter is genuinely urgent, these resolutions will receive immediate attention from committees and be directed to the Council, Commission, member state or appropriate international body. Green members have, through these means, introduced resolutions on nuclear waste and protection of the North Sea, amongst other issues. They are also active in arranging conferences and seminars on environmental and related concerns. Despite these successes, greens are hampered by both their own rooted objections to the structures they have to work within and the palpable way in which those structures flagrantly violate what they see as elementary democratic and participatory principles. As Bomberg asks: 'how can greens achieve "green" goals through structures that are deeply implicated in the *status quo* they seek to shift?' (Bomberg, 1996, pp. 329–30).

In Bomberg's opinion, three complications exacerbate the green paradox. The first is that in the Green Group's view, the subordinate position of the Parliament highlights the democratic deficit in the EU. The European Parliament is the EU's only directly elected body, and yet it wields the least amount of authority in a policy-making process dominated by the Commission and Council. Of course, many besides greens are concerned about the EU's democratic deficit, but most other groups do not share their radical emphasis on open democratic structures and grassroots participation. Second, policy making in the EU is technocratic, bureaucratic and largely centralised. It is centralised because it relies on interaction between national and EU bureaucracies to formulate and enact policies. This is perhaps inevitable given the task of coordinating policy across Europe; but the result, none the less, appears to be an EU run by an unaccountable technocracy. Green MEPs, therefore, by comparison with MEPs from traditional parties, have to face the dilemma of pushing for decentralised politics within the often centralised structures of the EU. Third, green MEPs face the difficulty of separation and distance from those they represent. This makes it especially problematic as they are committed to grassroots participation, the possibility of which is denied by geographical isolation and remoteness (ibid., p. 330).

Perhaps these are impossible challenges and maybe the greens, who have their own national and ideological divisions, are not yet in a position to conjure up a common view of a 'green Europe'. Despite this they have had successes and cooperated on issues such as anti-nuclear protest and biotechnology and, as Bomberg argues:

> Whether or not they alter fundamentally the course of EU policies, they at least offer a refreshing critique of the EU, and raise important questions concerning European policies, practices and democracy.
>
> (ibid., p. 330)[11]

TOWARDS SUSTAINABILITY? THE EU'S FIFTH ENVIRONMENTAL ACTION PROGRAMME (5EAP)

A new approach

EU environmental action from 1973 to 1992 was largely prescriptive and top-down. It typically consisted of the imposition of environmental legislation from the centre in response to what it perceived to be current pressing environmental concerns. The Fifth Environmental Action Programme (5EAP), covering the years 1993–2000, seeks to change this. As its extended title, *Towards Sustainability – A Community Programme of Policy and Action in Relation to the Environment and Sustainable Development*, indicates, sustainable development is identified as the main objective of environmental policy. This requires:

> a policy and strategy for continued economic and social development without detriment to the environment and the natural resources on the quality of which continued human activity and further development depend.
>
> (OJ, 1993, p. 18)

The 5EAP was adopted in 1992 and approved by a Council resolution in 1993. It was thus adopted only a few months before the Rio Earth Summit and, moreover, it was prepared in parallel with the main Rio agreements so that it shares most of their strategic objectives and principles (Wilkinson, 1997, p. 158). The 5EAP has been chosen as the main European vehicle for the implementation of Agenda 21 and other UNCED agreements. It is important in that it marks a change of direction in EU environmental policy. Previously programmes tended to be lists of proposed legislation. The focus of the 5EAP, by contrast, is anticipatory and committed to long-term sustainability

The 5EAP also signals a move away from traditional command and control legislation; there is a more explicit recognition of the concept of subsidiarity, and there is a move towards deregulation and market-based policies – using different policy instruments such as economic incentives and disincentives, taxation, and voluntary agreements with industry. In addition, an emergent key theme of the 5EAP is that of integration: the need to integrate the environment into the development and implementation of other policies. This integration is seen as a fundamental prerequisite for the achievement of sustainable development. However, this objective is hampered by the fact that the programme is not binding on EU member states or in practice on individual DGs in the Commission.

Issues and policy sectors

The first part of the 5EAP comprises a review of the state of the European environment and an assessment of the causes of environmental degradation in a number of areas: air, water, soil, waste, quality of life, high-risk activities and biological diversity. The second section, entitled *Towards Sustainability*, sets the objectives, policy and implementation programmes for the environment for 1993–2000. The report goes on to consider the five key sectors where integrated approaches to sustainable development are necessary. These sectors are agriculture, energy, industry, transport and tourism (see Table 8.1).

In addition to the target sectors there are also a number of priority issues identified in the programme. These are climate change, acidification, nature and biodiversity, water resources, the urban environment, coastal zones, and waste.

Table 8.1 Key sectors in the 5EAP

Sector	Policies
Agriculture	Reform of Common Agricultural Policy (CAP). Reduction of phosphate and pesticide use. Promotion of new forests. Establishment of agriculture/environment zones. Exchange of good practice between regions.
Energy	Moves to reduce energy demand and to control emissions. Use of economic instruments to ensure that the real cost of energy consumption is passed on to the consumer. Promotion of new technologies and use of renewable energy.
Industry	Implementation of strategic environmental impact assessment. Promotion of eco-audit; life-cycle analysis; BATNEEC. Introduction of eco-labelling. Promotion of self-regulation. Control of waste management. Increased public information.
Transport	Move towards sustainable mobility. Commitment to developing the Trans-European Network. Reduction of pollution and energy consumption. Promotion of integrated public transport. Reduced use of cars.
Tourism	Reconciling tourism with development. Protection of natural assets left to members states, regional and local authorities, the tourist industry and individual tourists – an application of the principles of shared responsibility and subsidiarity.

Principles and procedures

The 5EAP is based on the principle of subsidiarity and shared responsibility. It also recognises the EU's international obligations. Measures within the programme identify which level is responsible for implementation and provide target dates for implementation. Attention is also paid to enforcement. The success of the 5EAP is understood as depending on the contributions of public authorities, public and private enterprise, and the general public. For example, it is estimated by the EU that some 40 per cent of the 5EAP is the implementation responsibility of local government (LGMB, 1993a, p. 28). The programme goes beyond the traditional legislative approach by advocating the use of market-based measures such as charges, fiscal incentives, state aids, environmental auditing and an environmental liability regime. It also promotes the use of 'horizontal, supporting instruments' (for example, education, training, improvement of data and LIFE) which aim to increase the capacity of actors to exercise their 'shared responsibility'. In addition, environmental impact assessment is seen as necessary, not only for specific developments but also in relation to the framing of structural policies themselves. Hence there is support for the introduction of strategic environmental assessment (see Chapter 5).

Article 130r (amended by the TEU) requires the EU to promote international cooperation in dealing with environmental problems. Accordingly, the 5EAP states that already existing international activity should be furthered and supplemented. Hence there is added legitimacy for the participation of the EU as an independent actor in international regimes. This role has been played effectively in the UNCED process and recent climate change negotiations. It could even be argued that the EU may evolve into the hegemonic international environmental actor that so many international relations theorists believe is necessary for effective regime building (see Chapter 7).

To improve policy making and implementation, the 5EAP established three 'dialogue groups'. The General Consultative Forum comprises representatives of trade and industry, trade unions, environment and consumer organisations, and local and regional government. Members do not represent their organisation but speak for themselves. The Implementation Network is made up of national and Commission officials involved in implementing environmental policy and is concerned with information exchange and experience, and developing common approaches to implementation. The Environmental Policy Review Group comprises senior officials from member states and the Commission and is designed to facilitate understanding and the exchange of views on environmental policy and measures independently of specific proposals and infringement proceedings.

Towards what sort of sustainability?

Previous environmental programmes had taken the form of lists of proposed legislation, often selected in relation to specific events. This has been successful in many ways: for instance, over 200 pieces of legislation have been introduced. In comparison, the 5EAP attempts to address the fundamental causes of environmental degradation as a means of creating a more sustainable economy and society: it states that the principle of sustainable development should be incorporated into all other EU policies. However, what is clear is that its approach to sustainability is redolent of Brundtland – the rhetoric of ecological modernisation and weak sustainability is dominant (see Chapters 2 and 5). As Susan Baker argues: 'What is especially noticeable in the Fifth Action Programme is the centrality given to breaking the perception that there is a trade-off between environmental protection and economic development' (Baker, 1997, p. 97).

The Maastricht Treaty talks of sustainable progress, development and growth, using the terms interchangeably; thus, although the 5EAP contains the EU's most explicit commitment to sustainable development, it is a commitment to a weak rather than a strong conception. Why has the EU adopted such a weak view of sustainable development? The short answer is that it did so because of the context within which its environmental policies evolved and the extent to which EU policy making as a whole is incremental in character.

> Incrementalism makes the chances of successful translation of the commitment to sustainable development into actual policy dependent upon the extent to which the required policy changes can be fitted with existing policy commitments. Policy proposals that fit with the strategy of environmental quality management stand a greater chance of acceptance, while policies that fit more closely with the second, more radical, pattern have little, if any, chance

of success. The concept of sustainable development has been interpreted by the Union (and its member-states) to fit within the confines of managerial as opposed to radical policy solutions.

(Baker, 1997, p. 102)

However, even if the dominant understanding of sustainable development is ecological modernisation, this must be seen as progress given that the original EEC had absolutely no reference to environmental concerns. Even though it may not go far enough for many greens it may provide a critical standpoint from which to judge the continuing development of the EU. For example, the principles and policies with the 5EAP could be used to combat the tendency for member states to interpret the subsidiarity principle in a negative way and it may begin a move towards integration of environmental policy across policy sectors. However, as already noted, integration can imply a loss of control over environmental policy. No longer is it the exclusive reserve of DG XI but something which has to be encompassed by all DGs and is therefore subject to their discretion, interpretation and judgement.

DG XI's 1995 progress report on the 5EAP states that:

The measures so far have had limited impact ... progress has varied according to sectors, but the message of the Fifth Programme has not been sufficiently integrated in operational terms within the Commission. The process depends on persuasion and influence and will take time. In the longer term, change is likely to take place through increased education, training and changes of attitude. It will require continued adequate resources and sustained commitment.

(Quoted in Wilkinson, 1997, p. 164)

The achievement of sustainable development is in the balance. Much depends on interpretation of the term; on how the principles of subsidiarity and integration are interpreted and acted upon; on the activities of DG XI, the European Parliament and the leadership of the Council of Ministers; and the enthusiasm and enterprise of the member states in promoting environmental policy.

When originally introduced, the 5EAP was considered to be binding neither on the Commission nor the member states, as the Council had approved only the 'general approach and strategy of the programme' and not its detailed targets and timetables. This approval was given in the form of a non-binding resolution (Wilkinson, 1997, p. 169). However, under the provisions of Article 130s of the Maastricht Treaty a new legal status was given to general action programmes on the environment. This implies that future action programmes will be legally binding and also that the 5EAP will be interpreted in a stricter form than its formal status suggests. Further, the programme's promotion of sustainable development has recently been strengthened by the signing of the Treaty of Amsterdam. This contains a stronger and less equivocal commitment to sustainable development than any previous statement. In the new Article 2 it calls for 'a harmonious, balanced and sustainable development of economic activities', and the new provision in Article 3c states that 'environmental protection require-ments must be integrated into the definition and implementation of Community policies and activities ... in particular with a view to promoting sustainable de-velopment.' In a declaration attached to the treaty, the Commission has also promised to prepare 'environmental impact assessment studies when making proposals which may have significant environmental implications.' The Euro-pean Environmental Bureau (an umbrella organisation representing environ-mental groups in Brussels) described this as 'a radical change of course after forty years of placing economic growth at the top of the EC's political priorities' (ENDS, 1997a, p. 45). There may still be scope for optimism.

CONCLUSION

EU environmental policy is based on a notion of weak sustainable development – a conception of ecological modernisation. This should not be surprising. Although environmental policy now has an assured place, the origins of the EU as a commu-nity dedicated to promoting economic growth and prosperity limit the extent to which environmental policy can escape from or challenge that primary rationale. Despite the best efforts of DG XI, the tensions between its environmental con-cerns and the concerns of the policy makers in the Commission as a whole and in the Council of Ministers is always likely to limit its effectiveness in mounting a radical challenge to the status quo. It also means that to some extent the EU is always likely to lag behind the environmentally committed position of some of its member states which regard its policy as weak and ineffective. But this should all be placed in a broader perspective. We have already seen in this book that it is notoriously difficult to achieve agreement and action in environmental policy: perhaps we should therefore give credit to the EU for achieving what it has. In addition, the EU's adoption of sustainable development as a policy target (what-ever its own interpretation of the term) provides a criterion against which its suc-cess or failure can be judged in the future. Whichever way we look at it, a pan-European Union originally dedicated to economic growth and prosperity has become a major source of environmental policy, commitment and concern.

But before we get complacent it is important to recognise that the task has only just really got fully under way and there is much to be done. As the 1995 European Environmental Agency report on the 5EAP states:

> The European Union is making progress in reducing certain pressures on the environment, though this is not enough to improve the general quality of the environment and even less to progress towards sustainability. With-out accelerated policies, pressures on the environment will continue to ex-ceed human health standards and the often limited carrying capacity of the environment.
>
> (Quoted in Collier, 1997, p. 2)

CASE STUDY: THE ROLE OF THE EUROPEAN ENVIRONMENT AGENCY

Origins

The Fourth Environmental Action Programme suggested that the Commission should set up an environmental inspectorate. This suggestion was greeted with suspicion and some hostility, principally because few member states had sound enough environmental records to relish the prospect of its being overseen by a central EU inspectorate (ENDS, 1995b, p. 20). Despite this concern, in 1990 environment ministers adopted a regulation establishing the European Environment Agency (EEA). After further political disagreements as to its location, the EEA's headquarters in Copenhagen was eventually opened in November 1994. It began its substantive work in 1995 and now has a staff of about sixty and an annual budget of £12 million.

European Environment Agency

Objective:

To provide EC institutions and member states with information to enable them to take measures to protect the environment, assess the results of such measures, and ensure that the public is properly informed about the state of the environment and the pressures on it.

Key tasks:

- To establish and coordinate an Environmental Information and Observation Network (EIONET).
- To provide Community institutions and member states with the information they need to frame and implement sound and effective environmental policies.
- To collect and analyse data on the state of the environment and to provide uniform assessment criteria for the collection of data by member states which the Commission will use to determine compliance with EC legislation.
- To ensure environmental data is comparable and to encourage the harmonisation of monitoring methodologies.
- To ensure the broad dissemination of reliable environmental information, and in particular, publish a report on the state of Europe's environment every three years.

- To promote application of environmental forecasting techniques and preventive measures.
- To stimulate the development of methods to assess the costs of damage to the environment, prevention, protection and restoration.
- To stimulate information exchange on best available technologies.

(ENDS, 1995b, p. 22)

One of the key debates in the run-up to the formation of the EEA was whether it should have the powers of an inspectorate. ECOSOC and the European Parliament argued that it should have rights of inspection and of assessing compliance with legislation. They failed in this, but the Parliament was successful in forcing the inclusion of uniform assessment criteria for the collection of environmental data by all member states and in requiring a review of the agency's work after two years of operation (Collins and Earnshaw, 1993, p. 239). In the final version of the EEA regulation, the tasks of monitoring compliance and enforcing environmental law via inspectorates were specifically not included. There were three reasons for this: first, it was viewed primarily as an information gatherer; second, the view was taken that adding an inspectorate role at the outset would be too great a burden; third, there was a concern that it would not be able to sustain the contrasting roles of mediator and enforcer (Bailey, 1997, p. 149).

Although the EEA might be said to have limited powers, it is at the same time important not to underestimate the extent to which reliable information has a vital role to play in ensuring full and uniform compliance with environmental legislation. As we saw above, some countries such as the UK suffer at the hands of the Commission simply because their environmental reporting is better than that of other member states. Hence the UK supported the formation of the EEA:

The fledgeling EEA could improve this situation and remove the UK's vulnerability to being singled out by information-starved DG XI officials. Other EU states are likely to be revealed as more serious transgressors of Directives.

(Haigh and Lanigan, 1995, p. 29)

The executive director, Señor Domingo Jiménez-Beltrán, described the EEA as forming the tip of an iceberg made up of national information networks. In his view the problem lay not in securing information as such; it lay in securing good information. Accordingly he saw his primary task as establishing the EEA as an independent source of reliable data and knowledge as to the state of the European environment.

Europe's environment

The agency's first report on Europe's environment (The Dobris Assessment) was published in 1995. This provides a baseline picture of the state of Europe's (not merely the EU) environment and the pressures on it. It highlighted twelve issues as particularly important for the attainment of sustainability: climate change; stratospheric ozone depletion; loss of biodiversity; major accidents; acidification; tropospheric ozone and other photochemical oxidants; management of fresh water; forest degradation; coastal zone threats and management; waste reduction and management; urban stress; and chemical risks (Osborn, 1997, p. 256). The next report (Dobris plus 3) is due in 1998.

The first formal review of the agency's mandate was published in 1997. This showed that it is having some difficulties in persuading national networks to deliver information (ENDS, 1997b, p. 40). In building an environmental information network, the agency designated European topic centres. Each was to be a system of cooperating institutions led by a recognised national institute. The intention was to link experts in member states together (Jiménez-Beltrán, 1995, p. 267). However, of the eight planned topic centres, only those on air quality and atmospheric emissions have made a real impact. Others covering inland waters, soil quality, nature conservation, the marine and coastal environment, and land cover are just beginning to produce useful data. The waste management centre was only set up in 1997. Because the agency was having these difficulties in its information-gathering role, the Commission decided in its review that it would be inappropriate and premature to add major new tasks to the EEA's remit at that point (ENDS, 1997b, p. 40).

New roles for the EEA?

From its inception, there has been a debate about what the EEA's role should be. Although it was established primarily as an information-gathering agency, it is possible that at a later stage it could assume some sort of inspectorate role. Broadly speaking there are three possibilities. The first is the status quo: the EEA would remain as it is, a data-gathering and information service; the second is that it could become an 'inspectorate of the inspectorates', auditing the actions of national inspectorates such as the UK Environment Agency (see Chapter 8); the third is that it could become an inspectorate in its own right.

Could the EEA develop from being a passive recipient of information towards a stronger role in the coordination of environmental measurement and inspection in member states? Such a move would require it to have an oversight or audit function, inspecting the methods employed by national regulatory authorities (Collins and Earnshaw, 1993, p. 239). In 1995, the UK House of Lords Select Committee Report on the EEA took the view that while the work of the EEA would help by making the environmental action or inaction of member states more transparent, it would be of rather less help in securing enforcement. It concluded that an inspectorate of national inspectorates would eventually need to be formed. Such an inspectorate, in its role as auditor, would be allowed to visit a member state to take samples and to verify methods of data collection, compilation and analysis. It accepted that this was unlikely in the near future but that it should be established if patterns of persistent non-compliance are noted (Bailey, 1997, p. 150). Such a role would actively seek the cooperation of member states:

> While some analysts support the idea of an inspectorate, an inspectorate in the strict sense of the word may not be the best way to achieve compliance. Instead, the EEA could develop an inspectorate which works in conjunction with environmental ministries and enforcement bodies of the member states, thus operating in a more cooperative manner. In this way, the policies of the administrations of the member states can be used to affect implementation.
>
> (ibid.)

Could the EEA go further and become a full inspectorate? There are broadly two schools of thought here. On the one hand, the access to Europe-wide environmental information that it is developing would put it in a good position to do the job objectively; but on the other, because it is dependent on the goodwill of member states for the success of its existing projects and information gathering, it could jeopardise this relationship by becoming an inspectorate. A key issue is whether it could sustain the contrasting roles of mediator and enforcer (Bailey, 1997, p. 149; ENDS, 1995b, p. 22). In addition, it is often thought (as the 1997 report stated) that it is simply too soon for the agency to extend its activities. In 1992, the House of Lords Select Committee on the European Communities proposed that an environmental inspectorate should be established if the EEA discovered that member states are failing to comply. It would require powers to make spot checks on data collected by national authorities. However, such a move is now regarded as inappropriate given the 'current political mood in the member states' concerning the powers of EU institutions and a more incremental approach is now suggested. The EEA should recommend standards for data collection, sampling and analysis, publish annual reports on compliance, and if it finds persistent non-compliance, an inspectorate with the power to make spot checks should be brought into being (ENDS, 1995d, p. 31).

Future prospects for the EEA

Clearly, discussion about the role of the EEA goes beyond the narrow remit of environmental policy itself: it touches on and reflects broader issues concerning the nature of the EU, national sovereignty and the principle of subsidiarity. For example, it is often argued that member states would not accept an EU-level inspectorate, because it would have the power to intervene in national monitoring and policy (Collins and Earnshaw, 1993, pp. 238–9). However, such an inspectorate within the EU would not be unique:

> A common argument against inspectorates is that the sovereignty of the member states must be respected. But in reality, various forms of inspectorate can be found in other areas of the Community, such as competition policy, agricultural policies and fisheries management. Thus, an environmental inspectorate which audits both collection methods and methods of analysis would hardly intrude further on member states' sovereignty. None the less, member states are always resentful of any perceived intrusions on their sovereignty; creating an environmental inspectorate at Community level will certainly be difficult.
>
> (Bailey, 1997, p. 150)

A further set of arguments centres not so much on whether there ought to be an EU-wide inspectorate, but whether if there is to be one, should, or even could, the task be assigned to the EEA.

> The Commission might only give qualified support to the idea of the EEA taking on an audit inspectorate function. During the negotiations over the creation of the EEA the Commission was reluctant to assign monitoring or inspection functions to the EEA. Apart from the difficulty that it would have faced winning support in Council for such a development, the Commission also sought to defend its own role. It wanted to ensure that functions envisaged for the EEA were clearly distinct from, even if complementary to, its own role. The Commission

emphasised that the treaties give it specific responsibilities and prerogatives for the implementation and enforcement of EC environment legislation. In view of this it is also doubtful that the Commission was in a position in any case to sanction what could amount to a transfer of power to a new body.

(Collins and Earnshaw, 1993, pp. 239–40)

In May 1996, a European Parliament hearing on implementation and enforcement debated the issue of the desirability of an EU-level body to oversee the work of inspectorates. Three candidates were considered for the role: IMPEL (Network for the Implementation and Enforcement of Environmental Law – an informal network of pollution inspectorates), the EEA and the Commission. IMPEL does not consider itself ready to take on the role and MEPs were opposed to this idea as it is regarded as a secretive talking shop. The agency itself is wary, taking the view that an inspectorate role could jeopardise relationships with member states which are crucial for obtaining information. However, the EEA could monitor member states' inspection arrangements and thus be a natural institutional location for IMPEL. The Director-General of DG XI insists that the duty of ensuring compliance lies with the Commission. But the Commission itself regards it as premature to set up an EU inspectorate when some member states still need to build up their own inspectorate capacity (ENDS, 1996a, pp. 44–5).

Resolution of these debates is clearly still some way off; but, whatever the final outcome, it is worth heeding the remarks made by the chair of the European Parliament Environment Committee, Ken Collins: 'It is increasingly clear that without a well-resourced independent inspection and enforcement agency the job will never be done effectively' (ENDS, 1996a, p. 45).

SUGGESTIONS FOR FURTHER READING

David Judge (ed.), *A Green Dimension for the European Community* (1993), is a valuable collection of essays on the incorporation of environmental issues within European policy. Susan Baker *et al.* (eds), *The Politics of Sustainable Development* (1997), is a more contemporary collection of theoretical and practical considerations, relating EU policy to national and local actions. On the impact of green parties at the European level, see Elizabeth Bomberg, *Green Parties and Politics in the European Union* (1998).

9 National responses

There is sufficient evidence of institutional innovation occurring in the UK to be confident that there is a cautious shift towards addressing sustainable development beyond the rhetoric. Building on this capacity so that previously neglected policy areas and interests are included in a coherent transition is the current and continuing challenge.

(Voisey and O'Riordan, 1997, p. 49)

This chapter will focus on national attempts to respond to the environment and sustainable development agendas. The scope of policy options open to nation states is constrained by international obligations, particularly so for member states of the European Union (EU), an actor in its own right in environmental policy. However, national approaches still differ markedly in scope, effectiveness and approach. These differences can be explained by a number of factors, in particular the political culture of different nations – for instance, institutional arrangements, traditional approaches to policy formulation and implementation, party systems, the strength of different interest groups, and their access to policy networks. Such factors will be examined in light of the changing practice and policy of pollution control in the UK. The traditional British approach of consensual and secretive negotiations between industry and various agencies has been transformed into a much more standardised and integrated regime that bears more resemblance to other European traditions.

Achieving integrated pollution control is but one aspect of policy for sustainable development. At a more strategic level it is necessary to develop a coordinated strategy or plan that integrates national environmental, social and economic policy. By again focusing on the UK, which during the 1980s was ideologically opposed to economic planning, we can see just how far the green agenda has been addressed at the national level. A case study on the much praised Dutch *National Environment Policy Plan* (NEPP) affords the opportunity to compare the fortunes of two contrasting European liberal democracies.

ISSUES AFFECTING NATIONAL ENVIRONMENTAL POLICY MAKING

A number of factors influence the direction of environmental policy at a national level. These range from the nature of international agreements, regimes and organisations through to the activities of local NGOs. It is worth reflecting on some of these pressures as they are fundamental to understanding the development of pollution control policy and sustainability planning, which we shall look at in some detail in this chapter.

The growing number of international environmental agreements (see Chapter 7) creates a framework within which national environmental policy is formulated. Some of these agreements are legally binding, forcing a national response on issues such as carbon dioxide emission reductions or endangered species protection. Of equal importance, the very existence of international environmental regimes structures the way that nations approach environmental policy. In a positive sense, such regimes can be understood as creating the conditions for social learning – they provide an opportunity for states to gather information about environmental problems and possible solutions. On a more negative note, this learning is often done within a limited understanding of the nature of environmental problems and sustainable development. Typically, the prevailing economic orthodoxy is left unchallenged. Obviously not all international agreements and regimes result in positive environmental and developmental actions. Particularly for many Southern nations, attempts at developing effective environmental policies have often been overridden by the requirements of structural adjustment policies imposed by the IMF or the more immediate demands of widespread poverty and, in the extreme, famine and war. The new World Trade Organisation may also act against any unilateral national imposition of high environmental standards in the name of free-market international competition.

For member states, the expansion of the EU's competence into environmental policy (see Chapter 8) is perhaps the largest single influence on the direction of national environmental policy making. As the only currently existing supranational institution with legislative powers, its influence on member states has been quite profound. Much of the content of recent UK environmental legislation – for instance the Wildlife and Countryside Act (1981) and the Environmental Protection Act (1990) – was the legally required national implementation of relevant EU directives. It is questionable whether some of these environmental protection laws would have ever reached the statute book without the existence of the EU. Again, as we shall see below, the EU's influence on the emerging UK pollution control regime has been profound and indicates the influence of more environmentally forward-thinking states such as Germany.[1]

The recognition that there are diverse national traditions of environmental management and control is fundamental to any analysis of the formulation of environmental policy. At a quite basic level, different cultures display different attitudes to different environmental issues. It should be no surprise that the concern in North America, Australia and New Zealand over wilderness protection is not exactly replicated in more densely populated European nations. Even within Europe itself, there appears to be a broader conception of well-being, extending to environmental quality, in German and Scandinavian language and practices. Again, differences between European nations over attitudes to intensive animal farming practices vary, with the UK having a long tradition in animal welfare, whereas France, Spain and other Southern European nations appear to lack such sentiments.

A further factor that affects the fate of environmental policy is the ideological position of governments. A good example here, and one that will be returned to as the chapter progresses, is the ideological opposition during the 1980s of the Conservative Party in the UK to any comprehensive environmental policy which was seen as an impediment to economic development.[2] At the same time, the Prime Minister, Margaret Thatcher, was vehemently opposed to the inclusion of pressure groups within the policy-making process. Environmental NGOs found themselves in a most inhospitable political climate. The USA suffered a similar period of ideological opposition to environmental policy in the 1980s under Ronald Reagan and then George Bush.

However, Thatcher is a prime example of how national governments are to some extent also the creature of public opinion. The 'greening of Thatcher' in 1989 can be seen as a shrewd political manoeuvre given growing public concern over the environment and the Green Party's success in the European election, rather than as a deep political rethink (McCormick 1991; 1993). However, it did allow the political space for the relatively strong environment minister, Chris Patten, to produce a white paper, *This Common Inheritance* (DoE, 1990), which laid the ground for further progress in environmental policy making.

The capacity of Patten to produce this document from within a party whose leadership was ideologically opposed to the wider green agenda indicates two other important factors: leadership and the relative strength of the environment ministry. Certainly, the priority given to environmental policy has been affected by the standing and ability of the minister charged with this responsibility. In the UK, the re-emergence of the environment as a political issue coincided with the leadership given by successive Secretaries of State. Patten was followed by Michael Heseltine, an equally powerful figure within the Conservative Party. When Heseltine was replaced in 1993 by John Gummer, there was some disquiet amongst environmentalists as he was far from the image of a Tory 'rising star'. However, by the time of the Conservative Party's defeat in the 1997 general election, his standing had increased dramatically and he had proved to be a committed (although at times lone) environmental voice within the administration. During the mid-1990s, the Department of the Environment (DoE) played an important role in overcoming the power of the Department of Transport (DoT) and the vested interests of the roads lobby. Gummer played no small part in challenging the presumption that favoured increased road building and putting forward the idea of demand management. This needs to be placed in the context of a ruling party for which economic liberalisation and personal freedom were paramount: at times the private car was seen as a symbol of the Thatcherite political project. Again, under the recently elected

Labour administration, the responsibility for environmental policy is in the hands of the Deputy Prime Minister, John Prescott, and thus takes a high priority. Similarly, the fate of the much applauded Dutch *National Environmental Policy Plan* (NEPP) was tied to the leadership qualities of the environment minister, E.H.T.M. Nijpels. When he lost his position, the NEPP lost its political champion and fell down the national political agenda (see case study).

Also of great importance is the status of the environment ministry itself. In many liberal democracies, this ministry is not one of the more powerful departments, often lacking the economic power base which most politicians covet. Where the ministry is weak, it is unlikely that the cross-departmental working relationships and decision-making processes, so necessary for sustainable development, will be in place. Also, many environment ministries are not solely environment-focused. For instance, although the DoE was the first cabinet-level department of its kind, its title is perhaps a misnomer in that its focus is predominantly local government and housing. Its ability to coordinate policy on environmental issues is severely limited by the activities of other departments and agencies. For instance, the DoT has policy control over transport infrastructure with much of its resources centred on roads; the policies of the Ministry of Agriculture, Food and Fisheries (MAFF) have a large impact on the British countryside, with more emphasis being on food production rather than on conservation issues; the Department of Trade and Industry (DTI) covers energy policy; and obviously the Treasury is the lead department in terms of the direction of the economy, with the views of the business community often foremost in policy objectives. The recent election of Labour has led to a restructuring which should have a considerable effect on the future of environmental policy: John Prescott now heads the Department of the Environment, Transport and the Regions (DETR).[3] In principle this can only be positive from a green perspective as for too long transport policy has failed to address its environmental impact and, further, an integrated sustainable transport policy can only be planned within a regional framework (see Chapter 10). Given this focus on the power and status of the environment ministry, it is perhaps surprising that Sweden has no such department and yet is acclaimed as having some of the highest national environmental standards.

Other issues that have a bearing on the direction of environmental policy include the level of representation of green parties within national assemblies and the effectiveness of the wider green movement. An extended discussion of these issues can be found in Chapter 3, but it is clear that in countries without proportional voting systems, such as the USA and UK, there is little opportunity for green parties to penetrate representative structures. Where greens have been electorally successful, there is at the very least a consistent voice for environmental concerns in the legislature. Perhaps not surprisingly then, both the USA and UK have some of the most effective environmental pressure groups, with much focus being on lobbying. A final factor worth considering is the relative autonomy of local government in the environmental arena (see Chapter 10). Local political structures and competence vary throughout liberal democracies, but local authorities can be seen as agents for environmental change in their own right.

This is by no means an exhaustive account of the factors that influence national-level environmental policy making. Rather, it is an attempt to stress that it is not enough to simply analyse the substance of environmental policy alone – a variety of issues come into play and create the conditions within which environmental policy is generated and the direction of its development. It is worth bearing these sorts of factors in mind as the chapter progresses. Only then will we be able to generate a wider and deeper understanding of the development of pollution control policy and national sustainability planning.

TOWARDS INTEGRATED POLLUTION CONTROL (IPC)

> Environmental protection goes to the heart of the relationship between state and economy. … At the centre of these conflicting forces stand the pollution inspectorates. They have the day-to-day task of enforcing environmental legislation upon emitters and the longer-term task of evolving standards of environmental protection.
>
> (O'Riordan and Weale, 1989, pp. 277–8)

IPC: a definition

Environmental problems are by their very nature complex. It is rare for a discharge from a process to impact on one medium alone, be it air, water or land; more likely the impact will to some extent affect all media. Hence, it is no real answer to deal with impacts through analysing and licensing discharges to one medium only; such a response may lead to reductions and acceptable levels in that specific medium but often only at the expense of increased impacts on the others. Integrated pollution control (IPC) comprehends the holistic nature of pollution episodes and seeks systems of control that take into account all impacts on whatever medium; it aims to anticipate and prevent pollution rather than simply reacting to pollution incidents. Typically such control is stronger if there is a single permitting authority responsible for all factors.

In the UK, the creation of Her Majesty's Inspectorate of Pollution (HMIP) in 1987, the introduction of the Environmental Protection Act (1990) and, most recently, the establishment of the integrated Environment Agency in 1996 have all led to the UK taking a relatively large step towards the implementation of IPC practices. An analysis of the traditional approach to pollution control will show how both the structure and style have altered quite radically over a relatively short period of time.[4]

Traditional pollution control methods in the UK

Compared with the ideal of IPC, the structure of pollution control organisation in Britain has traditionally been fragmented. Pollution control authorities have tended

---

Integrated pollution control (IPC)

A system of pollution control would lack integration if:

- it is reactive rather than anticipatory in its policy making;

- it ignores problems of cross-media pollution;

- it fails to consider a sufficiently wide range of alternative solutions to problems;

- it displaces pollution across time and space;

- it fails to integrate environmental concerns with other areas of public policy.

(Weale *et al.*, 1991, p. xiv)

---

to focus on a single medium, irrespective of impacts outside their competence and jurisdiction. These authorities were built up over a period of time, often in response to contingent problems – beginning with the Alkali Inspectorate in 1863. This led to an unacceptable situation in which there were a variety of different agencies, incoherent structures and often overlapping responsibilities.[5] This not only had detrimental environmental consequences but also caused problems for industry, since it had to deal with more than one agency, some interested in specific aspects of plant operation, others only concerned with 'end-of-pipe' emission levels.

As with policy formulation affecting economic and industrial interests across all sectors of government, pollution control in the UK has tended to be 'discretionary, collaborative and secretive' (Jordan, 1993, p. 407). The norm has been close, confidential collaboration between public officials and representatives from industry resulting in 'negotiated consents' based on very loose national guidelines and the principle of best practicable means (BPM) to reduce or modify total wastes produced. The close relationship between regulator and regulated occurred in part because most inspectors of industrial processes have an engineering background – the same intellectual and sociological background as the industrialists they regulate.[6]

BPM was never adequately defined in court, in legislation or by the enforcement agencies and its vague nature suited the style of regulation. The stress on 'practicable' conformed to the discretionary style of control negotiations in that it required interpretation of a range of factors including the nature and state of the technology, the costs to the operator and wider environmental and social conditions. Without rigid standards, and based on a philosophy of 'partnership' between the regulator and industry, very few prosecutions occurred. The traditional politics of pollution control in many ways mirrored the rest of British political culture, with a close and often unspecified relationship between government and its agencies and the industrial and economic sector. As Jordan argues: 'The only way that this culture of collaboration, trusting co-operation and voluntary compliance could be sustained was on the basis of confidential dealings between regulators and the regulated' (ibid., p. 408).

Integrated pollution control in Sweden

Sweden has perhaps the most integrated system of pollution control dating back to 1969. Even though its organisation can be seen as highly fragmented, its success is in large part down to the Swedish political culture, which takes consensus, cooperation and non-adversarial problem solving to be of prime importance. There are three major structural levels:

• *National Environmental Protection Board*: sets national guidelines and coordinates policy implementation;

• *Franchise Board for Environmental Protection*: grants licences for processes;

• *Local authorities*: monitor and enforce licences.

Regulation is not based on uniform emission standards, but on a principle of lowest possible intervention into the environment with a commitment to the highest specification in technology. Central to the Swedish system is a high level of public scrutiny and decentralisation, with the involvement of local authorities and public participation in licensing and recourse to legal challenges.

Criticisms of traditional UK methods

This approach to pollution control in the UK was widely criticised for failing to adequately address environmental considerations in licensing procedures. Its fragmented structure led to a failure to consider the environment as a whole. For instance, in the control of atmospheric pollution there was much confusion, with agencies having overlapping powers; in other aspects of the environment there would be no control whatsoever. To add to these structural inconsistencies, the discretionary nature of control and a lack of public accountability meant that both industry and the enforcement agencies were discredited by a distrustful and ever more environmentally aware public.

One of the earliest and most insightful systematic criticisms of the UK's traditional system was the influential Royal Commission on Environmental Pollution's (RCEP) *Fifth Report: Air Pollution Control – An Integrated Approach*, published in 1976. As the title of the report suggests, the commission proposed the creation of a unified pollution inspectorate 'able to tackle in a comprehensive manner the waste of complex industrial processes' (O'Riordan and Weale, 1989, p. 248). It made clear the need to regulate not only the effect of, for instance, air pollution but also the overall environmental impact of industrial processes. To this end, the RCEP proposed the introduction of best practicable environmental option (BPEO) to supplement BPM. BPEO was again not clearly defined and possibly the most detailed definition did not appear until over a decade later, in the RCEP's twelfth report:

> A BPEO is the outcome of a systematic consultative and decision-making procedure which emphasises the protection of the environment across land, air and water. The BPEO procedure establishes, for a given set of objectives, the option that provides the most benefit or least damage to the environment as a whole, at acceptable cost, in the long as well as the short term.
>
> (RCEP, 1988, para 2.5)

Although the commission had proposed quite radical changes to the structure of the regulating authorities, it was reasonably supportive of the style and process of regulation, re-emphasising the important role that the consensual relationship between powerful and established interested parties – typically economic rather than environmental – played in British politics.

Vorsorgeprinzip: the German precautionary principle

In comparison with the UK's emphasis on confidentiality, pollution control in Germany since the early 1970s has explicitly evolved around the principle of precaution, *Vorsorgeprinzip*.[7]

> the principle of precaution is the notion that environmental policy should not be based simply upon dealing with known and certain problems, but should also be concerned with future and uncertain problems.
>
> (Weale *et al.*, 1991, p. 116)

Vorsorgeprinzip incorporates two basic ideas that refer to environmental quality and the nature of technology. First, any impact from a process should not have adverse effects on long-term environmental quality. Second, emissions standards should be set at as strict a level as possible bearing in mind the current state of available technology. A further general principle of German administrative law, the principle of proportionality, also has to be taken into account. This states that a balance between environmental improvement and costs is necessary. This interpretation of *Vorsorgeprinzip* formed the basis of the EU Directive on Atmospheric Emissions from Industrial Plants (84/360) where the phrase 'best available technology not entailing excessive cost' (BATNEEC) first appeared. BATNEEC was to become one of the foundational principles in the development of IPC in Britain.

Her Majesty's Inspectorate of Pollution (HMIP)

Even by the standards of Whitehall, the response to the RCEP's 1976 report was slow in the extreme. After equivocating for a decade, the government announced its decision to create a unified inspectorate and in 1987 HMIP emerged. HMIP, an agency answerable to the DoE, was a merger of four inspectorates that dealt with industrial air pollution, hazardous waste, radioactive chemicals and water quality. There were a number of reasons for this delay that reflect the issues raised at the beginning of the chapter. In the decade following the publication of the RCEP report, environmental issues had a relatively low political priority and this co-incided with the Thatcherite aversion to institutional reform and industrial regulation. At the same time, any possible momentum for change was lost as internal disputes deepened within Whitehall over the departmental location and powers of the amalgamated organisation.

In the late 1980s, however, the environment became a top political priority as public concern grew. The need for a unified inspectorate was taken up by the influential environment minister, William Waldegrave. His position was reinforced by the incompetent reaction of the existing pollution control agencies to a radio-active discharge at Sellafield in 1983 (O'Riordan and Weale, 1989, pp. 283–4). At the same time, the UK was under pressure to alter its enforcement practices by the European Community, which wished to develop a common, Community-wide pollution control process. However, the HMIP had to wait for the 1990 Environmental Protection Act to provide its legislative basis. It was not until April 1991, with the implementation of Part 1 of the Act, that the new agency was able to operationalise a version of IPC. Almost two decades after the RCEP's report, some of the first operators received IPC authorisations.

Environmental Protection Act (1990)

In terms of pollution control, the Environmental Protection Act is Britain's legislative response to a number of EU directives, in particular Directives 84/360 (emissions from industrial plants) and 88/609 (large combustion plants). From 1 April 1991, all new or substantially altered industrial processes required IPC authorisation – a fundamental shift in British pollution control philosophy. A rolling programme was set up to authorise existing processes, industrial sector by sector.

A successful IPC application requires prospective operators to prove in substantial detail that the process selected meets the objectives of the Act. This requires the operator to use the best practicable technique not entailing excessive costs (BATNEEC) to prevent, minimise or render harmless substances released and to control any releases with regard to the best practicable environmental option (BPEO), considering the environment as a whole. The operator must also comply with any relevant national or international environmental objectives. The procedure is rigorous and once an application is received it can take up to four months for a decision to be forthcoming. This time allows both statutory bodies and the public to make comments.

The Environmental Protection Act introduces a number of features that are novel to the UK. Embracing the principle of public access to information, local authorities are required to hold a register of the authorisations. Along with this, the public can comment on proposed licences and are able to take both the pollution control agency and the company to court if they believe the IPC authorisations are being ignored. The Act also introduces stricter emissions standards and higher penalties for offending operators.

The programme of IPC authorisation was somewhat delayed for a number of reasons. First, the HMIP inspectors had to adapt to completely new working practices and more formal working relations with industry. There was an enormous workload with over 5,000 prescribed processes requiring IPC authorisation and few new resources or staff to fulfil the original 1996 deadline. Second, industry itself often found the exercise problematic and costly – many applicants for IPC authorisation have been rejected on lack of detail. Not only is there a charging system in operation for the first time, but also the stricter guidelines in some cases entail expensive new plant. Third, a number of companies appealed to the Secretary of State for the Environment, who has enormous discretionary powers under the Act to determine standards, resolve disputes and decide what information is to be in the public domain – it is a common claim that too much public information on pollution standards will expose trade secrets.

For many commentators, the creation of HMIP and the introduction of the Environmental Protection Act were the foundation stone of an IPC system.

> For the first time there is in place a mechanism and a legal basis for looking at the impact which a process *as a whole* has on the environment *as a whole*, and for balancing the imperative of protecting the environment against the reality that the protection has a financial cost.
>
> (Slater, 1994, p. 4)

Clearly there was a definite move away from traditional UK methods and towards a more integrated, formal approach. The structure of HMIP had been envisaged in the 1976 RCEP report; its style and procedures were being influenced through growing European pressures. However, the question remains: could such an arrangement be truly classified as IPC?

The Environmental Protection Act did not make HMIP the sole permitting authority. The majority of more straightforward and less polluting processes were still authorised by local authorities' environmental health officers, who continued to operate a single-medium approach: their concern was only with atmospheric emissions. Of more importance though was that HMIP had little authority over discharge to water. Here the agency had to cooperate with the National Rivers Authority (NRA). The privatisation of the state water industry had exposed the UK government's poor record on pollution control and Thatcher's attempt to give the water companies a self-monitoring role was deemed illegal by the EU. The independent NRA was therefore established under the Water Act (1989). Under this legislation and the Water Resources Act (1991), the NRA was charged with safeguarding and improving the national water environment. This function was not only with reference to pollution control, but also to flood defence, regulation of rivers and ground water, protection and improvement of water stocks and promotion of water-based activities – a unique combination of pollution control, river management and conservation roles. In comparison with HMIP, which had moved some way from the more traditional secretive negotiated procedures, the NRA had a much more zealous philosophy on enforcement. Certainly it achieved a larger number of prosecutions, with the courts becoming more inclined to hand down stiffer penalties to persistent polluters. One of the largest of these was handed down to Shell (UK), which in February 1990 was fined and required to pay compensation of several million pounds for an oil spillage in the Mersey. The more arms-length approach to pollution control was in part a result of the NRA being a completely new inspectorate and not an amalgamation with inherited practices and associations with industry. Also its focus on water quality and what is discharged into water courses meant it had little interest and specialist engineering knowledge of the processes themselves: NRA inspectors did not necessarily share the technical sympathies that HMIP often had with operators.

Even with the new legislation, the concepts of BATNEEC and BPEO still require a large degree of interpretation. Although 'not entailing excessive cost' is more explicit than BPM it has still not been satisfactorily defined. What relative weight should be given to economic, social and environmental costs? How are they to be accounted for? As Jordan argues: 'Ultimately, the fate of many jobs, millions of pounds worth of investment and the welfare of people living in close proximity to industrial plant may ride on HMIP's interpretation of BATNEEC in any one case' (Jordan, 1993, p. 418). Again, with BPEO, which was fundamental in HMIP authorisations, similar problems can be exposed. Neither HMIP nor the RCEP developed a successful method by which the impact of emissions to different media can be balanced. The modelling required would necessarily include the carrying capacity or critical loading of the local environment, a notoriously difficult measure to determine.[8]

On a more positive note, the creation of HMIP and the legislative framework of the Environmental Protection Act required the regulators to develop a more formalised and open relationship with the regulated – a certain level of transparency was instituted. Further, polluters were being charged a growing proportion of the costs of HMIP's services – although this was far from the polluter-pays principle (PPP) – and there was higher public scrutiny and possibilities for recourse through the courts.

The Environment Act (1995) and a unified environmental agency

The Environment Act (1995) finally put in place the legislative framework for a unified environmental agency, which had been a commitment in the Conservative election manifesto of 1992. The Environment Agency and its Scottish equivalent, the Scottish Environmental Protection Agency (SEPA),[9] came into existence in April 1996. The agency is an amalgamation of the functions of the NRA, HMIP and local government's waste regulation authorities (WRAs)[10] and will be one of the largest organisations of its kind in the world, employing 9,000 staff with a budget of just over £500 million a year, much of it raised from charges on industry, commerce and anglers. Simply by virtue of being the responsibility of one large body instead of many smaller ones, environmental protection should be improved as it will allow a comprehensive, holistic approach to the regulation of industrial pollution, making possible overall assessments about net damage to air, land and water, rather than defending just one domain. That is, its introduction finally facilitates IPC. For industry, the Environment Agency has the advantage of a single consistent licensing and inspection regime.

The delay in the creation of the new Environment Agency can again be traced to intense Whitehall battles over its size, structure and remit. For instance, MAFF laid a claim to a number of the operating functions of the NRA, in particular its conservation responsibilities; and the DTI saw the process as an opportunity to reduce and narrow the regulatory remit of any new authority. Under pressure from NGOs, the NRA itself, and sympathetic MPs and peers, the Act was not weakened and retained most of the existing legislative responsibilities of the amalgamating inspectorates. However, the DTI and Treasury did force through a new requirement for the agency to carry out a cost–benefit analysis (CBA) of all its policies and practices. NGOs were joined by the RCEP and the Chairs of the Environment Agency Advisory Committee and the Panel on Sustainable Development (see below) in raising concerns that such a principle 'may expose the Agency unduly to judicial review, bog it down in bureaucracy, and stir up distracting disputes about valuation methodologies' (ENDS, 1995e, p. 2). Certainly there is no uncontroversial method for valuing many environmental costs and benefits (see Chapter 5). Further, there is some concern that any emphasis on CBA will mean that priority is given to the principle of cost-effectiveness rather than precaution or prevention.

If there is scepticism about this specification of CBA, the requirement, under the 1995 Environment Act, for the Environment Agency to concern itself with the achievement of sustainable development is an important recognition of the potential role of pollution control agencies. The Act states: 'in discharging its functions the Agency is required so to protect or enhance the environment, taken as a whole, as to make the contribution that Ministers consider appropriate towards achieving sustainable development.'[11]

Given the differing functional responsibilities of HMIP, NRA and WRAs, the statutory responsibilities of the Environment Agency are wide-ranging, from an obvious role in the prevention and minimisation of pollution, the regulation of radioactive waste and improvement of water quality, through to an advisory role in the development of national and local air quality strategies and plans and the maintenance of fish stocks.

The Environment Agency's statutory responsibilities are to:

- Regulate industrial processes to prevent or minimise pollution;
- Advise on the government's national air strategy and provide guidance to local authorities on their local air quality management plans;

- Regulate the disposal of radioactive waste, the keeping and use of radioactive material and the accumulation of radioactive waste;
- Regulate the treatment and disposal of controlled waste to prevent pollution or harm to human health;
- Implement the government's national waste management strategy for England and Wales in its waste regulation work;
- Preserve and improve the quality of rivers, estuaries and coastal waters;
- Conserve and secure proper use of water resources;
- Conserve the water environment and promote its use for recreation;
- Maintain and improve non-marine navigation;
- Regulate the management and remediation of contaminated land designated as special sites;
- Provide independent and authoritative views on environmental issues;
- Liaise with international counterparts and Governments to help develop consistent environmental policies.

In practice, there has been some criticism of the level of fines handed out to prosecuted companies. In 1996, the biggest fine was only £175,000 imposed on Severn Trent Water, which killed some 35,000 fish in a river in mid-Wales. Given that this was its forty-second pollution offence since privatisation in 1989, there has been some concern that such low-level fines will not deter large companies. This is not actually a criticism of the Environment Agency; rather there is a widespread view that magistrates and judges need to use their discretion and push the general level of fines upwards to act as a deterrent. However, there is also some disquiet that the agency has not prosecuted enough offenders.[12] For instance, there are fewer prosecutions for releases into water than in the days of the NRA. In response, the agency argues that it has adopted a 'two-track approach', providing guidance to those companies it believes genuinely wish to improve their environmental performance, and prosecuting those which blatantly disregard their responsibilities. This could be interpreted as a return to the previous cosy relationship with industry or, alternatively, a pragmatic approach that attempts to steer companies in the right direction. Further, there is clearly a wish not to unnecessarily alienate industry, since if inspectors are to assess whether a company is satisfying the principles of BATNEEC and BPEO, they will need to know the level of emissions, the nature of existing pollution abatement technology and financial information about the company. This knowledge is all in the hands of the industrial operator. So, even if the Environment Agency wished to, it could never completely regulate at arms length. The consequence of this is that even with a radical reorientation of pollution control methods in the last decade, the agency has been forced to allow companies back into a closer, more participative role in setting standards – although this time without the veil of secrecy that characterised the traditional approach to pollution control.

Just as the process of change in the UK's methods of pollution control seems to be coming to a conclusion with the unification of the major agencies in 1996, there are possibilities of more changes emanating from Europe. First, it is un-

The US Environmental Protection Agency

When the US Environmental Protection Agency (EPA) was established in 1970 as perhaps the earliest unified pollution control inspectorate, its mandate was based on taking a cross-media approach to regulation and enforcement. However, in terms of organisation and legislation the EPA has been unable to live up to the principles of integrated pollution control. In what may be seen as a lesson for the new UK Environment Agency, the EPA was founded on an amalgamation of existing agencies, each bringing its own traditions and styles, which it has never been able to adequately overcome. Rather than developing new integrated management structures and administrative processes, the agency was required to enforce a new wave of legislation responding to the heightened environmental awareness of the early 1970s. The fragmented structure of the EPA was reinforced by legislation, such as the Clean Air and Water Acts, which tended to focus on specific media.

> Since there is less political momentum in the US for consolidating legislation than for highly visible attacks on single-issue problems, it is perhaps not surprising that the organisational capacity of the EPA is hamstrung by its legislative mandate.
>
> (Weale, 1992, p. 102)

The Acts tended to legislate for comparatively strict environmental standards, the complexity of which often overwhelmed the under-resourced EPA. Along with this, a further feature of the US political system has acted against the effectiveness of the agency, namely the culture of litigation and appeal. The implementation and enforcement of much environmental legislation has been delayed by industry appealing against strict standards and interpretations of legislation in the courts, to Congress or to state governments. Finally, the success of the EPA has often been influenced to a large degree by the attitude to environmental issues of the President at any particular time. Certainly the EPA had a rough decade under the Ronald Reagan and George Bush administrations, where deregulation of industry was of central concern. The return of a Democrat President, Bill Clinton with his pro-environmentalist Vice President, Al Gore, has provided the EPA with much-needed high-level political support.

clear as to whether the European Environment Agency (EEA) will eventually take on a regulation function (see Chapter 8). Certainly a Europe-wide inspectorate would have implications for the UK Environment Agency. Second, an EU directive on integrated pollution prevention and control (IPPC) will soon have to be interpreted into British law. This will shift the focus of pollution thinking away from emissions standards and towards waste prevention. Finally, the phasing in of more economic instruments would also change working practices. Although the Environmental Protection Act (1990) introduced a charging system for operators applying for IPC authorisation and higher penalties for polluters, it is a long way from the polluter-pays principle (PPP). The UK system, as with most other nations, remains primarily a command and control arrangement (see Chapter 6). As we shall see below, there is a level of support in the government for economic instruments and we have recently witnessed the introduction of landfill taxes and recycling credits. However, the Treasury is unsure about the effect on macro-economic policy and again it may be that the EU takes a lead in introducing such measures.

Even though there are still criticisms from the green movement, there has definitely been a fundamental shift in the UK's approach to pollution control in the last two decades. As O'Riordan and Weale noted as early as 1989:

> Prominent features of this transition include the shift in emphasis from confidential flexibility towards greater openness and information, from single medium discharge control to multi-media waste management, from focus on end-of-pipe treatment towards a more comprehensive approach to good management practice, and from paternalism to a more structured accountability.
>
> (O'Riordan and Weale, 1989, p. 278)

A number of factors have been at play in this process and some – although by no means all –have been touched on here. Clearly the debate in Europe and the ensuing directives have been integral in forcing Britain's hand, particularly with the EU's emphasis on the need to prevent pollution rather than taking remedial action; the enforcement of strict standards and rules; and public access to information. At the same time, domestically, there is a growing aversion to, and distrust of, state secrecy, as well as the realisation that the quality of life is tied up with levels of pollution and environmental quality.

SUSTAINABLE DEVELOPMENT AND THE NATION STATE

> If pollution is to be controlled at source, rather than mitigated in terms of its effects, environmental considerations need to be integrated across the whole range of government policy. An emphasis upon controlling sources, rather than effects, therefore promises, or threatens, a substantial departure from many of the implicit assumptions of the 1970s.
>
> (Weale, 1992, p. 122)

Earlier in this chapter we highlighted a series of issues that can have an effect on the development of environmental policy at the national level. Many of these issues will be returned to in the analysis of what is possibly the most important area of national policy making – the development of national plans or strategies for sustainable development. Sustainable development planning requires governments to take a strategic stance towards environmental, social and economic questions across all policy areas – not an *ad hoc* approach as problems arise. In terms mentioned in the earlier discussion of IPC, it requires anticipatory and preventive rather than reactive policy making. In this section we shall focus on the UK's approach, which will then be followed in the case study by an analysis of the Dutch *National Environment Policy Plan* (NEPP).[13]

Environmental policy prior to Rio: *This Common Inheritance*

It was not until after the 1992 UNCED Earth Summit that the UK government seriously attempted to develop a coordinated response to the imperatives implicit in the idea of sustainable development. In fact it was not until September 1990 – over a decade after the Conservative administration first took office – that the government produced its first white paper on the environment, *This Common Inheritance* (DoE, 1990). The timing of this document is interesting in that it was the first official Whitehall document since the so-called 'greening of Thatcher' at the height of environmental awareness in the late 1980s. It was steered through by the sustained leadership of a strong environment minister, Chris Patten. However, its final form tells us much about the government's position at the time on environmental issues.

This Common Inheritance contains around 350 measures that the government was already undertaking in the environmental arena. Alongside this summary of existing policies and practices were a small number of new proposals. One of the potentially most interesting was a structural change: the creation of 'green ministers' in each department to take responsibility for environmental issues in their area of competence and the formation of a cabinet-level environment committee. However, the lack of transparency within Whitehall means that the effectiveness of these changes is extremely difficult to evaluate. The suspicion that the green ministers were having little impact on decision making across Whitehall was confirmed when John Gummer, the then Secretary of State for the Environment, admitted that the ministers had met only seven times in the five years from 1992 to 1996 (ENDS, 1996e, p. 24). Because of the secretive nature of British politics, it is not even clear how often the cabinet committee meets, what is on its agenda and what the outcome of its deliberations are. Of some importance, however, was the commitment to publish yearly updated White Papers to report on progress – or, as it more often turned out, lack of progress – on environmental proposals.

With Chris Patten as Secretary of State for the Environment, the environmental lobby had expected some quite radical and fundamental shifts in environmental policy; he was after all an open supporter of market-based environmental instruments and commissioned the environmental economist David Pearce to produce a report for his department.[14] The White Paper did not reflect this shift in thinking, and discussion of economic instruments was placed in an Annex with more research promised.[15] The fate of Patten's proposal for a carbon tax on fuel perhaps illuminates the problems he faced. Such a taxation policy was opposed by the energy minister on the grounds that increased prices would adversely affect the forthcoming electricity privatisation; by the Treasury because it might create inflationary pressures; and by the DoT as it would raise the cost of road haulage and motoring. At the same time, environmental concern appeared to be waning as a recession began to set in and Thatcher's conditional support for environmental issues was exposed. As a consummate politician she had tapped into the wave of public concern on such issues as pollution, but her true interest lay in short-term economic issues such as inflation, and with the reduction of industrial regulation and promotion of privatisation. Again, the Conservative administration showed itself to be closer to the established interests of the business and industrial lobby than to the environmental movement.

The final form of *This Common Inheritance* and its yearly updates exposed the lack of understanding of the radical nature of environmental problems amongst the majority of civil servants and ministers in Whitehall and further exposed the entrenched interests and strengths of established departments. It also highlighted the *ad hoc* and incremental nature of policy formulation and the lack of a comprehensive framework for environmental policy. Such a position would appear to be far from ideal for when questions of sustainable development were placed firmly on the agenda at the Rio Earth Summit. As Voisey and O'Riordan argue:

> The White Paper process appeared to have been a missed opportunity to address issues such as green taxation, the link between the environment, economic and social policies, and real institutional reform. It represents no strategic assessment of the needs of future society in environmental terms and lacks commitment to those measures it has considered. The opportunity for more accountability and openness was ignored.
>
> (Voisey and O'Riordan, 1997, p. 28)

Post-Rio: *The UK Strategy*

Shortly after his return from the Rio Earth Summit, the Prime Minister, John Major, made a commitment to publish a national plan to implement Agenda 21 by the end of 1993. He was also instrumental in persuading other G7 and EU countries to follow suit in order that the United Nations' Commission on Sustainable Development (CSD) would be able to fulfil its role (see Chapter 7).[16] On 25 January 1994, the UK government published four White Papers as the national response to the agreements signed at UNCED.

- *Sustainable Development: The UK Strategy*
- *Climate Change: The UK Programme*
- *Biodiversity: The UK Action Plan*
- *Sustainable Forestry: The UK Programme*

Of central concern here is *Sustainable Development: The UK Strategy*, the government's direct response to Agenda 21.

Throughout 1993, the government undertook a major consultation exercise inside and outside Whitehall, inviting agencies, local authorities, NGOs, businesses, individuals and any other interested parties to comment on a wide-ranging consultative paper (DoE, 1993b). The strategy eventually produced considers sustainable development over a twenty-year period.

Sustainable Development: The UK Strategy

- *Introduction and principles*: a brief explanation of the context and preparation of the strategy and a short interpretation of the principle of sustainable development.

- *Environmental media and resources*: a review of the state of the UK environment and trends and potential problems areas over the next twenty years.

- *Economic development and sustainability*: an analysis of different sectors of the economy highlighting policy options that it may be necessary to adopt to achieve sustainable development.

- *Putting sustainability into practice*: a discussion of the role of different levels of government and other sections of society in moving towards a sustainable future.

As with Agenda 21, *The UK Strategy* is littered with contradictions. At some points the necessity of demand management has been accepted, only for a later section to comment that it is not for the government to impose restrictions on citizens but only to persuade. To analyse the impact of the strategy it is worth considering a number of issues that are essential to any successful sustainable development plan: policy commitments, objectives and targets; demand management; institutional changes and implementation strategies; and integration across policy areas and departments.

Policy commitments, targets and objectives

Although the strategy sets out a number of policy options for the next twenty years, taking into consideration the forecasted impact of present policies on environmental resources, it has been widely criticised for lacking any commitment to new policies and targets on the problems it highlights. Further, it does not provide 'a clear vision of what sustainable development may mean to individuals, businesses and public bodies' (ENDS, 1994, p. 18). The necessity of targets against which progress towards sustainable development could be measured was fundamental in many of the consultation responses that the DoE received:

A very large proportion of those commenting on the principles of the strategy felt the Government should establish a rolling process to set, monitor and act on aims and targets. Many felt that the stated objectives in many areas were vague and sometimes complacent.

(DoE, 1994b, p. 249)

Unfortunately the DoE appeared to make no headway in persuading other departments that such a programme was necessary and the lack of targets and long-term objectives meant that most NGOs were eventually dismissive of the document and questioned whether it could be called a 'strategy' at all.

Demand management

In terms of policy formulation, the strategy is most notable in its acceptance of the principle that demand for energy, water, minerals and transport must be managed. This is a radical break from the Thatcherite, neo-liberal view that policy should be based on the presumption that individual demand ought to be satisfied. The DoE's promotion of demand management caused bitter interdepartmental conflict, particularly over transport. The strategy process can be seen as an integral part of the pressure that has been developing over the last few years on the DoT to rethink its policy on road building and private and commercial road transport. Prior to the publication of the strategy, the DoT continued to state that it was not the government's place to influence demand for transport. The strategy sets out starkly the consequences for sustainable development if increased traffic generation and road building is not tackled, despite the DoT's attempt to edit this out. The strategy is proof that the relative power and influence of the DoE and DoT is altering, with the former apparently in the ascendancy.

Institutional changes

Prior to the strategy, institutional change in the environmental arena had always been internal, for instance the cabinet committee and green ministers introduced in *This Common Inheritance* in 1990. The lack of transparency within Whitehall means that the effectiveness of such changes is extremely difficult to evaluate. The strategy has introduced new machinery that is external to Whitehall, which should therefore lead to greater public scrutiny and access.

The British Government Panel on Sustainable Development has already shown that it has the potential to become a major actor in the pressure for change, especially given the standing of its members. Its convenor, Sir Crispin Tickell, has already publicly intervened in the debate surrounding the remit of the recently formed Environment Agency and the panel includes two members of the Royal Commission on Environmental Pollution. The panel's first two reports (1995; 1996) are based on detailed work and submissions in areas where it contends that the government lacks a coordinated approach, including environmental pricing and economic instruments; environmental education; depletion of fish stocks; ozone

---

New institutions in *The UK Strategy*

British Government Panel on Sustainable Development: a group of five prominent individuals to provide independent advice to the Prime Minister and the government on strategic issues and priorities for sustainable development.

UK Round Table on Sustainable Development: involving representatives of central and local government, the business and industrial sector, voluntary groups, and the scientific and academic community.

Citizens' Environment Initiative (*Going for Green*): to increase the awareness of the impact of individual choices on sustainable development.

---

depletion; reform of the Common Agricultural Policy; environmental accounting; biotechnology; and disposal of radioactive waste. In agreement with the critics of *The UK Strategy*, it recommends that 'the Government should give higher priority to its environmental objectives and targets and how it intends to meet them' (British Government Panel on Sustainable Development, 1995, p. 11). The panel endorses the use of economic instruments where possible and calls for a radical shift in taxation policy away from labour and capital and on to pollution and resource use. In all areas it covers, the panel recommends a more strategic and comprehensive approach. The panel is in the position of selecting its own topics for consideration and as such it promises to be a highly visible and coherent critic of government policy on sustainable development.

The round table embodies a 'stakeholder' approach, attempting to include the most significant organisations in the sustainable development debate from all sectors.[17] As the DoE states:

> Its purpose will be to encourage discussion on major issues of sustainable development between people who approach them from different positions and who have different responsibilities. Members will be able to compare notes on what is being done in different sectors, to develop a better understanding of the problems faced by others, and to see how far a common perspective might be developed on various issues.
>
> (DoE, 1994b, p. 235)

The round table's *First Annual Report* highlights one of its central objectives as the development of 'new areas of consensus on difficult areas of sustainable development, and where this is not possible, to clarify and reduce difference' (UK Round Table, 1996, p. 4).[18] The effectiveness of this arrangement in dealing with areas of conflict will emerge over time.

Initially, it appeared that the major environmental NGOs were going to boycott the group as they believed it was simply 'a DoE talking shop' (ENDS 1995a, p. 6). In the end, only Greenpeace has failed to attend – it is putting its faith in the Panel on Sustainable Development. There is concern, however, as to the role and impact of the round table as departments and agencies outside the DoE do not appear to take the partnership initiative very seriously. This may change given that, under the new Labour administration, the Department of the Environment has been merged into a broader Department of the Environment, Transport and the Regions and other ministries, including the Foreign Office, have made strong overtures towards the emerging sustainable development agenda. The round table has produced a series of reports and recommendations, summarised in its two annual reports (1996; 1997), and although its initial recommendations on the restructuring of the energy market were swiftly rebuffed by the DTI (ENDS, 1995a; 1995c), some of its more recent interventions and reports have attracted significant short-term media and government attention. Some tensions remain as to the round table's rather ambiguous role and status within the decision-making process:

> The Round Table ... felt pressed to produce numerous reports in order to justify its existence to the outside world rather than taking its time to ponder the more intractable issues which some thought would be its role. ... In addition, it is aware that the need to produce reports by consensus has made it difficult to communicate any flavour of the sometimes heated debates among members.
>
> (ENDS, 1996b, p. 36)

The aim of the final institutional arrangement *Going for Green* is 'to increase people's awareness of the part their personal choices can play in delivering sustainable development, and enlist their support and commitment in the coming years' (DoE, 1994b, p. 236). As such, it focuses on individual environmental responsibility, often in terms of consumer choices. The initiative has fairly meagre funds and lacks any coordinated political support, although it has been involved in developing some small-scale, local projects (Voisey and O'Riordan, 1997, p. 37). Given that a more participatory role for citizens is at the heart of more radical interpretations of sustainable development, the only new initiative that aims to involve citizens directly is poorly supported and resourced and does not aim to open up opportunities for political engagement. This provides further evidence that the government's commitment to more radical grassroots change is shallow at best.

Finally, with regard to existing organisations and sectors, *The UK Strategy* stresses the need for the UK to play a more active international role in promoting sustainable development, as well as encouraging actors such as local authorities, business and voluntary bodies to become more involved in developing and implementing sustainable policies and practices. For instance, the strategy recognises that local councils are often at the forefront in developing locally based responses to sustainable development and as such offers its support for Local Agenda 21 initiatives. However, there are no new resources promised to already financially impoverished authorities (see Chapter 10). Given that the government failed to provide a coherent definition of the concept of sustainable development, it should not be too much of a surprise that it lacks any detailed implementation strategy.

Towards policy integration

Although *The UK Strategy* has been rightly criticised as lacking any vision, inspiration and long-term objectives, set against this is the deeper thinking about sustainable development that the process of preparation provoked across Whitehall. This may seem only a small advance but its significance should not be overlooked – for instance, it has helped provoke a rethink in transport policy and forced civil servants and ministers to consider environment and development issues. At the same time, the process increased the standing and influence of the DoE. Organisations such as the new Panel and Round Table on Sustainable Development can only help to strengthen its power base.

The need to integrate environmental considerations into other policy areas seems now to be well recognised even if institutional change has not been very effective. However, the strategy process has been unable to have any dramatic influence on the Treasury, whose policies set much of the framework for all other Whitehall departments. Fiscal and macro-economic policy do not receive any attention in the strategy and it is unclear as to whether this has been a terrible oversight or, more likely, an acknowledgement of the department's power and influence. The House of Lords Select Committee on Sustainable Development, set up in March 1994, recently called the Treasury to account for its apparent lack of interest in sustainable development. This, it seems, was 'the first occasion on which the Treasury had sent a team to defend its contribution to environmental protection before a parliamentary committee' (ENDS, 1995c, p. 29) – a telling fact in its own right. Its response showed that there was almost negligible action on developing new fiscal policies to protect the environment, its view being that such policy should be developed by the DoE. This runs firmly against the supposed cross-departmental nature of the strategy, exposes the lack of understanding and interest from the Treasury (the strongest of all Whitehall departments), and highlights the enormous task ahead of the green movement if it is to persuade the UK government to adopt coordinated policies across all sectors of the economy and wider society. This is particularly the case if it is serious about the principle of social justice implicit in sustainable development and the policies of redistribution that would flow from such a commitment. Given the political sensitivity to questions of resource redistribution, it should not be surprising that there is no real discussion of this aspect of sustainable development in *The UK Strategy*.

The yearly updates of the strategy have been low-key events and add little to existing policies and practices. However, there have been one or two interesting recent developments that may bode well for a more integrated approach. The creation of the unified Environment Agency in 1996 means that there is now a powerful actor for environmental protection and, as we have already noted, the promotion of sustainable development is seen as one of its fundamental objectives. In the same year, the government published *Indicators of Sustainable Development for the United Kingdom* (DoE, 1996b), which contained 118 indicators of resource use, pollution levels, species and habitats, human health, and the like.

This preliminary report was broadly welcomed by the environmental movement, although the sheer number of indicators means that it is difficult to get a clear sense of the situation. At present, through a process of consultation, the government is developing a more refined set of indicators, which it hopes to publish in 1998. The question remains, though, as to how much significance will be given to such indicators in comparison with economic indicators such as gross domestic product. What is encouraging is that the new Labour administration appears to be taking the integration of environmental considerations much more seriously. The Conservative Secretary of State, John Gummer, proved a champion of environmental and sustainable development issues but was marginalised within a government that had little interest in that agenda. The initial institutional changes that have seen the DoE merge into a more powerful and coordinated Department of the Environment, Transport and the Regions can only be a positive move toward integration. The Deputy Prime Minister, John Prescott, and his environment ministers have been applauded for their determination at the recent Kyoto climate change negotiations. They are soon to unveil an integrated transport policy, and also appear to have managed to persuade the Treasury that hypothecation of taxes is necessary so that charges on motor vehicles can be ploughed back into public transport initiatives. Even the Treasury itself is talking publicly of extending the use of green taxation.[19] The new government's own strategy for sustainable development should thus be a further step in the right direction.

CONCLUSION

In this chapter we have tended to focus on the practice and policies of the UK national government, although in the case study that follows we shall turn our attention to the Netherlands. Over the last two decades, the UK government has often been castigated for not giving enough attention to issues such as environmental protection and sustainable development. In many ways this is not surprising given the ideological outlook of the eighteen-year Conservative administration. However, even against the backdrop of a government committed to economic growth and deregulation, it must be acknowledged that there have been some advances made on the environmental front: our discussions of pollution control and sustainable development planning bear this out. It may have taken many years for the unified Environment Agency to be established, but it is now in place and operates a control regime which is a long way from the (much criticised) traditional secretive and collaborative approach. And the UK now has a sustainable development strategy. It may be weak in defining sustainable development and offering targets and objectives, but there have been significant steps forward, not least the recognition of demand management. And this is from an administration that was at times openly hostile to such issues.

What our analysis has shown is that all the factors isolated earlier in the chapter have at some time come into play. Certainly the influence of the EU and other member states has had a radical affect on pollution control practices and policy. Equally, the Rio Earth Summit set in motion steps toward the integration of policies on the environment, society and economy. We have shown that leadership is a key feature in achieving progress in the environmental protection and sustainable development agenda, although, by the same token, a lack of leadership could easily hinder future developments. But perhaps it is reasonable to hope that the process has gained enough momentum, with a sufficient number of influential politicians and civil servants coming to understand and perhaps even embrace the idea of sustainable development. Certainly this will be put to the test when it is recognised that the hard political choices lying ahead will challenge the traditional core priorities of the state, such as the promotion of existing patterns of economic growth. Only time will enable us to tell how far the sustainable development agenda has been grasped at the national level.

CASE STUDY: THE DUTCH *NATIONAL ENVIRONMENTAL POLICY PLAN*: TO CHOOSE OR TO LOSE?

The Dutch *National Environment Policy Plan* (NEPP) is frequently held up as by far the most successful attempt to date to plan nationally for sustainable development. Certainly, the Dutch government responded with apparent urgency to the Brundtland Report, *Our Common Future* (see Chapter 7), with the NEPP being presented to the Second Chamber of the States General as early as May 1989. A major factor here was the publication of *Concern for Tomorrow* by the National Institute of Public Health and Environmental Protection, which raised public awareness of the limitations of existing environmental measures. Even prior to the NEPP though, beginning in 1984, the Dutch had already brought forward a series of plans, the *Indicative Multi-Year Plans*, which attempted to coordinate environmental regulation and policy. By comparison, the UK does not share the same enthusiasm for detailed planning. Even though published six years earlier, the NEPP is a much more detailed and thoughtful document than its UK equivalent, although interestingly it suffers from similar problems, including a lack of attention to implementation strategies and policy instruments.

There are perhaps two areas in particular that illustrate why the NEPP has been seen by many as ground-breaking. The first is its comprehensive and detailed analysis of environmental problems and how they might be managed. The second is the detailed costing of alternative environmental policy scenarios and the defence of a relatively vigorous vision of the measures necessary to move towards a sustainable future.

Understanding sustainable development

The NEPP contains perhaps the most sophisticated analysis of sustainable development within a national strategy. It recognises the differences in scale – local through to global – of environmental problems as well as their multiple sources. The interconnected nature of environmental, social and economic factors is appreciated, as is the inconsistent nature of existing responses to environmental problems: too often impacts are treated as if they were isolated – this is misguided, as such an approach may lead to an even more deleterious effect in some other part of the environmental–social system. Commenting on the NEPP, Weale states:

> The natural and social worlds are seen as a large, complex, interlinked system in which disturbance at one point can cause malfunction at another. To the extent to which we can understand the system we should seek to rectify the malfunctioning not at the point of effects but at sources. This means modifying or eliminating the human activities that are responsible ultimately, as sources, for environmental degradation.
>
> (Weale, 1992, p. 128)

Action needs to focus on the initial cause of problems – the objective of policy ought to be preventive rather than reactive. Source-orientated rather than effect-orientated measures must be given preference.

The NEPP's case for source-orientated measures

Source-orientated measures are to be preferred to effect-orientated ones because the possibility to control is greatest at the source; one source may cause more than one effect; uncertainties about the cause–effect chain can exist; irreversible effects can occur; and it generally costs less to intervene at the source.

Source-orientated measures can be divided into:
- emission-orientated measures: add-on technology which reduces emissions and waste streams without changing the processes of production and consumption;
- volume-orientated measures: legal and organisational measures which reduce the volumes of raw materials and products without changing production and consumption processes as such;
- structure-orientated measures: structural changes of a technological or other nature which change the processes of production.

(Structural measures will also result in changes in volumes and emissions but target neither volumes nor emissions.)

Effect-orientated measures are taken only if:
- environmental quality has already been damaged by past developments or calamities, but the effects can still be mitigated;
- there are prospects for structure-orientated measures, but they cannot be taken at short notice;
- effect-orientated measures have significantly lower social costs and do not impede structural measures for other environmental problems.

(Ministry of Housing *et al.*, 1989, p. 13)

Possible scenarios and a vision for change

As well as promoting a widely respected, sophisticated theoretical analysis of the concept of sustainable development, the NEPP also provides a long, detailed list of policies and actions that need to be taken within the planning period 1990–94 if a sustainable future is to be achieved within twenty years. These measures were chosen from an analysis of the environmental and economic impacts of three policy scenarios:

1 a package of measures reflecting the continuation of current policy;
2 a package of measures reflecting maximum utilisation of currently known emission-orientated measures;
3 a package of measures reflecting a mix of emission-orientated and structural source-orientated measures such as:

- extended energy conservation in the household and business sector;
- shifts from private car use to public transport;
- more efficient use of minerals in agriculture;
- recovery of raw materials from waste streams;
- large-scale application of process-integrated clean technology.

The three scenarios are compared with the necessary reductions in emissions that the Netherlands needs to achieve for sustainable development. These reductions are extremely strict with, for instance, emissions of sulphur dioxide, nitrogen oxides, ammonia and hydrocarbons, discharges to the Rhine and North Sea, waste dumping, noise, and odour all required to be decreased by somewhere between 70 and 90 per cent. It is made clear that Scenario 1 cannot achieve such reductions. In Scenario 2, an ever-increasing investment and share of GNP would be required to achieve ever smaller environmental gains. Further, this emission-orientated approach can never lead to the required emission reductions. Such an end-goal requires much more radical policies, including structural changes. The measures outlined in Scenario 3 do achieve the required reductions in some areas, in others they come close. Interestingly, the calculations drawn up by the Central Planning Bureau 'demonstrate that even severe measures and strict norms will not have a significant effect on macro-economic variables' (Straaten, 1992, p. 58) – the economic case against the radical policies needed to achieve sustainable development appear not to hold. In the light of these results the NEPP argues for a gradual transition from the second to the third scenario – 'the reason for this choice is that Scenario 3 requires major technological and social adjustments which will take time to realise' (Ministry of Housing *et al.*, 1990, p. 15).

Problems of implementation

Although the NEPP offers a comprehensive analysis of the policy requirements for sustainable development it faced a number of problems in its implementation. We shall briefly discuss three issues: leadership; policy instruments; cooperation.

Despite being co-presented by the Ministers of Economic Affairs, Agriculture and Fisheries, and Transport and Public Works, the NEPP was driven mainly by the strong leadership of the Minister of Housing, Physical Planning and Environment, E.H.T.M. Nijpels, with the support of the Dutch Prime Minister. Nijpels was able to keep control of the emissions reduction targets and hence any strategy for change would need to be radical. However, the right-wing Liberal Party, a minority member of the Christian Democrat-led coalition government, was not prepared to support a number of the financial measures that the NEPP was to impose, in particular the abolishing of tax reductions for commuters and tax increases for home owners – the constituency of its core supporters. The Liberals forced an election – perhaps the first time that a government has fallen over an environmental policy – but had mistaken the mood of the electorate and the Christian Democrats were able to form a new Cabinet with the Social Democrats. Although this coalition was supportive of strong policy planning, unfortunately the leadership of Nijpels was lost: he himself being a Liberal.

Even with its radical vision, the use of economic instruments in the NEPP is fairly limited and it appears that (as in the UK) the Ministry of Economic Affairs and Finance was not prepared to sanction their widespread use. As well as the ministry's concern as to their effect on the economy, the business and industrial sector is a vociferous opponent of their intro-duction – the consensual nature of Dutch politics allows them some scope to negotiate standards (Straaten, 1992, pp. 66–7). A large number of the responses to the NEPP, particularly from NGOs, saw this political marginalisation of economic instruments as its major weakness (Ministry of Housing *et al.*, 1990, pp. 54–73).

Perhaps the greatest failing of the NEPP is its limited coverage of imple-mentation strategies. In fact there was a certain amount of resistance from the provinces, where local authorities found themselves presented with strict requirements from central government. Although there is stress on the ne-cessity of cooperation for sustainable development, the preparation of the NEPP appears not to have given much thought to achieving consensus on the way forward with other actors outside the ministries involved in its pro-duction. What the NEPP achieved, however, is the provision of a compre-hensive and widely supported framework of what is necessary to be done. The second NEPP focused more attention on such implementation meas-ures, although unfortunately a further election occurred and the new gov-ernment did not view the NEPP as a political priority (Straaten, 1994, pp. 231–2). Such is the fluid nature of Dutch coalition politics.

Divergent traditions: comparing the UK and the Netherlands

Why is it that when compared with *Sustainable Development: The UK Strategy*, the NEPP has a much more sophisticated conception of sustainable devel-opment and the necessary measures required to move towards it? Why was the Dutch government able to provide extremely stringent targets and objec-tives, cost the relevant policies and provide a clear vision of a sustainable future, whereas in the UK there was only a series of possible policy options? There would appear to be a number of possible reasons.

First, there is clearly a different attitude towards policy planning in the Netherlands. With its particular geographical and social situation – much of the Netherlands is below sea level and it has a dense population – land-use and development planning are well established. In the UK, the Thatcherite government was ideologically opposed to strict planning and it has only been in the last few years that the land-use planning system in the UK has begun to be strengthened again (see Chapter 10).

Second, the more sophisticated understanding of sustainable develop-ment and the reasonably broad support for the NEPP may stem from the more consensual and collective style of politics in the Netherlands. Much of this can be traced to the coalition governments that tend to be formed under the proportional representation voting system. The first-past-the-post system in the UK may lead to a single party in power with a majority in Parliament, but that in itself does not mean that the government will be environmentally enlightened. In the Netherlands, policy formulation appears more reasoned and debate amongst divergent interest is central. In the UK, by comparison, policy can be developed without any requirement for debate and opportunity for social learning.

Third, Dutch politics seems to embody a wider conception of well-being and a stronger conception of citizenship. The Dutch people appear to be more politically aware and have a more developed sense of their responsibility towards the environment. Again this could well be traced back to the consensual and collective nature of Dutch politics and to their geographical location. The idea of environmentally responsible citizenship is a central theme in the NEPP. In contrast, it is economic conceptions of well-being that dominate political debate in the UK and this is reinforced with the frequent portrayal of the electorate as individual consumers rather than citizens.

SUGGESTIONS FOR FURTHER READING

For a collection of essays looking at different areas of British environmental policy see Tim Gray, *UK Environmental Policy in the 1990s* (1995). Tim O'Riordan and Heather Voisey (eds), *Sustainable Development in Western Europe* (1997b), brings together a number of essays investigating national responses to sustainable development. Again, *Environmental Politics* is probably the single most authoritative source for up-to-date analysis of national approaches to environmental policy.

10 Local democracy and local authorities

Whether it is identified as subsidiarity, decentralisation, empowerment or participation, some component of democratisation is widely viewed as being integral to
the achievement of an environmentally sustainable future.

(Agyeman and Evans, 1994, p. 14)

The preceding chapters have focused attention on global, European and national
pressures for change and the differing reactions to the developing environment and
sustainable development agendas at these different levels. Much of the policy framework generated at these levels of political organisation requires implementation at a
more local level. It is thus local government that is often at the forefront of this
process. However, to view local action as solely consisting of the implementation of
policy generated from above would be to underestimate the practices and influence
of local authorities. In many countries, it is the experience of local government in
fashioning policies and actions and the day-to-day environmental problems that they
face that has driven them to adopt innovative practices and partnerships with other
sectors of the community. Their experiences, and the perceived inadequacies of
national and international directives and funding, has meant that it is often local
authorities which are developing a much more coherent approach to environmental
issues and, in turn, they have put pressure on their own nation states. This is particularly the case in the UK, where central government often finds itself 'between a rock
and a hard place': pressurised from above by the EU and from below by committed
and innovative local authorities and their associations.

Initially this chapter will look at the emerging pressure for the reinvigoration of
local democracy. Without doubt, greens stand alongside such a political programme.
However, there is a tension between this vision and recent reforms to local government. Particularly in the UK, local authorities find themselves faced with increased
economic and fiscal disciplines, which have the effect of fragmenting their responsibilities in the name of economic efficiency. This would appear to militate against
concerted environmental and democratic action. In response to these disciplines,
and in line with the emergence of environmental and sustainable development
concerns, many local authorities are beginning to reassess their relationship with
other local actors and the wider local community.

The final section of this chapter focuses on the emergence of the Local Agenda 21 process, perhaps the most important recent development in local environmental politics. Doubts about the UK national government's commitments to sustainable development have stimulated more enlightened local authorities to reinvigorate local democratic practices. Where Local Agenda 21 is embraced, local innovation and imagination become a real possibility.

Most of the chapter will focus on the experience of UK local authorities, which have been widely acknowledged as being at the forefront of developing Local Agenda 21. There may be a number of reasons for this. First, local authorities in the UK have lost a number of important functions in recent years and have seen local environmental action as an area where they can legitimately take a leadership role. Second, by comparison with other European countries, UK local authorities may have been latecomers to environmental politics. Local environmental policies and actions in, for instance, Germany and Norway were much further advanced in the 1980s (Sverdrup, 1997; Beuermann and Burdick, 1997; Voisey *et al.*, 1996).[1] However, this may mean that UK local authorities are in a particularly good position to respond to the wider sustainable development agenda that Local Agenda 21 represents. Where local authorities in other liberal democracies have responded to more traditional (and thus limited) 'environmental' concerns, UK authorities may well be in the forefront of responding to the wider environmental, social and economic implications of sustainable development.

THE CASE FOR LOCAL DEMOCRACY

Greens frequently celebrate 'the local' as a site of environmental action and appropriate democratic arrangements and engagement: one only has to reflect on the most famous of green slogans 'think globally, act locally'. Green politics can be seen as part of a wider project of democratisation, and more specifically local democratisation. Clearly, any study of local democratisation needs to attend to the role of local government. In the UK, unlike many other liberal democracies, the democratic and political features of local government have often been sidelined or ignored. The dominant strand in thinking about local government has emphasised its role in the efficient delivery of services. As Peter John argues, even before recent reforms, 'the national political consensus was that local government was more an agency administering welfare functions than an entrenched institution of the democratic polity' (John, 1997, p. 254). Under recent Conservative administrations, the focus on efficiency reached new heights with the embrace and celebration of market and quasi-market mechanisms in many areas of local government competence. The rationale here is to provide 'a more effective way of achieving efficiency. Competition between producers and choice for the consumer were to be the crucial weapons of reform' (Stoker, 1996b, p. 190). William Waldegrave, one of the more vociferous defenders of recent local government management reforms, argues: 'The key point ... is not whether those who run our public services are elected, but whether they are producer-responsive or consumer-responsive' (ibid., pp. 190–1). Local government in other liberal democracies may also be going through processes of reform, but in comparison with the UK, local democratic political principles and the idea of subsidiarity – taking decisions at the appropriate political level – remain fundamental (Wolman, 1996; Goldsmith, 1996; Chandler, 1993; Batley, 1991). We shall have more to say about the nature and effect of these reforms later in the chapter, but for now it is enough to recognise that calls for greater local democracy have gained added urgency in the light of shifts in local government thinking over recent decades and challenge the orthodoxy that local government should simply concern itself with local service delivery.

Local government in liberal democracies

Two aspects of the British experience of local government separate it from the practice of other liberal democracies.[2] The first is the preoccupation with service delivery; the second is its constitutional status. In the UK, local government is a creature of statute – it has only a limited legal and political status. Local government in the rest of Europe and the USA, on the other hand, has formal constitutional status. Within the rest of Europe, local authorities can be divided into two categories related to differing political traditions. First there is the 'Franco' model, with a tradition of strong centralised administration, but where local areas enjoy fundamental political status. The second is that typical of 'Northern and Middle Europe', where the principle of subsidiarity is embraced and a high value is placed on local self-government. Here local autonomy and financial independence are relatively important and local self-government has a constitutional status. By comparison with the UK, local authorities in the rest of Europe enjoy a much higher level of influence in the affairs of state and are seen as important political actors in their own right (Goldsmith, 1996, Batley, 1991). In the USA, local government operates in a formal constitutional context based on traditional American values of localism and local autonomy. Here individual rights and checks and balances on centralised power are taken as fundamental concerns, whereas the idea of public purpose is more common in Europe (Wolman, 1996). Looking at the capacity of local government to respond to contemporary environmental problems, it is clear that UK local authorities are in a relatively powerless position. If we take control over greenhouse gas emissions as an example, we find that in North America and Northern Europe local authorities typically have the capacity to develop more effective energy efficiency policies as they have some influence over energy production, distribution and consumption in their localities. In the UK, by contrast, the energy market is highly liberalised and the degree of local authority control correspondingly diminished (Nijkamp and Perrrels, 1994). In all liberal democracies there are tensions between local democracy and efficiency and between local autonomy and equality and justice. The interesting issue is the manner in which different traditions interpret and resolve these tensions.

Arguments for enhanced local democracy have a number of justifications.[3] First we find arguments based around the idea of 'localism': local problems are best dealt with by local decision-making processes. Local government is taken to have a sensitivity to local needs, interests, demands and conditions: its legitimacy rests on local knowledge and its responsiveness to individuals and communities to which it is democratically accountable. Often this 'localist' argument is linked with the question of efficiency. Because of its local knowledge and its ability to create alternative and innovative arrangements in the light of local conditions, local government can provide efficient and effective local service. Such arguments for localism are at the heart of arguments for subsidiarity. In a European context, the recent Conservative administration enthusiastically promoted the principle of subsidiarity, but only down to the level of the nation state, not below that to the level of local government.

A second defence of local democratic arrangements is the prudential argument that the enhancement of local democracy guards against the over-centralisation of power. In the UK it is a common argument that there need to be increased checks and balances on the powers of Whitehall and Westminster. In many ways the diminution of local democracy can be traced to the lack of any embedded constitutional status for local government in Britain.

A third set of arguments revolves around the celebration of public participation. Again this could be tied into arguments for diffusion of power. Increased opportunity for participation is taken as a way of transforming both the nature of politics and the way in which people act and think. Political participation is a transformative and educative process. Local government is taken to be the 'most accessible avenue of public participation' (Phillips, 1996, p. 26). Given that there is widespread dissatisfaction, cynicism and apathy amongst citizens (and even amongst councillors and officers) with the workings of existing representative structures (Gyford, 1991),[4] the forms of participation proposed are understood to require far more than periodic voting or standing for election as a councillor. Suggestions include developing the wider use of institutional arrangements such as public meetings, referendums, citizens' juries and electronic democracy. Local government is thus seen as having the potential to create the conditions within which divergent local interests can reveal and express their concerns and come to an understanding of competing claims.

These considerations by no means exhaust the justification for enhanced local democracy, but they do provide a flavour of the current debates on the topic. Greens draw on similar arguments. As we have already seen in Chapter 2, decentralisation is fundamental to much green political thinking. Local communities, particularly in anarchist streams of thinking, are taken to be the most appropriate level for political, social and economic relations, as well as relations with the non-human world.

Some green arguments for local democracy allow no place for local government. This view draws on anarchist principles, which regard relations of hierarchical authority as essentially implicated in both human and non-human subjugation. In Chapter 2, we rehearsed a number of problems with the eco-anarchist position, including the potential for parochialism, the lack of coordination between locali-

---

Green arguments for local democracy

- Decentralisation is related to a shift to a green consciousness.

- The corrosive effect of self-interest as displayed in the *Tragedy of the Commons* is best controlled by community-level political processes.

- Smaller-scale economic processes have a lower environmental impact.

- Grassroots democracy is a necessary condition for sustainability.

(Adapted from Ward, 1996)

---

ties, and the fact that the local is not always the most appropriate scale for economic, social and political action. Questions of distribution of resources and, as such, distributive justice, require government-type structures (not that the arrangements necessarily have to mirror current political arrangements and institutions). So, if we are to talk about government, greens take local authorities to be a prime site for political participation and action. And, as Ward argues, 'an increased environmental role represents an alternative to the Conservatives' minimalist vision of local government and gives a new basis of legitimacy in a period when older legitimacies are under constant attack' (Ward, 1996, p. 131).

A combination of these arguments for enhanced local democracy can be found at the heart of the Local Government Management Board's (LGMB) *A Statement to UNCED*, published in the run-up to the Rio Earth Summit. The concepts of subsidiarity and political participation are strongly affirmed in the light of contemporary environmental problems:

> the potential of local government in applying the principle of subsidiarity ... rests upon the following essential characteristics:
>
> - closeness to the issue;
> - a capacity for learning;
> - 'local choice and local voice';
> - local differences, local diversity, local innovation;
> - the basis for citizen participation;
> - an understanding of local interactions and impacts;
> - the starting point for actions leading to sustainable development within the community;
> - the ability to set conditions for local action;
> - a partner for global action across districts, regions and countries and a key player in the local economy.
>
> (Hams, 1994, pp. 31–2)

There is clearly a tension between arguments for enhanced local democracy (whether on the grounds of responsiveness to local needs, diffusion of power, or political participation and education) and arguments for economic efficiency in allocation and service provision. The potential resolutions of these tensions mirror alternative visions of local government and democracy. As this chapter develops, it will become clear that local government has become just one of a number of organisations operative at the local level. Thus any conception of local democracy requires us to attend to the relationships between these different public, private and voluntary organisations and to recognise that local authorities have become one actor amongst many in networks of *local governance*. Green arguments for enhanced participation need to be sensitive to these new conditions. Local democracy cannot simply be equated with the actions of local government alone.

STRUCTURE AND PRACTICE OF LOCAL GOVERNMENT

The case for enhanced local democracy and for the important role that local authorities will be called on to perform in reinvigorating local democratic practices has been made above. However, this is but one vision of the nature and purpose of local authorities and by no means the dominant one. Clearly there is always, in local government, a state of tension between different important values, for instance between the values of 'democracy' and 'efficiency'. As we shall see, the reforms of local government brought about in the last two decades have tended to give priority to efficiency. Again we can observe tensions between 'centralisation' and 'localism': it is often argued that a strong centralised state is necessary in order to promote social justice, welfare, equity and comprehensive environmental protection.

Over the past decade or so the functions and remit of local government have become the site of ideological confrontation. The reforms of local government brought about under recent Conservative administrations have led to fragmentation and a differentiated pattern of structure, management and service provision. Local government often seems to be under constant reform and reorganisation, typically *ad hoc* and based on political expediency rather than firm principles. The level of change has been unprecedented, but as we move into the twenty-first century, there is a great deal of uncertainty and disagreement about the nature of these changes and the direction local government is moving in. A number of competing (and conflicting) options and visions have been proposed. We shall briefly look at the manner in which the structure of local government has altered and the introduction of economic disciplines such as compulsory competitive tendering (CCT) before discussing these alternative visions.

Structure

The 1972 Local Government Act created a fairly consistent two-tier system throughout England and Wales – forty-seven shire county councils and 333 district councils; and six metropolitan county councils and thirty-six metropolitan districts. A similar structure was introduced in Scotland in 1975 with a two-tier system of regional and district authorities. The 1980s saw local government become a site of increased ideological confrontation, in particular between Conservative central government and Labour-controlled urban authorities. The so-called 'militant' metropolitan county councils, such as the Greater London Council (GLC) and Greater Manchester Council, were abolished in 1986 and their functions transferred to the lower tiers (metropolitan districts) and joint planning boards. From a green perspective, these changes were criticised on the grounds that the large cities now lacked the capacity for strategic planning in areas such as transport, economic development and education and that there was a 'democratic deficit' at the heart of the UK's largest urban areas: small metropolitan districts simply did not have the capacity to respond to many of the city-wide environmental, social and economic pressures.

A further reorganisation of local government began in 1992 led by the Local Government Commission. Government guidance for the commission stressed the criteria of efficiency, accountability, responsibility and localness. Although the Conservative administration originally favoured the creation of a single tier of local government, the final outcome is a 'patchwork' of unitary and two-tier authorities – often Whitehall ignored the commission's advice because of political expediency and opportunism. A number of problems have been noted with the commission's terms of reference: for instance, it was not given the option of promoting regional authorities or rearranging political boundaries so that unitary city authorities would include their conurbations; and the fate of metropolitan areas was left out of its remit (Leach, 1996a, pp. 164–5). At the same time, the review process led to increased animosity between councils, particularly between districts and counties vying for control of each other's functions – working relationships on cross-authority issues such as environmental problems became increasingly soured. Second, funding and political support for responses to long-term environmental concerns found themselves squeezed by short-term publicity and marketing-style campaigns by authorities hoping to impress the commission. Third, the review criteria did not refer explicitly to environmental management issues but primarily to financial and social concerns. Against this antagonistic and often highly competitive backdrop it is perhaps a surprise that the environmental agenda has moved forward at all. The review process can be seen as a lost opportunity not only because a future central government has to attend to the ambiguous and inconsistent structures which resulted from it, but also because 'the Local Government Review has not really been an exploration of the future of local government as an institution' (Leach and Davis, 1996, p. 2).

From 'provider' to 'enabler'

Without any doubt, the reforms introduced since the 1980s challenged 'traditional' understandings of the role of local authorities as direct service providers and also further undermined their local democratic credentials. As we have already mentioned, the traditional view of local authorities has emphasised their administrative rather than democratic capacities. Three areas of change are worth mentioning as they provide a brief sketch of the situation of local authorities in the late 1990s:

the extension of central government control in finance and revenue; the introduction of compulsory competitive tendering (CCT) for certain functions and service provision; and the weakening of the powers of local authorities to coordinate local actions and the rise of quangos as an increasing number of their responsibilities have been lost or fragmented. To a certain extent, the philosophy of the Conservative government can be seen as fundamentally reorientating local authorities away from being 'providers' towards being 'enablers'. This is emphasised in the 1991 White Paper *Competing for Quality*:

> The Government's model for local government in the 1990s and into the 21st century is that of the *enabling authority*. Here the task of local authorities lies in identifying requirements, setting priorities, determining standards of service and finding the best way to meet these standards and ensuring that they are met. This implies a move away from the traditional model of local authorities providing virtually all services directly and a greater separation of the functions of service delivery from strategic responsibilities.
>
> (Quoted in Pratchett and Wilson, 1996, p. 3, emphasis added)

Local government's primary purpose is thus taken to be 'specifying service requirements in relation to a discrete range of services which cannot be directly provided by the market, and then "enabling" these services to be provided through increased use of external agencies (including private contractors)' (Leach and Davis, 1996, p. 3). More than any other reform, it has been the introduction of CCT that has forced local authorities towards this enabling role. CCT requires a split between the roles of purchaser and provider, with the primary role of local authorities being the former – 'contracting out' service provision. This has happened in refuse collection and disposal, leisure management, building cleaning, and school catering, although more recent developments have seen its extension into 'white collar' areas. Although in many cases the contracts are won by council-created direct service organisations, critics have argued that the fragmentation of responsibilities (local authorities have often been split into client and contractor relations) has led to a loss of the public service ethos and lessened the influence of elected councillors on service provision. More importantly perhaps, CCT has been charged with creating low-cost services at the expense of quality, good working conditions and sound environmental practice (Patterson and Theobald, 1996, pp. 9–18; Whitehead, 1996, pp. 20–1). The new Labour government, whilst recognising the potential efficiency savings of CCT, has committed itself to ending the 'compulsory' element of tendering and introducing a 'best value' criterion, which promotes the idea of public–private partnerships (John, 1997, p. 274).

In the area of waste management, for example, CCT has brought about a number of changes. The Environmental Protection Act (1990) forced local authorities to separate their waste regulation, collection and disposal functions. CCT has affected the latter two roles.[5] For example, the waste collection authorities (WCAs) are required to both open collection to tender – around 25 per cent of collections are now run by private companies (Cooper, 1994, p. 133) – and produce a recycling plan. The

DoE's target of 25 per cent of all household waste to be recycled by the year 2000 is a highly ambitious target in its own right and progress is hampered by problems in incorporating such environmental criteria within contract specifications. Waste disposal authorities (WDAs) are responsible for the management of collected waste and often the day-to-day running of disposal facilities such as incinerators and landfills. Again, with the expansion of CCT policy into white collar areas, many local authorities have created arms-length local authority waste disposal companies (LAWDCs). Clearly, waste management is an area of local authority activity that has felt the effects of CCT, which is frequently criticised for undermining the relatively expensive environmental options of recycling and the promotion of waste minimisation. While there may have been some positive aspects of the changes in that the separation of collection, disposal and regulation functions should have the effect of avoiding corruption, new incentives will have to be introduced into the system if environmental good practice is to emerge.[6]

Recent years have also witnessed a substantial weakening in the financial autonomy of local authorities. Their revenue-raising capacity has been substantially decreased by, for instance, the removal of locally determined business charges; strict borrowing limits; and the introduction of the standard spending assessment (SSA) and 'capping'. Central government now assesses the level of grant that authorities will receive and places an upper limit on the level of local tax that can be collected. 'In the mid-1980s, 60 per cent of local expenditure was covered by locally determined taxes. Today that figure has declined to under 20 per cent' (Pratchett and Wilson, 1996, p. 7). As the Commission for Local Democracy argues, such financial control is 'wholly incompatible with democratic accountability. It is as offensive to local government as capping by Brussels would be to a national government' (Commission for Local Democracy, 1995, p. 42).

Finally, local government no longer finds itself in a monopoly situation – the fragmentation of responsibilities means that local authorities can no longer take strategic control of service provision alone. The Conservative reforms created a whole raft of quangos[7] that took control of certain services and functions, for example urban development corporations, training and enterprise councils, housing action trusts, grant-maintained schools and health trusts: 'there are now some 5,750 agencies (90 per cent operate at the local level) which take about a third of public expenditure and have some 50,000 appointed people sitting on them' (John, 1997, p. 267). These organisations, whose boards are typically directly appointed by ministers, are rightly criticised for a lack of democratic accountability and legitimacy (J. Stewart, 1996). What is clear is that with the reduction of its monopoly on coordination, local authorities have had to enter into new forms of relations with private, public and voluntary organisations. As Peter John argues:

> local government has been transformed from being the dominant legitimate local public institution to just being one body which participates in a more complex framework of governing. In short, local government has been succeeded by local governance.
>
> (John, 1997, p. 253)

There has been a severe fragmentation of responsibilities, a lessening of local authorities' ability to coordinate action, a reduction in the available areas of discretion and a continuing vulnerability to central government legislation and policy changes. However, the Conservatives' interpretation of the concept of 'enabling' does not necessarily restrict local authorities to quite the extent it might first appear, and it also fails to take account of the capacity of local authorities to respond to local problems in ways which *transcend* service provision. Leach and Davis argue that:

> its characterisation in these terms virtually ignores other important local government functions – planning, regulation, promotion and advocacy – which have increased in significance since the 1974 reorganisation. It is a gross simplification of the current position to equate local government with service provision *per se*, and to assume that arguments about enabling (i.e. the way in which services are provided) are applicable to the whole range of local government activity.
>
> (Leach and Davis, 1996, p. 4)

Local authority 'environmental' responsibilities typically cut across different types of functions. As Leach and Davis contend: 'Land-use planning involves planning *and* regulation; environmental health involves regulation *and* promotion and advocacy' (ibid.). We shall discuss land-use planning in more depth below, but for now it is enough to recognise that local authorities' functions go well beyond simple direct service provision.

Does 'enabling' entail the disempowering of local government? Should we understand the local government reform process as a process of 'disabling'? What becomes clear when we begin to look at the actual practices of different local authorities is that there are different and competing visions or interpretations of the meaning of 'enabling' and of the role of local government.

> There are unmistakable contrasts between the political priorities and organisational cultures of Tower Hamlets, where the devolution of power to neighbourhoods was taken so far that the role for the authority itself became residual and Birmingham where in recent years the city council has attempted to transform Birmingham into an 'international city'. ... There is a similarly striking contrast between Rutland, which has developed the involvement of the private sector (and other alternative sources of service provision) well beyond what is required by law, and many South Wales authorities which, whilst acting within the law, have attempted to minimise the impact of CCT on their operations and organisational structures and maximise the chance of winning contracts internally.
>
> (Leach, 1996b, p. 160)

The vision of 'enabling' as an alternative to direct service provision lies at the heart of Conservative local government philosophy and practice in the 1980s. But other interpretations of 'enabling' are possible, and Clarke and Stewart, for instance, have extended the idea beyond the limited service provision debate and towards 'enabling the community to meet the needs and opportunities and problems faced *in the most effective way*' (quoted in Gyford, 1991, p. 186). Such an interpretation is based on the ideas of community governance and the reinvigoration of local democracy that we have already touched on.

Leach offers four illustrative examples of the strategic choice that local authorities can make with respect to service provision and local governmental intervention; although there may be a loss of traditional local authority activity and discretion, there is even greater room for manoeuvre at the strategic level. The first option for local government is to attempt to maintain *direct service provision* based on the traditional ethos of public service. The second is the *commercial approach*, which celebrates the Conservative interpretation of 'enabling' and maximises the role of the private sector. The third model is that of *community governance*, in which the local authority develops partnerships and networks with external organisations from all sectors to respond to the different needs of the community. It plays a pro-active leadership and coordinating role to overcome gaps in strategic planning and service delivery. Finally, the *neighbourhood approach* respects the diversity of local communities and aims to decentralise activities and responsibilities into localities. These different strategies display different attitudes to governance, the market and to local populations (Leach, 1996a, pp. 29–37) and raise interesting questions about democratic accountability and the capacity of local authorities to respond to growing environmental pressures. In light of the agenda for reasserting local democracy, it is the last two approaches that are of most interest and these will be returned to when we discuss the emergence of Local Agenda 21. Before then, however, we shall briefly focus on the planning and transportation responsibilities of UK local authorities, both of which have considerable impact on the local environment.

Land-use planning

Where there is a two-tier system, planning control and development plans are instituted through structure plans and local plans. Structure plans are statements of general policy produced by county councils which are applied in a more detailed manner by the local plan produced by district councils. Unitary authorities apply the planning process through a unitary development plan, which combines general policies and detailed proposals for land use in a single document. Both structure and unitary development plans require approval from the Secretary of State for the Environment.

It is perhaps not surprising that a land-use planning system dating back to the 1947 Town and Country Planning Act has problems dealing effectively with many contemporary environmental issues. Typically, the environment has been compartmentalised and treated within a separate chapter in such plans, usually focusing on historic monuments and nature conservation. As a 1993 Town and Country Planning Association (TCPA) report states, the planning system 'has been an effective instrument for achieving the policy objectives of the 1940s, particularly the demarcation of built-up areas from the countryside and the

designation and protection of national parks, landscape areas, and nature reserves. ... But it has been far less successful in responding to new kinds of environmental concerns' (Hall *et al.*, 1993, p. 20). So, for instance, the planning system
has to a certain extent protected rural areas from development pressures, but has
no influence on the direction of agricultural policy: 'the town and country planning system has protected the rural land resource from building development
but not from some of the uglier side-effects of agribusiness' (ibid.). Andrew Blowers
of the TCPA argues that the planning system needs to be modernised so that it
can deal effectively with 'the integrated nature of environmental processes and
policies' (Blowers, 1993b, pp. 14–17). This requires a response to the transmedia,
transsectional and transboundary nature of environmental problems. The
transmedia nature of environmental problems (see Chapter 9) requires the integration of, for instance, pollution control, waste management and land-use planning. Environmental problems are transsectional: environmental policy should
not be a discrete area within plans, but rather should be fundamental to the
planning of issues such as energy, transportation and agriculture. Along similar
lines, environmental problems do not recognise existing political boundaries and
as such a structure plan cannot be seen as an independent document – the impacts on other localities must be recognised. The development of independent
plans for a city and its hinterlands, each under the control of different authorities, has caused much concern. A strategic approach to planning is required
which integrates local planning within regional, national and even European
policy frameworks. For instance, the relation between structure plans and the
European Union's Fifth Environmental Action Plan[8] needs to be formalised (Lusser,
1994, pp. 126ff). Existing counties and unitary authorities are not always the
most appropriate political units for planning purposes.

The 1980s saw a definite step towards the 'liberalisation' of planning, with the
presumption being in favour of development over environmental concerns, perhaps the most vivid example being the rise in out-of-town retail and business developments. Local authorities have consistently lost appeals against such developments,
with the result that the vitality of city centres has been much reduced and traffic
(principally private vehicle) movements have increased. At the same time, local
authorities have competed with each other to attract economic development, often
without taking any account of the strategic impact. Particularly in urban areas, the
introduction of enterprise zones and simplified planning zones and the activities
of quangos such as unitary development corporations removes many of the traditional planning controls and discretion from local authorities and at the same time
raises questions of accountability (M. Stewart, 1996, pp. 149ff).

In the early 1990s there was a general recognition that the planning system
needed to be refocused as it was unable to protect localities from unsustainable
incursions, such as out-of-town retail and business developments.[9] The Policy Planning
Guidance (PPGs) provided by the DoE began to treat issues such as energy, transport and tourism in a more integrated manner. For example, PPG12, *Development
Plans and Regional Planning Guidance*, published in 1992, introduces the concept of
sustainable development into the planning process.

The government has made clear its intention to work towards ensuring that development and growth are sustainable. It will continue to develop policies consistent with the concept of sustainable development. The planning system, and the preparation of development plans in particular, can contribute to the objectives of ensuring that development and growth are sustainable. The sum total of decisions in the planning field, as elsewhere, should not deny future generations the best of today's environment. This should be expressed through the policies in development planning.

(DoE, 1992b, para.1.8)

Similarly, the 1994 and 1995 revisions of PPG6, *Town Centres and Retail Development*, promote development in town centres in preference to out-of-town retailing, while PPG13, published in 1993, allows local authorities to take into account, in judging the merits of development projects, their effect on the volume of vehicle emissions.[10] Sustainability has become a common theme in many PPGs, although the definitions are often contradictory and there still remains a presumption in favour of economic development. Also, 'developers can still effectively play competing suburbs off against city-based local authorities, as the recent contretemps between Eastleigh and Southampton on shopping and leisure facilities, and between Norwich and Broadlands DC on the development of a business park amply illustrate' (Whitehead, 1996, p. 20). However, planning guidance has allowed a number of local authorities to produce land-use plans which approach environment and development issues in a much more comprehensive manner and to halt certain grossly unsustainable developments.

The DoE has also published *Policy Appraisal and the Environment* (1991a) and *Environmental Appraisal of Development Plans* (1993c), which continue the trend towards a more environmentally integrated approach to development planning. However, Whitehall has not yet come out in support of a statutory duty for local authorities to apply a strategic environmental assessment to all plans and policies (see Chapter 5) and has actually blocked a possible EU directive in this area. Again, local authorities are receiving mixed signals from central government. The most significant use of strategic environmental assessment on a structure plan is almost certainly by Lancashire County Council, which 'devised a matrix comprising environmental indicators and allocated to each policy a sustainability score in relation to the indicators' (Hill and Smith, 1994, p. 83). As a result of the assessment, a number of the policies in the structure plan were altered.

The planning system is being slowly reformed by central government, but clearly in an *ad hoc* manner. The new Labour administration is without doubt more sympathetic to planning problems and, with the creation of the Department of the Environment, Transport and the Regions, is expected to introduce a more consistent and comprehensive approach with particular emphasis on the need for regional strategic planning. A fundamental overhaul of a rather outdated system is what is required in order to take into account the nature of relatively new environment and development pressures and to affirm sustainable development as a central guiding principle.[11]

Transportation

The changes in control over transportation policy is an area where the Conservatives' belief in liberalisation and the superiority of the market and the private sector can be clearly seen. The last decade or so has seen a loss of discretion and capacity for coordination on the part of local authorities. At the same time, there has been a substantial increase in road vehicle usage – both private car and freight – and an associated increase in pollution problems, along with a modal shift away from public transport. The direction of government legislation has meant that local authorities have not been in a position to develop sustainable and integrated transport policies.[12] As Alan Whitehead states: 'The Transport Act 1985 has deprived cities of the ability to regulate public transport for social rather than economic purposes, and produce any sort of integrated transport plan that links in car parking, buses and trains' (Whitehead, 1996, p. 19).

Again, we can see the transboundary problem arising in the provision of, for example, 'park-and-ride' schemes where, because the territorial control of urban authorities may not extend to their hinterlands, such schemes require cooperation between authorities which may be in direct competition with one another. Examples of this kind reinforce the strength of the arguments both for a review of existing political and administrative boundaries and for the adoption of a strategic regional approach to planning issues.

Unitary and county councils are the highway authorities for all roads except trunk roads and motorways. In that capacity they produce Transport Policy and Programmes (TPPs) to bid for resources from Whitehall. Traditionally this has been purely for highway construction and improvements. In response to growing congestion and pollution episodes in certain areas and pressure for reform, local authorities have been allowed to put forward a more balanced and integrated 'package' approach including road traffic management and public transport schemes. A difficulty is that in many authorities the highway construction department dominates the transport agenda and this results in conflict between transport engineers and environmental planners; this problem mirrors the influence of roads-based interests in Whitehall (Hamer, 1987). Entrenched interests in road transport will need to be overcome for any change to succeed.

Although the package approach is a step in the right direction and has allowed cities to bid for grants for public transport schemes such as the modern Manchester and Sheffield tram systems, local authorities are far from being able to adopt an integrated, sustainable approach to local transport policy. Such schemes are incredibly costly and authorities depend heavily on private investment or limited government grants. Other aspects of the transport network are out of their control. For instance, bus deregulation, another service opened up by CCT legislation, means that all routes are open to the private sector and local government has little control over timetabling. Against this backdrop some councils have attempted to utilise the planning system to develop more sustainable and environmentally sensitive transport infrastructure. PPG13 has provided some encouragement. A number of areas have witnessed the development of extensive cycle routes and pedestrianisation zones although often in the face of claims by business pressure groups that this will have an impact on commerce. In fact from wider European experience, pedestrianisation appears to boost the local economy as urban centres become more attractive and safer places. In apparent contradiction of recent trends, a small number of authorities have even found the finances, often through public–private partnerships, to open new sections of rail network, such as the Robin Hood Line in Nottinghamshire.

LOCAL AGENDA 21: LOCAL AUTHORITIES AND SUSTAINABLE DEVELOPMENT

> Because so many of the problems and solutions being addressed by Agenda 21 have their roots in local activities, the participation and cooperation of local authorities will be a determining factor in fulfilling its objectives. ... As the level of governance closest to the people, they play a vital role in educating, mobilising and responding to the public to promote sustainable development.
>
> (UNCED, 1992, Chapter 28)

Agenda 21, signed at the Rio Earth Summit (see Chapter 7), appears to be having a quite profound effect on the practices of a number of UK local authorities. Faced, in the 1990s, with a central government that reduced their powers and influence and responded to the growing sustainable development agenda with only weak commitments and few new policies, local authorities have looked beyond Whitehall and towards the emerging post-Rio sustainable development agenda. Chapter 28 of Agenda 21, 'Local Authorities' Initiatives in Support of Agenda 21', recognises local authorities as the closest level of government to the general population and, as such, their functions and ability to mobilise support are seen as essential if moves towards a more sustainable future are to be successful. It has been estimated that over two-thirds of Agenda 21 'cannot be delivered without the commitment and cooperation of local government' (LGMB, 1992, p. 1).[13] But, UK local authority activity in the areas of environmental change and sustainable development did not simply emerge as a response to Rio – its emergence can be traced back to the late 1980s. To understand the manner in which Local Agenda 21 is progressing, it is important to briefly analyse these earlier initiatives.

The emergence of the environmental agenda

Prior to Agenda 21 and the EU's Fifth Environmental Action Programme, a number of enlightened authorities in the UK had already begun to question their response to environmental issues. These authorities began to recognise the need to move beyond simply fulfilling day-to-day statutory duties in such areas as planning, transport and waste disposal, and towards a more coordinated, corporate approach to environmental problems. For these authorities the international agreements and programmes provide a legitimate basis for their more radical policies, and for others they may act as an inspiration to move from token responses to a more holistic appreciation of the sustainable development agenda. Initially this will often be through action within the authority's own structure and then out into the wider community through education, partnerships and consultation.

The publication of Friends of the Earth's *Environmental Charter for Local Government* in 1988 is often regarded as a seminal initiative in making the transition to a more corporate approach to environmental issues. The charter – a general statement of intent – was adopted in one form or another by many local authorities and it had the effect of introducing the idea that environmental issues permeate all departments, policies and service delivery areas.

At the same time as promoting the concept of an environmental charter, FoE was working with Kirklees Metropolitan Council to produce the UK's first state of the environment (SOE) report in 1989. The collation of all available information and knowledge on local environmental conditions can be seen as essential if local authorities wish to act as stewards of the local environment. Such a report provides a clear indication of the background environmental conditions against which the local authority can measure the impact of its policies and take informed decisions on what are priority areas for action. The process of developing an SOE report is not simply a matter of collating and coordinating in-house knowledge, itself spread throughout different departments, but requires the cooperation of other sectors in providing information, for example the pollution control agencies, privatised utilities and voluntary organisations. Such a process is often an early stage in the development of local partnerships and relationships of trust between actors.

Many local authorities began to recognise that if they were to take a more activist, leadership role in solving local environmental problems then they should start by getting their own house in order. Many have thus subjected themselves to internal environmental audits and attempted to develop awareness training programmes, often simply focusing on such areas as energy consumption, purchasing practice and paper usage. For some this is an important first step in recognising the huge impact that councils can have on the environment.

A natural step forward from such audits, SOE reports and charters is the development of a more comprehensive environmental strategy which defines broad environmental priorities, indicates responsible actors (not always the local authority itself) and provides timetables for action. The content of these strategies varies, but typically they focus on areas such as energy, transport, waste, environmental education and awareness raising. These strategies have been complemented by more systematic environmental management systems – a number of authorities have piloted the recent British Standard 7750 and its European counterpart, the Eco-Management and Audit Regulation.[14]

Also prior to Rio was the designation of Leicester as Britain's first 'Environment City'. This was part of an initiative established by the Royal Society for Nature Conservation, Civic Trust and UK2000 which aimed to create a network of British cities as models of environmental excellence. A number of other cities competed for the designation and many of them retained the structures and mechanisms even when they were unsuccessful. Typically, as in Leicester, a number of 'specialist working groups' were set up in areas such as energy, transport, waste and pollution, and the natural and built environment. These involve individuals and representatives from the private, public and voluntary sectors, who together develop an environmental strategy for the city (ICLEI, 1993, pp. 38–9). As we shall see, Environment City has had quite an impact on the manner in which local authorities in the UK have responded to the post-Rio agenda.

Local authorities and the Rio process

Given that the post-Rio agenda is beginning to have an incredibly positive effect on the work of local authorities in the environmental field, it is perhaps surprising that only three months before UNCED there was no mention of the role of local government in any of the documents being prepared. It was not until the fourth prep-com in March/April 1992 that they achieved any recognition. From that point, when Job Brugman from the International Council for Local Environmental Initiatives (ICLEI) was able to introduce the text for Chapter 28 of Agenda 21, the essential role of local authorities in attaining sustainable development patterns has been brought to the fore of the environment and development debate. As we have already noted, it is claimed that up to two-thirds of Agenda 21 cannot be delivered without the commitment of local authorities and the communities they serve.

A week before UNCED, a meeting of leaders of local authorities from around the world endorsed the *Curitiba Commitment*, a declaration calling for local authorities to develop a local action plan for sustainable development centred on principles of community education and democratic participation. In the UK, this international commitment was shadowed by the LGMB's *A Statement to UNCED*, which stressed that the 'local democratic mandate enables local authorities to inform, mobilise and speak on behalf of their communities. ... They can use these powers both to enforce and to encourage good environmental practice' (Hams, 1994, p. 31).

The important coordination, education and advocacy role that ICLEI and the LGMB have played in promoting local authority action, and Local Agenda 21 in particular, should not be understated. Both organisations aim to build local government's institutional capacity to respond to environmental problems. At the international level, ICLEI continues to provide information on successful local environmental practice through research in its Local Agenda 21 Model Communities Programme and is at present concentrating its work on supporting the development of Local Agenda 21 processes in developing and transitional countries (Brugman, 1997; Hams *et al.*, 1994, pp. 45–6; ICLEI, 1993). In the UK, a similar role is played by the LGMB, under the guidance of the Local Agenda 21 Steering Group, comprising representatives of local government and other private, public and voluntary sector organisations. The LGMB not only provides guidance on good practice – for instance it commissioned research on sustainability indicators (LGMB, 1995b) – but also has been heavily involved in lobbying central government (LGMB, 1993b) and providing reports to the United Nations Commission on Sustainable Development (see Chapter 7) (LGMB, 1993c).

The Local Agenda 21 process

Within Chapter 28 of Agenda 21 there is a recommendation that most local authorities should have produced a Local Agenda 21 through consultation with all sectors of their communities by 1996.

> Each local authority should enter into a dialogue with its citizens, local organisations and private enterprises and adopt 'a local Agenda 21'. Through consultation and consensus-building, local authorities would learn from citizens and from local, civic, community, business and industrial organisations and acquire the information needed for formulating the best strategies.
>
> (UNCED, 1992, Chapter 28)

Local Agenda 21 can be understood as 'the process of developing local policies for sustainable development and building partnerships between local authorities and other sectors to implement them' (LGMB, 1994, p. 1). Rather than being seen as a single, standard approach, the process will involve different initiatives and priorities in different localities. What is clear is that Local Agenda 21 requires action within the authority itself and a new working relationship between the authority and other actors in the local community.

The key elements of Local Agenda 21: steps in the process

Action within the local authority

1   Managing and improving the local authority's own environmental performance.

2   Integrating sustainable development aims into the local authority's policies and activities.

Action in the wider community

3   Awareness raising and education.

4   Consulting and involving the general public.

5   Partnerships.

6   Measuring, monitoring and reporting on progress towards sustainability.

(LGMB, 1994, pp. 2–3)

It is beyond question that Agenda 21 requires a radical change in practice by committed local authorities. Julian Agyeman and Bob Evans emphasise four linked themes that are essential for the achievement of the overall policy goal of sustainability: community environmental education; democratisation; balanced partnerships; and integrated and holistic policy making (Agyeman and Evans, 1994, pp. 20–2). These can be seen as fundamental to any successful attempt by local authorities to develop a comprehensive and coordinated response to local environmental, social and economic issues. The success or failure of initiatives often depends upon whether these themes have been embraced and understood. To this end, committed authorities are looking to promote new working relationships with different sectors of their communities.[15] There is a growing recognition that the adversarial nature of many existing local political institutions, particularly in the planning process, needs to be altered if participation is to become more meaningful. As Chris Church argues, 'the needs and justifiable aspirations of local people are rarely taken into account. Traditional "adversarial" planning processes often offer no more than a chance to object to proposals prepared in private' (Church, 1995, p. 3). For those authorities committed to the Local Agenda 21 process, a range of institutional designs and initiatives have been developed to enhance community participation, including forums, round tables, focus groups, visioning, audits and appraisals, 'planning for real' initiatives, community arts projects and information services (LGMB, 1994, p. 5; Young, 1996, pp. 17ff; Whittaker, 1995).

One of the most celebrated Local Agenda 21 initiatives to date is coordinated by Lancashire County Council. In 1989, three years before the Earth Summit, the council published a *Green Audit*, a sophisticated state of the environment report. It identified areas of environmental concern and exposed where information and knowledge was limited. In the same year, the council established the Lancashire Environment Forum to be a focus for decision making in developing a plan of action to follow up the audit's findings. Four specialist groups were created by the forum to develop proposals.[16] These were discussed, debated and challenged in a full forum meeting and eventually converted into the Lancashire Environmental Action Programme (LEAP). Published in 1993, LEAP makes some 200 recommendations aimed at, amongst others, central government, local authorities, industry, the voluntary sector and the general public.

Aspects of Lancashire's Local Agenda 21 programme

- *Green Audit*: Published in 1989, this is one of the most sophisticated state of the environment reports, produced using a Geographic Information System (GIS). It identifies areas of environmental concern and exposes where information is limited.

- *Lancashire Environmental Action Programme*: LEAP was launched in 1993 and takes into account the next fifteen years. It makes 200 recommendations aimed at, amongst others, central government, local authorities, industry, the voluntary sector and the general public.

> • *Lancashire Environment Forum*: Set up by the county council in 1989, this is
> the focus of decision making for the Green Audit and LEAP. It com-
> prises 85 organisations from all sectors and has four specialist working
> groups that have developed the LEAP recommendations from an analy-
> sis of the audit.

Lancashire County Council is one of the more forward-thinking authorities
with respect to the development of Local Agenda 21 and sustainable practices.
Central to its programme is the Lancashire Environment Forum, a 'stakeholder'
design involving major local actors.

> Consensus through partnership had to be an underlying principle. The exer-
> cise concerns the environment of Lancashire in which the whole population,
> and the organisations which represent them, are stakeholders. To facilitate
> this from the outset, the Lancashire Environmental Forum was created. Now
> comprising 85 organisations drawn from the public, private and NGO sec-
> tors, the Forum has guided the whole initiative.
>
> (Whittaker, 1995, p. 158)[17]

Tensions in the Local Agenda 21 process

It is interesting that Leicester Environment City and Lancashire County Council
both created a 'two-track' institutional approach. An inclusive process is developed wherein major actors and interest groups are involved in some form of forum
– typically there will be a steering committee with smaller forums or specialist
working groups concentrating on particular issues and feeding proposals back. At
the same time local meetings and initiatives will be developed to raise awareness
and promote initiatives within the wider community.[18] The initial success of this
approach led to its widespread employment by other authorities, particularly when
Agenda 21 emerged. This Environment City heritage may in some ways be problematic, however, as the issues tackled and stakeholders involved often have an
'environment' bias rather than a sense of the wider 'sustainable development'
agenda. Too often Local Agenda 21 involves those groups and individuals who
have worked together purely on environmental matters. This is not to suggest that
the environment does not cut across all other social and economic matters, rather
that those involved tend to have more traditional 'environmentalist' backgrounds
and perspectives. Thus Chris Church notes, in a review of current Local Agenda
21 activity:

> Crime, poverty and health are three areas where, as yet, there is little 'good
> practice' emerging out of Local Agenda 21. ... If they have not emerged in
> discussions on Local Agenda 21 it is perhaps because people are not being
> given sufficient opportunity to raise their real concerns.
>
> (Church, 1995, p. 19)

For Agenda 21 to be a meaningful exercise it needs to move beyond the limited (but important) 'environmentalist' concerns, such as energy, transport and land-use planning, and open up the process so that issues such as social justice are confronted and a broader number of 'stakeholders' involved in the process. Local Agenda 21 must not simply follow traditional environmental protection lines, but begin to link environmental, social and economic agendas (O'Riordan and Voisey, 1997a, p. 20).

At the same time, Local Agenda 21 faces widespread disillusionment, cynicism and alienation within large sections of the community. Contemporary surveys often reinforce the perception that trust and confidence in politicians and political institutions is extremely low (Miller *et al.*, 1996, p. 47).[19] Should we be concerned about the growing lack of trust in, and political alienation from, political authority? Contrary to the belief of some green radical democrats, passivity may have a role to play in stable democratic systems: 'A free society implies a freedom not to participate' (Parry *et al.*, 1992, p. 416). However, passive citizens must be given the opportunity to participate and engage with political processes when they believe that the values they hold are not being adequately represented. Citizens must be able to cross the threshold into public action. Contemporary democratic institutions, including local authorities, appear to engender a passivity based on cynicism and distrust. As Dunn argues, we ought to be concerned since distrust, 'if held with any pertinacity and clarity of mind, will crush political energy and creativity in a sense of overwhelming futility' (Dunn, 1990, p. 38). Distrust and apathy are unlikely to be fertile ground for political institutions to engage citizens in collective action. This should be of particular concern for environmentalists. As recent research carried out for Lancashire County Council shows, there is a definite problem for political institutions to overcome if they wish to promote innovative environmental practice:

> People display a pronounced degree of fatalism and even cynicism towards the country's public institutions, including national and local government. This is reflected in an apparently pervasive lack of trust in the goodwill and integrity of national government, and in doubts about the ability or willingness of local government to achieve positive improvements in the quality of people's lives (not least because local authorities' powers are seen as diminishing). ... There is a danger that, because of people's largely negative attitudes towards (and apparent recent experience of) such official bodies, proposals by the latter for specific measures to advance sustainability will be interpreted as self-interested, and even more likely to marginalise people further (particularly those in lower income groups). ... Overall, whilst there is substantial latent public support for the aims and aspirations of sustainability, there is also substantial and pervasive scepticism about the goodwill of government and other corporate interests towards its achievement.
>
> (Macnaghten *et al.*, 1995, pp. 3–5)

Sustainable development requires widespread changes in contemporary practices across all areas of society. Without doubt there is a substantial role to be played by local government in coordinating such action, but it is unlikely that citizens will respond positively to proposals when there is such a profound sense of apathy, cynicism and mistrust abroad.

A further problem for the successful development of Local Agenda 21 processes is the financial restrictions and new forms of management imposed on local authorities. The UK national government's *Sustainable Development: The UK Strategy* (DoE, 1994b) officially supported and encouraged the development of Local Agenda 21 and yet no extra revenue has been made available. Where Local Agenda 21 requires a holistic approach to policy making and practice, CCT and other fiscal measures tend towards the fragmentation of local authority responsibilities. As Patterson and Theobald argue:

> CCT, linked with tight fiscal restraint on local government capital and recurrent spending, is having a considerable negative impact on the ability of local authorities to plan long term and to implement new environmental strategies such as those required by Local Agenda 21, and even on their ability to deliver more traditional environmental services to an acceptable standard. ... the means by which the principles of sustainability, subsidiarity and strategy can be implemented are being weakened or removed.
>
> (Patterson and Theobald, 1996, p. 18)

Local Agenda 21, community governance and decentralisation

We have highlighted three problems which any Local Agenda 21 process must overcome: the emphasis on 'environment' rather than sustainable development; alienation and distrust at the community level; and new financial disciplines. What is required is to confirm the links between Local Agenda 21 and the reinvigoration of local democracy and local government. We have already stressed the necessity to look beyond the isolated actions of local authorities and towards the emergence of new networks and partnerships with different sectorial actors – local governance. At the same time, these new forms of governance must be sensitive to local community concerns, concerns that may not necessarily be articulated by dominant actors in local politics. So, the alternative model of decentralisation needs to be accommodated so that individuals, groups and communities, at present frequently alienated from the decision-making process, are able to give voice to their needs, interests and values. Too often the early development of Agenda 21 is 'expert'-led. Dominant actors in local authorities, the private sector and voluntary sector (whether third-force or pressure groups) are active in forums and specialist groups developing action plans, which the local community is then expected to implement. To counter this, there needs to be participation not only at the implementation stage but also at the development and vision stages: the local community must truly 'own' Local Agenda 21 if it is to be effective in overcoming alienation and distrust. This will require experimentation with innovative institutional designs such as citizens' juries (Stewart *et al.*, 1994; Kuper, 1997) that can provide for citizen engagement at earlier stages of the decision-making process. Such an approach to Local Agenda 21 corresponds to what Gerry Stoker characterises as 'community governance':

> Local governance should be open so that people are recognised as having the right and opportunity to act in local public life. There should be a capacity for deliberation about the key issues confronting a community both on the part of civic leaders and 'ordinary' citizens. Finally the system requires a capacity to act. It should enable institutions and actors from public, private and voluntary sectors to blend their resources and skills to achieve common purposes.
>
> (Stoker, 1996b, p. 189)

Local authorities need to create conditions for mutual understanding and cooperation – decision-making and implementation structures and strategies that build trust and develop the capacity of organisations to act in response to the sustainable development agenda.[20] Local Agenda 21 is thus part of the concern within green politics for *transformation* – a 'vibrant' local democracy has a crucial role to play in the politics of innovation that sustainable development requires.

CONCLUSION

> Environmental concern has the dual advantage of being able to provide some justification for the defence of some locally-produced services, whilst simultaneously allowing a demonstration of a new enabling role. It provides an opportunity to prove to a sceptical local electorate and an unsympathetic central government that they have a useful, popular role in a democratic society. Developing and promoting environmental policies is therefore a way of creating new political space for local authorities through the concept of local guardians of the environment and equally a way of defending their traditional service role.
>
> (Ward, 1993, p. 466)

It would appear that there are a number of stages through which a local authority passes as it develops its response to environmental problems and the principle of sustainability (Stoker and Young, 1993, pp. 89–90; Hams *et al.*, 1994, pp. 13–14). These seem to map on to the idea that there are competing approaches to, and interpretations of, sustainable development (see Chapters 2 and 5). The initial phase is *business as usual*, where environmental policy and response to problems is fragmented. The council fulfils only its statutory duties and takes the minimal necessary notice of PPGs and pressures from the community. It pursues economic goals irrespective of the environmental impacts. In phase two, *superficial tokenism* arises as local authorities begin to appreciate the significance of environmental issues but are only willing to tackle specific issues without taking into account the wider, overall effect of their policies. The council will normally act on high-profile issues such as cycle paths and wildlife protection, seeing these as vote winners. In the third phase, the *holistic policy approach*, councils recognise the integrated nature of the environmental impact of their policies. SOE reports, internal management systems and environmental strategies are developed to make all policies more environmentally sensitive. Sustainable development becomes a guiding principle. The final phase is the development of a *Local Agenda 21 process*. Local councils realise that they must work in partnership with and involve all sectors of the community to achieve sustainability. Local Agenda 21 is then crucially tied to the reinvigoration of local democracy and to the idea of community governance. As such, the emerging environmental and sustainable development agenda is at once radically democratic and a challenge to international and national economic, social and environmental practice. Whether local authorities and local communities will be able to realise this agenda is another matter. What is clear is that some enlightened authorities are beginning to tread this path and that local governance will become one of the most important sites of environmental and democratic innovation.

CASE STUDY: THE SUSTAINABLE SEATTLE PROJECT

Seattle is a metropolitan area on the north-west coast of the United States with a population of about 1.5 million, only a third of whom live in the city itself. Common to most large American cities, Seattle has experienced a process of 'urban sprawl' or 'suburbanisation', with the population in the city itself steadily declining and larger numbers of households becoming almost entirely dependent on their cars for mobility. This population movement has resulted in increasing economic differentials with concentrations of high levels of poverty in the inner city.

Since the late 1980s a series of initiatives, focusing on the goal of making Seattle a more sustainable place to live, have been developed. These initiatives, involving different sections of the community, have gained widespread recognition in the United States and beyond, as many local authorities and their populations begin to develop Local Agenda 21.

Ongoing elements of the Sustainable Seattle project

- The Waste Reduction and Recycling Programme;
- The Environmental Priorities Project;
- The Comprehensive Plan;
- The Sustainable Seattle Citizen's Initiative.

The first of these initiatives, the Waste Reduction and Recycling Programme, emerged in 1988 initially as a citizens' campaign against the incineration policy of the city council. The programme has set a recycling target of 60 per cent and 'has blossomed into one of the world's most progressive and successful. Forty-two per cent of the city's solid waste is now recycled; 90 per cent of all single-family households participate in the programme' (Lawrence, 1994, p. 15).

The second initiative, the Environmental Priorities Project, began in 1990 with the objective of identifying Seattle's most serious environmental and social problems and developing an action plan to address these issues. The process is ongoing, with the first environmental action agenda adopted by the city council in 1992.

The Comprehensive Plan was also initiated in 1990 as an attempt to produce an integrated and anticipatory land-use and development planning process. Both this and the Environmental Priorities Project were initiated by the Seattle Mayor, Norman Rice, who has given influential political leadership in the development of the local sustainable development agenda. One of his most interesting acts was his early appointment of Gary Lawrence as Director of the Planning Department. He readily admits to not being a trained planner and he has made the department's procedures more understandable and accessible to the Seattle public.

The fourth element, dating back to late 1990, is the citizen-driven Sustainable Seattle, 'a voluntary network and civic forum, bringing together citizens from many different sectors of the community to promote the concept and practice of sustainability. Business, environmental groups, city and county government, labor, the religious community, educators and social activists have all been represented' (Sustainable Seattle, 1993, p. 3). Its most ambitious and well-documented project is its attempt to develop sustainable development indicators for the Seattle area against which the effectiveness of other initiatives can be judged.

What makes a good indicator?

These Indicators of Sustainable Development have been selected because they meet the following criteria, which were developed by the Task Team:

Good indicators
- *are bellwether tests of sustainability* and reflect something basic and fundamental to the long-term economic, social, or environmental health of a community over generations;

> • *can be understood and accepted by the community* as a valid sign of sustainability or symptom of distress;
> • *have interest and appeal for use by local media* in monitoring, reporting and analysing general trends toward or away from sustainable community practices;
> • *are statistically measurable* in our geographic area, and preferably comparable to other cities/communities; a practical form of data collection or measurement exists or can be created.
>
> The geographic scope of an indicator depends on the context and accessibility of the data, with some indicators referring to Seattle city limits, others to King's County (our first choice, when available), and still others placing Seattle in a statewide context.
>
> (Excerpt from Sustainable Seattle, 1993, p. 4)

In its first report, *The Sustainable Seattle 1993 Indicators of Sustainable Community*, the first twenty indicators were detailed. They covered four areas: environment; population and resource; economy; and culture and society. In all four areas there are a few indicators that show some improvement or little measurable change, but overall, over half indicate moves away from sustainability.

> Recent years have seen improvements in such key indicators as overall air quality, water consumption, and the diversity of the local economy. There has been little measurable change in adult literacy rates or the numbers of hours one has to work at the average wage to support a family's basic needs. But many other trends are carrying us away from sustainability and toward an uncertain – and potentially unpleasant – future.
>
> Increasing numbers of children are being born with low birth weights, or being raised in poverty, or turning to crime. Fewer people are voting. Wild salmon are disappearing. More of us are driving more miles, consuming more energy, and producing more garbage per person every year.
>
> Overall, the Seattle area is not moving toward the goal of long-term sustainability. Instead, it is moving in the wrong direction.
>
> (Sustainable Seattle, 1993, p. iii)

The trends that the report highlights are worrying, but in the long term, the partnerships and participative initiatives that have been developed in the Seattle area may well begin to reverse some of these negative tendencies.

A spirit of realism pervades the various initiatives. There is a recognition that any long-term turnaround will require major changes in citizen and organisational attitudes. The city council has devoted a lot of resources researching the values and attitudes of the community and, not surprisingly, has discovered that although the public holds many political themes in common (environmental stewardship, economic security and social equity), their values often conflict. For instance, citizens value highly their freedom to drive and any reduction in that freedom is viewed as an attack on the individual's liberty. But, at the same time environmental degradation is also viewed in a similar manner – 'attacks on the environment are perceived to be the same as an attack on the person' (Lawrence, 1994, p. 12). Private cars are a major cause of pollution and so any action to alter mobility patterns needs to tread carefully between these two perceived freedoms. In the long term though, the first of these freedoms will need to be rearticulated, although in such a way as not to alienate the citizens whose participation and political support is vital. It would appear that Seattle may have the initiatives in place through which such a reinterpretation of values might be achievable.[21]

So why Seattle? Why should this area of America be taking such innovative steps towards a more sustainable future? Why do citizens appear to be more inclined to participate? First, there is a strong cultural connection with the local environment, which can perhaps be traced to such factors as its geographical setting (the region is dominated by the sea and hills), a strong connection to native Indian traditions, and high educational standards. Second, the city council has greater control over fiscal and planning issues by comparison with similar cities in other countries, especially in the UK. Rather than receiving most of its resources from central government, American cities raise a large proportion from local taxes. This in itself makes the council more accountable to its local population, which tends to be more interested and involved in local planning and fiscal issues. Perhaps the most important reason, however, is the political vision and leadership of Mayor Norman Rice. He has a clear understanding of the links between economic, social and environmental injustices and has developed and supported initiatives which aim to make Seattle a more equitable and livable city. Central to his vision is the idea of sustainable development and the necessary involvement, partnership and political support of all sectors of an economically and socially divided community. His influence, it seems fair to say, cannot be underrated.

The political, cultural and geographical features of Seattle make it a location where the concept of sustainable development resonates amongst the local communities. Although in many ways the political and cultural situation is unique, the initiatives and experiences of Seattle have become the focus of attention for other areas around the world also looking to develop towards a more sustainable future.

SUGGESTIONS FOR FURTHER READING

Julian Agyeman and Bob Evans (eds), *Local Environmental Policies and Strategies* (1994), examines the response in different areas of local government policy to growing environmental concern. Tony Hams *et al.*, *Greening your Local Authority* (1994), considers similar ground, but from the perspective of local government officers responsible for Local Agenda 21. The Department of the Environment's *First Steps: Local Agenda 21 in Practice* (1995b) contains a wealth of information on local actions around the world.

Conclusion

In this book we have followed the path of environmental concern from thought to action. We have sought to portray the relationships and connections between green philosophical and political thought and environmental action and policy making. One of our central aims has been to illuminate how concepts such as sustainable development – so central to environmental theory and practice – function in various and sometimes contradictory ways depending on their use within philosophical, economic, political or activist discourse. We have also demonstrated some of the opportunities, difficulties and (perhaps) dangers facing attempts to engage with environmental issues. Throughout the book, two areas of general concern have constantly re-emerged in different guises: these can broadly be described as the vulnerability of contemporary environmental politics in the face of, first, the *politics of cooption and assimilation*; and, second, the *politics of gesture*. In this conclusion we shall briefly rehearse some of our anxieties as to the future direction and success of environmental politics.

The last couple of decades have seen an unprecedented number of actions in the name of environmental protection. The environment is now clearly recognised as a serious political issue: witness, for instance, the number of world leaders attending the Rio Earth Summit; the intense lobbying tactics of industrialists in the run-up to the Kyoto climate negotiations; the different types of people who belong to environmental pressure groups. Certainly, given the relatively short period of serious environmental awareness, the response at all levels of policy making has been fairly impressive. The environment is an issue that resonates at all levels of political action, from the local everyday practices of individuals and communities through to international diplomacy and regime building. The point, therefore, is not whether governments and other significant actors have responded, but how they have responded.

As should be clear by now, there is a lack of consensus amongst greens themselves as to what sort of response would be adequate to contemporary environmental problems. In general terms, however, any significant move towards a sustainable society would require a fundamental reassessment of what is understood by 'development'. Within green writing there is a near unanimous censure of existing uneven capitalist development patterns and the values that underpin the logic of continued economic growth. Greens call for a re-evaluation of what we understand by the term 'progress': ever-increasing levels of economic wealth do not necessarily equate to increased well-being and environmental protection. A more complete understanding of development requires us to seriously address the values we associate with non-human nature, as well as a re-evaluation of more 'mainstream' political values and ideals such as democracy, and social and intergenerational justice. Environmental politics requires a fundamental reappraisal of ethical and political decision making.

But what of the response by governments and other dominant actors? In recent years we have seen a situation of undisguised opposition to the challenge of environmental politics melt into an apparent recognition that a response is required. But what form of response? We have characterised the most influential response to environmental concern as 'ecological modernisation'. Fundamental to the discourse of ecological modernisation is the belief that there is no necessary trade-off between economic growth and environmental protection: both can be achieved if environmental costs and benefits are incorporated into economic decision-making processes. Such a paradigm is related to a 'weak' interpretation of sustainable development. The dominance of the discourse of ecological modernisation is manifest in the development of environmental economics: the attempt by economists to quantify in monetary terms the values we associate with the non-human world. It is further manifest in current planning for sustainable development, in international documents ranging from *Agenda 21* to the European Union's *Fifth Environmental Action Plan*, and national sustainability plans such as *Sustainable Development: The UK Strategy* and the Dutch *National Environmental Policy Plan*. The content of these documents has been discussed in some depth already; what interests us here is that their existence could be explained in terms of the politics of cooption. As environmental issues have become more significant to decision makers they have been reinterpreted or assimilated into the dominant paradigm of development. Capitalism is in the process of being 'greened'; it is not in the process of being fundamentally challenged and reassessed. Green activists are drawn into what could be considered peripheral political institutions such as the United Nations Commission on Sustainable Development or the UK Round Table on Sustainable Development. The result is that, inadvertently, greens legitimise this green capitalism and, at the same time, 'dull' the radical edge of environmental protest and politics. And we find here, in this process of cooption, an irony within the modern environmental movement itself. It is quite possible that, in their push for radical change, greens might make consumer capitalism more environmentally efficient, and thereby prolong the life of a fundamentally non-sustainable way of life. If their demands for sustainable development are met by a move towards ecological modernisation which allows industrial capitalism an extended lease of life with green credentials, more radical and challenging interpretation of the concept will go unheeded.

Again, a further threat to a meaningful politics of the environment can be characterised as the politics of the gesture. Direct action sometimes succumbs to this temptation, with the protest sometimes becoming more important than the consequences. High-profile actions by well-known environmental pressure groups fall into this trap at times. In a similar vein the appearance of firm and decisive legislative action can sometimes fall short of meaningful action. Under the pressure of intense lobbying and the sway of strong public opinion, governments can sometimes be induced to act in ways which are practically ineffectual or even counterproductive, but have the appearance of commitment. Again, the international 'grand gesture' is cause for concern. Many greens argue that the Rio Earth Summit acted simply as an electoral platform for world leaders desperate to cash in on the 'green vote'. International conferences and regimes may not be able to deliver what they promise. Although symbolic action can be positive, we must not mistake gesture for action.

None the less we have witnessed real and significant changes at all levels of policy making. Internationally, regimes are being developed that have begun to limit some of the excesses of environmental degradation and pollution. Further, the very values out of which such regimes evolve can be seen to conflict with the logic of existing patterns of development. Here, perhaps, we can begin to offer a different and less pessimistic reading of the state of environmental politics. The emergence of international regimes creates a tension within global economic and political relations; at the local level, direct action, DIY culture and the growth of not-for-profit third-force organisations create space for the development of alternative practices. The emergence of more democratic governmental institutions and practices, from the Commission on Sustainable Development through to Local Agenda 21, may themselves have a transformative effect. National environmental planning may begin to awaken decision makers to the limits of the existing development paradigm. In this more optimistic scenario, ecological modernisation is understood simply as a necessary stepping stone to more sustainable policies and practices embracing the democratic and cooperative principles of Agenda 21. This would doubtless lead to a reassessment of uneven patterns of development, consumption, poverty and environmental degradation.

In this book we have sought to explore the extent to which there might be reasonable expectations of moves towards a more sustainable future, towards this second scenario. Our own response to this investigation has to be that the prospects for environmental politics are in the balance: enough progress has been made so far to reassure us that further progress in the future, whilst not inevitable, is at least possible. Environmental politics, although vulnerable to cooption and gesture, presents a powerful critical perspective from which current political and economic arrangements can be challenged. Perhaps more importantly, it offers prospects for the development of sustainable economic, political and social practices.

Notes

Introduction

1 In this book, unless explicitly stated, we will use the terms 'green' and 'environmental' and 'greens' and 'environmentalists' largely interchangeably.

1 Environmental philosophy

1 In addition, Genesis 1:29 seems to indicate that our diet should be a vegetarian one: 'And God said, behold, I have given you every herb bearing seed, which is upon the face of all the earth, and every tree, in which is the fruit of a tree yielding seed; to you it shall be for meat.'

2 *Which* actions in the case of act utilitarianism; which *type* of actions performed as a rule in the case of rule utilitarianism. For our present purpose the distinction will be ignored. For an introductory discussion of the various forms of utilitarianism see Plant, 1991, Chapter 3.

3 Utilitarian reasoning can be seen to be the basis of welfare economic decision-making procedures such as cost–benefit analysis (CBA). The extension of such procedures to incorporate environmental values is a central concern in Chapter 5.

4 By contrast, Regan's defence of animal rights leads to the ascription of rights to individual animals. This itself is problematic: for a discussion see the case study at the end of this chapter.

5 The political implications of deep ecology are explored in Chapter 2.

6 For a discussion of moral pluralism and environmental ethics, see Stone, 1987; Brennan, 1988; 1992. For a contrary view, see Callicott, 1990.

7 Different interpretations of intrinsic value are discussed by O'Neill, 1993, pp. 8–25.

8 Further, attempting to ignore human claims is also politically flawed in its contradictory hope for a mobilisation of human support and action whilst at the same time ignoring the legitimacy of human claims. Public policy requires public support and needs to be seen as justifiable by those affected by its implementation. Unjust policies, or policies with unjust outcomes, should be opposed not only because they are unjust but also because injustice generates opposition which renders policies unworkable and hinders the achievement of environmental goals and aspirations.

9 The nature of collective action problems is explored in Chapter 4; the politics of international environment and development issues is dealt with in Chapter 7.

10 Published by the World Commission on Environment and Development (WCED) in 1987 and otherwise known as the Brundtland Report after its chair, Gro Harlem Brundtland. For more on this, see Chapter 7.

11 This point is contested by O'Neill, 1993, pp. 26–43. Whilst his is a valuable discussion it does not substantially affect what is argued for here, although his remarks concerning damage to the reputation of the present generation is a strong one.

12 The reason Rawls did not do this is because of the strong tendency in his work to see justice as a relation of mutual advantage based on reciprocity, and there can of course be no reciprocity if the contracting parties do not belong to the same generation.

13 Passmore holds a similar position (Passmore, 1980, pp. 91ff).

14 Distinguishing needs from wants is not as simple a matter as the Brundtland definition appears to suggest. See Plant, 1991, pp. 184–220.

15 Most prominently Descartes, who argued in the seventeenth century that animals were no more than machines. More recently see Leahy, 1994.

16 This is not, however, to deny that there may be a point to granting rights to some animals. For example, the extension of rights to the higher primates can be couched in terms of the extension of *human* rights to the great apes precisely because of their common links with humankind. This approach sidesteps some of the theoretical and practical difficulties raised by the general extension of rights to other animals. The rights granted to apes would not extend to the full catalogue of human rights, but still would be of equal seriousness and worth. Thus the great apes would be granted some full rights and these would not be easily overridden. This solves the dilemma in principle because (1) it is limited to a recognisably near human group of animals; (2) it restricts itself to a specified list of rights which are granted in the same way as they would be to humans.

2 Green ideology

1 At this point we can simply take 'ideology' to be a coherent set of principles explaining the world and intended to guide political action. We shall return to its essentially contested nature later in the chapter.

2 As we shall see later, this criticism can be levelled particularly at deep ecology – the ethical and political status of the ecological concepts diversity, symbiosis and complexity are central to Arne Naess's seminal article on the deep ecological movement (Naess, 1973).

3 Even before the publication of *The Limits to Growth*, a number of authors, notably Rachel Carson in *Silent Spring* (1962), had been instrumental in raising the level of environmental awareness. However, it was the Club of Rome's report which provided the first comprehensive attempt to analyse the connections between economy, society and environment which now forms the basis of much environmental thought.

4 Malthus, writing in 1798, argued that the exponential growth of population would outstrip food supply. Hence he was a forerunner of present-day concerns with the limits to growth.

5 So successful is this feedback mechanism that Beckerman claims that we are better-off in respect of all of the resources covered by the Club of Rome. Beckerman amusingly entitled the box in which he gave the reserve figures 'How we used up all the resources that we had and still finished up with more than we started with' (Beckerman, 1995a, p. 53). His point is that although resources are finite, we do not know what their *absolute* quantity is: it is easy to assume that we have reached an absolute limit when we have reached only a *relative* limit; a limit relative to present prices, technological ability, desire for the resources and so on. Once feedback mechanisms come in to play, he argues, we might find that the resource is in effect rationed, that we develop suitable alternatives, or that it is now worth developing techniques for gaining access to hitherto inaccessible resources.

6 Chapter 3 will highlight the 'broad church' of organisations and approaches which constitute the environmental movement. This diversity derives from the wide variety of political and ethical commitments that greens can and do endorse.

7 Bookchin has been developing the principles and practice of social ecology for around three decades. Two of his more important works are *Toward an Ecological Society* (1980) and *The Ecology of Freedom* (1991).

8 For an example of Bookchin's vitriolic outpourings against deep ecology, see 'Social Ecology versus "Deep Ecology" ' (1987).

9 Sale is perhaps better described as a decentralist communitarian than as an anarchist.

10 Essentially contested concepts are ones where their 'proper use ... inevitably involves endless disputes about their proper uses on the part of their users' (Gallie, 1964, p. 158). Dobson discusses the contested nature of the concept of ideology in the Introduction of *Green Political Theory* (Dobson, 1995, pp. 1–13).

11 Other influential writers who offer a well-defined green ideological position include Arne Naess, whose distinction between 'deep' and 'shallow' ecology motivates much green writing and action (Naess, 1973), and Tim O'Riordan, whose differentiation between 'ecocentrism' and 'technocentrism' is illustrated in the quote at the beginning of this chapter (O'Riordan, 1981, p. 1). For further distinctions and classifications, see Eckersley, 1992, pp. 60–71; Young, 1992; and Vincent, 1993. Such classifications can be useful, but they do seem to caricature and fix what often prove to be rather fluid and in some cases inconsistent positions (Barry, 1994).

12 See, for example, Dryzek, 1987; 1990; 1995; Hayward, 1995; and some of the essays in Doherty and Geus, 1996.

13 Deliberative democracy is not the same as direct democracy. The former does not necessarily require total participation of all citizens, but rather a reasoned decision-making process to which all voices have access.

14 This case study has been distilled from a number of sources including Dobson, 1991; 1995; Ekins, 1986; Goodin, 1992; Irvine and Pontin, 1988; Jacobs, 1996; Porritt, 1984; Robertson, 1989.

15 Although as Dobson recognises, the classification of basic human needs is itself problematic (Dobson, 1995, p. 91). For a general discussion of this problem, see Plant, 1991, pp. 184–220.

3 The environmental movement

1 This equates to approximately 8 per cent of the total population. However, it is important to remember that many people will belong to more than one organisation, so these figures may be an over-estimate caused by double counting. Further, more decentralised, direct action-orientated organisations such as Earth First! and Reclaim the Streets do not have 'membership' in the same sense as more orthodox groups.

2 Details taken from McCormick, 1991 and *Office for National Statistics*, 1992–97.

3 Witness the length of time it took for the British government to admit that emissions in the UK were responsible for the acidification of lakes in Scandinavia; and the intransigence of the US government over climate change negotiations which would result in binding reductions in carbon dioxide emissions.

4 In fact, the Green Party could be said to have had 'half' an MP: Cynog Dafis was elected to the House of Commons in 1992 on a joint Plaid Cymru/Green Party platform.

5 The wave of public enthusiasm for environmental issues that resulted in this level of support for the Green Party was the background to Mrs Thatcher's Royal Society speech.

6 For a compelling insider's account of the divisions in the Green Party since its inception, see Wall, 1994.

7 It will be interesting to see which organisations are able to sustain or gain insider status with the new Department of the Environment, Transport and the Regions (DETR), formed by the new Labour administration.

8 The relationship between the British Roads Federation and the DoT provides a good example.

9 The Third Battle of Newbury is the group protesting against the construction of the Newbury bypass.

10 These trends will be addressed in more detail in Part III of this book.

11 It is noticeable that the recent (July 1997) protests by Greenpeace against BP developing the new Atlantic Frontier oilfield only received extensive media coverage after BP sued for £1.4 million.

12 For a discussion of the events surrounding Twyford Down, see the case study at the end of this chapter.

13 For a moving account of such a campaign, see 'Closed Mined, Open Cast' on *Undercurrents 4*, the alternative news video.

14 In a recent Gallup poll survey in the UK, 68 per cent of respondents were prepared to entertain the idea of civil disobedience in defence of a cause they believed in (Bryant, 1996, p. 302).

15 For an accessible guide to using and running LETS, see Peter Lang's *LETS Work: Rebuilding the Local Community* (1994). The New Economics Foundation's magazine *New Economics* has regular articles on LETS and similar community-based initiatives.

16 As was argued in Chapter 2, however, certain advocates of green communes, particularly bioregionalists, are not at all concerned with the establishment of democratic forms of self-governance; living within ecological limits takes precedence over political arrangements. In practice, though, existing communes have largely been founded on a principle of democratic renewal.

17 During the 1970s, John Tyme became a well-known figure at public inquires both presenting the case against road building and inciting disruptions. His book *Motorways Against Democracy* (1978) is a detailed account of his fights against road proposals and the lack of accountability of the then Department of Transport.

18 Although the DoT has recently been merged into the Department of the Environment, Transport and the Regions, it is unclear whether this has had any effect on the decision-making processes. For the sake of clarity we shall continue to refer simply to the DoT.

19 Objectors do have the right to challenge the accuracy of the actual figures within the COBA9 calculation. However, they cannot challenge the use of COBA9 itself. Occasionally, inquiries have been won or at least abandoned on the basis of inaccurate figures.

20 English Nature estimated that the DoT's 1989 *Roads for Prosperity* road programme threatened 161 Sites of Special Scientific Importance (SSSIs), and English Heritage calculated that over 800 important archaeological sites could be affected.

21 Private security firms, such as Brays in Southampton, have become established actors in the present political climate, collecting information on direct action activists for the DoT and the contractors.

22 See the recently published *Road Raging: Top Tips for Wrecking Roadbuilding* produced by Road Alert! for a description of the techniques and organisations involved in direct action.

4 Collective action, power and decision making

1 'Rational choice' is a broad term which includes 'public choice' and 'social choice' theory. The former studies political and bureaucratic processes on the assumption that people engaged in politics and administration behave in the same way as they do when making choices in a market; the latter concentrates on the formal aspects of decision-making procedures by studying the problems of aggregating individual preferences into a rational and acceptable social choice. See Heap *et al.*, 1992; and Mueller, 1989, for a complete overview of the territory.

2 These assumptions can of course be challenged. It can be denied that people are really like this; or it can be argued that they are like this some, but not all, of the time; or that they only behave in this way under special circumstances; or that it is wrong to think of preferences as always fixed and immutable; and so on. We will look at some

of these objections at the end of the chapter and in Chapter 5. However, it is clear that collective agreement and action is often threatened by the existence of free riding, and that this has significance for environmental politics: this concession is enough to show that these theories may have something to offer.

3 This is not a hypothetical example: it is based on events in Liverpool in the early 1980s. The example is taken from Laver, 1983, pp. 152–4.

4 Strictly speaking the problem is not one of 'the commons' but of open access to resources owned by no one. Given such ownership status, we can perhaps understand why authoritarian solutions to environmental problems have been proposed by certain elements of the green movement.

5 The detail and adequacy of Lukes' account can be challenged, as it is for example by Wrong (1979) and Morriss (1987), but commentators would agree that the aspects of power which he investigates need to be addressed. See Clegg, 1989, for a good introductory overview of the debates around the concept of power.

6 For further discussion of such bias within the politics of transport, see the case study at the end of Chapter 3.

7 See the case study at the end of this chapter for an extended example.

8 The 1990 UK White Paper, *This Common Inheritance*, which largely consisted of a repackaging exercise of this sort, received extensive criticism on exactly these grounds. It promised much but delivered little. Most of its more radical proposals were consigned to an appendix on the use of economic instruments in environmental policy despite the commissioning of David Pearce as an adviser. Here it is important to remember that what was considered radical was the use of economic instruments, rather than any more fundamental questioning of the UK's patterns of production and consumption. For more on *This Common Inheritance*, see Chapter 9.

9 The concept of discounting is examined in Chapter 5.

10 Some of the related ethical issues regarding future costs are discussed in Chapter 1.

11 This example is for the most part adapted from McLean, 1987, pp. 62–80.

12 For a full account of 'privileged' and 'latent' groups, see Olson, 1971, pp. 48–52.

13 The main environmental organisations involved were the Sierra Club and the Natural Resources Defense Council (NRDC).

5 Valuation of the environment

1 For a detailed discussion of the rationale behind cost–benefit analysis, see Mishan, 1988, or Pearce, 1983.

2 This book has proved so popular that Pearce and his colleagues have developed a series of *Blueprint* texts on different aspects of economic valuation of environmental issues, from global environmental change to the cost of transport.

3 Where policies and projects are constrained by the need to fulfil environmental targets or objectives, such as air or water quality standards, the decision-making tool is known as cost-effectiveness analysis (CEA). See DoE, 1991a, p. 19.

4 The concept of externalities was originally developed by A.C. Pigou (1932).

5 However, representatives of the neo-liberal school of free-market economics attempt to follow through Coase's argument to its logical end by introducing the idea of property rights for the atmosphere and the oceans; see for instance Anderson and Leal, 1991.

6 For an account of the issues at Twyford Down, see the case study at the end of Chapter 3.

7 Not all commentators use exactly the same typology, although that need not concern us here. For a more detailed discussion of direct and indirect techniques, see Winpenny, 1991, pp. 42–72; Pearce and Turner, 1990, pp. 141–159; OECD, 1989, pp. 25–58.

8 See, for example, Pearce and Turner, 1990, p. 149–53; Winpenny, 1991, pp. 59–61; Jacobs, 1991, pp. 205ff, for more detailed discussions of the biases inherent within

CVM. There are also numerous articles in the *Journal of Environmental Economics and Management* devoted to the results and refinement of CVM and other valuation techniques.

9 For a discussion of the different meanings of commensurability, see O'Neill, 1993, pp. 110ff.

10 For more on this directive and on the nature and impact of European Union environmental policy, see Chapter 8.

11 See in particular the work supported by the New Economics Foundation. Its magazine *New Economics* and other publications provide a wealth of information.

12 Fourteen countries were selected – the USA, Canada, Japan, France, West Germany, Italy, the UK, China, India, USSR, Indonesia, Brazil, Nigeria and Bangladesh. Together these nations represent 66 per cent of the world's population (Anderson, 1991, p. 75).

13 As mentioned in Chapter 2, the origins of steady-state economics can be traced back to the nineteenth century and the writings of John Stuart Mill (Mill, 1909, pp. 746–51).

14 Bioeconomists frequently refer to the second law of thermodynamics, which holds that useful low entropy energy always eventually dissipates into an inaccessible high entropic state. Bioeconomists argue that traditional forms of economic theory abstract to such an extent from physical and social reality that their theories are almost worthless and, in many cases, potentially dangerous. They aim to forge theories that are multidisciplinary, working with physicists, biologists and the like. See, for example, Georgescu-Roegen (1971).

15 For a taste of the ongoing debate around weak and strong sustainability, see the entertaining and somewhat polemical exchanges in *Environmental Values* between Beckerman (1994; 1995b), Daly (1995) and Jacobs (1995c).

6 Choosing the means

1 For further details of the way in which such technological standards are applied in the UK, see Chapter 9.

2 Whether this is done in practice depends on a number of factors. In the UK, for example, hypothecation of taxes (earmarking their revenue for a particular use) has hitherto been virtually unknown; in other countries, such as Germany, the Netherlands and Sweden, it is more common.

3 Technically it would be proper to refer both to taxes and to charges and to distinguish between them. However, for the sake of simplicity we shall use the term 'tax' as a general term. See Jacobs, 1991, pp. 120–4, for more on this distinction.

4 For an extended discussion, see Tindale and Holtham, 1996.

5 It could also be argued that there is a problem in that we are being asked to place an economic value on the environment – the problems with this were discussed in Chapter 5. However, it could be argued that this is not the case: all that is required is that an environmental standard is set according to whatever are regarded as relevant criteria. This does not require placing an economic value on the environment, merely agreement about acceptable limits – and this applies as much to command and control or other solutions as it does to green taxes or tradeable permits.

6 We do not mean to suggest that private ownership is a panacea; on the contrary, in Chapter 4 we explored some of the reasons for thinking otherwise.

7 For a discussion of the issues surrounding the economics and ethics of setting up a global carbon dioxide permit scheme, see Markandya, 1991.

8 For fuller details both of the terms employed and of the results of trading, see Turner *et al.*, 1994, pp. 182–5.

9 These types of questions have been addressed in Chapter 1 and will be returned to in Chapter 7.

10 If we are thinking solely in terms of carbon dioxide reduction, nuclear energy is without doubt superior to most other energy sources. However, other problems with nuclear power certainly outweigh this advantage.

7 International dimensions

1 Some writers such as Gareth Porter and Janet Walsh Brown argue that the system of
norms and rules that underpin regimes should be 'specified by a multilateral agreement among the relevant states' (Porter and Brown, 1996, p. 16). This has the merit of
allowing us to explicitly identify the existence of regimes, although it fails to appreciate the informal aspects of many regimes – the informal development of norms through
which actors (be they states and/or other organisations) develop mutual understanding and relations of trust (Paterson, 1996, pp. 182–3).
2 For a more detailed analysis of the state of a number of environmental regimes, see
Porter and Brown, 1996, pp. 67–106. There are a number of collections that cover a
range of environmental issues (some are listed in the bibliography) and a growing
number of texts on the international politics of particular problems, for example,
Matthew Paterson's *Global Warming and Global Politics* (1996).
3 As we shall emphasis later, this figure tells us nothing of the distribution of wealth
within the North or the South.
4 Clearly the European Union (EU) is a special case in that it is a supranational institution. We shall have more to say about the EU in Chapter 8, but for the purpose of this
analysis it can be ignored.
5 This is only a brief discussion of international relations theory. For a much more
sophisticated introduction to traditional and contemporary theories, see Brown, 1997.
For an analysis of international relations theory in light of global climate politics, see
Paterson, 1996, and for a more general collection of essays, see Vogler and Imber,
1996.
6 In one of the more sophisticated analysis of power in international politics, Susan
Strange argues that there are four sources of structural power: security, production,
financial and knowledge structures (Strange, 1988, pp. 29ff). According to this account, the USA is still by far the dominant nation in terms of structural power, even if
it is unwilling to take a leadership role in international environmental regimes.
7 Also known as multinational corporations (MNCs).
8 This was the final round of negotiations of the General Agreement on Tariffs and
Trade (GATT), which had been set up in the 1940s as a precursor of the WTO. However, it was five decades later that the WTO was finally created.
9 We shall have more to say about the Global Environment Facility later in this chapter.
10 It is perhaps a fair criticism of green international political economy that the role of
the financial markets is under-theorised and researched.
11 For a disturbing account of the economic plight of Africa in the face of growing debt,
see Mihevc, 1995, and de la Court, 1990.
12 We need to be aware of 'the existence of a growing "South" in the "North" ' (Thomas, 1997, p. 3) and similarly, a growing 'North' in the 'South'.
13 For a sophisticated critique of contemporary globalisation theories, see Hirst and
Thompson, 1996.
14 A more complete analysis would also look at the work of international organisations
such as the United Nations Development Programme (UNDP), the Food and Agriculture Organisation (FAO) and the World Health Organisation (WHO) amongst others.
15 For a comprehensive discussion of the IPPC and its findings, see Paterson, 1996,
pp. 40ff.
16 Questions have been raised about the nature and significance of 'epistemic communities'. For instance, they are only likely to be effective in so far as they do not challenge
the core interests of the state (Brown, 1997, p. 234) and as such their role in bringing

into question the very structures of the international political and economic systems is limited. This ties in with the recognition that science and politics are intimately linked in international negotiations and that, as we discussed briefly in Chapter 4, it is difficult to separate out the manner in which scientific investigation is taken forward and the political ends to which it is used. For an extended discussion of the limits of the epistemic communities approach, see Paterson, 1996, pp. 134–56.

17 Maurice Strong was the chair of the 1972 United Nations Conference on the Human Environment and was Secretary-General of UNCED two decades later.

18 Dr Töpfer will also serve as Director of Habitat at the UN Centre for Human Settlement, also based in Nairobi.

19 The workings of the CSD are discussed in some detail in the case study at the end of this chapter.

20 See for instance *Third World Resurgence*, the magazine produced by the Third World Network, 'an international network of groups and individuals involved in efforts to bring about a greater articulation of the needs and rights of peoples in the Third World; a fair distribution of world resources; and forms of development which are ecologically sustainable and fulfil human needs.'

21 These can be seen to mirror some of the tensions within the green movement discussed in Chapter 3.

22 The G77, formed in the 1970s, is a coalition of Southern states pressing for North–South economic reform.

23 For a more detailed discussion of the political negotiations surrounding the GEF, see Porter and Brown, 1996, pp. 141–4, and Chatterjee and Finger, 1994, pp. 151–7.

24 For a summary of the first four annual sessions of the CSD, see Bigg and Dodds, 1997, pp. 23–29. A new five-year programme of work for the CSD (1988–2002) was agreed at the Earth Summit II (Bigg, 1997).

8 European integration

1 In 1957, the organisation was known as the European Economic Community (EEC). In 1967, a number of European organisations merged to form the European Community (EC). When the Treaty on European Union (Maastricht Treaty) came into effect in 1993, the name changed again to the European Union (EU). In this chapter we shall use all three terms depending upon the time period referred to.

2 The five larger states appoint two commissioners each.

3 Qualified majority voting is a weighted voting system that gives larger member states a higher value vote. So, for example, the UK, France, Italy and Germany have ten votes; Luxembourg has only two. For approval, a minimum of sixty-two out of eighty-seven votes is required. As such, an individual government can be overruled.

4 The idea of a European bubble was not new to these negotiations. Haigh points out that agreement on the Large Combustion Plant Directive (which concerned emissions of sulphur dioxide and other contributors to acid rain) required the acceptance of different national targets within an overall 'bubble' (Haigh, 1989, p. 227).

5 For instance, there is not a single member state which has fully complied with the requirements of the Directive on Drinking Water Quality (80/778) (Krämer, 1997, p. 17). The Commission acted against the UK for non-compliance and found it to be in breach of the directive in a ruling by the ECJ in 1992; the UK was also found in breach of directive 76/160 on Bathing Waters in 1993 (Bell, 1997, p. 91).

6 The role of the UK regions on the committee is likely be increased as the new Labour administration supports increased regionalisation of policy making and implementation. The most obvious practical instantiation of this is the devolution of power to a Scottish Parliament and Welsh Assembly. Regional institutions for England are also planned and will replace the existing regional offices. Whether these will become elected assemblies is a moot point.

7 The use of statutory instruments is the most common mechanism for introducing EU legislation into UK national law. Many Acts of Parliament contain clauses which empower the minister to issue directives and regulations (statutory instruments) at a later time. Much EU environmental policy is thus enacted through delegated rather than primary legislation.

8 Ludwig Krämer of DG XI estimates that out of forty-seven pieces of environmental legislation, compliance is as low as about 25 per cent. To date, the UK and Denmark have the most impressive implementation records. (Haigh and Lanigan, 1995, p. 29).

9 This mirrors the concern expressed in Chapter 7 that TNCs will often relocate for competitive advantage in Southern nations where environmental standards are low.

10 As we shall see in Chapter 10, the UK government has tended to support subsidiarity down to the level of the nation state, but not below that level to local authorities.

11 Some of the dilemmas and difficulties faced by green parties were addressed in general terms in Chapter 3.

9 National responses

1 Although after German reunification, the environment has slipped down the political agenda – the economic redevelopment of former East Germany is taking priority.

2 Historically, however, Britain can be seen as an innovator in the environmental field, with policies often instigated by earlier Conservative administrations. Britain was responsible for the world's first piece of anti-pollution legislation in 1273 (a decree prohibiting the burning of sea coal); the first government environment agency, the Alkali Inspectorate established in 1863; the first private environmental group, the Commons, Open Spaces and Footpaths Preservation Society, founded in 1865; the first comprehensive air pollution control Act, the Clean Air Act of 1956; and the first cabinet-level environment department created in 1970 (McCormick, 1991, p. 9).

3 In many ways this is reminiscent of the original 1970 DoE, which included transport policy in its remit. A fully independent (and environmentally insensitive) DoT was created in 1976.

4 For a comparative analysis of progress towards IPC in Europe and North America, see Haigh and Irwin (1990).

5 For a description of the variety of pollution control agencies and their responsibilities prior to the creation of HMIP, see O'Riordan and Weale, 1989, p. 282.

6 A similar argument is made by Hamer in his study of the relationship between the roads lobby and the DoT, *Wheels Within Wheels*. He argues that the emphasis on road building can partly be traced to the fact that the road lobbyists and civil servants tend to have similar backgrounds – 'overwhelmingly male and middle-class ... share the seemingly trivial details of social conditioning – a car, a house with a garden in the suburbs – that are so important in prejudicing attitudes in transport policy' (Hamer, 1987, p. 112).

7 The precautionary principle is discussed in Chapter 4.

8 There may be a tension in the heart of pollution control philosophy given that at the same time as there is a move towards formalised, national standards, BPEO and BATNEEC require sensitivity to local environmental conditions.

9 Unlike its English and Welsh counterpart, SEPA also includes the local authority environmental health officers, who previously dealt with pollution control.

10 The separation of waste regulation, disposal and collection functions within local authorities is discussed briefly in Chapter 10.

11 The current objectives, policies and practice of the Environment Agency can be found on its website http://www.environment-agency.gov.uk/.

12 Much of what is said in this paragraph is taken from an interview with Ed Gallagher, the agency's chief executive, on *File on Four*, Radio 4, December 1997.

13 For a comparison of the UK's approach to sustainable development with that of

Norway, Germany, Portugal, Greece and the European Union, see the special issue of *Environmental Politics* edited by O'Riordan and Voisey (1997a). For a discussion of the Canadian Green Plan, see Toner and Doern, 1994.

14 This was later published as *Blueprint for a Green Economy* (Pearce *et al.*, 1989) which is discussed in Chapter 5.

15 For instance, the DoE later produced *Making Markets Work for the Environment* (DoE, 1993a).

16 The UK was 'one of only 13 countries that had submitted a national report for 1996 to the CSD by the end of January 1996' (Voisey and O'Riordan, 1997, p. 48).

17 For a full list of the members of the round table, see its *Second Annual Report* (1997). In order to work efficiently, the round table breaks up into smaller sub-groups to develop its recommendations, often coopting expert advisers and other interested parties.

18 To avoid charges of partiality and cooption, the round table was originally co-chaired by the Secretary of State for the Environment and Richard Southwood, former Chairman of the Royal Commission on Environmental Pollution. Under the new Labour administration, Southwood has become the sole chair, with John Prescott being afforded the role of President.

19 This may be mainly because the Labour government is looking for alternative revenue sources, other than income tax, in an attempt not to alienate middle-class voters; but greens should welcome any changes in this direction, whatever the political intention.

10 Local democracy and local authorities

1 For a comparative analysis of sustainable development in different European nations, see the 1997 special issue of *Environmental Politics* (vol. 6, no. 1), *Sustainable Development in Western Europe: Coming to Terms with Agenda 21* (1997b), edited by Tim O'Riordan and Heather Voisey. This compares British national and local practice with that of Norway, Germany, Portugal, Greece and the European Union.

2 In general terms, the British 'style' of local government is also present in the Republic of Ireland, Canada, Australia and New Zealand.

3 These arguments are drawn from a number of sources, including Phillips, 1996; Stoker, 1996a; 1996b; Commission for Local Democracy, 1995; Pratchett and Wilson, 1996; Parry *et al.*, 1992; Barber, 1984.

4 This is most obviously expressed in the consistently low turnouts for local elections (Pratchett and Wilson, 1996, p. 7).

5 The waste regulation authority (WRA) function has now been merged into the new Environment Agency (see Chapter 9). The WRA has the responsibility for enforcing the 'duty of care' requirements for controlled wastes and for licensing, inspecting and enforcing remedial action on landfills. Duty of care 'applies to any person who produces, imports, carries, keeps, treats or disposes of controlled waste, or, who, as a broker, has control of it' (Bell, 1997, p. 421). Such persons are responsible for the containment of the waste and for ensuring it is transferred to an authorised person.

6 For a more detailed discussion of waste management, see Cooper, 1994; and Blowers, 1993a.

7 Quasi-autonomous non-governmental organisations.

8 The EU Fifth Environmental Action Programme (5EAP) is discussed in Chapter 8.

9 For a brief discussion of the problem of land value that has led to out-of-town developments, see Hall *et al.*, 1993, pp. 22–3.

10 A list of PPGs is provided in Hams *et al.*, 1994, p. 57.

11 For a detailed discussion of what is required to make the planning process more sustainable, see *Planning for a Sustainable Environment*, a report by the Town and Country Planning Association (Blowers, 1993a). Also see Lusser, 1994.

12 For an overview of different problems facing the development of an integrated

transport policy, see Roberts *et al.*, 1992, and the Royal Commission on Environmenal Pollution, 1995.

13 Similarly, the European Commission has calculated that some 40 per cent of the EC Fifth Environmental Action Programme, *Towards Sustainability*, is the implementation responsibility of local government (LGMB, 1993a, p. 28). See Chapter 8.

14 For further discussions of these initiatives, see Ward, 1993; Webber, 1994; Hams *et al.*, 1994.

15 As a rough guide, in 1996, 38.5 per cent of local authorities claimed that they strongly supported the development of Local Agenda 21 and were 'committed to change in [the] authority's operations'; 49.1 per cent gave more 'tentative support' to the process (Tuxworth, 1996, p. 281).

16 The four specialist working groups are: air, energy, transport and noise; water, waste, land and agriculture; wildlife, landscape, townscape and open space; education and public awareness.

17 Of the eighty-five members, the forum is broken down into equal numbers of representatives from local government, industry, central government, and NGOs, and a smaller number of academic representatives (Whittaker, 1995, p. 162).

18 For discussions of such approaches to Local Agenda 21, see Whittaker, 1995; Young, 1996; LGMB, 1994; Church, 1995; Agyeman and Evans, 1994; Hams *et al.*, 1994; Brugman, 1997.

19 Only 33 per cent of respondents agreed that 'most politicians can be trusted to do what they think is best for the country' (Miller *et al.*, 1996, p. 47).

20 In many ways the role of local authorities in community governance can be compared to the role of international organisations in developing international environmental regimes (see Chapter 7) (Ward, 1996, p. 142).

21 It is interesting to note that the community consultation exercise threw up results that the city planners did not expect and as such is a lesson that strategies for sustainable development need to be aware of the way in which the community perceives problems. The planners in Seattle believed that one of the first problems that needed solving was peak hour congestion on major routes in Seattle: 'Yet citizen consultation revealed that people didn't necessarily want a lot spent on solving peak hour congestion because they view it as part of the working day and "the roads are supposed to jam!" For them what was imperative was finding solutions to congestion on Saturday mornings when delays cut into their own quality time' (Church, 1995, p. 50).

Bibliography

Ackerman, B. and Hassler, W.T. (1981) *Clean Coal, Dirty Air: or How the Clean Air Act became a Multibillion-dollar Bail-out for High-sulphur Coal Producers and What should be Done about it*, New Haven, Conn., Yale University Press.

Adams, J. (1995) *Cost Benefit Analysis: Part of the Problem, Not the Solution*, Oxford: Green College Centre for Environmental Policy and Understanding.

Agyeman, J. and Evans, B. (1994) 'The New Environmental Agenda' in Agyeman, J. and Evans, B. (eds) *Local Environmental Policies and Strategies*, Harlow: Longman.

Alarm UK (1996) *Roadblock: How People Power is Wrecking the Roads Programme*, London: Alarm UK.

Alarm UK (no date) *A Rough Guide to the Roads Programme*, London: Alarm UK.

Andersen, M. (1996) 'The Impact of New Member States on EU Environmental Policy', *Environmental Politics*, vol. 5, no. 2, pp. 339–44.

Andersen, S. and Eliassen, K. (1993) *Making Policy in Europe: The Europeification of National Policy-making*, London: Sage.

Anderson, T.L. and Leal, R.L. (1991) *Free Market Environmentalism*, San Francisco: Pacific Research Institute for Public Policy.

Anderson, V. (1991) *Alternative Economic Indicators*, London: Routledge.

Atkins, S.T. (1990), *Unspoken Decrees: Road Appraisal, Democracy and the Environment*, London: South East Wildlife Trust.

Attfield, R. (1991) *The Ethics of Environmental Concern* (second edition), Athens, Georgia: University of Georgia Press.

Attfield, R. (1994) *Environmental Philosophy: Principles and Prospects*, Aldershot: Avebury.

Attfield, R. and Belsey, A. (eds) (1994) *Philosophy and the Natural Environment*, Cambridge: Cambridge University Press.

Bachrach, P. and Baratz, M.S. (1962) 'Two Faces of Power', *American Political Science Review*, 56, pp. 947–52 (reprinted as Chapter 1 of *Power and Poverty*).

Bachrach, P. and Baratz, M.S. (1970) *Power and Poverty: Theory and Practice*, New York: Oxford University Press.

Bailey, P. (1997) 'The Changing Role of Environmental Agencies', *European Environmental Law Review*, vol. 6, no. 5 (May), pp. 148–54.

Baker, S. (1996) 'Environmental Policy in the European Union: Institutional Dilemmas and Democratic Practice.', in Lafferty, M. and Meadowcroft, J. (eds) *Democracy and the Environment.* Aldershot: Edward Elgar.

Baker, S. (1997) 'The Evolution of European Union Environmental Policy: From Growth to Sustainable Development?' in Baker, S. *et al.* (eds) *The Politics of Sustainable Development: Theory, Policy and Practice Within the European Union*, London: Routledge.

Baker, S., Kousis, M., Richardson, D. and Young, S. (eds) (1997) *The Politics of Sustainable Development: Theory, Policy and Practice Within the European Union*, London: Routledge.

Barber, B. (1984) *Strong Democracy: Participatory Politics for a New Age*, Berkeley: University of California Press.

Barde, J. and Pearce, D. (1991) *Valuing the Environment*, London: Earthscan.

Barry, B. (1973) *The Liberal Theory of Justice*, Oxford: Oxford University Press.

Barry, B. (1991) *Liberty and Justice: Essays in Political Theory 2*, Oxford: Clarendon Press.

Barry, J. (1994) 'The Limits of the Shallow and the Deep: Green Politics, Philosophy, and Praxis,' *Environmental Politics*, vol. 3, no. 3, pp. 369–94.

Bateman, I. (1991) 'A Critical Analysis of COBA and Proposals for an Extended Cost Benefit Approach to Transport Decisions', in *What Are Roads Worth?* London: Transport 2000/New Economics Foundation.

Batley, R. (1991) 'Comparisons and Lessons' in Batley, R. and Stoker, G. (eds) *Local Government in Europe: Trends and Developments*, Basingstoke: Macmillan.

Beckerman, W. (1990) *Pricing for Pollution* (second edition), Institute for Economic Affairs.

Beckerman, W. (1994) 'Sustainable Development: Is it a Useful Concept?' *Environmental Values*, vol. 3, pp. 191–209.

Beckerman, W. (1995a) *Small is Stupid*, London: Duckworth.

Beckerman, W. (1995b) 'How Would You Like Your "Sustainability", Sir? Weak or Strong? A Reply to My Critics', *Environmental Values*, vol. 4, pp. 169–79.

Beder, S. (1996) *The Nature of Sustainable Development* (second edition), Newham, Australia: Scribe Publications.

Bell, S. (1997) *Ball and Bell on Environmental Law* (fourth edition), London: Blackstone.

Bentham, J. (1960) *An Introduction to the Principles of Morals and Legislation*, Oxford: Blackwell.

Benton, T. (1993) *Natural Relations: Ecology, Animal Rights and Social Justice*, London: Verso.

Beuermann, C. and Burdick, B. (1997) 'The Sustainability Transition in Germany: Some Early Stage Experiences', *Environmental Politics*, vol. 6, no. 1, pp. 83–107.

Bigg, T. (1994) *Report on the Second Session of the UN Commission on Sustainable Development*, London: UNED-UK.

Bigg, T. (1997) *Report on 'Earth Summit II', the UN General Assembly Special Sessions to review outcomes from the Rio Summit: A UNED-UK Report*, London: UNED-UK.

Bigg, T. and Dodds, F. (1997) 'The UN Commission on Sustainable Development', in Dodds, F. (ed.) *The Way Forward: Beyond Agenda 21*, London: Earthscan.

Bigg, T. and Mucke, P. (1996) 'NGO Priorities and Concerns for the 1997 UN GA Session', in *Priorities for Earth Summit II*, London: UNED-UK.

Blowers, A. (ed.) (1993a) *Planning for a Sustainable Environment*, London: Earthscan.

Blowers, A. (1993b) 'The Time for Change', in Blowers, A. (ed.) *Planning for a Sustainable Environment*, London: Earthscan.

Bomberg, E. (1996) 'Greens in the European Parliament', *Environmental Politics*, vol. 5, no. 2, pp. 324–31.

Bomberg, E. (1998) *Green Parties and Politics in the European Union*. London: Routledge.

The Book: Directory of Active Groups in the UK (1995) Brighton.

Bookchin, M. (1980) *Toward an Ecological Society*, Montreal: Black Rose Books.

Bookchin, M. (1987) 'Social Ecology versus "Deep Ecology": A Challenge for the Ecology Movement,' *Green Perspectives*, 4/5.

Bookchin, M. (1991) *The Ecology of Freedom* (second edition), Montreal: Black Rose Books.

Boutros-Ghali, B. (1992) *An Agenda for Peace*, New York: United Nations.

Bray, J. (1995) *Spend, Spend, Spend: How the Department of Transport Wastes Money and Mismanages the Roads Programme*, London: Transport 2000.

Braybrooke, D. and Lindblom, C. (1963) *A Strategy of Decision*, New York: The Free Press.

Brennan, A. (1988) *Thinking About Nature*, Athens, Georgia: University of Georgia Press.

Brennan, A. (1992) 'Moral Pluralism and the Environment', *Environmental Values*, vol. 1, no. 1, pp. 15–33.

British Government Panel on Sustainable Development (1995) *First Report*, London: DoE.

British Government Panel on Sustainable Development (1996) *Second Report*, London: DoE.

Brown, C. (1997) *Understanding International Relations*, Basingstoke: Macmillan.

Brown, L., Flavin, C. and Kane, H. (1996) *Vital Signs 1996–1997*, London: Earthscan.

Brugman, J. (1997) 'Local Authorities and Local Agenda 21', in Dodds, F. (ed.) *The Way Forward: Beyond Agenda 21*, London: Earthscan.

Bryant, B. (1996) *Twyford Down: Roads, Campaigning and Environmental Law*, London: E. & F.N. Spon.

Bunyard, P. and Morgan-Grenville, F. (eds) (1987) *The Green Alternative*, London: Methuen.

Cairncross, F. (1991) *Costing the Earth*, London: Business Books.

Callicott, J.B. (1990) 'The Case Against Moral Pluralism', *Environmental Ethics*, vol. 12, no. 3, pp. 100–24.

Cameron, J.R. (1989) 'Do Future Generations Matter?' in Dower, N. (ed.) *Ethics and Environmental Responsibility*, Aldershot: Avebury.

Carruthers, P. (1992) *The Animals Issue*, Cambridge: Cambridge University Press.

Carson, R. (1962) *Silent Spring*, Boston: Houghton Mifflin.

Chandler, J. (1993) *Local Government in Liberal Democracies*, London: Routledge.

Chappell, T.D.J. (ed.) (1997) *The Philosophy of the Environment*, Edinburgh University Press.

Chatterjee, P. and Finger, M. (1994) *The Earth Brokers: Power, Politics and World Development*, London: Routledge.

Church, C. (1995) *Towards Local Sustainability: A Review of Current Activity on Local Agenda 21 in the UK*, London: United Nations Association/Community Development Foundation.

Clark, S.R.L. (1977) *The Moral Status of Animals*, Oxford: Oxford University Press.

Clegg, S. (1989) *Frameworks of Power*, London: Sage.

Coase, R. (1960) 'The Problem of Social Cost', *Journal of Law and Economics*, vol. 3, no. 1, pp. 1–44.

Cohen, C. (1970) 'Defending Civil Disobedience', *The Monist*, vol. 54, no. 4, pp. 469–87.

Cohen, J. (1989) 'Deliberation and Democratic Legitimacy' in Hamlin, A. and Pettit, P. (eds) *The Good Polity*, Oxford: Blackwell.

Collier, U. (1997) 'Sustainability, Subsidiarity and Deregulation: New Directions in EU Environmental Policy', *Environmental Politics*, vol. 6, no. 2, pp. 1–23.

Collier, U. and Golub, J. (1997) 'Environmental Policy and Politics', in Rhodes, M. *et al.* (eds) *Developments in West European Politics*, London: Macmillan.

Collingwood, R.G. (1946) *The Idea of Nature*, Oxford: Clarendon Press.

Collins, K. and Earnshaw, D. (1993) 'The Implementation and Enforcement of European Community Environment Legislation', in Judge, D. (ed.) *A Green Dimension for the Economic Community*, London: Frank Cass.

Commission for Local Democracy (1995) *Taking Charge: The Rebirth of Local Democracy*, London: Municipal Journal Books.

Commission of the European Communities (1985) *Council Directive on the Assessment of the Effects of Certain Public and Private Projects on the Environment*, Brussels: CEC.

Commission of the European Communities (CEC) (1992) *Towards Sustainability: The Fifth Environmental Action Programme*, Luxembourg: CEC.

Cooper, J. (1994) 'Waste Reduction and Disposal' in Agyeman, J. and Evans, B. (eds) *Local Environmental Policies and Strategies*, Harlow: Longman.

Craven, J. (1992) *Social Choice*, Cambridge: Cambridge University Press.

Crenson, M. (1971) *The Un-Politics of Air Pollution*, Baltimore: Johns Hopkins University Press.

Dahl, R. (1957) 'The Concept of Power', *Behavioural Science*, vol. 2, July, pp. 201–50.

Daly, H. (1991) *Steady State Economics* (second edition), New York: Island Press.

Daly, H. (1995) 'On Wilfred Beckerman's Critique of Sustainable Development', *Environmental Values*, vol. 4, pp. 49–55.

Daly, H. and Cobb, J. (1990) *For the Common Good*, London: Green Print.

de la Court, T. (1990) *Beyond Brundtland: Green Development in the 1990s*, London: Zed Books.

Department of the Environment (DoE) (1989) *Environmental Assessment: A Guide to Procedures*, London: HMSO.

DoE (1990) *This Common Inheritance: Britain's Environmental Strategy*, London: HMSO.

DoE (1991a) *Policy Appraisal and the Environment: A Guide for Government Departments*, London: HMSO.

DoE (1991b) *This Common Inheritance: The First Year Report*, London: HMSO.

DoE (1992a) *This Common Inheritance: The Second Year Report*, London: HMSO.

DoE (1992b) *PPG12: Development Plans and Regional Planning Guidance*, London: DoE.

DoE (1993a) *Making Markets Work for the Environment*, London: HMSO.

DoE (1993b) *UK Strategy for Sustainable Development: Consultation Paper*, London: HMSO.

DoE (1993c) *Environmental Appraisal of Development Plans*, London: HMSO.

DoE (1994a) *This Common Inheritance: The Third Year Report*, London: HMSO.

DoE (1994b) *Sustainable Development: The UK Strategy*, London: HMSO.

DoE (1995a) *This Common Inheritance: UK Annual Report*, London: HMSO.

DoE (1995b) *First Steps: Local Agenda 21 in Practice*, London: HMSO.

DoE (1996a) *This Common Inheritance: UK Annual Report*, London: HMSO.

DoE (1996b) *Indicators of Sustainable Development for the United Kingdom*, London: HMSO.

Department of Transport (DoT) (1987) *Values for Journey Time Savings and Accident Prevention*, London: DoT.

DoT (1989) *Roads for Prosperity*, London: HMSO.

DoT (1991) *The Role of Investment Appraisal in Road and Rail Transport*, London: HMSO.

DoT (1992) *The Government's Expenditure Plans For Transport 1992–3 to 1994–5*, London: HMSO.

Devlin, J. and Yap, N. (1993) 'Structural Adjustment Programmes and the UNCED Agenda: Explaining the Contradiction', *Environmental Politics*, vol. 2, no. 4, pp. 65–79.

Dobson, A. (ed.) (1991) *The Green Reader*, London: Andre Deutsch.

Dobson, A. (1993) 'Critical Theory and Green Politics', in Dobson, A. and Lucardie, P. (eds) *The Politics of Nature: Explorations in Green Political Theory*, London: Routledge.

Dobson, A. (1995) *Green Political Thought* (second edition), London: Routledge.

Dobson, A. and Lucardie, P. (eds) (1993) *The Politics of Nature: Explorations in Green Political Theory*, London: Routledge.

Dodds, F. (ed.) (1997) *The Way Forward: Beyond Agenda 21*, London: Earthscan.

Doherty, B. (1997) 'Direct Action Against Road-Building: Some Implications for the Concept of Protest Repertoires', in Stanyer, J. and Stoker, G. (eds) *Contemporary Political Studies*, Political Studies Association.

Doherty, B. and de Geus, M. (eds) (1996) *Democracy and Green Political Thought*, London: Routledge.

Dower, N. (ed.) (1989) *Ethics and Environmental Responsibility*, Aldershot: Avebury.

Dryzek, J. (1987) *Rational Ecology*, Oxford: Blackwell.

Dryzek, J. (1990) 'Green Reason: Communicative Ethics for the Biosphere', *Environmental Ethics*, vol. 12, pp. 195–210.

Dryzek, J. (1992) 'Ecology and Discursive Democracy: Beyond Liberal Capitalism and the Administrative State', *Capitalism, Nature, Socialism*, vol. 3, no. 2, pp. 18–42.

Dryzek, J. (1995) 'Political and Ecological Communication', *Environmental Politics*, vol. 4, no. 4, pp. 13–30.

Dryzek, J. (1996) 'Democracy and Environmental Policy Instruments', in Eckersley, R. (ed.) *Markets, the State and the Environment*, London: Macmillan.

Duff, A. (ed.) (1997) *The Treaty of Amsterdam: Texts and Commentary*, Federal Trust.

Dunn, J. (1990) 'Trust and Political Agency', in *Interpreting Political Responsibility*, Oxford: Blackwell.

Dworkin, R. (1977) *Taking Rights Seriously*, London: Duckworth.

Eckersley, R. (1992) *Environmentalism and Political Theory*, London: UCL Press.

Eckersley, R. (ed.) (1995a) *Markets, the State and the Environment*, London: Macmillan.

Eckersley, R. (1995b) 'Liberal Democracy and the Rights of Nature: The Struggle for Inclusion', *Environmental Politics*, vol. 4, no. 4. pp. 169–98.

Eckersley, R. (1996) 'Greening Liberal Democracy: The Rights Discourse Revisited' in Doherty, B. and de Geus, M. (eds) *Democracy and Green Political Thought*, London: Routledge.

The Ecologist (1993) *Whose Common Future*, London: Earthscan.

Ehrlich, P. (1972) *The Population Bomb*, London: Pan/Ballantine.

Ekins, P. (ed.) (1986) *The Living Economy: A New Economics in the Making*, London: Routledge & Kegan Paul.

Ekins, P. (1995) 'Economics and Sustainability', in Ravaioli, C. *Economists and the Environment*, London: Zed Books.

Elkington, J. and Burke, T. (1987) *The Green Capitalists*, London: Gollancz.

Elkington, J. and Hailes, J. (1988) *The Green Consumer Guide*, London: Gollancz.

Elliot, R. (ed.) (1995) *Environmental Ethics*, Oxford: Oxford University Press.

Environmental Data Services (ENDS) (1994) 'Advancing the Sustainable Development Agenda', *ENDS Report*, no. 228 (January), pp. 18–21.

ENDS (1995a) 'Round Table on Sustainable Development starts work', *ENDS Report*, no. 240 (January), p. 6.

ENDS (1995b) 'European Environment Agency gets under way', *ENDS Report*, no. 240 (January), pp. 20–3.

ENDS (1995c) 'Treasury put to test over sustainable development', *ENDS Report*, no. 242 (March), p. 29.

ENDS (1995d) 'Lords urge step-by-step move to EC environment inspectorate', *ENDS Report*, no. 242 (March), pp. 30–1.

ENDS (1995e) 'Taking cost/benefit analysis too far', *ENDS Report*, no. 243 (April), p. 2.

ENDS (1996a) 'Commission outlines ideas for improving implementation', *ENDS Report*, no. 257 (June), pp. 44–5.

ENDS (1996b) 'Disappointing response to Round Table report', *ENDS Report*, no. 258 (July), pp. 35–6.

ENDS (1996c) 'Breaches of EC environmental rules remain commonplace', *ENDS Report*, no. 261 (October), pp. 39–40.

ENDS (1996d) 'Commission treads softly on decentralisation of enforcement', *ENDS Report*, no. 261 (October), pp. 40–1.

ENDS (1996e) 'Green ministers who barely meet', *ENDS Report*, no. 263 (December), p. 24.

ENDS (1997a) 'Sustainable development becomes treaty goal for EC', *ENDS Report*, no. 269 (June), pp. 44–5.

ENDS (1997b) 'Commission proposals to ease work of European Environmental Agency', *ENDS Report*, no. 270 (July), pp. 40–1.

Environment Challenge Group (1994) *Green Gauge: Indicators for the State of the UK Environment*, London: ECG.

Environmental Politics, London: Frank Cass.

European Environmental Agency web page, http://www.eea.dk

Falk, R. (1995) *On Humane Governance*, Cambridge: Polity.

Feinberg, J. (1991) 'The Rights of Animals and Unborn Generations' in White, J. (ed.) *Contemporary Moral Problems*, St Paul, Minn.: West Publishing Co.

Foster, M.B. (1992) *Creation, Nature, and Political Order in the Philosophy of Michael Foster* (edited by C. Wybrow). Lewiston: Edwin Mellen Press.

Fox, W. (1990) *Towards a Transpersonal Ecology*, Boston: Shambhala.

Frankena, W. (1979) 'Ethics and the Environment', in Goodpaster, K.E. and Sayre, K.M. (eds) *Ethics and Problems of the Twentieth Century*, Notre Dame, Ind.: University of Notre Dame Press.

Freeden, M. (1995) *Green Ideology: Concepts and Structures*, OCEES Research Paper no. 4, Mansfield College, Oxford.

Friends of the Earth (1988) *Environmental Charter for Local Government*, London: FoE.

Friends of the Earth (1996) *Earthmatters: 25th Anniversary Issue*, no. 30, Summer.

Gallie, W.B. (1964) *Philosophy and the Historical Understanding*, London: Chatto & Windus.

Garner, R. (1996) *Environmental Politics*, Hemel Hempstead: Prentice-Hall/Harvester Wheatsheaf.

Gaventa, J. (1982) *Power and Powerlessness: Quiescence and Rebellion in an Appalachian Valley*, Oxford: Clarendon Press.

George, S. (1996) *Politics and Policy in the European Union* (third edition), Oxford: Oxford University Press.

Georgescu-Roegen, N. (1971) *The Entropy Law and the Economic Process*, Cambridge, Mass.: Harvard University Press.

Golding, M.P. (1972) 'Obligations to Future Generations', *The Monist*, vol. 56, pp. 85–99.

Goldsmith, E. *et al.* (1972) *Blueprint For Survival*, Harmondsworth: Penguin.

Goldsmith, M. (1996) 'Normative Theories of Local Government: A European Comparison', in King, D. and Stoker, G. (eds) *Rethinking Local Democracy*, Basingstoke: Macmillan.

Golub, J. (1996a) 'Sovereignty and Subsidiarity in EU Environmental Policy', *Political Studies*, vol. 44, no. 4, pp. 686–703.

Golub, J. (1996b) 'British Sovereignty and EC Environmental Policy', *Environmental Politics*, vol. 5, no. 4, pp. 700–28.

Goodin, R. (1992) *Green Political Theory*, Cambridge: Polity Press.

Goodpaster, K.E. (1978) 'On Being Morally Considerable', *Journal of Philosophy*, 75, pp. 308–25.

Gorz, A. (1980) *Ecology as Politics*, London: Pluto.

Grant, W. (1989) *Pressure Groups, Politics and Democracy in Britain*, London: Philip Allan.

Gray, J. (1993) *Beyond the New Right: Markets, Government and the Common Good*, London: Routledge.

Gray, T. (ed.) (1995) *UK Environmental Policy in the 1990s*, Basingstoke: Macmillan.

Gruen, L. and Jamieson, D. (eds) (1994) *Reflecting on Nature*, Oxford: Oxford University Press.

Gyford, J. (1991) *Citizens, Consumers and Councils*, Basingstoke: Macmillan.

Haas, P. (1989) 'Do Regimes Matter: Epistemic Communities and Mediterranean Pollution Control', *International Organisation*, vol. 43, pp. 377–403.

Haas, P., Keohane, R. and Levy, M. (eds) (1993) *Institutions for the Earth*, Cambridge, Mass.: MIT.

Haigh, N. (1989) *EEC Environmental Policy and Britain* (second edition), London: Longman.

Haigh, N. and Irwin, F. (eds) (1990) *Integrated Pollution Control in Europe and North America*, Washington, DC: The Conservation Foundation.

Haigh, N. and Lanigan, C. (1995) 'Impact of the European Union on UK Environmental Policy Making', in Gray, T.S. (ed.) *UK Environmental Policy in the 1990s*, London: Macmillan.

Hall, D., Hebbert, M. and Lusser, H. (1993) 'The Planning Background', in Blowers, A. (ed.) *Planning for a Sustainable Environment*, London: Earthscan.

Hamer, M. (1987) *Wheels Within Wheels*, London: Routledge.

Hams, T. (1994) 'Local Environmental Policies and Strategies After Rio', in Agyeman, J. and Evans, B. (eds) *Local Environmental Policies and Strategies*, Harlow: Longman.

Hams, T., Jacobs, M., Levett, R., Lusser, H., Morphet, J. and Taylor, D. (1994) *Greening Your Local Authority*, Harlow: Longman.

Handler, T. (1994) *Regulating the European Environment*, London: Wiley.

Hardin, G. (1968) 'The Tragedy of the Commons', *Science*, vol. 162, pp. 1243–8.

Hardin, G. (1977) 'Lifeboat Ethics: The Case Against Helping the Poor', in Aiken, W. and La Follette, H. (eds) *World Hunger and Moral Obligation*, Englewood Cliffs, NJ: Prentice-Hall.

Hay, P.R. (1988) 'Ecological Values and Western Political Traditions: From Anarchism to Fascism', *Politics*, 8, pp. 22–9.

Hayward, T. (1995) *Ecological Thought*, Cambridge: Polity Press.

Heap, S.H., Hollis, M., Lyons, B., Sugden, R. and Weale, A. (1992) *The Theory of Choice: A Critical Guide*, Oxford: Blackwell.

Helm, D. (ed.) (1991) *Economic Policy Towards the Environment*, Oxford: Blackwell.

Henry, R. (1996) 'Adapting United Nations Agencies for Agenda 21: Programme Coordination and Organisational Reform', *Environmental Politics*, vol. 5, no. 1, pp. 1–24.

HM Treasury (1991) *Economic Appraisal in Central Government: A Technical Guide for Government Departments*, London: HMSO.

Hill, D. and Smith, T. (1994) 'Environmental Management and Audit', in Agyeman, J. and Evans, B. (eds) *Local Environmental Policies and Strategies*, Harlow: Longman.

Hirst, P. and Thompson, G. (1996) *Globalisation in Question*, Cambridge: Polity Press.

Holm, J. and Bowker, J. (eds) (1994) *Attitudes to Nature*, London: Pinter.

Hurrell, A. (1993) 'The 1992 Earth Summit: Funding Mechanisms and Environmental Institutions', *Environmental Politics*, vol. 1, no. 4, pp. 273–79.

Hurrell, A. and Kingsbury, B. (eds) (1992) *The International Politics of the Environment*, Oxford: Clarendon Press.

Imber, M. (1993) 'The United Nations' Role in Sustainable Development', *Environmental Politics*, vol. 2, no. 4, pp. 123–36.

Ingham, A. (1993) 'The Market for Sulphur Dioxide Permits in the USA and UK', *Environmental Politics*, vol. 2, no. 4, pp. 98–122.

International Council for Local Environmental Initiatives (ICLEI) (1993) *Local Initiatives: ICLEI Members in Action 1991–1992*, Toronto: ICLEI.

Irvine, S. and Ponton, A. (1988) *A Green Manifesto: Policies for a Green Future*, London: MacDonald Optima.

Jacobs, M. (1991) *The Green Economy*, London: Pluto.

Jacobs, M. (1994) 'The Limits to Neoclassicism', in Redclift, M. and Benton, T. (eds) *Social Theory and the Global Environment*, London: Routledge.

Jacobs, M. (1995a) 'Sustainable Development: Assumptions, Contradictions, Progress', in Lovenduski, J. and Stanyer, J. (eds) *Contemporary Political Studies: Proceedings of the Annual Conference of the Political Studies Association*, London: PSA, pp. 1470–85.

Jacobs, M. (1995b) 'Financial Incentives: The British Experience', in Eckersley, R. (ed.) *Markets, the State and the Environment*, London: Macmillan.

Jacobs, M. (1995c) 'Sustainable Development, Capital Substitution and Economic Humility: A Response to Beckerman', *Environmental Values*, vol. 4, pp. 57–68.

Jacobs, M. (1996) *The Politics of the Real World*, London: Earthscan.

Jiménez-Beltrán, D. (1995) 'The Process of Sustainable Development and the Role of the European Environment Agency', *European Environmental Law Review*, vol. 4, no. 10 (October), pp. 265–9.

John, P. (1997) 'Local Governance', in Dunleavy, P. *et al.* (eds) *Developments in British Politics*, Basingstoke: Macmillan.

Johnson, G. and Corcelle, S. (1995) *The Environmental Policy of the European Communities* (second edition), London and The Hague: Kluwer Law International.

Jordan, A. (1993) 'Integrated Pollution Control and the Evolving Style and Structure of Environmental Regulation in the UK', *Environmental Politics*, vol. 2, no. 3, pp. 405–27.

Jordan, G. and Richardson, J. (1987) *British Politics and the Policy Process*, London: Allen & Unwin.

Judge, D. (ed.) (1993) *A Green Dimension for the European Community*, London: Frank Cass.

Justice? (1996) *SchNEWS reader*, Brighton: Justice?

Kant, I. (1963) *Lectures on Ethics*, New York: Harper Torchbooks.

Kay, P. (1992) *Where Motor Car is Master: How the Department of Transport Became Bewitched by Roads*, London: CPRE.

Kemp, R. (1985) 'Planning, Public Hearings, and the Politics of Discourse', in Forester, J. (ed.) *Critical Theory and Public Life*, Cambridge, Mass.: MIT Press.

Khor, M. (1992) 'Development, Trade and the Environment: A Third World Perspective', in Goldsmith, E. (ed.) *The Future of Progress: Reflections on Environment and Development*, Bristol: International Society for Ecology and Culture.

Khor, M. (1994) 'CSD Still Alive, But Not Yet Kicking into Action', *Third World Resurgence*, no. 47 (July), pp. 3–4.

Khor, M. (1997) 'Effects of Globalisation on Sustainable Development after UNCED', *Third World Resurgence*, no. 81/82 (May/June), pp. 5–11.

Kinrade, P. (1996) 'Towards Ecologically Sustainable Development: The Role and Short-comings of Markets', in Eckersley, R. (ed.) *Markets, the State and the Environment*, London: Macmillan.

Knetsch, J. (1990) 'Environmental Policy Implications of Disparities between Willingness to Pay and Compensation Demanded Measures of Values', *Journal of Environmental Economics and Management*, vol. 18, pp. 227–37.

Krämer, L. (1993) *European Environmental Law Casebook*, London: Sweet & Maxwell.

Krämer, L. (1995) *E.C. Treaty and Environmental Law* (second edition), London: Sweet & Maxwell.

Krämer, L. (1997) *Focus on European Environmental Law* (second edition), London: Sweet & Maxwell.

Krasner, S. (ed.) (1983) *International Regimes*, Ithaca, NY: Cornell University Press.

Kunzlik, P. (1994) *Environmental Policy*, London: Longman.

Kuper, R. (1997) 'Deliberating Waste: The Hertfordshire Citizens' Jury', *Local Environment*, vol. 2, no. 2, pp. 139–53.

Lamb, R. (1996) *Promising the Earth*, London: Routledge.

Lang, P. (1994) *LETS Work: Rebuilding the Local Economy*, Bristol: Grover Books.

Lang, T. and Hines, C. (1993) *The New Protectionism: Protecting the Future Against Free Trade*, London: Earthscan.

Laver, M. (1983) *Invitation to Politics*, Oxford: Blackwell.

Lawrence, G. (1994) 'Sustainable Seattle, USA', in Department of the Environment (ed.) *Partnerships for Change*, London: HMSO.

Leach, S. (1996a) 'The Dimensions of Analysis: Governance, Markets and Community', in Leach, S. *et al.* (eds) *Enabling or Disabling Local Government*, Milton Keynes: Open University Press.

Leach, S. (1996b) 'Conclusion: Scenarios for Change', in Leach, S. *et al.* (eds) *Enabling or Disabling Local Government*, Milton Keynes: Open University Press.

Leach, S. and Davis, H. (1996) 'Introduction', in Leach, S. *et al.* (eds) *Enabling or Disabling Local Government*, Milton Keynes: Open University Press.

Leahy, M. (1994) *Against Liberation*, London: Routledge.

Lee, K. (1994) 'Awe and Humility: Intrinsic Value in Nature', in Attfield, R. and Belsey, A. (eds) *Philosophy and the Natural Environment*, Cambridge: Cambridge University Press.

Lee, N. (1989) *Environmental Impact Assessment: A Training Guide* (second edition), Occasional Paper no. 18, EIA Centre, Department of Planning and Landscape, University of Manchester.

Lee, N. and Walsh, F. (1992) 'Strategic Environmental Assessment: An Overview', *Project Appraisal*, vol. 7, no. 3, pp. 126–36.

Levy, M., Keohane, R. and Haas, P. (1993) 'Improving the Effectiveness of International Environmental Institutions', in Haas, P. *et al.* (eds) *Institutions for the Earth*, Cambridge, Mass.: MIT Press.

Liberatore, A. (1997) 'The Integration of Sustainable Development Objectives into EU Policy-making: Barriers and Prospects', in Baker, S. *et al.* (eds) *The Politics of Sustainable Development: Theory, Policy and Practice Within the European Union*, London: Routledge.

Lindblom, C. (1959) 'The Science of Muddling Through', *Public Administration Review*, vol. 19, pp. 79–88.

Lindblom, C. (1965) *The Intelligence of Democracy*, New York: Free Press.

Local Government Management Board (LGMB) (1992) *Agenda 21: A Guide for Local Authorities in the U.K.*, Luton: LGMB.

LGMB (1993a) *Towards Sustainability: A Guide for Local Authorities*, Luton: LGMB.

LGMB (1993b) *A Framework for Local Sustainability*, Luton: LGMB.

LGMB (1993c) *The UK's Submission to the UN Commission on Sustainable Development: An Initial Submission by UK Local Government*, Luton: LGMB.

LGMB (1994) *Local Agenda 21 Principles and Processes: A Step by Step Guide*, Luton: LGMB.

LGMB (1995a) *The Sustainable Management of Solid Waste*, Luton: LGMB.

LGMB (1995b) *Sustainability Indicators Research Project: Consultants Report of the Pilot Phase*, Luton: LGMB.

London Economics (1992) *The Potential Role of Market Mechanisms in the Control of Acid Rain*, Department of the Environment, Environmental Research Series, London: HMSO.

Lovelock, J. (1979) *Gaia: A New Look at Life on Earth*, Oxford: Clarendon Press.

Lowe, P. and Goyder, J. (1983) *Environmental Groups in Politics*, London: Allen & Unwin.

Lukes, S. (1974) *Power: A Radical View*, London: Macmillan.

Lusser, H. (1994) 'Environmental Planning', in Agyeman, J. and Evans, B. (eds) *Local Environmental Policies and Strategies*, Harlow: Longman.

McCormick, J. (1991) *British Politics and the Environment*, London: Earthscan.

McCormick, J. (1993) 'Environmental Politics', in Dunleavy *et al.* (eds) *Developments in British Politics 4*, London: Macmillan, 1995.

McKay, G. (1996) *Senseless Acts of Beauty: Cultures of Resistance since the Sixties*, London: Verso.

McLean, I. (1987) *Public Choice*, Oxford: Blackwell.

Macnaghten, P., Grove-White, R., Jacobs, M. and Wynne, B. (1995) *Public Perception and Sustainability in Lancashire*, Preston: Lancashire County Council.

Malthus, T. (1968) *An Essay on the Principles of Population*, Harmondsworth: Penguin.

Marin, A. (1997) 'EC Environmental Policy', in Stavridis, S. *et al.* (eds) *New Challenges to the European Union: Policies and Policy-Making*, Aldershot: Dartmouth.

Markandya, A. (1991) 'Global Warming: The Economics of Tradeable Permits', in Pearce, D.W. *et al.* (eds) *Blueprint 2: Greening the World Economy*, London: Earthscan.

Marman, K. (1996) 'Road Rave', *Green Line*, no. 137 (September), pp. 3–5.

Martell, L. (1994) *Ecology and Society*, Cambridge: Polity Press.

Mathews, F. (1991) *The Ecological Self*, London: Routledge.

Mayo, E. (1994) 'What Happened When We Measured "Real" Wealth', *New Economics*, no. 29 (Spring), pp. 6–7.

Meadows, D.H., Meadows, D.L., Randers, J. and Behrens, W.W. (1972) *The Limits to Growth*, London: Pan.

Mensah, C. (1996) 'The United Nations Commission on Sustainable Development', in Werksman, J. (ed.) *Greening International Institutions*, London: Earthscan.

Midgley, M. (1983) *Why Animals Matter*, Harmondsworth: Penguin.

Midgley, M. (1994) 'The End of Anthropocentrism?', in Attfield, R. and Belsey, A. (eds) *Philosophy and the Natural Environment*, Cambridge: Cambridge University Press.

Mihevc, J. (1995) *The Market Tells Them So: The World Bank and Economic Fundamentalism in Africa*, London: Zed.

Mill, J.S. (1874) *Three Essays on Religion*. London: Longman.

Mill, J.S. (1909) *Principles of Political Economy*, London: Longman.

Miller, W., Timpson, A. and Lessnoff, M. (1996) *Political Culture in Contemporary Britain*, Oxford: Clarendon Press.

Ministry of Housing, Physical Planning and Environment (1989) *National Environmental Policy Plan: To Choose or To Lose*, The Hague: SDU.

Ministry of Housing, Physical Planning and Environment (1990) *Report Recommendations on and Responses to the NEPP*, The Hague: SDU.

Mishan, E.J. (1988) *Cost-Benefit Analysis*, London: George Allen & Unwin.

Moran, A. (1995) 'Tools of Environmental Policy: Market Instruments versus Command-and-control', in Eckersley, R. (ed.) (1995) *Markets, the State and the Environment*, London: Macmillan.

Morriss, P. (1987) *Power: A Philosophical Analysis*, Manchester: Manchester University Press.

Mueller, D. (1989) *Public Choice II*, Cambridge: Cambridge University Press.

Naess, A. (1973) 'The Shallow and Deep Ecology Movement', *Inquiry*, vol. 16, pp. 265–70.

Naess, A. (1989) *Ecology, Community and Lifestyle*, Cambridge: Cambridge University Press.

Nijkamp, P. and Perrels, A. (1994) *Sustainable Cities in Europe: A Comparative Analysis of Urban Energy-Environmental Policies*, London: Earthscan.

Norton, A. (1994) *The International Handbook of Local and Regional Government: A Comparative Analysis of Advanced Democracies*, Aldershot: Edward Elgar.

Offe, C. and Preuss, U.K. (1991) 'Democratic Institutions and Moral Resources', in Held, D. (ed.) *Political Theory Today*, Cambridge: Polity Press.

Office for National Statistics (1992–7) *Social Trends*, 22–7.

Official Journal of the European Communities (OJ) (1993) C138.

Olson, M. (1971) *The Logic of Collective Action* (second edition), Cambridge, Mass.: Harvard University Press.

O'Neill, J. (1993) *Ecology, Policy and Politics: Human Well-Being and the Natural World*, London: Routledge.

O'Riordan, T. (1981) *Environmentalism* (second edition), London: Pion.

O'Riordan, T. and Jordan, A. (1995) 'The Precautionary Principle in Contemporary Environmental Politics', *Environmental Values*, vol. 4, pp. 191–212.

O'Riordan T. and Voisey, H. (1997a) 'The Political Economy of Sustainable Development', *Environmental Politics*, vol. 6, no. 1, pp. 1–23.

O'Riordan, T. and Voisey, H. (eds) (1997b) *Sustainable Development in Western Europe: Coming to Terms with Agenda 21: Special Issue of Environmental Politics*, vol. 6, no. 1.

O'Riordan, T. and Weale, A. (1989) 'Administrative Reorganisation and Policy Change: The Case of Her Majesty's Inspectorate of Pollution', *Public Administration*, vol. 67, Autumn, pp. 277–94.

Ophuls, W. (1973) 'Leviathan or Oblivion', in Daly, H. (ed.) *Toward a Steady-State Economy*, San Francisco: W.H. Freeman.

Organisation for Economic Co-operation and Development (OECD) (1989) *Environmental Policy Benefits: Monetary Valuation*, Paris: OECD.

Osborn, D. (1997) 'The Way Forward Beyond Agenda 21: Perspectives on the Future from Europe', in Dodds, F. (ed.) *The Way Forward: Beyond Agenda 21*, London: Earthscan.

Parkin, S. (1989) *Green Parties: An International Guide*, London: Heretic Books.

Parry, G., Moyser, G. and Day, N. (1992) *Political Participation and Democracy in Britain*, Cambridge: Cambridge University Press.

Parson, E. (1993) 'Protecting the Ozone Layer', in Haas, P. *et al.* (eds) *Institutions for the Earth*, Cambridge, Mass.: MIT Press.

Passmore, J. (1980) *Man's Responsibility for Nature* (second edition), London: Duckworth.

Paterson, M. (1992) 'The Convention on Climate Change Agreed At the Rio Conference', *Environmental Politics*, vol. 1, no. 4, pp. 267–72.

Paterson, M. (1996) *Global Warming and Global Politics*, London: Routledge.

Patterson, A. and Theobald, K. (1996) 'Local Agenda 21, Compulsory Competitive Tendering and Local Environmental Practices', *Local Environment*, vol. 1, no. 1, pp. 7–20.

Peacocke, A. and Hodgson, P. (1989) 'The Judaeo-Christian Tradition', in Attfield, R. and Dell, K. (eds) *Values, Conflict and the Environment*, Oxford: Ian Ramsey Centre.

Pearce, D. (1983) *Cost-Benefit Analysis* (second edition), London: Macmillan.

Pearce, D., Markandya, A. and Barbier, E.B. (1989) *Blueprint for a Green Economy*, London: Earthscan.

Pearce, D.W. *et al.* (1991) *Blueprint 2: Greening the World Economy*, London: Earthscan.

Pearce, D. and Turner, R.K. (1990) *Economics of Natural Resources and the Environment*, London: Harvester Wheatsheaf.

Pearce, F. (1991) *Green Warriors*, London: Bodley Head.

Pepper, D. (1993) *Eco-Socialism: From Deep Ecology to Social Justice*, London: Routledge.

Phillips, A. (1996) 'Why does Local Democracy Matter?', in Pratchett, L. and Wilson, D. (eds) *Local Democracy and Local Government*, Basingstoke: Macmillan.

Pigou, A. (1932) *The Economics of Welfare* (fourth edition) London: Macmillan.

Plant, R. (1991) *Modern Political Thought*, Oxford: Blackwell.

Plumwood, V. (1986) 'Ecofeminism: An Overview and Discussion of Positions and Arguments', *Australasian Journal of Philosophy*, vol. 64 (Supplement), pp. 120–38.

Porritt, J. (1984) *Seeing Green: The Politics of Ecology Explained*, Oxford: Blackwell.

Porter, G. and Brown J. (1996) *Global Environmental Politics* (second edition), Boulder, Colo.: Westview Press.

Pratchett, L. and Wilson, D. (1996) 'Local Governance under Siege', in Pratchett, L. and Wilson, D. (eds) *Local Democracy and Local Government*, Basingstoke: Macmillan.

Princen, T. and Finger, M. (1994) *Environmental NGOs in World Politics*, London: Routledge.

Quinton, A. (1982) *Thoughts and Thinkers*, London: Duckworth.

Raghavan, C. (1996) 'TNCs Control Two-Thirds of World Economy', *Third World Resurgence*, no. 65/66 (Jan/Feb), pp. 31–2.

Rawls, J. (1972) *A Theory of Justice*, Oxford: Clarendon Press.

Real World (1996) *Real World Action Programme for Government*, London: Real World.

Regan, T. (1984) *The Case for Animal Rights*, London: Routledge.

Renn, O., Webler, T. and Wiedemann, P. (eds) (1995) *Fairness and Competence in Citizen Participation*, Dordrecht: Kluwer.

Richardson, D. and Rootes, C. (eds) (1995) *The Green Challenge: The Development of Green Parties in Europe*, London: Routledge.

Ritchie, D.G. (1894) *Natural Rights*, London: Allen & Unwin.

Road Alert! (1997) *Road Raging: Top Tips for Wrecking Roadbuilding*, Newbury: RA!

Roberts, J., Cleary, J., Hamilton, K. and Hanna, J. (eds) (1992) *Travel Sickness: The Need for a Sustainable Tranport Policy for Britain*, London: Lawrence & Wishart.

Robertson, J. (1989) *Future Wealth*, London: Cassell.

Robinson, M. (1992) *The Greening of British Party Politics*, Manchester: Manchester University Press.

Roddick, J. (1994) 'Second Session of the Commission on Sustainable Development', *Environmental Politics*, vol. 3, no. 3, pp. 503–12.

Roddick, J. and Dodds, F. (1993) 'Agenda 21's Political Strategy', *Environmental Politics*, vol. 2, no. 4, pp. 242–49.

Roemer, J.E. (1989) 'A Public Ownership Resolution of the Tragedy of the Commons', in Paul, E.F, Miller, F.D. and Paul, J. (eds) *Socialism*, Oxford: Blackwell.

Rolston, H. (1981) 'Values in Nature', *Environmental Ethics*, vol. 3, pp. 113–28.

Rolston, H. (1994) 'Environmental Ethics: Values in and Duties to the Natural World' in Gruen, L. and Jamieson, D. (eds) *Reflecting on Nature*, Oxford: Oxford University Press.

Rootes, C. (1995) 'Britain: Greens in a Cold Climate' in Richardson, D. and Rootes, C. (eds) *The Green Challenge: The Development of Green Parties in Europe*, London: Routledge.

Routley, R. and Routley, V. (1995) 'Against the Inevitability of Human Chauvinism', in Elliot, R. (ed.) *Environmental Ethics*, Oxford: Oxford University Press.

Rowell, A. (1996) *Green Backlash*, London: Routledge.

Royal Commission on Environmental Pollution (RCEP) (1976) *Fifth Report: Air Pollution Control – An Integrated Approach*, London: HMSO.

RCEP (1988) *Twelfth Report: Best Practicable Environmental Option*, London: HMSO.

RCEP (1995) *Transport and the Environment*, Oxford: Oxford University Press.

Ryle, M. (1988) *Ecology and Socialism*, London: Century Hutchinson.

Sachs, W. (ed.) (1993) *Global Ecology: A New Arena of Political Conflict*, London: Zed Books.

Sagoff, M. (1988) *The Economy of the Earth*, Cambridge: Cambridge University Press.

Salih, M. (1997) 'Global Ecologism and Its Critics', in Thomas, C. and Wilkin, P. (eds) *Globalisation and the South*, Basingstoke: Macmillan.

Sandbrook, R. (1996) 'Rio plus Five – What has Happened and What Next?' in *Priorities for Earth Summit II*, London: UNED-UK.

Sandler, T. (1997) *Global Challenges: An Approach to Environmental, Political and Economic Problems*, Cambridge: Cambridge University Press.

Scheffler, S. (1994) *The Rejection of Consequentialism*, Oxford: Clarendon Press.

Schumacher, E.F. (1973) *Small is Beautiful*, London: Sphere.

Sen, A. (1977) 'Rational Fools', *Philosophy and Public Affairs*, vol. 6, pp. 317–44.

Sen, A. (1987) *On Ethics and Economics*, Oxford: Blackwell.

Shiva, V. (1988) *Staying Alive: Women, Ecology and Development*, London: Zed Books.

Shiva, V. (1992) 'Recovering the Real Meaning of Sustainability', in Cooper, D.E. and Palmer, J.A. (eds) *The Environment in Question: Ethics and Global Issues*, London: Routledge.

Singer, P. (1983) *Animal Liberation*, London: Thorsons.

Slater, D. (1994) 'How IPC is Facilitating Environmental Protection', in Drake, J.A.G. (ed.) *Integrated Pollution Control*, Cambridge: Royal Society of Chemistry.

Soper, K. (1995) *What is Nature?* Oxford: Blackwell.

Sprigge, T.L.S. (1997) 'Respect for the Non-Human', in Chappell, T.D.J. (ed.) *The Philosophy of the Environment*, Edinburgh: Edinburgh University Press.

Spretnak, C. and Capra, F. (1986) *Green Politics: The Global Promise*, London: Paladin.

Standing Advisory Committee on Trunk Road Assessment (SACTRA) (1992) *Assessment of the Environmental Impact of Trunk Roads*, London: HMSO.

Stewart, M. (1996) 'Urban regeneration', in Leach, S. *et al.* (eds) *Enabling or Disabling Local Government*, Milton Keynes: Open University Press.

Stewart, J. (1996) 'Reforming the New Magistracy', in Pratchett, L. and Wilson, D. (eds) *Local Democracy and Local Government*, Basingstoke: Macmillan.

Stewart, J., Kendall, E. and Coote, A. (1994) *Citizen Juries*, London: IPPR.

Stoker, G. (1996a) 'Introduction: Normative Theories of Local Government and Democracy', in King, D. and Stoker, G. (eds) *Rethinking Local Democracy*, Basingstoke: Macmillan.

Stoker, G. (1996b) 'Redefining Local Democracy', in Pratchett, L. and Wilson, D. (eds) *Local Democracy and Local Government*, Basingstoke: Macmillan.

Stoker, G. and Young, S. (1993) *Cities in the 1990s*, Harlow: Longman.

Stone, C. (1987) *Earth and Other Ethics: The Case for Moral Pluralism*, New York: Harper & Row.

Stone, C. (1988) 'Moral Pluralism and the Course of Environmental Ethics', *Environmental Ethics*, vol. 10, pp. 139–54.

Straaten, J. van der (1992) 'The Dutch National Environmental Policy Plan: To Choose or To Lose', *Environmental Politics*, vol. 1, no. 1, pp. 45–71.

Straaten, J. van der (1994) 'Recent Developments in Dutch Policy', *Environmental Politics*, vol. 3, no. 4, pp. 226–32.

Strange, S. (1988) *States and Markets*, London: Pinter.

Sunstein, C.R. (1991) 'Preferences and Politics', *Philosophy and Public Affairs*, vol. 20, pp. 3–34.

Sustainable Seattle (1993) *The Sustainable Seattle 1993 Indicators of Sustainable Community: A Report to Citizens on Long-Term Trends in Our Community*, Seattle: Sustainable Seattle.

Sverdrup, L.A. (1997) 'Norway's Institutional Response to Sustainable Development', *Environmental Politics*, vol. 6, no. 1, pp. 54–82.

Third World Network (1992) *Earth Summit Briefings*, Penang, Malaysia: TWN.

Thomas, C. (1992) *The Environment in International Relations*, London: Riia.

Thomas, C. (1993) 'Beyond UNCED: An Introduction', *Environmental Politics*, vol. 2, no. 4, pp. 1–27.

Thomas, C. (ed.) (1994) *Rio: Unravelling the Consequences*, Newbury: Frank Cass.

Thomas, C. (1997) 'Globalisation and the South', in Thomas, C. and Wilkin, P. (eds) *Globalisation and the South*, Basingstoke: Macmillan.

Thompson, J. (1990) 'A Refutation of Environmental Ethics', *Environmental Ethics*, vol. 12, no. 2, pp. 147–60.

Tietenberg, T.H. (1991) 'Economic Instruments for Environmental Regulation', in Helm, D. (ed.) *Economic Policy Towards the Environment*, Oxford: Blackwell.

Tindale, S. and Holtham, G. (1996) *Green Tax Reform: Pollution Payments and Labour Tax Cuts*, London: IPPR.

Toner, G. and Doern, B. (1994) 'Five Political and Policy Imperatives in Green Plan Formation: The Canadian Case', *Environmental Politics*, vol. 3, no. 3, pp. 395–420.

Turner, R.K., Pearce, D. and Bateman, I. (1994) *Environmental Economics*, London: Harvester Wheatsheaf.

Tuxworth, B. (1996) 'From Environment to Sustainability: Surveys and Analysis of Local Agenda 21 Process Development in UK Local Authorities', *Local Environment*, vol. 1, no. 3, pp. 277–98.

Tyme, J. (1978) *Motorways versus Democracy*, London: Macmillan.

UK Round Table on Sustainable Development (1996) *First Annual Report*, London: DoE.

UK Round Table on Sustainable Development (1997) *Second Annual Report*, London: DoE.

United Nations Association Sustainable Development Unit (UNA SDU)/Community Development Foundation (CDF) (1995) *Towards Local Sustainability: A Review of Current Activity on Local Agenda 21 in the UK*, London: UNA.

United Nations Conference on Environment and Development (UNCED) (1992) *Agenda 21: A Programme for Action for Sustainable Development*, New York: United Nations.

United Nations Conference on Trade and Development (UNCTAD) (1995) *World Investment Report 1995*, New York: United Nations.

United Nations Environment and Development UK Committee (UNED-UK) (1996) *UNED-UK Annual Report 1995/96*, London: UNED-UK.

Vidal, J. (1996) 'The Seeds on Stony Ground', *The Guardian 2*, 16 October, pp. 2–3.

Vincent, A. (1992) *Modern Political Ideologies*, Oxford: Blackwell.

Vincent, A. (1993) 'The Character of Ecology', *Environmental Politics*, vol. 2, no. 2, pp. 248–76.

Vogel, D. (1993) 'The Making of EC Environmental Policy', in Andersen, S. and Eliassen, K. (eds) *Making Policy in Europe: The Europeification of National Policy-making*, London: Sage.

Vogler, J. and Imber, M. (eds) (1996) *The Environment and International Relations*, London: Routledge.

Voisey, H. and O'Riordan, T. (1997) 'Governing Institutions for Sustainable Development: The United Kingdom's National Level Approach', *Environmental Politics*, vol. 6, no. 1, pp. 24–53.

Voisey, H., Beuermann, C., Sverdrup, L.A. and O'Riordan, T. (1996) 'The Political Significance of Local Agenda 21: The Early Stages of Some European Experience', *Local Environment*, vol. 1, no. 1, pp. 33–50.

Wall, D. (1994) *Weaving a Bower Against Endless Night ... An Illustrated History of the UK Green Party*, Green Party.

Ward, S. (1993) 'Thinking Global, Acting Local? British Local Authorities and Their Environmental Plans', *Environmental Politics*, vol. 2, no. 3, pp. 453–78.

Ward, S. (1996) 'Green Arguments for Local Democracy', in King, D. and Stoker, G. (eds) *Rethinking Local Democracy*, Basingstoke: Macmillan.

Warren, K.J. (1987) 'Feminism and Ecology: Making Connections', *Environmental Ethics*, vol. 9, no. 1, pp. 3–20.

Warren, K.J. (ed.) (1994) *Ecological Feminism*, London: Routledge.

Warren, M.A. (1991) 'The Rights of the Non-human World', in White, J. (ed.) *Contemporary Moral Problems*, St Paul, Minn.: West Publishing Co.

Wathern, P. (ed.) (1988) *Environmental Impact Assessment: Theory and Practice*, London; Unwin Hyman.

Watson, M. and Sharpe, D. (1993) 'Green Beliefs and Religion', in Dobson, A. and Lucardie, P. (eds) *The Politics of Nature*, London: Routledge.

Weale, A. (1992) *The New Politics of Pollution*, Manchester: Manchester University Press.

Weale, A., O'Riordan, T. and Kramme, L. (1991) *Controlling Pollution in the Round*, London: Anglo-German Foundation.

Webber, P. (1994) 'Environmental Strategies', in Agyeman, J. and Evans, B. (eds) *Local Environmental Policies and Strategies*, Harlow: Longman.

White, J. (ed.) (1991) *Contemporary Moral Problems*, St Paul, Minn.: West Publishing Co.

White, L. (1994) 'The Historical Roots of our Ecologic Crisis', in Gruen, L. and Jamieson, D. (eds) *Reflecting on Nature*, Oxford: Oxford University Press.

Whitehead, A. (1996) 'Can Local Authorities Deliver Local Agenda 21?' *Interdisciplinary Strands*, vol. 5, no. 2, pp. 17–21.

Whittaker, S. (ed.) (1995) *First Steps: Local Agenda 21 in Practice*, London: HMSO.

Wilkin, P. (1997) 'New Myths for the South: Globalisation and the Conflict between Private Power and Freedom', in Thomas, C. and Wilkin, P. (eds) *Globalisation and the South*, Basingstoke: Macmillan.

Wilkinson, D. (1997) 'Towards Sustainability in the European Union?', *Environmental Politics*, vol. 6, no. 1.

Williams, B. (1973) 'A Critique of Utilitarianism', in Smart, J. and Williams, B. (eds) *Utilitarianism: For and Against*, Cambridge: Cambridge University Press.

Williams, B. (1985) *Ethics and the Limits of Philosophy*, London: Fontana.

Williams, B. (1995) 'Must a Concern for the Environment be Centred on Human Beings?' in *Making Sense of Humanity*, Cambridge: Cambridge University Press.

Williams, C.C. (1995) 'Local Currencies *Are* Getting Through', *New Economics*, no. 35 (autumn), p. 4.

Winpenny, J.T. (1991) *Values for the Environment: A Guide to Economic Appraisal*, London: HMSO.

Winter, G. (ed.) (1996) *European Environmental Law: A Comparative Perspective*. London: Dartmouth.

Wolman, H. (1996) 'Theories of Local Democracy in the United States', in King, D. and Stoker, G. (eds) *Rethinking Local Democracy*, Basingstoke: Macmillan.

Wood, C. and Dejeddour, M. (1992) 'Strategic Environmental Assessment: EA of Policy, Plans and Programmes', *Impact Assessment Bulletin*, vol. 10, no. 1, pp. 3–22.

World Commission on Environment and Development (WCED) (1987) *Our Common Future*, Oxford: Oxford University Press.

Wrong, D. (1979) *Power: Its Forms, Bases and Uses*, Oxford: Blackwell.

Wynne, B. (1996) 'May the Sheep Safely Graze? A Reflexive View of the Expert–Lay Knowledge Divide', in Lash, S., Szerszynski, B. and Wynne, B. (eds) *Risk, Environment and Modernity: Towards a New Ecology*, London: Sage.

Yearley, S. (1991) *The Green Case*, London: HarperCollins.

Yearley, S. (1994) 'Social Movements and Environmental Change', in Redclift, M. and Benton, T. (eds) *Social Theory and the Global Environment*, London: Routledge.

Young, S.C. (1992) 'The Different Dimensions of Green Politics', *Environmental Politics*, vol. 1, no. 1, pp. 9–44.

Young, S.C. (1993) *The Politics of the Environment*, Manchester: Baseline Books.

Young, S.C. (1996) *Promoting Participation and Community-Based Partnerships in the Context of Local Agenda 21*, Manchester: Manchester University Press.

Young, S.C. (1997) 'Community-based Partnerships and Sustainable Development: A Third Force in the Social Economy', in Baker, S. *et al.* (eds) *The Politics of Sustainable Development*, London: Routledge.

Index